Phonetic Interpretation

Phonetic Interpretation presents innovative work from four core areas: phonological representations and the lexicon, phonetic interpretation and phrasal structure, phonetic interpretation and syllable structure, and phonology and natural speech production. Written by major figures in the fields of phonetics, phonology and speech perception, the chapters in this volume use a wide range of laboratory and instrumental techniques to analyse the production and perception of speech, their aim being to explore the relationship between the sounds of speech and the linguistic organisation that lies behind that. The chapters present evidence of the lively intellectual engagement of laboratory phonology practitioners with the complexities and richness of human language. The book continues the tradition of the series, Papers in Laboratory Phonology, by bringing linguistic theory to bear on an essential problem of linguistics: the relationship between mental models and the physical nature of speech.

JOHN LOCAL is Professor of Phonetics and Linguistics at the Department of Language and Linguistic Science, University of York. He is co-author of *Doing Phonology* (1989) and is co-editor of the *Journal of the International Phonetics Association*.

RICHARD OGDEN is Lecturer in Phonetics and Phonology at the Department of Language and Linguistic Science, University of York. He has published in a number of journals including *Phonology, Computer Speech & Language, Journal of Linguistics* and *Journal of the International Phonetics Association*.

ROSALIND TEMPLE is Lecturer in French Language and Linguistics at the Department of Language and Linguistic Science, University of York. She is co-author of *Problems and Perspectives: Studies in the Modern French Language* (2000) and co-editor of *The Changing Voices of Europe* (1994).

PAPERS IN LABORATORY PHONOLOGY
SERIES EDITORS: MARY E. BECKMAN AND JOHN KINGSTON

Phonetic Interpretation
Papers in Laboratory Phonology VI

Phonetic Interpretation
Papers in Laboratory Phonology VI

EDITED BY JOHN LOCAL
University of York

RICHARD OGDEN
University of York

AND ROSALIND TEMPLE
University of York

CAMBRIDGE
UNIVERSITY PRESS

PUBLISHED BY THE PRESS SYNDICATE OF THE UNIVERSITY OF CAMBRIDGE
The Pitt Building, Trumpington Street, Cambridge, United Kingdom

CAMBRIDGE UNIVERSITY PRESS
The Edinburgh Building, Cambridge, CB2 2RU, UK
40 West 20th Street, New York, NY 10011–4211, USA
477 Williamstown Road, Port Melbourne, VIC 3207, Australia
Ruiz de Alarcón 13, 28014 Madrid, Spain
Dock House, The Waterfront, Cape Town 8001, South Africa

http://www.cambridge.org

First published 2003

Printed in the United Kingdom at the University Press, Cambridge

Typeface Times 10/12 pt.   *System* LaTeX 2_ε [TB]

A catalogue record for this book is available from the British Library

ISBN 0 521 82402 8 hardback

Contents

viii

Contents

Part IV: Phonology and natural speech production: tasks, contrasts and explanations

Contributors

MARY E. BECKMAN — Department of Linguistics, Ohio State University

PAUL CARTER — Department of Language and Linguistic Science, University of York

TAEHONG CHO — Max Plank Institute for Psycholinguistics, Nijmegen

JOHN COLEMAN — Phonetics Laboratory, University of Oxford

GERARD J. DOCHERTY — Department of Speech, University of Newcastle upon Tyne

BRYAN GICK — Department of Linguistics, University of Vancouver

BARBARA GILI FIVELA — Scuola Normale Superiore, Pisa

CÉCILE FOUGERON — Section de Psychologie Université de Genève

JONATHAN HARRINGTON — Speech, Hearing and Language Research Centre, Macquarie University

JOHN HARRIS — Department of Linguistics and Phonetics, University College London

SARAH HAWKINS | Department of Linguistics, University of Cambridge

JENNIFER HAY | Department of Linguistics, University of Canterbury, NZ

KATRINA HAYWARD | Department of Languages and Cultures of South East Asia and the Islands, School of Oriental and African Studies, University of London

CHAI-SHUNE HSU | Department of Linguistics, University of California, Los Angeles

MARIAPAOLA D'IMPERIO | LORIA, Nancy

KENNETH DE JONG | Department of Linguistics, Indiana University

PATRICIA KEATING | Department of Linguistics, University of California, Los Angeles

D. ROBERT LADD | Department of Theoretical and Applied Linguistics, University of Edinburgh

PETER LADEFOGED | Department of Linguistics, University of California, Los Angeles

TERRANCE M. NEAREY | Department of Linguistics, University of Alberta

NOËL NGUYEN | Laboratoire Parole et Langage, CNRS & Université de Provence

AKIN OYÈTÁDÉ | Department of Languages and Cultures of South East Asia and the Islands, School of Oriental and African Studies, University of London

JANET PIERREHUMBERT | Department of Linguistics, Northwestern University

ROBERT F. PORT | Department of Linguistics, Indiana University

JAMES M.SCOBBIE | Department of Speech and Language Sciences, Queen Margaret University College, Edinburgh

DANIEL SILVERMAN | Department of Linguistics, University of Illinois

List of contributors

KEIICHI TAJIMA   ATR Human Information Science Laboratories,
                         Kyoto

JUSTIN WATKINS   Department of Languages and Cultures of South
                         East Asia and the Islands, School of Oriental and
                         African Studies, University of London

RICHARD WRIGHT   Department of Linguistics, University of
                         Washington

BUSHRA ADNAN ZAWAYDEH   BBN Technologies, Massachusetts

Acknowledgements

This collection of papers is drawn from the Sixth Conference in Laboratory Phonology which was held at the University of York in 1998.

We are especially grateful to the Department of Language and Linguistic Science at the University of York and the British Academy for their generous financial support of the conference. Thanks also go to Judy Weyman, secretary in the Department of Language and Linguistic Science, for her tireless efforts, to Paul Carter for his much appreciated work, to our graduate-student assistants, ably led by Helen Lawrence, who helped with the day-to-day running of the conference, and to Mary Beckman and John Kingston, the series editors, for their sharp linguistic observations, their practical suggestions and their encouragement. We would particularly like to acknowledge all those who undertook, with such professionalism and care, the anonymous refereeing of the original abstracts for the conference and the papers which appear in this volume. An anonymous Cambridge University Press reviewer provided very helpful comments on an earlier version of the book. Traci Curl provided invaluable help with indexing.

Finally, we thank all the participants at the conference for their enthusiasm and creativity in pursuit of Laboratory Phonology.

John Local
Richard Ogden
Rosalind Temple

Acknowledgements

The publisher has used its best endeavours to ensure that the URLs for external websites referred to in this book are correct and active at the time of going to press. However, the publisher has no responsibility for the websites and can make no guarantee that a site will remain live or that the content is or will remain appropriate.

Introduction

JOHN LOCAL, RICHARD OGDEN AND
ROSALIND TEMPLE

There is a long tradition in Europe and North America of employing laboratory techniques to explore questions within phonetics (Hardcastle and Laver 1997; Ohala, Bronstein, Busà, Lewis and Weigel 1999). However, the coherent use of laboratory techniques to address phonological questions has a somewhat shorter history. Indeed the term 'Laboratory Phonology' (LP), which features in the title of this book, was coined by Janet Pierrehumbert only some ten years ago to characterise a growing body of experimental research on sound structure, its representation and its physical exponents (Kingston and Beckman 1990; Pierrehumbert, Beckman and Ladd 1996). Up to that point it had been typical for workers in other areas such as psychology to borrow the ideas from phonology and apply them within experimental settings to address the concerns of their own disciplines rather than to illuminate linguistic theory *per se*.

Nonetheless, over forty years ago the linguist, phonetician and phonologist J. R. Firth wrote of taking 'linguistics into the laboratory' (1957: 25). The point of doing this, Firth was at pains to emphasise, was not to engage in an 'experimental phonetics' ('a very different scientific procedure') but rather to support the exploration of the relationships between phonetics, phonology and the 'grammar' of language. Revisiting this matter in 1959, he writes: 'The linguist will, of necessity, have in mind tentative analysis at the phonological and grammatical levels, and unless the results of laboratory experiments throw light on findings at these levels there is no profit in them' (Firth 1959: 34–5).

Firth was pursuing a research agenda which sought to provide an understanding of the nature of phonological and phonetic categories: 'The

1

theory of *exponents*, linking the phonic data phonetically described with *categories* of phonology and grammar is a central necessity of linguistic analysis at congruent levels' (1957: vi). In undertaking this exploration he too was reacting against what he saw as the artificial and damaging separation of phonology from phonetics wherein neither gained benefit from developments in the other. He insisted that 'No phonetician listens fruitfully without what nowadays would be called a theory of phonology of some kind and indeed of general linguistics' (1957: vi). Indeed Firth argues that it is only by dealing with pieces of language which are clearly specified and constrained in terms of their phonological (and grammatical and lexical) structure that sensible interpretation of laboratory experimentation can be achieved. He also reminds us that no matter how sophisticated the experimental paradigms and techniques are, we need to reflect carefully on the *linguistic* adequacy of proposed categories being modelled: 'It is obvious that the validity of statistical methods and of other applications of mathematics depends on the elements of structure and units of systems set up by competent linguistic analysis' (1959: 29).

It goes without saying that since Firth's time phonological and phonetic theory have advanced, as has our understanding of the potential of 'laboratory' work to illuminate linguistic enquiry. It is all the more remarkable, then, that so many of Firth's concerns should resonate in the research agenda of LP characterised by Kingston and Beckman in 1990 and in the research presented in this volume.

What then is the enterprise of contemporary LP? Pierrehumbert *et al.* (1996) argue that 'Laboratory Phonology' is not a theoretical framework but rather a research community' (537). It might be more accurate to say that LP is constituted by 'the practices' of a research community that is seeking specifically to build bridges between experimental phonetics and theoretical linguistics in understanding the complex nature of language and the system(s) of constraints that govern it. Nonetheless, it is clear that while members of this particular research community may have different views on, say, the precise architecture of phonological theories, they do share aspirations, goals and approaches which impact on what kinds of phonological theories might be entertained and how claims might be tested. While LP is not prescriptive as to what constitutes 'laboratory investigation' or what constitutes a phonological theory, it does insist that if formal phonological claims are to be testable they need to be grounded in careful empirical *linguistic*-phonetic investigation and subjected to systematic laboratory experimentation which can provide for explicit modelling of results. The emphasis here on *linguistic*-phonetic investigation is important. Alongside the strong commitment to experimental research LP has always emphasised the need to ground such research in specific pieces of linguistic structure.

These concerns are well exemplified in the present volume, as are a number of recurrent themes in LP work. From its inception LP's central concern with finding ways of making robust, predictive statements about the way in which the sound systems in language function and are constrained has led it to explore three key areas:

- the question of what is the division of labour between phonetics and phonology – which phenomena belong where;
- the extent to which phonology is phonetically grounded – the extent to which language as a cognitive object can be/is to be accounted for in terms of general facts about the physical world;
- the nature of phonetic and phonological categories – the relationship between putatively discrete phonological categories and units and dynamic, continuous phonetic parameters.

These themes are enthusiastically taken up by the authors in present volume. They explore recurrent topics in LP (the phonetics–phonology interface, the physical constraints on phonological systems) and introduce new perspectives on issues such as lexical representation, linguistic constraints on phonetic variation and the extent to which phonological and lexical categories and structures constrain phonetic interpretation. Developments in LP are reflected in this volume by the increasing emphasis on perception rather than articulation and the role of functional considerations in shaping sound systems. A sense of the maturity and breadth of the work in LP can be gauged from the wide varieties of languages treated here which include Arabic, English (British and American), Danish, French, Italian, Korean, Japanese and Yorùbá.

One of the major contributions of LP which is reflected in this volume is the perspective on fundamental questions in phonology offered by paying attention to fine-grained phonetic detail. This has been achieved by its explicit goal of bringing phonology into the laboratory, and thus rooting phonology in the concrete world of what people/speakers do when they produce and perceive speech. The diversity and ingenuity of experimental design in the present volume testify to the richness of responses to this challenge. Approaches range from acoustic analysis of the speech waveform (e.g. Carter; Ladd and Scobbie; D'Imperio and Gili Fivela) to analysis of articulatory data using laryngography (Hayward, Watkins and Oyètádé), laryngoscopy (Zawaydeh) and electropalatography (Keating, Cho, Fougeron and Hsu) and from measuring reaction times to cross-spliced stimuli (Hawkins and Nguyen) to word-association tasks (Pierrehumbert, Hay, and Beckman) and perceptual simulation by training a recognition device (Nearcy). The speech materials used in production experiments range from those read at the subjects' leisure (e.g. Carter; Ladd and Scobbie; D'Imperio and Gili Fivela) to the highly constrained speech-cycling task used by Tajima and Port. Equally, the interpretation of results is frequently contextualised in ways which are not normally applied to phonological analysis. Thus Carter provides a convincing case for a particular model of phonetic interpretation by making reference to cross-dialectal patterning. Wright and Beckman and Pierrehumbert incorporate non-canonically phonological information of a very different kind in the form of sophisticated lexical frequency measures (and illustrate, by their co-occurrence in this volume, the application of such information in both production and perceptual studies).

In considering wider issues of lexical representation, Beckman and Pierrehumbert discuss the nature of phonological categories. They see phonological categories as formal syntactic objects which have three defining relations: (1) their semantics (cf. Pierrehumbert 1990), which is the phonetic interpretation of the category; (2) their paradigmatic relations with other items in the same system; (3) their syntagmatic relations with other items, i.e. their position in linguistic structure. This view is very like that of the Firthian prosodic analysts, whose theory had 'exponents', 'terms in system' and 'units in structure' as axiomatic. Like Beckman and Pierrehumbert, they viewed phonology as being part of a larger system, encompassing the lexicon, syntax, and wider, non-linguistic contexts, which includes the society in which a given language is spoken and the context in which it is used.

This view of phonology raises profound and challenging questions which have been themes in the discipline for decades. What is the nature of the relation between phonological categories and their phonetic interpretation? How many systems (and subsystems) can a language have, and how do we establish what they are? How is structure organised? What are the implications of system and structure for phonetic interpretation?

While the papers in this volume are very diverse, many are concerned with phonetics and its relation to phonology. One classic question of phonology is 'what constitutes a possible phonological inventory?', and several papers look at this issue, showing that phonological inventories can be shaped by phonetic constraints. The papers by Silverman and Hayward *et al.* investigate the relation between tone and voice quality. They look at issues of production and perception which constrain the combination of voice quality and tones in tonal inventories. Zawaydeh's paper considers the place of pharyngeals in Arabic. Other papers in the volume look at issues of timing. Gick and de Jong examine the possible interpretation of 'onset' and 'coda' in gestural accounts of American English, while Tajima and Port investigate the rhythmic structure of English and Japanese. As well as exploring relations between phonetics and phonological organisation, these papers provide new facts about the phonetic details of specific languages. This has been, and clearly continues to be, one of the main outcomes of Laboratory Phonology.

Another way to understand how phonetics is related to phonology is to consider *Grenzsignale*, phonetic stretches that unambiguously signal a particular phonological structure. Attention is drawn to this by Harris who argues that prosodic and morphological structures can be signalled by particular phonetic events because these structures differentially license the occurrence of interpretable phonological elements. Thus the phonetic signal is rich in information about phonological structure, which in turn characterises other linguistic structures. The paper by Keating *et al.* provides a more subtle understanding of this: they show that there is a significant systematic effect of higher-level prosodic structure on segment duration. D'Imperio and Gili Fivela show that the phonetic interpretation of structures which might have been subject to *Raddoppiamento Sintattico* is a complex product of the intersection of prosodic structure and information focus. They argue that the durational characteristics of consonants and vowels are constrained where the structures under consideration fall within particular kinds of information focus domain. Hawkins and Nguyen show that the temporal and spectral characteristics of onsets depend on codas; this is a smaller domain than those dealt with by Keating *et al.* and D'Imperio and Gili Fivela, but in each case, phonetic detail is closely associated with prosodic structure. Findings like these imply a close association of prosodic structure with phonetic detail, and they are more refined examples of classic *Grenzsignale*. As phonology continues its move away from rule-based frameworks to more structure-based frameworks, structure and the things that make it manifest become increasingly important.

The phonetic details reported in this volume are, in their very diverse ways, closely related to linguistic structure. Linguistic structure and the speech signal are in a symbiotic relationship with each other. Linguistic structure contains information of many types: syntactic structure, lexical frequency, semantic information, and so forth. This structure is part of the human cognitive system; the speech signal is its audible manifestation.

Many of the papers in the current volume are concerned with systematic phonetic detail. Some of this detail is subtle and hard to detect. But its systematic presence challenges traditional notions of what we mean by 'linguistic phonetics', which has generally cast aside 'detail'. Some of the details reported in this volume are clearly part of speakers' grammar, even though they do not contribute in any obvious way to establishing or maintaining lexical contrast, which has been the backbone of much phonology. These effects are more subtle: no doubt speech without them would be intelligible, but we can only hypothesise that without them, speech does not sound natural. The fact that even good speech synthesis often sounds unnatural is one way in which we can tell that systematic phonetic details contribute to overall impressions of 'naturalness'.

5

In other words, many of the systematic details we can observe in speech are a kind of syntagmatic glue: these details in some sense hold language together. Why might language be structured like this? One answer is that these details, however subtle, reflect and signal structural information. This facilitates the process of communication, since the speech signal contains information that relates to linguistic structure on many levels. In Hawkins' (1995) terms, they make speech 'perceptually coherent'. The challenge for phonology is how to explain such details. Perhaps if the notion of 'inventory' (a systematic listing of elements) is refined and a more polysystemic approach is taken, some of the frequency effects and variability observed in this volume and elsewhere would turn out to be artefacts of focusing too widely.

What are the types of thing which systematic phonetic detail is sensitive to? The papers in this volume give several different but complementary answers. Some of the details we can observe, such as those already remarked upon, relate fairly straightforwardly to linguistic structure. But others relate to things that are less conventionally thought of as important in phonological theory.

Wright shows that some details of vowel quality also depend on lexical frequency. Less frequent words have more peripheral, more hyperarticulated vowels than more frequent words, which have more central, more hypoarticulated vowels. Combined with the stochastic model of knowledge representation proposed in Hay *et al.*'s and Beckman and Pierrehumbert's papers, here we have evidence that phonetic detail reflects not only the discrete properties of the linguistic system, but also its continuous ones. Nearey's analysis of the factorability of phonological units (particularly syllables) into their parts takes a different point of departure. He explores the possibility that that symbolic units of no larger than a phoneme size play a major role in speech perception and argues that this role is modified by higher-order elements such as words in a 'highly limited and stylized way'.

Carter's paper shows that the exponents of 'clear' and 'dark' depend on the system in which these terms occur. Two laterals that in absolute, quantifiable, terms are the same count as 'clear' in one dialect but as 'dark' in another. Carter argues that words like 'clear' and 'dark' have no intrinsic semantics. In other words, the details of phonetic interpretation are language-specific; and the details may be far more complex than has traditionally been thought. This complexity, and its implications for phonological representation and phonetic interpretation, is highlighted by the fact that many 'mono-dialectal' speakers have passive knowledge of many varieties. In a wider social context, listeners partly identify dialects by details of this sort: as Firth put it, 'part of the meaning of an American is to sound like one' (Firth 1951: 120).

One of the conclusions to be drawn from this discussion is that speech is highly controlled behaviour. Phonetic details are closely associated with particular languages. To talk of some kind of universal or straightforward phonetic interpretation of phonological categories is naive; and we have barely begun to scratch the surface of the systematic details of naturally occurring talk. But this is not a surprising conclusion given that the identity of a phonological category is bound up with its place in the overall system. At what level might phonological categories be 'universal', if any, if their 'meaning' is defined in terms of their interpretation as well as the paradigmatic and syntagmatic relations they enter into? If a well-studied language like English still provides us with intriguing details, laboratory phonologists have plenty of work left to do.

Yet some of the principles of linguistic organisation are more generally applicable. Systems of contrast and the possibilities of phonological structure impose constraints on phonetic interpretation: the positive outcome of this is that speech is rich in information about the cognitive system that generates it and the speaker that produces it. In this respect, Harris's paper is particularly helpful, since it makes explicit a theory of phonological structure and contrast which is intimately tied in with expectations about the interpretation of that structure. Harris argues for a rather abstract phonology but one which is strongly grounded in phonetics. He makes the important point that the 'features' that are often assumed are not necessarily the appropriate ones and in doing so he encourages a re-examination and re-evaluation of the nature of the phonetics–phonology interface and the nature of phonetic interpretation of phonological categories.

A further set of issues raised by the papers in this volume concerns the kinds of data and data collection employed in LP and its consequences for interpreting research outcomes. The very fact of bringing phonology into the laboratory and seeking to expand its foundations in observable phonetic reality has opened a Pandora's box. The question has to be faced of how real that concrete reality is. To what extent do the findings of LP provide an insight into the characteristics of language and its phonetic interpretation in everyday talk and natural speech production?

This question turns around the closely interrelated key issues of variability and authenticity. For instance, how does the sample size of speakers in a production experiment impact on the kinds of variability we observe and model? Variationist linguistics has provided plenty of evidence over the past forty years that this variability can be highly structured and this raises questions of representativity which have to be taken into account as much by the laboratory phonologist as by the sociolinguist (see e.g. Docherty and Foulkes 1999; Docherty, Foulkes, Milroy, Milroy and Walshaw 1997). Similarly the results of close phonetic examination of extensive (non-laboratory collected) data-bases with large numbers of speakers reveal patterns of delicately controlled phonetic detail (see e.g. Local 1996; Shriberg 1999; Temple 1999; Ogden 1999b).

However, the very act of bringing phonology into the laboratory is problematic. The fact that the majority of the production experiments reported here have fewer than five subjects raises questions of representativeness; but in some cases at least this is clearly an artefact of the pragmatic limitations imposed by the experimental techniques used. Thus, the expense of providing artificial palates and the availability of subjects willing and able to don one or undergo the insertion of a nasal catheter for the purposes of laryngoscopy are highly limiting. Moreover, the use of such experimental techniques raises the question of just how close to real speech is the speech observed using such techniques. This question can equally well be applied to the speech obtained by elicitation techniques such as the reading of real and nonsense word lists in a laboratory setting. Given the demonstrable sensitivity of speakers and listeners to the probability characteristics of the phonotactic organisation of languages (Beckman and Pierrehumbert and Hay *et al.*) and word frequency (Wright) we clearly need to be sharply aware of the effects particular kinds of experimental design and data elicitation have on the kinds of phonetic events (and judgements) we get from our 'experimental participants'.

We must of course be careful not to interpret apparent 'contextual' characterisations such as 'laboratory setting/speech' or 'experimental context' in too a simplistic fashion (see for instance the discussion in Schegloff 1991, especially 54–7). Certainly the tasks set to participants impact on the way they shape their talk. But there is no guarantee that for two pieces of research reporting on, say 'prescripted and read laboratory speech' the participants understood and did the same kinds of things. One of the clear responsibilities of LP practitioners is to determine precisely *how* such tasks, 'settings' and 'context' have a consequential impact on the phenomena that are being investigated and modelled. That has to be shown rather than assumed. Interpreting the results of LP research and extrapolating them to the everyday productions and understandings of language users is not a trivial matter; it is however, one that LP has yet to face full-on.

More subtle problems may be present, too. The grammar and constraints of natural language may vitiate attempts to obtain veridical data in the laboratory (see e.g. the discussion in Schegloff 1993 for some of the constraint systems which arise from the sequential organisation of talk-in-interaction). For instance, Ladd and Scobbie's discussion of external sandhi in Sardinian highlights the difficulties which arise when trying to design 'laboratory' materials to investigate the properties of language in its situated context. In a series of experiments they seek to provide empirical grounds for analysing protection from lenition of consonants at word edges in Sardinian as either phonological (creating postlexical geminates) or phonetic (incomplete realisation of the final consonant). However, they find that the lexical and postlexical geminates do not occur in the same prosodic context and observe that 'the facts of the language make it almost impossible to design "materials"'.

These are not concerns exclusive to LP; they are have implications for the wider world of experimental phonetics and for the practice of normative laboratory sciences in general (Garfinkel 1967; Schegloff 1993). Many of the issues involved are discussed by Docherty in his commentary on four of the papers in this volume, but they are applicable more widely than to those papers. In some respects these methodological paradoxes are insoluble. And the value of existing methodologies in providing insights into phonetic and phonological phenomena cannot be denied. However, given that LP seeks to develop an explanatory theory of language and to strengthen the scientific foundations of phonology by improved methodological practices (Pierrehumbert *et al.* 1996), it nevertheless behoves its practitioners to address them and seek to address the issues.

One of the strengths of LP has been to rise to challenges like this. Its willingness to embrace an eclectic range of methodological approaches and experimental techniques has generated substantive insights into the phonetic interpretation of linguistic structure(s) and has allowed LP researchers to clear away much of the metaphorical debris which has littered the phonological landscape for years.

The papers in this volume present evidence of the lively intellectual engagement of LP practitioners with the complexities and richness of human language. In tackling a wide range of issues such as the nature of the lexicon, the relationship between form and function, comprehension and production and articulatory and acoustic/auditory representations LP continues to address seriously the 'need to recognise a wide variety of theories of linguistics and methods of analysis and to take them all into the laboratories' (Firth 1959: 29).

9

I

Phonological representations and the lexicon

1

Interpreting 'phonetic interpretation' over the lexicon

MARY E. BECKMAN AND JANET PIERREHUMBERT

1.1 The metaphors invoked

The phrase 'phonetic interpretation' (included in both special themes of the 6th Conference on Laboratory Phonology) invokes a particular view of language sound structure in which phonetics is defined as the semantics of phonology, which implies, conversely, that phonology is the syntax of phonetics. (See Pierrehumbert 1990, *inter alia*, for earlier explicit articulations of this view.) The paired metaphors are characteristic of a class of phonological theories built on symbolic formalism, just as the theory of 'ordinary' syntax is. They also delineate a class of psycholinguistic theories about how our memory of past experiences constrains our own phonological behaviour and our understanding of others' phonological behaviour. The utterances of other speakers are not apprehended and remembered as a collection of unanalysed audio-visual patterns. Nor are our own utterances produced by dredging up from memory the unanalysed articulatory records of some collection of previously produced utterances. Rather, utterances are decomposed into (or composed from) smaller parts that can be recognised as instances of particular syntactic categories standing in particular syntactic relationships to other categories in the context. Thus, phonological behaviour (like 'ordinary' syntactic behaviour) can be seen as a particularly elaborate type of categorisation, which allows for very complex and flexible stimulus generalisation. In this paper, we explore the cognitive function of categorisation, to try to understand its ecological advantage.

Shepard (1987) defines stimulus generalisation as the cognitive act of determining the probability that a newly encountered stimulus will have a particular consequence, given that a similar stimulus previously encountered had that consequence. For example, a bear becomes ill after eating nightshade berries. Later encountering similarly small, scarlet berries on another similar-looking plant, it might infer that eating these will have a similar effect. Shepard proposes a theory of stimulus generalisation in which a particular consequence is represented as a connected region in the relevant sensory dimensions in the organism's mind. The organism evaluates the probability that the new stimulus falls into this 'consequential region' by estimating the region's location and size. Shepard applied his theory to explain results of multidimensional scaling analyses of identification responses to stimuli that are systematically varied in dimensions that are known to be relevant for identifying some target category. Myung and Shepard (1996) show that, given certain simplifying assumptions about the shape of the consequential region of the category, the estimations of its location and size can be based on observed distances between 'consequential' stimuli, ignoring regions occupied by 'non-consequential' stimuli.

In nature, however, these simplifying assumptions often do not hold, and there is no experimenter to specify the targeted response category. Imagine the difficulty for the bear if one variety of nightshade produced fruit larger than the smallest wild tomatoes. Does the bear forgo eating ripe edible fruit of intermediate size? Does it set up two independent consequential regions for the smaller and larger varieties associated with the common consequence? Also, how does 'illness' become identified as a common consequence to identify these berries as 'illness-causing' in the first place? Unless it is innate, this category must be learned from the sensory dimensions representing experiences of illness. That is, the bear must generalise a class of encounters in the sensory space for nausea and nausea-related events in order for 'illness-causing' to become an index for equating different berry stimuli.

Categorisation thus seems typically to be a more elaborate cognitive act than simple stimulus generalisation. It involves a space of intervening consequences, which allows the organism to learn robust, efficient and potentially quite arbitrary associations between otherwise incommensurable domains of experience. This is the ecological advantage of phonological categorisation, which is the theme of this paper. The organism recognises the immediate stimulus as a member of one of several contrasting conceptual classes. These classes then stand as an independent conceptual space between the sensory representation of the proximal stimulus and the sensory representation of its associated distal consequence. Because the dimensions of this intermediate conceptual space are not isomorphic to those of either stimulus space, categorisation promotes more robust stimulus generalisation in two ways.

First, even limited experience with categorisation in a particular domain promotes selective attention to regions of the stimulus space where there are salient consequences for some classificatory dimension of the conceptual space. This differential attentional weighting sharpens perceptual acuity at boundaries between categories and blurs distinctions around prototypical values well within a category. For example, the bear quickly learns to pay attention to size when a berry is a bit small (for a tomato). Second, accumulated experience with categorising stimuli in their natural environments promotes a flexible, context-dependent partitioning of the stimulus space. Sensory dimensions of the context can be associated with the competing categories in the conceptual space, so that different attentional weights can readily alternate for each other in different contexts. The bear attends to size for red berries growing on small plants with large, dark-green, lobed leaves, but not for blue berries growing on woody shrubs with pale, smooth, round leaves. The noxious berry is a bit small, *for a tomato*.

Syntactic structure allows a further elaboration on this type of intervening conceptual space, in which the category of a stimulus itself constitutes a relevant dimension of the context of another stimulus at a comparable level of description. Syntactic classes have a contextual (syntagmatic) categorisation as well as an 'ordinary' (paradigmatic) categorisation. A syntactic object is classified as being the same as or different from other stimuli that have been previously encountered in similar contexts, and also as belonging to a particular context class for the recognition of other syntactic objects. For example, the element /æ/ is classified in an utterance of the wordform *cat* by being different from /e/, /ɑ/, etc., and also by the way that members of its syntagmatic class provide a recurring environment for differentiating /k/ from /g/, /p/, etc.

As stated above, categorisation moulds attention to the most relevant available stimulus dimensions. Categorisation also allows the listener to make inferences about hidden stimulus dimensions. If a listener recognises a region of the signal as an example of /æ/, he can infer from the spectral peaks in the signal that the speaker lowered the tongue body. This inference can be made even if he is listening to the speech on a tape recording and has no direct information about the articulation. Equally, however, a speaker can articulate an example of an /æ/ while having the auditory percept of her own speech blocked by white noise played through headphones. In this case, she can infer the existence of spectral peaks that she cannot observe directly. In the terms of formal semantics, complexes of events in the physical world which provide examples of the category /æ/ are elements of the 'extension' of /æ/. Because /æ/ is a syntactic object, moreover, part of its extension involves the relationships in the physical world which can be inferred from its syntagmatic class. When the listener recognises a region of the signal as an example of /æ/, he also recognises it as providing a potential following context for a /k/. He then can infer from changes in the spectral peaks over time that, just before the speaker lowered the tongue body, she first raised it to momentarily contact the palate.

A robust linguistic generalisation that falls out of adopting this phonetics-as-semantics metaphor is that phonological objects and relationships should be 'natural' ones. The conceptual structures that acquiring a human language imposes on the child's mind reflect often very robust correlations with properties and events in nature. This is why a child can acquire the phonetic and phonological concepts of the ambient culture. This is true also of the correlations between semantic and syntactic properties that define the 'lemma', the conceptual category that a wordform names. (See, e.g., Levin and Rappaport Hovav 1996; also, Malt 1996, for a review of the anthropological linguistics literature on this point.) It is unlikely that language could have evolved otherwise.

We can contrast the naturalness of these phonology- or syntax-specific associations to the typically arbitrary nature of the cross-domain association between wordform and lemma. Although speech communities can (and do) exploit recurring associations, in both sound symbolism and word play, these correlations between wordform and lemma are not predictive in the way that domain-internal associations typically are. A new member of the community (such as the field linguist) can use his native-language categories to guess the approximate relationship between phonological categories and their observed phonetic referents. Similarly, after encountering enough verbs of motion, he might be able to guess, for example, that the language has distinct words for running in place and running toward a goal. However, unless the language is closely related to his own, he is not likely to be able to predict what the two wordforms are for these two lemmas. The lack of strong correlations between the phonological and phonetic properties of wordforms and the homologous properties of their associated lemmas is a very robust generalisation, the principle of *l'arbitraire du signe*. To acquire the language of the ambient culture, a child has to make many such associations, most of which are entirely conventional – i.e., arbitrary and culturally specific.

L'arbitraire du signe seems to be related to another important generalisation about the organisation of the human memory for words, the property of 'duality of patterning' (Hockett 1960): The principles of compositionality on the wordform side of the 'primary' semantic association are different from those on the lemma side. Even the smallest 'meaningful' forms in a language – the wordforms and grammatical morphemes that associate to lemmas and recurring syntactic relationships among lemmas – can be decomposed further into smaller elements which have no 'meaning' on their own in the sense of associating to some category on the other side of the *signe–signifiée* divide.

Because humans who share a common culture share the categories on both sides of this divide, existing categories of various orders of complexity can be combined to make new categories. These new composite categories will have predictable syntactic and semantic properties, derived from the syntactic and semantic associations of the smaller objects that were combined to make the larger ones. This is true not just of 'ordinary' syntactic objects such as lemmas and combinations of lemmas, but also of the syntactic objects internal to wordforms such as phonemes and gestures. Hearers and talkers can productively apply their knowledge of the internal composition of known wordforms to recognise and reproduce novel wordforms such as the name of a person met at a party, a newly encountered technical term, or the name of a novel object borrowed from another culture. Also, the syntax and semantics of phonological categories such as /æ/, /k/, and /t/, and of their composition into /kæt/, are independent of the 'ordinary' syntax and semantics of lemmas and lemma combinations. Therefore, hearers can 'understand' a new wordform in terms of categories and properties internal to the phonology. Moreover, they can do so even if the new wordform names an object or event that does not fit naturally into any existing lemma category – indeed, even if the new wordform does not name any conceptual category at all, as in the nonce 'words' presented in many speech experiments.

Another fundamental linguistic principle – that of 'positional contrast' – falls out from the fact that wordforms are structured in time. Recognising the syntagmatic context of a syntactic object such as the /k/ in *cat* involves learning such temporally defined properties as 'the beginning of the wordform' and 'before /æ/' as well as the relationships between this dimension of classification and various different sensory dimensions. Such syntactic properties must be abstracted away from the semantics of the /k/ itself. Abstracting away the temporal syntax is important, because the mapping between our experience of articulatory manoeuvres and our audio-visual experience of the consequences of these manoeuvres is not always the same for different positions. For example, the audible consequences of lowering the tongue dorsum after forming a /k/ closure typically will differ between 'before /æ/' as in *cat* and 'before /s/' as in *axe*.

To recapitulate, then, we view a phonological category, such as the phoneme /æ/ or /k/, as a formal syntactic object. It exists in memory not simply by virtue of its semantics. It is not stored or accessed just via the indexical associations to sensory representations of real-world events, such as the gesture of making and releasing a closure that blocked airflow and the burst that results. Rather, it is remembered and invoked from memory by virtue of two other kinds of indexical relationship to other categories in memory. These relationships are the syntagmatic associations to other syntactic objects which can occur in the object's context, and the paradigmatic associations to other syntactic objects which can occur in the object's place in the given context. Moreover, in adopting the metaphor, we attribute to the human mind – to the language user and not simply to Language – the four principles characterising the phonological organisation of all human languages: (1) the 'naturalness' of phonological categories, (2) *l'arbitraire du signe*, (3) duality of patterning, and (4) positional contrast. We propose that a formal model of phonological competence will accurately mimic human performance only if it provides an account of how these four characteristics can emerge in acquisition as attributes of the memory store for wordforms of the ambient language. While no one has yet offered a formal model that can account for acquisition and control of a reasonably large lexicon, it is possible to find evidence that these principles govern individual phonologies using very simple experiments, such as the following priming test.

1.2 The word-association experiment

Priming refers to experimental observations suggesting that retrieving a word or other item from memory also activates related items that might be associated with it in memory. We devised a word-association task to see whether accessing two words together could differentiate between associative links among similar wordforms and associative links among related lemmas, as predicted by the principle of *l'arbitraire du signe*. We also examined the priming effects that we found to see whether they suggested a simple all-or-none association between similar wordforms, or a more complex network of associations that is structured by the principles of duality of patterning and positional contrast.

We presented 60 Ohio State University undergraduates with 24 pairs of priming words (see Table 1.1), each followed by a blank in which to write down the first word that came to mind. In each pair, the second word (the one immediately preceding the blank) had 5 phoneme-sized segments, as transcribed in the *Hoosier Mental Lexicon* (*HML*, Pisoni, Nusbaum, Luce and Slowiaczek 1985) and a familiarity rating of 7 on the *HML* scale of 1–7. We will refer to this word as the 'immediate prime.' The paired non-immediate primes also were all highly familiar words, and each was either a wordform associate (a word with 2 to 4 segments in common with the immediate prime) or a lemma associate (a word with a related meaning). We chose wordform associates from different semantic domains (to minimise semantic relatedness) and lemma associates with no shared segments in identical positions. A split-plot design insured that each participant saw an equal number of lemma associates and wordform associates, without any individual participant seeing both pairings for the same immediate prime. Pairs containing lemma associates and pairs containing wordform associates were interleaved in pseudo-random order.

18

Table 1.1 *Stimulus words for the association test. Transcriptions of the target and wordform associate from the* HML, *with segments in common underlined*

target word	*HML*	no shared segments	wordform associate	*HML*	lemma associate
splash	spl@S	3	split	splIt	fountain
juggler	J^gLX	2	jumbo	J^mbo	circus
sermon	sRmxn	2	syrup	sRrxp	bible
package	p@kIJ	2	panda	p@ndx	mail
pleasure	plEZX	2	plant	pl@nt	vacation
strong	strcG	3	stripe	strYp	muscle
usual	yuZuL	2	youth	yuT	never
balloon	bxlun	2	tycoon	tYkun	party
crank	cr@Gk	4	drank	dr@Gk	pull
friend	frEnd	3	attend	xtEnd	hug
snicker	snIkX	3	wicker	wIkX	tease
excel	IksEl	2	lapel	lxpEl	grade
treaty	triti	2	fifty	fIfti	war
motive	motIv	3	octave	aktIv	excuse
wrinkle	rIGkL	3	ritual	rICuL	forehead
staple	stepL	3	simple	sImpL	tack
Chinese	CYniz	3	cheese	Ciz	Greek
cancel	k@nsL	3	camel	k@mxl	renew
famous	femxs	3	focus	fokxs	star
clamp	kl@mp	3	cap	k@p	wood
filling	fIlIG	3	footing	fUtIG	cavity
desert	dEzXt*	3	dart	dart	sand
kitchen	kIC|n	2	keen	kin	stove
machine	mxSin	2	moon	mun	gear

*Before tabulating forms in common, we changed this from the homograph verb [d\|zRt]. However, responses such as 'pie', 'pastry' and 'chocolate' to 'dart, desert' suggest that many of our subjects read *desert* as the verb's homophone *dessert*.

Response forms for participants who were not self-identified as native speakers of English were discarded, as were forms in which any blanks were unfilled or filled with long proper nouns (e.g. 'Emancipation Proclamation (document)' in response to 'fifty, treaty, _____'). The remaining responses were scored for their similarity in form and meaning to the immediate prime.

For similarity in form, three different objective scores were computed, based on the *HML* transcriptions (see below). Similarity in meaning was determined by obtaining judgements from a second pool of Ohio State University undergraduates. New response sheets were created, each containing all 24 immediate primes, but paired this time with the corresponding response words written down by one of the participants in the association task rather than with the other (non-immediate) prime. Participants in the scoring task rated each pair on 'how closely related their meanings are' using a scale from 1 (for '*not* related') to 7 (for '*very* related'). Again, a response form was discarded if there were missing ratings or if the rater was not self-identified as a native speaker of English. This left 39 sets of responses, about evenly divided between the two lists on the association task. The mean semantic relatedness rating was then calculated by averaging over the 18 or 21 similarity judgements obtained for each immediate prime in each pairing condition in the association task.

To compute wordform similarity, we looked up the *HML* transcription for each response word from the association task, and tabulated the number of responses that shared at least one segment with the immediate prime. We also calculated the number of segments shared, in two different ways – once without regard for position in the word and once counting only identical segments in identical position relative to either the beginning of the word, the end of the word, or the stressed vowel in the word. Since the *HML* transcription system encodes some allophonic and positional features directly in the symbols used, we first recoded some symbols. For example, we recoded syllabic 'R' and its unstressed counterpart 'X' as 'r'. This uncovered, for example, the shared 'r' in 'lover' [l^vX]=[l^vr] as a response to 'hug, friend', as well as the 'r' segment shared by the wordform associates 'dart, desert' (hence the count of 3 rather than 2 segments in common for this pair in Table 1.1).

Figure 1.1 shows the results. In each panel, the x-axis plots the mean semantic relatedness rating between the response and the immediate prime, and the y-axis plots some measure of wordform relatedness. For example, the top left panel shows the proportion of responses that shared a phoneme with the immediate prime. Note that this count disregards position in the wordform, so that the non-initial 'k' symbols in 'book', 'subscribe', 'check' and 'smoking' and the initial ones in 'credit', 'keep', 'caramel', 'cancer', etc., all count as equivalent to the initial 'k' of the immediate prime in the 'renew, cancel, _____' and 'camel, cancel, _____' priming pairs. The distribution of filled and open circles suggests the robustness of *l'arbitraire du signe* as a principle organising the remembered properties of these words. The proportion of responses sharing a segment with the target word is generally somewhat higher for the wordform associate pairs, whereas the mean semantic relatedness rating is generally higher for the same words in lemma-associate pairs. When the clear and filled datapoints for each immediate prime are compared to each other, the proportion of responses containing shared segments is shown to be higher in the wordform associates' condition for all but four items, and the mean semantic relatedness rating is higher for the responses in the lemma associates' condition for all 24 items. (Both of these differences, as well as the effects described below for the other panels of Figure 1.1, are significant at p<0.0001, by a Wilcoxon test.)

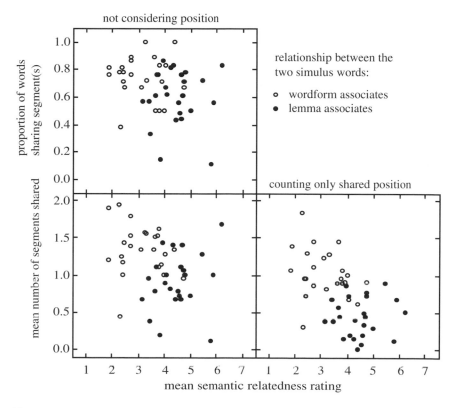

Figure 1.1 Three measures of mean wordform relatedness plotted against mean lemma relatedness between each immediate prime and all participants' responses to wordform priming pairs (open circles) and to lemma priming pairs (filled circles). Measures: (a) proportion of responses sharing a segment with the immediate prime, (b) mean number of segments shared between responses and immediate prime, and (c) mean number of shared segments in identical position with respect to the wordform's beginning, end, or stressed vowel

The y-axis in the lower left panel shows a somewhat finer measure of phonological relatedness – the mean number of segments in common between the response and the immediate prime, again without regard to position in the wordform. The responses to the two types of associates become better differentiated. When a priming pair prompted a response with any phoneme in common with the immediate prime, that was typically the only phonological similarity for lemma associates, whereas there were typically more segments in common when they were wordform associates. This suggests that duality of patterning also plays a role. Not only are wordforms remembered as separate entities from their lemmas, they are also parsed into smaller phonological elements such that degree of phonological association or activation is not all or none.

The last panel in the figure refines the measure of wordform similarity further by counting a segment in the response as identical to a segment in the immediate prime only if it occurred in the same position relative to the stressed vowel or to either of the wordform's edges (except when counting blindly from the edge would equate prevocalic and syllabic consonants as in 'breakfast' as a response to 'syrup, sermon, _____'). When phonemes in common are tabulated using this positionally specific criterion, there is even less overlap between filled and open circles, suggesting that positional contrast constrains associations between phonologically related items in memory. Links among wordforms are sensitive to the forms' internal syntactic structure, so that the most accessible paradigmatic associations are between elements that share not just gestural content but also syntagmatic position.

1.3 Lexical neighbourhoods and the emergence of structure

A useful metaphor for understanding these three results combines two ideas. One is the idea of spreading activation as a way to model retrieval of information from long-term memory (Morton 1969). The other is the idea of the lexical neighbourhood as a way to account for the roles of semantic and phonological similarity in the spread of activation through the relevant part of the long-term memory store (Goldinger, Luce and Pisoni 1989). The composite 'neighbourhood activation' metaphor developed in the 1980s as psycholinguists working on lexical access explored ways around the impasse of trying to reconcile the older metaphor of dictionary lookup with experiments suggesting multiple entry points to the lexicon. If words are stored in memory as a one-dimensional list organised by order of relative lexical frequency, one can explain the advantage that more frequent words have in naming and lexical decision tasks by the relative amount of time it takes for the lookup mechanism to reach a word that is entered earlier or later in the list. But then there is no easy way to explain semantic priming. By contrast, if the lexicon is organised along the principles of a thesaurus, with ample and easily traversed cross-reference links, then each word is a cell defined by the intersection of all of the links in this multi-dimensional space. And one can explain semantic priming as the result of increased activity in one cell activating all the connected neighbouring cells. Moreover, if phonologically similar words are also connected together to make a phonological neighbourhood for each wordform, then phonological priming is no more miraculous than semantic priming. As Dell (1999) puts it, 'processing a word affects its neighbours, and vice versa. It is impossible to sneak into the lexicon and take out the word you want without the neighbours getting all excited'. Rousting a word out of its bed requires a ruckus that wakes up the rest of the neighbourhood.

The development of the neighbourhood activation metaphor was a critical step in the application of connectionist models to the understanding of lexical access in several different linguistic domains. Some of these applications, such as Dell (1988), build on Morton's original conception (and the description above) in identifying words as actual cells or 'nodes' in the connectionist network. Others, such as Bybee (2000), instead equate the nodes of the network only with the shared properties of words (i.e. conceptual features such as 'past tense' or phonological properties such as 'having the phoneme /k/ in initial position'). Words then are represented only as distributed patterns of activation across the associations between these primary feature category nodes. The first conception seems more consistent with our results, and there are a functional argument and a formal (architectural) argument in favour of it.

Interpreting the first result of our experiment in terms of Dell's (1999) description of the neighbourhood activation metaphor suggests the following elaboration. The two sets of neighbours – wordform and lemma – are connected via the word. Picture the word as a terraced house with a kitchen (the wordform) and a living-room (the lemma). The living-room side of the word sits on a street with one set of neighbours, and the kitchen side of the word sits on an alley with a different set of neighbours. Recognising a wordform in the stream of speech means that the revellers (the activity invoked by recognising phonetic cues and phonological categories) have passed through the kitchen and out through the living-room door to the word's lemma neighbourhood. Producing a word, conversely, means that the revellers in the lemma neighbourhood have passed through the living-room and out the kitchen door into the word's phonological neighbourhood. The only way that the neighbours on one side of the house can hear the ruckus in the other neighbourhood is if the word opens the front door and the service door to let the mob of revellers pass through. Each word is its own little bottleneck for the spread of activation. A synonym for 'bottleneck' is 'channel' – which does better justice to the advantages of this structural design. By localising structure in this way, the spread of activation is effectively channelled. If no close neighbour is rousted out of bed by mistake to open her living-room and kitchen doors, the revelling crowd will pass through the correct house into a smaller neighbourhood on the other side. The intended lemma will be recognised or the intended wordform produced without requiring extensive soothing of the word's closest wordform and lemma neighbours. The fact that slips of the ear or tongue are more common for words that are both lemma and wordform neighbours thus suggests the ecological advantage afforded by *l'arbitraire du signe*.

(a)	[FEMALE]	[SIBLING]	[LABIAL CLOSURE]	(b) input		XOR output
mother	1	0	1	1	0	1
father	0	0	0	0	0	0
sister	1	1	0	1	1	0
brother	0	1	1	0	1	1

Figure 1.2 (a) Fragment of semantic-to-phonetic mappings for words in a semantic neighbourhood (b) Input-output mappings for the possible inputs to the logical function exclusive-OR

As Dell, Schwartz, Martine, Saffran and Gagnon (1997) point out, the formal characterisation of this bottleneck is very similar to the characterisation of the XOR ('exclusive or') function, as illustrated in Figure 1.2. The two wordforms that start with a labial closing gesture correspond to the lemmas for the female parent and the male sibling. If semantic properties [FEMALE] and [SIBLING] are the input, the labial-closure output must be activated for the input that is either a female or a sibling, but not both. As Elman (1990) has pointed out, the XOR function requires that a layer of hidden nodes intervene between the input and the output. To model *l'arbitraire du signe* using a connectionist architecture, similarly, there must be hidden nodes – i.e. words as discrete, local cells – in between the nodes that encode semantic and syntactic properties (lemma features), and the nodes that encode phonological and phonetic properties (wordform features).

These word nodes are needed so that the patterns of co-activation on the word's lemma side can be represented by changing the weights of the lemma associations without affecting the weights of the wordform properties that trigger co-activations of phonologically similar wordforms. Examination of the hidden nodes after training should show the emergence of dedicated wordform and/or lemma nodes, representing linguistic structure at this level. After sufficient exposure, co-activation patterns for words should be localised enough to support robust processing on just the relevant side of the bottleneck. In this way, a new (or less frequent) word can be produced or perceived by activating the subnetwork of intersecting properties that define its wordform, without activating the lemma neighbourhoods of the closest attested (or more frequent) words. The child can recognise the wordform as novel, and learn its associated semantic and syntactic properties without undue interference from the lemmas of similar wordforms.

1.4 The bottleneck between articulatory and acoustic representations

As we have just seen, duality of patterning is ecologically functional. It results in channelling of activation at the word level between wordform properties and the lemma properties. However, this is not the only channelling in the system. In this section, we argue that channelling between articulatory and acoustic representations is one source of sublexical units such as the phoneme. Figure 1.3 illustrates the formal similarity between this bottleneck and the one discussed in the previous section. We posit channelling between acoustic and articulatory representations because research efforts to establish an isomorphism between them have generally failed. Several types of problems have arisen.

One is the clear differences between the most accessible semantic properties of some categories. The phonetic correlates of some features, such as [±cont], [±voice], or [±nasal], can be defined articulatorily in terms of a constriction degree 'gesture' at some oral aperture, the glottal aperture, or the velic aperture. The phonetic correlates of the feature [⊥sonorant], on the other hand, cannot be unified in terms of any single articulatory constriction. Rather, the feature refers to the 'effective constriction degree' (Browman and Goldstein 1989), the acoustic consequence of how the resulting airflow channels are coupled in the gestural ensemble as a whole. Similarly, because many vowels can be implemented using more than one articulatory strategy, traditional vowel features of height and frontness are highly problematic as articulatory features. Vowel categorisation in the acoustic domain is more perspicuous.

	[cont]	[voice]	[nasal]	[son]
/b/	0	1	0	0
/m/	0	1	1	1
/w/	1	1	0	1
/ʍ/	1	0	0	0
	lip aperture	glottal aperture	velic aperture	effective const. deg.

Figure 1.3 Logical structure for sample mappings from articulatorily motivated features describing close or critical constriction degree values to an acoustically motivated feature describing effective constriction degree for four gestural ensembles

More generally, the relation of acoustic to articulatory levels of description is, as Nearey (1995, this volume) points out, 'doubly weak'. This means that each entity in the acoustic description corresponds to more than one entity in the articulatory description, and vice versa. Because of this double weakness, it is impossible to establish the kind of invariant, or one-to-one relationship between acoustics and articulation, which many speech researchers previously hoped to find. To model this relationship in a connectionist architecture, it is necessary to posit a layer of hidden nodes. This layer of hidden nodes is, we would argue, the segmental level. If the relationship of acoustics to articulation were simple, there would be no impetus for anything as abstract as the phoneme.

Stops provide an especially clear example. In making or watching someone else make a /b/, the somatosensory or visual representations of oral and glottal constriction degree and of oral constriction location are continuously available, but during the closure, the spectral dynamics do not tract the articulatory dynamics. Building a layer of hidden nodes to stand between these disparate stimulus spaces allows the auditory cues to associate to the temporally localised gestural ensemble, and to do so even when the preceding or following environment is not conducive for carrying place or voicing cues. In other words, one of the reasons why an infant might acquire phonemes is that the articulatory-to-acoustic mapping is not invertible. (See Plaut and Kello 1999 for a pilot implementation of this idea.) Thus, the articulatory-to-acoustic bottleneck is relevant to the bootstrapping question: how can localised representations of sublexical structure emerge for the infant to begin acquiring words? It is by now well established that perceptual responses begin to be attuned to the phonological categories of the ambient language well before the infant begins to make associations between recurring wordforms and their lemmas (e.g. Kuhl, Williams, Lacerda, Stevens and Lindblom 1992). How can this attunement occur before the infant has a large enough lexicon for the wordform–lemma bottleneck to enforce an analysis of similarities finer than identity across the whole utterance?

1.5 The third hidden layer

A third bottleneck also is relevant to the bootstrapping question. Sublexical structure emerges not just because of the double-weak relationship between the articulatory and acoustic properties of consonants and vowels, but also because speech unfolds in time. This means that many of the contextual (syntagmatic) dimensions of the conceptual space for speech have as their semantic extensions such inherently temporal relationships as 'occurs after' or 'is contained within'. We have already outlined above how categorisation in intelligent animals such as the bear is more robust than Shepard's simple stimulus generalisation model, because the intermediate conceptual space allows the organism to assess the likelihood of a category relative to apprehended properties of its context. For the syntactically structured categories of speech, then, the relevant contextual properties include the category types that are identified for preceding time intervals and for larger time intervals containing the target stimulus. Thus, a good way to characterise the acquisition of the syntagmatic categories relevant for speech is that the child is 'Finding structure in time' (Elman 1990).

Devising some way to model structure in time is one of the most challenging problems in applying connectionist models to speech. The formal similarity to the XOR problem is illustrated in the two mappings in Figure 1.4. The first shows how the context vowel category constrains the interpretation of the spectrum during a sibilant fricative. The centre of gravity is in the ambiguous middle region of the speaker's range (where the listener must attend carefully to its precise value) when the consonant is likely to be /s/ or the vowel is likely to be /u/, but not both. The second example shows how contextual categories can not only lead to more efficient attentional strategies for processing the semantics of the target stimulus, but can also constrain expectations about the identity of the target category more directly. Given the transitional probabilities for English obstruents and liquids, an alveolar cluster is a likely onset when the first consonant is a stop or the second is a lateral, but not both. While Figure 1.4(b) illustrates the point with an extreme case (in English, /sr/ and /tl/ have a near zero probability of occurring without an intervening morpheme boundary), there is a growing body of research showing that such 'absolute' phonotactics are qualitatively similar to the effects of more gradient differences in transitional probability. (See Hay *et al.*, this volume, for a review.)

(a)	/s/	/i/	mid-frequency mean spectrum	(b)	C1 is /t/	C2 is /l/	likely onset
see	1	1	0 (high)	/tl/	1	1	0
sue	1	0	1	/tr/	1	0	1
she	0	1	1	/sl/	0	1	1
shoe	0	0	0 (low)	/sr/	0	0	0
				/kl/	0	1	1

Figure 1.4 Logical structure for sample mappings (a) from context classifications to expected acoustic property, and (b) from context classifications to expected following paradigmatic category

Elman (1990) shows that a recurrent neural network (RNN) connectionist model can learn some complex syntactic systems by exploiting such transitional probabilities. The RNN architecture stores a temporary buffer of 'context units' to build associations between immediately preceding elements and the input element currently being processed. In the English syntactic subsystem illustrated in Figure 1.4(b), for example, the low probability of the /tl/ sequence can override the acoustic semantics of the alveolar stop burst, to cue a /kl/ instead of the intended /tl/. The RNN architecture can model such structure in time, as long as the transitional probabilities that are exploited to predict the next element in a sequence are stated over input and output units that are of the same structural type – e.g. using the previous one or two words to predict the next word in a phrase or the previous one or two segments to predict the next segment (Elman 1990). If transitional probabilities for phoneme sequences contained within wordforms differ systematically from those that cross word boundaries, these probabilities can be used to generalise the syntax of the composite phonological structure. Thus, phonotactics can be exploited to establish the probable word count and the most probable points for the edges of words in continuous speech.

Many recent experimental findings demonstrate the importance of transitional probabilities in language acquisition as well as in adult speech processing. For example, Jusczyk, Luce and Charles-Luce (1994) show that by 9 months, infants are sensitised to word-internal transitional probabilities for the ambient language. That is, already at the point when they begin to learn arbitrary wordform–lemma associations, they have established conceptual structures that are relevant for phonological parsing. These structures allow them to interpret novel wordforms by using phonotactic generalisations over remembered prior experiences of particular wordforms. Thus, another reason why there must be phonemes is that many of the transitional probabilities that establish the phonotactics of possible words in the language involve syntactic objects that are sequenced at this grain of time. The existence of robustly localised memory structures at this temporal grain can explain why the effectiveness of phonological priming is systematically gradient and why the size of the effect can be measured by counting the number of phonemes in common between the prime and the response. This is in keeping with the results of our association test, and of word-identification experiments in Pisoni *et al.* (1985).

Of course, the infant typically is presented with other systematic variation that correlates with positionally specified transitional probabilities, variation that helps him to pick out likely places for a wordform to begin. For example, in many languages the acoustic semantics of stop-vowel sequences are systematically differentiated between initial and other positions in the wordform (Keating, Linker and Huffman 1983). Some of this semantic variation picks out structural positions defined on elements that can have a larger or smaller temporal grain than the wordform – e.g., elements such as the accentual phrase or syllable in Korean (Jun 1998) or the stress foot in English and German (Keating 1984). In connectionist models of lexical access, we might expect to see more or less localised representations of these other structures in the hidden nodes as well. (The separate nodes for prosodic 'frames' and the positionally specific nodes for consonant 'phonemes' in Dell's 1988 model are an example.)

Infant perception research supports the idea that such hidden nodes will emerge early in speech acquisition. Saffran, Aslin and Newport (1996a) show that a 2-minute exposure to an extended synthetic passage containing trisyllabic CVCVCV nonce wordforms is all that is required to sensitise 8-month-old infants to different transitional probabilities for CV syllables within versus between wordforms. However, infants are sensitised to syllable count considerably earlier than this (Bertoncini, Floccia, Nazzi and Mehler 1995), no doubt because of the typically very salient alternation in effective constriction degree that defines the canonical CV syllable. English-acquiring infants also show a well-established sensitivity to the alternation between strong and weak syllables and to the differing transitional probabilities for these two syllable types between and within wordforms (Jusczyk and Aslin 1995). They do so several months before they begin to be sensitive to the transitional probabilities of segment sequences for the language. Thus, well before the infant has acquired any words *qua* words, structures are emerging in memory for the typical prosodic word 'frames' of the ambient language. These structures will channel the child's attention so as to efficiently exploit positional allophony in remembering and accessing the phoneme strings of the thousands of wordforms that the child will learn in the first few years of life. The results of our association test suggest that positionally specific semantic properties of wordform-internal elements remain an important component of the definition of a wordform's phonological neighbourhood even in adulthood. The phonological priming effect of the wordform-associate pairs emerged most clearly when we counted only identical segments that also stood in identical positions relative to such salient points as the word's stressed vowel.

1.6 Granularity effects and reductionism

As the above discussion suggests, we believe that an important component of language sound structure is the channelling of information flow between different dimensions of the sensory and classificatory spaces. This channelling accounts for the appearance of 'autonomy' or 'modularity' that both the Structuralists and the later Generative Phonologists have noted. That is, there are granularity effects at each of the three bottlenecks described above, which structure the representations available for different phonological tasks. In looking for adequate formal models of these effects, it is important to avoid false reductionism. In particular, it is important to resist the temptation to try to explain all of the phonological generalisations that are available to the child in terms of the observed or expected granularity effects at just one of the bottlenecks.

For example, the exigencies of lexical contrast interact with the discontinuities in the mapping from articulation to acoustics to constrain probability distributions in the articulatory space (Stevens 1989). This provides a natural, universal basis for bootstrapping into the phonemic structure of the lexicon. It is mistake, however, to try to reduce generalisations about segmental structure to the universal aspects of these constraints. Excessive reductionism in this direction results in the common misapprehension that the sequential elements that must be conceptualised to acquire a particular lexicon are properties of the signal *per se* – i.e. that discrete segments and their feature specifications pre-exist in nature. This makes it difficult to appreciate the role of the lexicon in structuring the phonological categories that the child sets up in order to reliably apprehend and reproduce the wordforms of the ambient language. Put simply, different languages use different phonological inventories to make up wordforms. For almost any phonetically robust contrast, it is possible to find a language in which that contrast is not exploited. But many very marginal contrasts are exploited in at least a few languages.

To see the false reductionism here it is important to appreciate why the child should abstract away discrete segments. In the preceding section, we outlined the advantages for the infant who is first learning to pick out recurring acoustic patterns in the ambient stream of speech. This first impetus toward abstraction will be reinforced when the child later on begins to associate the perceived acoustic patterns with his emerging word-motor schema. Consider, for example, the gestural dynamics that differentiate English *cap* from *cab* and *seat* from *seed*. The labial versus alveolar closing gestures harness different articulatory subsystems. But there are useful generalisations to be abstracted away from that difference in place of oral constriction. Some of these generalisations involve the timing of the oral gesture relative to the laryngeal and pharyngeal postures that will either inhibit or promote the continuation of voicing into closure. For English, however, an even more important set of generalisations involves the stiffness of the oral gesture and its timing relative to the oral target for the preceding vowel. The English-acquiring child learns the appropriate motor dynamics and the mapping to the resulting acoustics, and in the space of a few years is able to parse, remember and reproduce novel wordforms such as *seep* and *cad* even after just one encounter with them. Making the right generalisations for this 'fast mapping' (Carey 1978) means that the properties and events in the articulatory and acoustic stimulus spaces are partitioned into those that belong to the vowel and those that belong to the following stop. This partitioning is specific to the language. The syntax and semantics of the voiced versus voiceless final stop contrast in Hindi, for example, differ considerably. Unlike in English, voicing is maintained during closure for Hindi voiced stops even in utterance-final position. Also, vowel length is phonologically contrastive, and is not co-opted to be a phonetic cue to the voicing category of the follow stop.

Another advantage of partitioning the signal into the properties that come from a vowel and those that come from an adjacent consonant is that the child can class together rather different acoustic properties or events in terms of the

30

similar gestural ensembles that produced them. For example, the young child can parse the spectral distribution of energy in an /s/ before /u/ into the contribution of the consonant constriction (coupled with the velic closure and glottal opening) and the contribution of the rounding from the contextual vowel. Moreover, the older child can do so even for a synthesised fricative (Nittrouer 1992).

The advantage of this syntagmatic partitioning becomes even more apparent when a familiar wordform is encountered in a novel sentence context. For example, the English-acquiring child can recognise and fluently mimic the different instantiations of /t/ at the end of *put* – with a lateral release in *Put lettuce on the list*, no release in *Put juice in the cup*, a strident release in *Put your feet on the floor*, and a hyperarticulated alveolar burst in *I said PUT the forks on the table, not THROW them*. The conceptual structures that arise from well-rehearsed parallel associations across the articulation-to-acoustic bottleneck, as the child learns to produce and perceive *put* in all these contexts, support the common phonological classification of the word as invariably ending with a /t/. Moreover, abstracting the /t/ away from the preceding vowel allows the generalisations about variable acoustic patterns to be applied to correctly perceive other wordforms that end in /t/ in analogous contexts, and thus to infer the articulatory structure of their rhymes. The nonlinearities in the mapping between the articulatory and acoustic dimensions of the phonetic space constrain the partitioning of these spaces, but they do not fully determine it. The listening child cannot apprehend articulatory structure that is never supported by the acoustics, but he can adjust attentional weights to glean all relevant available information from the signal. The speaking child, conversely, can organise her articulations to insure that others apprehend the intended wordform.

Excessive reductionism here stems from focusing too narrowly on the structure that nature provides in this interchange of information between the speaker and listener. Because of the discontinuities in the mapping between the articulatory and the acoustic spaces, the language user typically has a finer-grained phonetic representation of her own utterances than of another's utterances. This difference in granularity across that bottleneck is sometimes mistaken for evidence that one or the other set of phonetic dimensions is somehow more primary in the representation of the wordform – for example, to argue that lexical representations need refer only to acoustic properties, because the probability distributions along articulatory dimensions are determined entirely by the nonlinearities (e.g. Stevens 1989).

This kind of reductionism often is associated with a particular type of modular processing model, whereby the categorical specifications for the 'primary' (i.e. acoustic) categories are retrieved from lexical memory and transformed into independent control parameters for the secondary articulatory space in the course of producing or apprehending an utterance. When two

31

'natural' categories in the acoustic space are not contrastive in a language, however, the discretised probability distributions in the articulatory space are assumed to still be available for the production module to use in the independent categorical control of 'enhancing' features (Stevens, Keyser and Kawasaki 1986). This type of model locates the discretisation into segments and features entirely at the articulatory-to-acoustic bottleneck that nature provides, and attributes to the lexicon only the function of determining whether a particular (naturally discrete) acoustic feature is distinctive in the language. Because it effectively ignores the role that the third bottleneck plays in discretising the phonetic space, the model fails to predict the different syntagmatic organisations (the different patterns of 'coarticulation') that acquiring the lexicon promotes for children acquiring different languages (see Manuel 1999 for a review). Trying to explain all of phonetic structure in terms of the natural granularity of the acoustic space makes it difficult to appreciate that articulatory-to-acoustic nonlinearities do not deterministically partition the articulatory space.

Reductionism at this level, however, is not limited to models that take the acoustic space as primary in lexical representation. It also characterises Fowler's Direct Realism (Fowler 1990). In this framework, phonological elements and their associated phonetic properties are equated with macroscopic versus microscopic levels of control for skilled movement. Phonemes in relationship to their phonetic extensions are homologous to different reaching tasks in relationship to the specification of degrees of joint rotation at the shoulder, elbow and wrist. There is a similar claim about lexical memory in Articulatory Phonology. But Direct Realism goes further in also making strong claims about perception and word recognition. Gestures can be perceived directly. One can perceive the gestures of the /t/ just as one perceives the movement of a door, when one hears the sound of it being slammed shut. The articulatory gestures that compose a wordform are transparently available in the acoustic signal, and no language-specific model of the other's intentions is required to apprehend their structuring of the acoustics.

This framework cannot account for the way in which the acoustic robustness of lexical contrast shapes articulation. Where the developers of Articulatory Phonology acknowledge that acoustic events and properties that are distinctive for the ambient lexicon play some role in organising the articulators into gestures and gestural scores (Goldstein 1989; Browman and Goldstein 1989: 226), Fowler must assume a drive toward granularity that is not ecologically situated in lexical memory. Because she does not recognise gestures as syntactic objects, her model cannot account for the effects on the conceptual motor space of learning a particular set of wordform–lemma associations. It cannot account for the fact that gestures and gestural scores reflect the particular set of syntagmatic and paradigmatic categories that come from generalising acoustic and articulatory patterns across the wordforms of a particular language. Like

32

Chomsky (1986), Fowler must assume a predisposition for language that is purely structural, and not built on the more general cognitive functions of symbolic categorisation.

1.7 Granularity effects at the first bottleneck

In the preceding section, we described how well-rehearsed parallelism in the associations across the articulation–acoustics bottleneck interacts with differential transitional probabilities to give rise to (often highly language-specific) patterns of coarticulation and positional allophony. There are homologous granularity effects at the wordform–lemma bottleneck. Well-rehearsed parallelism across the *signifiant–signifié* divide interacts with lexical frequencies to give rise to more or less productive morpho-phonological patterns.

A particularly well-studied case is the regular past-tense affix in English. Work by Marchman and Bates (1994) and others suggests that the child acquires the regular, productive pattern by generalising from parallels in wordform and lemma neighbourhoods across many different present-tense and past-tense wordforms. In a connectionist model, this generalisation can be made if the wordform lemma associations are encoded as activation patterns over separate sets of hidden nodes for lemmas and for their wordforms. In this way each regular verb contributes to the type frequency that establishes the coronal stop affix as the more frequent pattern despite the higher lexical token frequencies of many irregular verbs in English. That is, the parallel association between a past-tense and a present-tense verb lemma on one side of the divide, and between the shorter and longer wordforms on the other side of the divide, promotes the development of an independent but related morphophonological dimension of categorisation. The child learns to recognise the ensemble of gestures at the ends of utterances of the wordforms *played, planned, cried, laughed, skipped,* and so on, not only as tokens of the phoneme types /d/ and /t/, but also as tokens of the regular past-tense affix.

The granularity effects here stem from the relationship between allomorphy and sound change. The phonetic reductions in Old English that led eventually to the loss of the vowel in many post-tonic syllables juxtaposed the voiced coda of what was a fully syllabic affix against a root-final consonant. The synchronic pronunciations of *laughed* and *skipped* treats these wordforms in conformity with the otherwise nearly exceptionless phonological generalisation that within words, obstruent sequences agree in voicing. To make the most useful paradigmatic and syntagmatic partitions of the articulatory and acoustic spaces on the wordform side of the divide, the child should categorise the endings of *laughed* and *skipped* together with the endings of *left, apt, plant* and *plate* and distinguish them from the endings of *played* and *planned*. To make the most useful morphosyntactic partitions on the lemma side, on the other hand, the child should categorise *laughed* and *skipped* together with *played* and *planned*. Because of the way that the first type of categorisation moulds attention and discretises the motor control space, the dissimilarities that obtain between different positional allophones of a phoneme are typically more fine-grained than those between the allomorphs of a morpheme. Where English word-medial /d/ and word-initial /d/ differ merely in 'subphonemic' detail – the one being 'redundantly voiced' (Jakobson, Fant and Halle 1952) relative to the other – the shapes of the past-tense affix in *played* versus *laughed* differ 'phonemically'.

Classical Generative Grammar tries to explain both types of categorisation in terms of the same device – transformational rules operating on minimal phonological representations of wordforms in the lexicon. The child stores the different allomorphs of the past-tense affix as a single lexical entry, which is productively added to (or parsed away from) the verb root each time the past-tense form is produced (or perceived). In thus attempting to reduce allophony and allomorphy to the same phenomenon, accounts of specific languages often are forced to impute to the native speaker, extremely abstract and potentially unlearnable underlying representations. (For elaborations of this point, see Broe 1993; Odden 1992; Steriade 1995.) Equating allophony with allomorphy is an example of false reductionism. The false reductionism here makes it difficult to account for performance in lexical-recognition tasks that differentiate the native speaker's knowledge of the phonological categories from his or her knowledge of the morphophonological categories.

The difficulty comes out especially clearly in the treatment of 'incomplete neutralisation' – i.e. cases where a differentiation between two phonological classes for one set of wordforms is not robustly supported by the phonetics, but is nevertheless maintained by salient associations on the lemma side to another set of wordforms in which the differentiation is robustly supported by the associated phonetic properties. For example, the contrast between /d/ and /t/ in word-medial position in German wordforms such as *Bünde* versus *bunte* supports the maintenance of very subtle 'subphonemic' differences between the associated forms *Bund* and *bunt*. Native speakers' sensitivity to these differences can be uncovered in simple identification tasks (Port and O'Dell 1985). The differences apparently can be exaggerated in some discourse contexts (Charles-Luce 1985). Dressler (1985: 93) also reports a 'clear' differentiation by many speakers of syllable-final obstruents in abbreviations such as *Log* 'logarithm' versus *Lok* 'locomotive', suggesting that the parallel associations across phonological and semantic neighbourhoods need not involve obligatory morphosyntactic categories to support morpho-phonological generalisation.

In a model of lexical representation that reduces allophony and allomorphy to a single transformational process, the phonologist is forced to choose between the 'underlying' and the 'surface' consonant to encode the speaker's lexical representation of each wordform. The fact that morphophonological generalisations can sometimes result in finer-grained rather than coarser-grained categorisation is an embarrassment (e.g. Manaster Ramer 1996). A model of lexical representation that places the grammar square within the lexicon, by contrast, can easily explain the different granularity effects. It does so by distinguishing between categories that are made by generalising over patterns of phonetic similarity among all wordforms in a phonological neighbourhood and categories that are made by generalising over patterns of similarity among sets of wordforms that are also associated on the lemma side. Given a frequent enough rehearsal of the relevant associations, very detailed phonetic representations of the 'underlying' category and of the 'surface' category can co-exist in a single speaker's mind.

This understanding of how lexical memory is structured might also help to explain the ways in which lexical frequency affects both regular sound change and analogical levelling. Research on sound changes in progress has shown that a regular sound change first yields competing variant pronunciations for a segment in a particular phonological context in one set of words, and then spreads through the communal lexicon in ways that are influenced by the relative lexical frequencies of the individual wordforms. This influence exists because a more frequent target word presents speakers with more opportunities to exercise an analogical extension of the pattern of variation from the originally affected words. If the conditioning context is internal to the wordform, a more frequent word is affected sooner because it provides both the target and the context each time it is produced. If the conditioning context is external to the word, a more frequent word is again affected sooner, because its chances of being produced in the relevant external context are also higher (Bybee 2000).

When the candidate set of wordforms is related also on the lemma side of the bottleneck, by contrast, the pattern of frequency effects is rather different. The spread of the change through the lexicon is conditioned by the frequency of the parallel association – i.e. the frequency of the pattern of phonological relationships between wordforms that are also linked by other kinds of relationship. This conditioning is most obvious in sets of inflectionally related wordforms that express obligatory morphosyntactic categories. The conditioning of a sound change by such robustly localised parallelism leaves traces that can be interpreted as 'analogical levelling' even millennia after the sound change has spread through the community. A less frequent pairing of associations across the wordform–lemma divide will leave less clear traces, in keeping with the less robustly localised representation of the joint associations.

An example is the analogical change resulting in the American pronunciations of adjectives such as *hostile* and *ductile*, with a weak /əl/ or syllabic /l/ in place of the strong /ajl/ of standard southern British. This change must have been conditioned by the association to another wordform ending in /ɪlɪti/ – i.e. *hostile* is associated with *hostility*, *ductile* with *ductility*, and so on. Phonologically related wordforms such as *profile* and *textile*, which have no parallel association to a noun ending in *-ility*, are unaffected. To understand this change, we note the low frequency of the analogical link between an originally tense vowel and a lax vowel in these *-ile/-ility* form pairs relative to the higher frequency of the link between an originally reduced vowel in the adjective and the lax vowel in the related noun in *civil–civility*, *national–nationality*, *noble–nobility*, and many other pairs involving the suffixes *-ible* and *-able*, as in *navigable–navigability*. A search of such adjective–noun pairs in the *Hoosier Mental Lexicon* found more than six times as many pairs in which there is an originally reduced vowel in the adjective. The very high frequency of the linking of a reduced vowel in the adjective with a lax vowel in the noun apparently overwhelmed the less frequent correspondence, so that the reduced vowel replaced the original diphthong in most of the adjectives ending in *-ile*. This change affected many very infrequent words such as *ductile*, *contractile*, and *motile* (each with only 1 occurrence per million words in the Kučera–Francis corpus), and was not limited to the higher-frequency adjectives such as *hostile* (at 19 ppm) and *mobile* (at 44 ppm). Conversely, the three adjectives in these pairs for which the *HML* gives the diphthong as the preferred American reading for the vowel in *-ile* also span the range of frequencies for the set. They are *puerile* (1 ppm), *senile* (2 ppm), and *juvenile* (18 ppm). However, the change did not affect other phonological neighbours such as *profile* and *textile*, which are at least as high in frequency as *hostile*, but are not adjectives paired to a noun form ending in *-ility*.

Thus, phonological pattern frequency plays a role in the spread of a regular sound change through the phonological neighbourhood. It also plays a role in analogical levelling – although the frequencies at play are not the same. In the first case, the associations among words that contain the target pattern for the change are all on the wordform side of the *signifiant–signifié* divide. Here it is the frequency of the word itself that affects its susceptibility to change. In the case of analogical levelling, by contrast, there are crucially relevant associations across the wordform–lemma divide. Here it is the frequency of the parallel correspondences in the two different 'semantic' domains that shapes the outcome. The fact that frequency affects both types of changes highlights the common cognitive organisation. By understanding what it means to say that phonological categories are syntactic objects, we can recognize the 'purely phonological analogy' that makes regular sound change regular. The associations in lexical memory that are involved here are not qualitatively different from the associations that drive 'irregular' morphophonologically conditioned changes. There is 'syntactic structure' involved in both types of change; the only difference lies in whether the relevant syntagmatic associations lie only in the wordform neighourhood or also in the lemma neighourhood.

This affinity between the two types of change was impossible to capture in older Structuralist models, where a completely autonomous phonology was encapsulated away from the morphology. However, the exact nature of the affinity is just as difficult to capture in many, more recent phonological frameworks. The different frequencies that are at play cannot be predicted by any framework which reduces the granularity effects at the wordform–lemma bottleneck to a distinction between underlying and surface forms (King 1969) or between lexical and postlexical rules (Kiparsky 1995).

In summary, the multiple dimensions along which subparts of wordforms can be classified together or separately cannot be reduced to a neat hierarchy of derivational strata, each operating at a different grain of specification. Phonetic interpretation is a set of indexical associations between parts of wordforms and their semantic properties. These associations provide real-world extensions for all syntactic objects and functions on the wordform side of the wordform–lemma bottleneck, not just for the last set of phonological categories spewed out by a grammar of rules or ordered constraints. Structure is not learned in isolation from content. Children build on the semantics on both sides of the wordform–lemma divide in constructing the grammar and other conceptual structures appropriate for the culture that they come to share.

2

Effects on word recognition of syllable-onset cues to syllable-coda voicing

SARAH HAWKINS AND NOËL NGUYEN

2.1 Introduction

It is well known that syllables in many languages have longer vowels when their codas are voiced rather than voiceless (for English, cf. Jones 1972; House and Fairbanks 1953; Peterson and Lehiste 1960; for other languages, including exceptions, see Keating 1985). In English, the durational difference in stressed syllables can be 100 ms or more, and it is well established as one of the strongest perceptual cues to whether the coda is voiced or voiceless (e.g. Denes 1955; Chen 1970; Raphael 1972). More recently, van Santen, Coleman and Randolph (1992) showed for one General American speaker that this coda-dependent durational difference is not restricted to syllabic nuclei, but includes sonorant consonants, while Slater and Coleman (1996) showed that, for a British English speaker, the differences tended to be greatest in a confined region of the syllable, the specific location being determined by the syllable's segmental structure.

In a companion study to the present paper (Nguyen and Hawkins 1998; Hawkins and Nguyen, submitted), we confirmed the existence of the durational difference and showed that it is accompanied by systematic spectral differences in four accents of British English (one speaker per accent). For three speakers/accents, F_2 frequency and the spectral centre of gravity (COG) in the /l/ were lower before voiced compared with voiceless codas, as illustrated in Figure 2.1. (The fourth speaker, not discussed further here, had a different pattern, consistent with the fact that his accent realises the /l/-/r/ contrast differently.) Since F_1 frequency in onset /l/s did not differ due to coda voicing, whereas both F_2 frequency and the COG did, we tentatively concluded that our measured spectral differences reflect degree of velarisation, consistent with impressionistic observations. Thus the general pattern is that onset /l/ is relatively long and dark when the coda of the same syllable is voiced, and relatively short and light when the coda is voiceless.

Do these differences in the acoustic shape of onset /l/ affect whether the syllable coda is heard as voiced or voiceless? If they do, the contribution of the onset is likely to be small and subtle, because the measured acoustic differences are small (mean 4.3 ms, 11 Hz COG, 16 Hz F_2 over three speakers). However, though small, the durational differences are completely consistent and strongly statistically significant. Spectral differences are more variable but also statistically significant. Moreover, at least some can be heard. Even if only the more extreme variants provide listeners with early perceptual information about coda voicing, there are far-reaching implications for how we model syllable and word recognition, because the acoustic-phonetic properties we are concerned with are in *non*adjacent segments and, for the most part, seem to be articulatorily and acoustically independent of one another. So, by testing whether these acoustic properties of onset /l/ affect the identification of coda voicing, we are coming closer to testing the standard assumption that lexical items are represented as sequences of discrete phonemic or allophonic units, for in standard phonological theory, longer duration and greater darkness of a sonorant are not considered to be fundamental attributes of a voiced stop at the other end of a syllable.

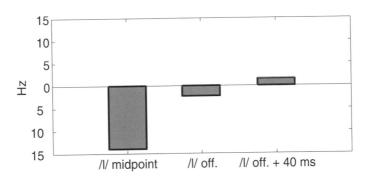

Figure 2.1 Difference in mean spectral centre of gravity (COG) at three points during the onset /l/ and vowel of all syllables produced by one speaker. The COG was computed from a DFT spectrum (49 ms Hanning window) converted to an auditory excitation pattern with decibel magnitude (Moore and Glasberg 1987) in the range 50–3500 Hz. /l/ midpoint = COG centred at the midpoint of the periodic portion of /l/; /l/ off. = COG centred at the offset of the /l/; /l/ off. + 40 ms = COG centred 40 ms after vowel onset

We argue, then, that whereas the durational pattern simply extends the well-established distinction in vowel length due to coda voicing into another sonorant part of the syllable, the association of darkness in the onset with voicing in the coda potentially adds a different dimension. There is good evidence that decisions about segmental and lexical identity are heavily context-dependent. But to the best of our knowledge, there is no documented evidence that information in nonadjacent phonetic segments influences perception, except when the information either changes the number of lexical candidates or directly reflects a property fundamental to the articulation of the upcoming segment. Thus vowel-to-vowel coarticulation reflects tongue movements essential to the two vowels (cf. Öhman 1966; Fowler and Smith 1986), just as long-domain spectral influences due to /r/ or /l/ reflect the spread of attributes essential to the liquids (Kelly and Local 1989; Hawkins and Slater 1994; Tunley 1999; West 1999). Similarly, although a lip-rounded vowel can affect the identity of an (ambiguous) fricative across an intervening stop (Mann and Repp 1980), the acoustic properties that spread to the fricative are fundamental to the identity of the conditioning vowel. The current case also differs from documented instances of word identification being delayed until after the acoustic offset of a syllable (cf. Grosjean and Gee 1987): our effects are tautosyllabic, and do not depend on the identification of one versus two words. Perhaps the case most like our own is work by Raphael and Dorman, cited by Fowler (1983), in which the type of syllable onset caused shifts in /d-t/ boundaries in the coda, but these data were interpreted as due to changes in vowel duration consequent on different onsets. The properties we are discussing are different in two crucial ways: they involve changes in the *same* onset segment dependent on coda voicing, and, as noted above, in standard phonetic theory, longer duration and greater darkness are not fundamental attributes of a voiced obstruent articulation, nor even an associated secondary articulation; hence they cannot spread to a sonorant elsewhere in the utterance. We argue below that longer and darker onset sonorants could in fact contribute fundamentally to perception of coda voicing, but the argument cannot be couched in terms of standard phonetic theory.

If information about coda voicing is available to listeners in the syllabic onset, then coda voicing could reasonably be modelled as a property of the entire syllable. Such an approach has a number of consequences, one of them being that speech might be analysed and matched in a nonsegmental way to words in the lexicon, which might itself be represented nonsegmentally. The investigation described here was intended to provide data that could justify our developing these arguments.

We cross-spliced /l/s in pairs of monosyllables differing in both coda voicing and lexical status (e.g. /l/ of *larg* was cross-spliced with that of *lark*) and presented original and cross-spliced syllables in a speeded lexical decision task. We expected longer reaction times (RTs) for cross-spliced syllables than originals if acoustic properties of /l/ provide information about the voicing of the coda (cf. studies of coarticulatory cues in word recognition: Marslen-Wilson and Warren 1994; Streeter and Nigro 1979; Whalen 1991).

2.2 Experiment 1: Method

2.2.1 Material

Stimuli were isolated monosyllables spoken by S1 in Nguyen and Hawkins (1998) and Hawkins and Nguyen (submitted), which may be consulted for more details. S1, the first author, has lived in several regions of England and the USA; she maintained an Educated Northern British accent, with clear initial /l/. The data were part of a larger dataset recorded directly into a Silicon Graphics computer (16 kHz SR) in a sound-treated room with high-quality equipment. S1 spoke as naturally as possible while keeping pitch, intonation and rate as constant as possible. Although her average spectral differences were smaller than those of Hawkins and Nguyen's S2 and S3, durational differences were the largest, and stress and F_0 were especially consistent.

2.2.1.1 Test stimuli
The test stimuli were 39 pairs of (C)lVC monosyllables differing in the voicing of the final stop (voiced for one member of the pair and voiceless for the other). For 14 pairs, the voiced member was an English word, e.g. *load*, and the voiceless member a nonword, *loat*, while the reverse was true for the other pairs. All words had frequencies of less than 50 per million (mean 4.41 in the Brown Corpus). We controlled as far as possible the frequencies of the lexical competitors for each pair, defined as other English monosyllables with the same onset and nucleus: 33 pairs had only low-frequency lexical competitors (<100 per million); three had one high-frequency competitor, and three had two. Syllable onsets were /l bl pl gl kl fl sl/; vowels were /i ɪ eɪ eə e æ aɪ ɑ ʌ ɒ əʊ u/. Tokens were selected from the dataset on grounds of greater-than-average differences in /l/ duration and F_2 frequency, yet small differences in F_0 at the cross-splicing point. The /l/ was longer (mean +23 ms), and had a lower F_2 (mean −17 Hz) in voiced-coda syllables.

2.2.1.2 Control stimuli
There were 39 pairs of FVC stimuli, constructed identically to the test stimuli except that F is a fricative. Thus the FVC pairs differed in the voicing of the final stop, and were matched with the (C)lVCs for phonemic structure, lexical status, word frequency and frequency of lexical competitors. These FVCs were intended as a control set for which cross-splicing was not expected to have any effect.

2.2.1.3 Filler and practice stimuli

There were 89 pairs of filler items; and 38 other monosyllables to be used as practice items. The fillers fell into two categories. (i) 32 word–nonword pairs of (C)lVC and FVC monosyllables. Unlike the test and control stimuli, their codas were either both voiced or both voiceless, but differed along some other phonetic dimension, e.g. *chafe–chayshe*. (ii) 57 word–nonword monosyllabic pairs whose onset contained neither /l/ nor a fricative, and whose codas were both voiced or both voiceless e.g. *noon–noove*. All filler words were low frequency. The test, control and filler sets all contained the same proportions of voiced and voiceless words. The 38 practice pairs fitted some of the above patterns, but were otherwise chosen at random.

2.2.1.4 Cross-splicing of test and control stimuli

To avoid cutting right at the acoustic discontinuity at /l/ release, each (C)lVC pair was cross-spliced at the zero-crossing 4 periods after the end of /l/ (defined as an abrupt rise in formant amplitudes and, usually, frequencies). Thus cross-spliced *lark* had the /l/ + 4 periods from *larg,* while cross-spliced *larg* had /l/ + 4 periods of *lark.* The average duration between the offset of /l/ and the splicing point was 18.6 ms (sd = 3.6 ms, n = 78). The FVC stimuli were cross-spliced at the boundary between aperiodic and periodic excitation. Four stimuli were derived from each pair, the two original syllables and two cross-spliced ones. Both members of each pair came from the same repetition of the production study. (C)lVC pairs were rejected and replaced by others if the cross-splicing resulted in audible discontinuities in pitch, vowel quality, or loudness. At the cross-splicing point, mean F_0 was 181 Hz; the mean absolute difference in F_0 between the members of each pair was 5.7 Hz (σ 3.8 Hz, n = 39); mean absolute difference in intensity was 1.09 dB (σ 0.89 dB). For comparison, measurements made at the same location in the unspliced stimuli (that is, on either side of the putative cross-splicing point) were as follows: mean absolute difference in F_0 was 1.4 Hz (σ 1.3 Hz, n = 78); mean absolute difference in intensity was 0.34 dB (σ 0.32 dB). Thus, although cross-splicing produced bigger differences in F_0 and intensity than in the original stimuli at the same location, these differences seem to be limited within a reasonable range, given the nature of the experiment. As noted above, pairs with noticeable discontinuities were rejected.

2.2.2 Tapes

The stimuli were recorded onto two DAT tapes, each containing either the original or the cross-spliced version of each test and control item. Each tape began with the 38 practice stimuli, followed by two further blocks, with one member of each pair in each of these two blocks. The four blocks (2 × 2 tapes) were balanced for proportion of words *versus* nonwords, voiced *versus* voiceless codas, and original *versus* cross-spliced syllables. Stimuli were randomised within blocks. ISI was 4 s. A warning beep sounded 1 s before the onset of each stimulus. For each test and control item, a 5 kHz pulse coinciding with the cross-splicing point was recorded onto the other track of the tape. This pulse (inaudible to the subject) triggered the millisecond clock used to measure RTs.

2.2.3 Procedure

Each subject heard one tape over headphones in a sound-treated room, so each person heard only the original or the cross-spliced version of each pair of test and control items, counterbalanced and randomised with the other stimuli. Subjects indicated whether each item was a real word by pressing the appropriate one of two buttons; they were asked to respond as quickly and accurately as possible. Right/left positions of the 'yes' and 'no' buttons were counterbalanced. RT was measured from the cross-splicing point.

2.2.4 Subjects

Eighteen paid subjects (nine per group) completed the experiment, all native speakers of English aged 18–31 years with no known hearing impairment. Six further subjects (three per group) were rejected for low percentage of correct fast responses (< 1200 ms).

2.3 Results of Experiment 1

Of the 2808 total possible responses to the test and control items, 6 were missing, 259 (9.2%) were discarded as incorrect, and 98 (3.5%) with RTs longer than 1200 ms were discarded after inspecting the RT distribution. Unless otherwise specified, statistical significance was assessed by ANOVAs with splice type (original/cross-spliced), lexical status (word/nonword) and coda voicing (voiced/voiceless) as fully crossed within-group IVs, and subjects as a between-groups random factor. A preliminary ANOVA showed that cross-splicing did not affect the percentage of correct responses.

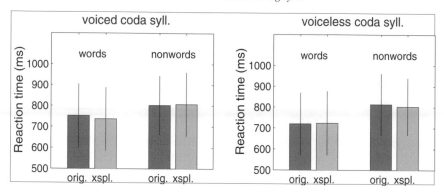

Figure 2.2 Mean reaction times and standard deviations for (C)lVC syllables. Left panel = voiced codas; right panel = voiceless codas; orig. = original syllables; x-spl. = cross-spliced syllables

Figure 2.2 shows RTs for (C)lVC syllables. As expected, RTs were significantly faster for words than nonwords: mean 734 ms *versus* 808 ms, F(1,17) = 30.61, p < 0.001. However, cross-splicing did not affect RTs: original and cross-spliced syllables had mean RTs of 774 ms and 769 ms respectively. Although this testifies to the success of our splicing technique, it does not support our main prediction. Because there was no difference between the cross-spliced and original test stimuli, responses to these stimuli were not compared with those to the controls (FVCs), which are not discussed further. No other differences between conditions were significant.

Since RTs to cross-spliced syllables were not longer overall, we tested whether they were sensitive to the *magnitude* of changes resulting from cross-splicing, such that responses might be slower when cross-splicing entailed greater modification of the acoustic shape of the syllable onset. If so, then RTs should increase in proportion to the acoustic difference in duration and F_2 frequency between the two /l/s in a cross-spliced pair. (The COG could be substituted for F2.) In a standard linear statistical framework, hereafter the voicing-cue model, this prediction can be stated as follows:

(1)   RT(x-spliced) − RT(original) = 0.5(a_1[dur(voiced) − dur(voiceless)] + a_2[F_2(voiceless) − F_2(voiced)] + b)
         where $a_1 > 0$ and $a_2 > 0$

In (1), b is the intercept in a standard linear regression equation; a_1 and a_2 are greater than 0 in order to satisfy the requirement that the relationship is positively correlated; and the constant 0.5 is used because two single-parameter models are combined. Fitting the model to the empirical data involves finding the set of coefficients, a_1, a_2 and b, that minimises the squared deviations between the observed differences in RT, and those predicted from the durations and F_2 frequencies for /l/. These coefficients were estimated in four multiple

44

linear regressions, for voiced-coda words, voiceless-coda words, voiced-coda nonwords and voiceless-coda nonwords, as shown in Figure 2.3.

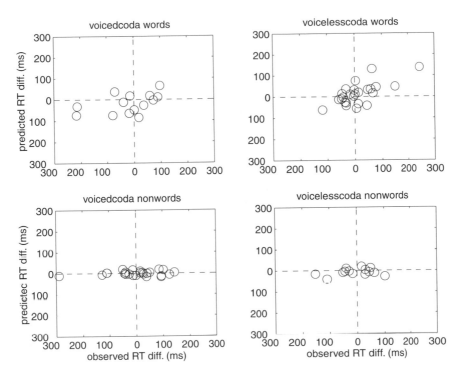

Figure 2.3 Predicted difference in RT between cross-spliced and original versions of stimuli, as a function of observed differences. Predicted differences were based on the difference between the original and cross-spliced /l/s in duration and F_2 frequency

Listeners' RTs were positively correlated with the magnitude of the acoustic change that cross-splicing introduced for real words, whereas they were completely unrelated for nonwords. That is, whereas the data points for words rise towards the right, those for nonwords lie along a horizontal line. Amongst real words, listeners' RTs were only strongly correlated when the coda was voiceless (multiple R = 0.689, F(2,22) = 9.95, p < 0.001, Spearman rho(25) = 0.59, p < 0.01, one-tailed). In other words, when a real word ended with a voiceless coda e.g. *lark*, the longer and darker its cross-spliced /l/, then the slower were listeners' responses. The correlation for voiced-coda real words is weaker. The parametric test does not achieve statistical significance at the 5% level (multiple R = 0.465, F(2,11) = 1.52, p = 0.261), but the rank-order Spearman correlation does (rho(14) = 0.49 p << 0.05). Responses to real words with voiceless codas thus appear to be most affected by cross-splicing, but it seems reasonable to conclude that both voiced- and voiceless-coda real words were processed in a qualitatively different way from nonwords in this experiment.

A number of factors might account for the pattern of these data. First, the difference between words and nonwords (positive correlations for words but zero correlations for nonwords), suggests that these phonetic mismatches were processed at the lexical level, which is in keeping with a nonsegmental view of speech perception. Second, the long vowel of voiced-coda words may have been long enough to override the perceptual salience of small changes in onset /l/. Some support for this point lies in the slight (though nonsignificant) tendency for RTs to be longer when the coda was voiced (777 ms *versus* 768 ms, $F(1,17)$ = 1.61, p = 0.222). On this account, the voiceless-coda words offered the highest probability of finding a correlation between the acoustical measures and RTs.

Alternatively, the longer RTs (mean +75 ms) for nonwords than words may have prevented fine acoustic details of /l/ from measurably influencing RT to nonwords, analogous to a ceiling effect. This explanation is not very convincing since, at around 800 ms, the RTs to nonwords were not especially long. A more convincing possibility is that responses to some stimuli were delayed because the cross-spliced stimuli sounded unnatural. This 'general-disruption' hypothesis differs from the voicing-cue hypothesis on one point. If cross-splicing itself interferes with processing the syllable, then it should interfere regardless of whether the coda is voiced or voiceless. Only the size of the acoustic differences between the two /l/s should matter. For example, cross-splicing should increase RT even when onset /l/ is shorter in the voiced-coda syllable, provided that the durational difference is large enough. In keeping with the linear statistical framework adopted above, the general-disruption hypothesis can be stated thus:

(2) $RT(\text{x-spliced}) - RT(\text{original}) = 0.5(a_1 \times |\text{dur(voiced)} - \text{dur(voiceless)}| + a_2 \times |F_2(\text{voiced}) - F_2(\text{voiceless})| + b)$ where $a_1 > 0$ and $a_2 > 0$

The general-disruption hypothesis cannot be properly tested because /l/ was always longer in the voiced-coda syllables. However, since F_2 frequency in /l/ was higher in the voiced-coda than the voiceless-coda syllable in a few pairs, the general-disruption model could be fitted to the RT data as described above, though only the influence of F_2 is really being assessed. As with the voicing-cue model, predicted and observed RTs were only significantly correlated for the voiceless-coda words, using these parametric tests. However, the multiple correlation coefficient was lower than with the voicing-cue model (R = 0.50), and achieves a much lower level of significance ($F(2,22) = 3.58$, p < 0.05). Thus, the voicing-cue model accounts more reliably than the general-disruption model for the reaction-time data.

2.4 Discussion of Experiment 1

These data show that onset /l/ by itself does not provide a strong indication of coda voicing: cross-splicing affected neither the percentage of items correctly identified nor average RT. On the other hand, the regression analyses suggest that the acoustic properties of onset /l/ can disrupt lexical decisions in the right circumstances, namely when the onset of a real word indicates a voiced coda but the syllable rhyme is consistent with a voiceless one. Though these results show only a small perceptual influence, they deserve attention.

First, they are unlikely to be artifacts of the cross-splicing itself. Although splicing did introduce some differences in F_0 and intensity (see Section 2.2.1.4), the fact that its effect was not significant in the ANOVAs testifies to the acceptability of the experimental manipulation. Likewise, the general-disruption model does not account for the data as reliably as the voicing-cue model. Moreover, had splicing introduced significant artifacts, one would expect differences in RT for the nonwords. Instead, the restriction of positive correlations to real words is consistent with Whalen, Best and Irwin's (1997) finding that people are sensitive to allophonic errors in real words but not nonwords.

Second, work by Wolf (1978) and Summers (1988) demonstrates differences in vowel onset spectra that provide weak perceptual information about the voicing of the coda obstruent that conditions them. If vowel onsets can cue coda voicing, then syllable onsets could be expected to as well, at least if they are sonorant.

Third, if acoustic properties of onset /l/ provided strong cues to coda voicing, then they would be expected to have been well known for years, as have durational properties of the preceding vowel. Since they are not well known, it seems reasonable to assume that perceptual influences from onset /l/ should be small. But if they exist at all, there could be important implications for theories of how we understand words.

We thus interpret these results as promising, but we need more supportive data before developing the theoretical implications. A second experiment was thus carried out to directly test whether acoustic properties of onset /l/ can indicate the voicing of the coda. This experiment is briefly described in the next section.

2.5 Experiment 2

The purpose of Experiment 2 was to check in a more controlled way than Experiment 1 allowed that the duration and F_2 frequency of onset /l/ can cue the voicing of a coda obstruent. Pilot studies suggested that F_0 might also be influential, so, since this has theoretical interest (cf. Kingston and Diehl 1995), F_0 was a third variable. (Recall that in Experiment 1, F_0 differences were minimised in order to avoid discontinuities at the cross-splicing point.) The word *led* was synthesised using Sensimetrics' Sensyn (similar to KLSYN88) from a token spoken by S1. The impressionistic quality of synthesis was good. From this stimulus, five more were made such that the duration of /l/ varied in 20-ms steps over the range 70-170 ms. At each of the six durations a total of 4 stimuli were made by using different combinations of F_2 frequency and F_0 during the /l/. F_2 was constant during the /l/, at either 1850 Hz or 1740 Hz; in each case it jumped to 1860 Hz at vowel onset, from where it rose to 2080 Hz over the next 110 ms. Likewise, F_0 began at either 180 Hz or 168 Hz, and fell linearly to 162 Hz at vowel onset, from which point on it fell over identical values in all stimuli. Thus there were 24 (6 durations x 2 F_2 x 2 F_0) stimuli, identical except for properties of the initial /l/.

Each stimulus was truncated 80 ms after vowel onset, and 300 ms of white noise (rise time 20 ms, decay time 50 ms) was added to it, starting 70 ms from vowel onset. Thus the end of each stimulus seemed to be obliterated by noise: only its initial /l/ and 70-80 ms of the vowel could be heard. The stimuli were randomised in ten blocks of 24, preceded by 16 practice items, and played one at a time to 12 listeners using a Tucker-Davis DD1 D-to-A system controlled by a PC computer. Other conditions were as in Experiment 1. Listeners pressed one response button when they thought the word heard was *let*, and another if they thought it was *led*. ISI was 3 s.

Both duration and F_0 had the predicted effect on responses, but F_2 frequency did not: shorter /l/s and higher F_0 produced more *let* responses. Duration had by far the most influence, with a mean of 73% *let* responses when /l/ was shortest, falling roughly linearly to 36% when /l/ was longest ($F(5,55) = 16.21$, $p < 0.0001$). F_0 alone had a much smaller effect – only about 8% difference: 59% *versus* 51% *let* to stimuli with high *versus* low F_0 respectively ($F(1,11) = 12.12$, $p = 0.005$). There were no significant interactions, although F_0 tended to exert less influence as /l/ lengthened: responses to stimuli with high and low F_0 differed by 13% when /l/ was shortest (70 ms: 80% *versus* 67% *let*) but only 4% when /l/ was longest (170 ms: 38% *versus* 34%). The possibility that non-durational differences may exert most influence when /l/ is short is worth pursuing, since F_2 frequency, whose influence was far from significant, shows the same pattern as F_0 in this respect. That F_2 frequency did not significantly affect responses bears more study in any case, in view of our measurements of natural speech, and other perceptual data (Newton 1996). For example, the influence of large durational and F_0 differences may outweigh that of F_2 frequency in this paradigm, or there may be interactions with vowel height.

In summary, listeners knew about and could use acoustic properties of onset /l/ to help predict the voicing of the coda of the same syllable. Although the properties of onset /l/ did not unequivocally signal the voicing of the coda, they were salient enough to swing decisions by as much as 17-35% on either side of chance.

2.6 General discussion

2.6.1 Preliminary comments

Experiment 1, using natural speech, showed that lexical decisions could be disrupted when an onset appropriate for a voiced coda was followed by the nucleus and coda appropriate for a voiceless obstruent. There is some evidence for a similar but much weaker effect in the opposite case, when the onset was appropriate for a voiceless coda but the rhyme was appropriate for a voiced coda. Experiment 2, using variants on a good-quality synthetic *led*, confirmed that, in the absence of other cues, both the duration of the /l/, and its F_0, influence listeners' responses about the voicing of the coda. F_2 frequency, however, did not. More experiments are planned to further explore influences of F_0 and F_2 frequency.

It seems, then, that the acoustic shape of onset /l/ indicates the voicing of the coda and affects the speed of lexical access. These acoustic properties of onset /l/ are subtle and have only a limited influence on perception when pitted against strong perceptual cues. But it is precisely because they are subtle that we find them interesting. In the cross-spliced syllables, we would not expect /l/ to always play a decisive role in perception of the coda as voiced or voiceless, given that differences in the vowel are still associated with the appropriate coda. In their original contexts, however, there seems no question that they could significantly contribute to the percept of coda voicing. Acoustic evidence in the onset increases the total duration in which coda voicing is consistently indicated, and its presence in more than one phonological unit might enhance the percept further.

2.6.2 Implications for perception of low-level phonetic contrasts

Our findings fit well with assumptions of Auditory Enhancement Theory (AET: Kingston and Diehl 1994 1995). In AET, many acoustic properties combine to form complex Intermediate Perceptual Properties (IPPs), which in turn combine to contribute in varying proportions to the identification of a distinctive feature. Longer onset /l/s before voiced codas could contribute to the (slightly redefined) IPP of the C:V duration ratio. The darkness of the /l/ could contribute to the IPP called the low-frequency (LF) property, since that is associated with a lower spectral centre of gravity. In AET, the C:V duration ratio and LF property are the two IPPs that feed into the phonological feature [voice]. Their physical parameters combine to form a unitary percept, defined as an abstract feature.

Both these IPPs are defined in terms of adjacent acoustic segments. It is trivial to extend the definition of the C:V duration ratio to include durations of sonorant syllable onsets, and the LF property to include F_0 in the onset. But Kingston and Diehl would be justified in objecting to our lumping darkness with the LF property, which is currently defined as a psychoacoustic blending of high-amplitude energy in F_1 and F_0 in the vicinity of a vowel-obstruent boundary: F_1 frequency at vowel offset, and periodicity in the obstruent closure. Our 'dark' property is different: darkness is a property of the entire frequency spectrum, or perhaps the mid-frequencies, and it is distributed across the syllable onset or the onset and nucleus. It remains to be seen whether we are looking at one IPP or two in the LF property and onset darkness, but at some level of analysis we are almost certainly looking at a property of the whole syllable. Nevertheless, our durational and spectral findings seem compatible with AET's principles, and thus with an interesting model of the perception of low-level phonetic contrasts. Since our findings are also compatible with principles of psycholinguistic models of word recognition, we have a potential link between two disciplines that traditionally pursue separate paths.

2.6.3 Implications for lexical access

We have shown that lexical decisions were most likely to be disrupted when an onset appropriate for a voiced coda was followed by the nucleus and coda appropriate for a voiceless obstruent. This pattern might arise because the perceptual system is, metaphorically, taken by surprise when the vowel is short. One might characterise this process in terms of a Weber ratio, involving the contrast between a long onset and short rhyme. A short rhyme may allow properties of the onset /l/ to be discriminated better.

Figure 2.4 illustrates our argument. It shows actual parameter values for one unspliced token of *led* and one of *let*, spoken in isolation by S1. Consider for now only the spectral centre of gravity, calculated as described for Figure 2.1 from the beginning of /l/ to the end of the vowel. The COG is higher throughout the /l/ and the first half of the vowel in *let* (open circles). In the cross-spliced version of *let*, the syllable-onset would be taken from the other syllable, *led*, so the onset would be relatively long and dark, and the rhyme would have a short vowel paired appropriately with its voiceless coda. The long dark /l/ would presumably lead listeners to initially expect a voiced coda. When they hear the end of the vowel sooner than expected, listeners discover that their initial interpretation was wrong: RT increases while the interpretation changes as the vowel suddenly ends.

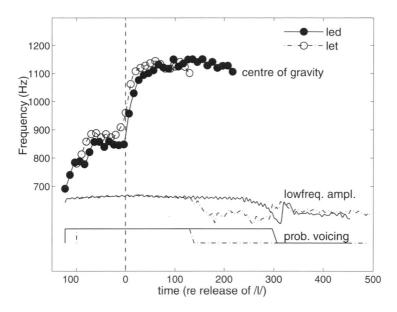

Figure 2.4 Time-course of centre-of-gravity, low frequency amplitude, and probability of voicing for *led* and *let*, aligned at /l/ offset. See text for explanation

In contrast, when the cross-spliced onset is short and followed by a long vocalic nucleus, the likelihood that the coda is voiced will rise as more of the vowel is heard beyond a certain minimum duration. By the end of the word, the relatively weak initial cues to coda voicelessness lose out to stronger contradictory evidence from the syllable nucleus and the coda itself. There is no need for sudden late readjustment, because of the length and consistency of the cues for coda voicing in the syllable rhyme; decisions are thus not significantly slower. Of the explanations we have looked at, this one fits the data best.

There are at least three ways of conceptualising this process. (1) The listener makes early decisions about coda voicing but backtracks when she or he discovers an error. (2) The listener continually predicts what is about to occur, based on past and current information, and makes late decisions. (3) The listener continually predicts what is about to occur, makes early decisions, and corrects them later if necessary – in other words, early decisions are continually updated. Our work cannot speak to the first possibility, but one way to distinguish between the second and third possibilities could be to pit these acoustic–phonetic differences against a context effect that is generally thought to take place late in the decision process (cf. Frauenfelder and Tyler 1987: 8–17). If the acoustic–phonetic properties are used in perception, they should presumably be used early, and so should reduce the magnitude of postlexical effects. These issues must be addressed in future work. Here, we focus on the type of model that these data seem to support, although we point out where our views have implications for the above questions.

Our general approach is uncontroversial: from the input signal, the system identifies properties that are linguistically relevant, combines them into higher-order categories, and identifies their linguistic status in a matching process based on activation of and competition between representational units. This process repeats as long as the signal continues. What distinguishes our model from others is the emphasis on the acoustic signal's fine structure, our consequent conceptualisation of how words are first recognised, and the implications for lexical and phonological structure.

In our model, the fine structure of the sensory signal contributes crucially to spoken word recognition. Consider Figure 2.4 again. In addition to the COG data, there are measures for low-frequency amplitude and the probability of voicing. These parameters extend through the ends of the stops and show the expected differences between the two words. They are just some of many parameters that can be readily calculated from the acoustic signal. In reality there would presumably be many channels, whose nature and initial structuring into auditory streams could be subject to psychoacoustic principles (cf. Bregman 1990). Such fluctuating, multichannel streams of information may resemble what the auditory system transmits to the brain's word-recognition system. There, they can be matched against similar representations stored in memory, which might comprise or include abstract templates, or prototypes, developed from the statistical distribution of items that have been heard over many years. (Such abstract representations presumably include multimodal information derived from nonauditory as well as auditory input channels (cf. Remez, Fellowes, Pisoni, Goh, and Rubin 1998), but for simplicity the present description refers only to the acoustic/auditory modality.) In other words, we are suggesting that the first contact stage of spoken word recognition involves matching incoming auditory shapes with memories of other auditory shapes. And that in at least the initial stages of word recognition, lexical representations are simply time-varying auditory shapes.

We propose that distributional evidence accumulated over repeated hearings allows additional classes of specification to develop from the unsegmented lexical representation that the auditory signal initially contacts (cf. Figure 2.4). One such class is abstract features whose time-varying, phonetically unsegmented values vary continuously between 0 and 1. These can be thought of as fuzzy truth values (Massaro 1998) or as probabilities (cf. McClelland and Elman 1986; Norris 1994). Unlike feature values in those models, which roughly speaking represent the expected degree to which that feature is or should be present, feature values in our model represent a range of acceptable values depending on speech style. Other information derived from statistical evidence includes syllabic and prosodic structure, and links to grammatical and semantic systems. From the spoken signal, the mature listener can identify elements at all levels of the structure simultaneously. For example, an onset /l/ whose acoustic properties were indicative of a voiced coda would raise activation associated with coda voicing throughout the syllable while having no effect on features associated with manner or place of coda articulation. Likewise, the presence of a stressed syllable could be identified before the place of articulation of its initial consonant, or *vice versa*, depending on context and clarity of the signal.

The incoming speech signal is continuously monitored for information on each unit, giving rise to continuous modulation of feature values and structural relationships, and the best match with lexical items is sought. The model allows for the system to track time functions and hence vocal-tract dynamics and their acoustic consequences. It also allows for information that is relatively weak to provide an unambiguous percept, as long as it is consistent over time (cf. Warren and Marslen-Wilson 1987; Hawkins and Warren 1994). Disruption of this consistency delays perceptual decisions, as demonstrated in Experiment 1.

If the first stage of word recognition is based on relatively nonsegmental principles, how then do we get to segments, and to other discrete higher-order linguistic units? Discrete units presumably have some sort of mental representation, since they play a part in people's linguistic lives – consider speech errors, writing systems, pig Latin, poetry, and so on. We envisage that each person gradually builds up a system of discrete categories, corresponding to the familiar levels of linguistic analysis, from the distribution of sensory patterns stored in memory. So, for example, features which regularly co-occur become bound into segments as phonology develops. How exactly this might happen is still largely a matter of opinion, with the two main schools of thought involving either exemplar-based or idealised prototype-based systems. In our view, we cannot yet expect to distinguish between the two, and indeed the distinction may not be clearcut, but it seems undeniable that the process of category formation depends initially on identifying repeated patterns over many instances of like items (cf. Jusczyk 1993).

In our view, processes dependent on episodic memory should be important in the early contact stages, when information-rich sensory patterns are matched against similar time-varying, streamed, but otherwise unsegmented mental representations. Research in cognition suggests that episodic memory contributes significantly to how humans form categories in nonlinguistic systems. It may similarly contribute to speech perception (Pisoni, Lively, and Logan 1994; Lively, Pisoni and Goldinger 1994). The perceptual learning and attunement approach of direct realists, described for speech by Best (1994a, b, 1995), likewise ascribes the formation of abstract cognitive categories to the individual's observation of repeated co-occurrences between events. Eventually, the individual learns to attend to certain types of information and to ignore others. This approach is compatible with the principle that a wide variety of higher-order classes can be formed from a smaller number of individual streams in the sensory input, by weighting and binding them together in different combinations.

The episodic memory and perceptual learning/attunement approaches could be compatible. They may describe the same processes from different viewpoints, though we tend to favour the idea that attunement may begin to operate on more abstract categories, when episodic memory exerts less influence on lexical access. Conceivably, they have somewhat complementary roles in different types of memory. For example, episodic memory of instances could be a primary aspect of memories for speakers and for vocally expressed emotions, while processes better described in terms of attunement might have more influence in representations of lexical items and accents. The present data on /l/ would presumably be relevant to all four types of memory. Amongst the advantages of both approaches are, first, that access to exemplars in memory easily allows access to knowledge of acceptable ranges of variation in feature values for particular lexical items, and second, that different people may develop slightly different phonologies and grammars due to exposure to different input, just as they develop different lexicons and word associations, and as bilinguals' experiences affect how they organise their languages. Although these processes are presumably most plastic in an individual's early years, we envisage them as continuing throughout life, thus allowing for accommodation to new accents, for example.

This type of model can easily accommodate our perceptual results. At the end of the cross-spliced *voiceless* word in Experiment 1, the voiced coda is still activated to a certain degree, for the vowel is short enough that coda activation caused by the onset has not yet decayed. Hence the delay in the response, because the cross-spliced stimulus is more ambiguous than the original voiceless-coda word. In contrast, at the end of the cross-spliced *voiced* word, the activation of the voiceless coda (produced by the cross-spliced onset) has already been reduced to (or towards) 0 because of the relatively long vowel duration. In Experiment 2, the nature of the task presumably activates both words, but the acoustic properties of the /l/, relative to those of the vowel, provide enough evidence in favour of just one word for responses to differ significantly from chance.

Although there are other ways to explain these data, the proposed model has several advantages. Most specifically, because it maps fine acoustic detail onto nonsegmental whole-word memories, it economically accounts for properties of the syllable onset being able to cue the phonological status of the coda. Moreover, in Experiment 1, nonwords did not show the positive correlations found for words (Figure 2.3), which suggests that the mismatches were processed at the lexical level. This in turn supports a nonsegmental perceptual model in which fine phonetic detail distributed across the entire syllable is encoded in the lexicon. More generally, the proposed explanation is relatively simple: it invokes only the notions of activation, decay and some sort of competition. The questions raised at the beginning of this section – at what point in the decision process the increase in RTs occur, and whether the increases reflect a slowing in the decision time itself, or a backtracking and explicit error correction – lose their importance, for this model does not require concepts like 'early decision strategies' and 'backtracking' to correct errors induced by early decisions. A 'lexical decision' can be made at whatever time circumstances demand, for it always reflects the same thing: the current best match to a lexical representation, based on all the available evidence.

2.6.4 Some connections

Although we advocate a nonsegmental and phonetically detailed approach to modelling, our data could be described within a segmental framework. However, that is less appealing because it makes more assumptions, e.g. that coarticulatory effects must be 'undone' through perceptual compensation for coarticulation (cf. Mann and Repp 1980). Our perceptual findings may not be incompatible with a TRACE-like model, with the addition of a set of connections between detectors for syllable-initial phonemes and detectors for syllable-final ones. In a sense, however, such connections would make the model a little less segmental, given that they would have to represent syllable constituents explicitly. More generally, accounting for how distributed acoustic cues are perceived in the framework of a phonemic model such as TRACE seems counterintuitive to us, for we see no convincing reason why distributed acoustic information should be fed into short-domain detectors (phonemes), only to be redistributed again as these detectors in turn activate long-domain units (words).

Our basic ideas are implicit or explicit in most statistically based continuous-information models of speech perception and word recognition, as indicated above. However, our approach is novel in its focus on the role of fine phonetic detail. By contrast, most models in practice assume a phoneme input, so they ignore the perceptual salience of systematic variation in acoustic–phonetic fine detail and thus begin at a level considerably higher than our conceptualisation of initial lexical contact. An exception amongst models of adults' spoken word recognition is the revised cohort model (Marslen-Wilson 1993; Marslen-Wilson and Warren 1994), but even this work has not examined how particular acoustic–phonetic properties correlate with perceptual responses. Grossberg's adaptive resonance theory (Grossberg, Boardman and Cohen 1997), although it uses phonemes as obligatory units, likewise tackles a number of issues relevant to our concerns, including word recognition at different speech rates (see also Protopapas 1999).

Superficially, our model resembles LAFS (Klatt 1979), but there are crucial differences. The most obvious is that phoneme strings are central to LAFS, whereas they are non-essential in ours, usually a by-product of literacy in an alphabetic writing system, and only loosely associated with lexical representations. Second, our input and initial contact representation is nonsegmental, but not unanalysed: sensory information is analysed into streams, which is attended to and further processed in different ways. This is true also for LAFS, but the emphasis is different. In particular, prosodic phonological structure seems to be secondary in LAFS, whereas by its nature it is fundamental to systems like ours, which must take account of syllabic structure, for example. Finally, to reduce errors, LAFS prefers lexical decisions to be made late, but not too late, whereas our hierarchical, nonsegmental model should be less affected by these constraints. Undoubtedly however, some differences between the two models are due to the twenty-year gap between them.

Our position is compatible with work in a number of other disciplines. Early antecedents in phonological acquisition include the nonsegmental approaches of Waterson (1971) and Ferguson and Farwell (1975); see also MacNeilage and Davis (1990). More recently, Jusczyk's (1993) WRAPSA model of how infants learn to recognise words is especially compatible, as are aspects of Suomi's (1993) DAPHO, especially in the status it accords phonemes. By showing that perceptual cues to segmental phonological contrasts can be present in non-adjacent phonological segments, the particular contribution of the present study is to provide supportive data for models such as these, and thereby to underline the likelihood that adults may also recognise spoken words by reference to holistic rather than segment-by-segment analyses. The usual processes that adults use to recognise spoken words may be much the same as the processes young children use, not only because young children begin that way because they have no phonology, but also because speech itself is structured to facilitate or even demand the use of those processes.

There are implications of the present work for increasing the naturalness and robustness of speech synthesis, inasmuch as properties that influence speech perception by humans are presumably broadly similar to those that produce natural-sounding synthetic speech that is robust in adverse listening conditions. However, although our approach would seem to be compatible with statistically based techniques in machine speech recognition, current systems do not use long- as well as short-term dependencies, and it is not currently clear how they could be made to do so (S. Young, T. Robinson, pers. comm.; Nguyen and Hawkins 1999).

2.6.5 Concluding remarks

This demonstration of the influence of fine acoustic detail in a syllable onset on perception of the phonological status of the coda is unusual in combining psycholinguistic methods with phonetic materials and principles. We have shown that tampering with fine acoustic detail in nonadjacent phonetic segments can disrupt lexical access, and supported these observations with more direct evidence of their perceptual cueing power. We argued from this evidence that the initial contact stage of word recognition involves matching relatively unanalysed auditory streams with memories of such streams, or with closely related representations constructed from such streams. Discrete units, and abstract representation, could be built up from these auditory representations (cf. Beckman and Pierrehumbert, this volume), but if they are, then they function later in the process of lexical access. This viewpoint lends itself naturally to models of speech perception based on statistical (distributional) principles and identification via processes of excitation and decay of perceptual units.

Note

We are grateful to Dennis Norris for use of his TSCOP equipment in the perceptual experiment, and to a number of other people for various types of help, especially John Coleman, Eric Fixmer, Ruth Kearns, John Local, Richard Ogden and an anonymous reviewer.

3

Speech perception, well-formedness and the statistics of the lexicon

JENNIFER HAY, JANET PIERREHUMBERT AND
MARY E. BECKMAN

3.1 Introduction

The speech literature abounds in evidence that language-specific phonotactic patterns affect perception. Phonotactics affect placement of phoneme category boundaries (Massaro and Cohen 1983), segmentation of nonce forms (Suomi, McQueen and Cutler 1997), and speed and accuracy of phoneme monitoring (Otake, Yoneyama, Cutler and van der Lugt 1996). Papers in previous volumes in this series (Pierrehumbert 1994; Treiman, Kessler, Knewasser and Tincoff 2000) have provided evidence that perceived well-formedness of phoneme combinations is related to their frequency in the language. Coleman (1996) also found that speakers rated neologisms with attested clusters higher than those containing unattested clusters.

These results indicate that speakers generalise over the entries in their lexicons, and respond differently to patterns which are exemplified versus ones which are not. However, patterns may be exemplified to different degrees. This raises the question of whether knowledge of phonotactics is categorical, distinguishing only possible from impossible forms (as predicted by classical generative models), or whether it is gradient, tracking lexical statistics more finely. Some evidence is available from studies which report different outcomes for high- and low-frequency configurations.

Jusczyk, Luce and Charles-Luce (1994) found that 9-month-old infants prefer frequent phonotactic patterns in their language to infrequent ones. Saffran, Aslin and Newport (1996a) showed that 8-month-old infants are

58

sensitive to transitional probabilities in nonsense speech streams. Saffran, Newport and Aslin (1996b) show similar sensitivity in adults. Treiman *et al.* (2000) found that high-frequency rhymes were judged better, and were more likely to be preserved in blending tasks, than low frequency rhymes. Vitevitch, Luce, Charles-Luce and Kemmerer (1997) demonstrate that subjects rate nonsense words with high-probability phonotactics more highly than nonsense words with low-probability phonotactics, and processing times are also faster for the high-probability set. Pitt and McQueen (1998) explore a phoneme boundary effect reported in Elman and McClelland (1988). They show that the decision between /t/ and /k/ is biased by transitional frequencies, and argue for a model in which transitional frequencies are encoded in a pre-processor which parses the speech signal for access to the lexicon.

Coleman and Pierrehumbert (1997) found that rates of acceptance of neologisms as possible English words correlated with log likelihood, as determined by a probabilistic parse of the form. A low r^2 for this correlation indicates their parser did not adequately model all the important factors. However their major claim – that well-formedness of a neologism reflects its cumulative likelihood as a function of its subparts – has been subsequently validated by Frisch, Large and Pisoni (2000).

These studies all make comparisons between attested patterns and either less attested or unattested patterns. Thus, they do not distinguish between two alternatives for the status of unattested patterns. One possibility is that they are a smooth extrapolation – the limiting case of less and less attested patterns, as expected if the phonological grammar is a simple projection of the lexical statistics. The other possibility is that unattested patterns are processed in a qualitatively different manner, supporting models in which lexical statistics contribute more indirectly.

This paper explores the perception and well-formedness of nonsense words containing nasal-obstruent (NO) clusters. Morpheme internally, these clusters are subject to a homorganicity constraint in English, which would be represented in a conventional phonology by a feature-spreading rule. Yet such a rule does not do justice to the lexical statistics. The strength of the homorganicity requirement depends on the manner of the obstruent and the place of articulation of both the nasal and the obstruent. Some NO clusters are therefore extremely frequent (e.g. /nt/), others are unattested (/mθ/), and yet others fall between these two extremes (/nf/). Because NO clusters are a phonetically coherent set, and sample the range of frequencies finely, they make it possible to assess not only the existence, but also the mathematical character, of perception and well-formedness effects related to lexical statistics.

In all experiments reported here, subjects heard nonsense words containing NO clusters, and rated them as possible additions to the English vocabulary. In the first and third experiments, they also transcribed what they had heard in ordinary spelling. We created NO clusters by cross-splicing because the phonetic interpretation of naturally produced ill-formed clusters is problematic. They may prove disfluent because the speaker has little practice with them. Or they may display so much coarticulation that their identity is unclear.

Experiment 1 demonstrates that nasal homorganicity is psychologically real, gradient and related to lexical frequency. Both the well-formedness judgements and the pattern of corrections in the transcriptions support this conclusion. The next two experiments follow up residual issues related to these results.

First, there was a remote possibility that the quality of cross-splicing was correlated with lexical frequency. The well-formedness ratings would then display the observed pattern even if subjects only attended to the speech quality and not to the phonotactics. Experiment 2 eliminated this possibility by inducing multiple parses for ambiguous compounds. A single stimulus (e.g. *zanplirshdom*) is rated better with a likely parse (*zan-plirshdom*) than with an unlikely parse (*zanp-lirshdom*).

Second, the two unattested clusters in Experiment 1 received anomalously high ratings. Experiment 3 explores the hypothesis that unattested clusters are vulnerable to both reanalysis of the place of the nasal, and to morphological decomposition. We allow for the possibility that the stimulus is interpreted as affixed (as in *camp#er*) or as a compound (*sweet#pea*). The well-formedness ratings are found to be predicted by the log probability of the best morphological parse of the word transcriptions. In Section 3.3 we argue that these results support a model in which perception, production and well-formedness depend on the statistics of the lexicon.

3.2 Experiments

Experiment 1

Experiment 1 involved five series of nine trochaic nonsense words, with each of the nine words containing a different target nasal-obstruent cluster. None of the words begin with a real-word substring; we also tried to avoid beginnings which were reminiscent of real words. All non-target onsets, rhymes, and phoneme-to-phoneme transitions are attested. It was not possible to design balanced stimuli in which no word ended in a substring constituting a real word. However, the pitch accent was on the first syllable, and the second syllable was clearly subordinated.

Transcriptions of the stimuli are shown in Table 3.1, with the log probabilities of the target clusters, given the set of bisyllabic monomorphemic trochees.[1] Two of the clusters have a probability of zero, and so the log cannot be calculated for these – their log probability is represented in the table as simply ln(0). Similarly, on the figures to follow, these clusters appear to the left of a disjunction on the x axis, indicating that no log probability value was calculated for these stimuli.

All calculations presented in this paper are based on type frequency in the CELEX lexical database. We believe that it is type frequency, rather than token frequency, which is most directly related to phonotactic well-formedness. The stimuli here were not constructed to directly test this hypothesis, and in fact, for the set of nasal-obstruent clusters discussed here, type and token frequency are highly correlated. However post-hoc analysis revealed that despite this fact, type frequency out-performs token frequency in predicting the distribution of well-formedness judgements in our data.

Table 3.1 *Simuli Experiment 1, with log probabilities of target clusters*

Set 1	Set 2	Set 3	Set 4	Set 5	ln P
zæntɚ	stɹɪnti	krɛntɪk	ɡɹontəlt	slɛntu	-4.2
zæmpɚ	stɹɪmpi	krɛmpɪk	ɡɹompəlt	slɛmpu	-4.5
zænfɚ	stɹɪnfi	krɛnfɪk	ɡɹonfəlt	slɛnfu	-6.87
zæmfɚ	stɹɪmfi	krɛmfɪk	ɡɹomfəlt	slɛmfu	-7.16
zæmkɚ	stɹɪmki	krɛmkɪk	ɡɹomkəlt	slɛmku	-7.57
zæmsɚ	stɹɪmsi	krɛmsɪk	ɡɹomsəlt	slɛmsu	-8.26
zænkɚ	stɹɪnki	krɛnkɪk	ɡɹonkəlt	slɛnku	-8.26
zænpɚ	stɹɪnpi	krɛnpɪk	ɡɹonpəlt	slɛnpu	ln(0)
zæmθɚ	stɹɪmθi	krɛmθɪk	ɡɹomθəlt	slɛmθu	ln(0)

All stimuli were created by cross-splicing. First, a naïve male speaker of General American English produced nonsense words containing homorganic clusters. These nonsense words mixed beginnings from one stimulus set with endings from another set; for example, the words included both /zænti/ and /stɹɪmpɚ/ in order to support creation of /zænpɚ/. Two stems for each set were excised: one in which the nasal originally appeared before a stop, and one in which it appeared before a fricative. Word endings were excised starting at the voiceless obstruent. Stimuli were constructed by splicing the stem to the relevant ending. Three randomised blocks of all 45 stimuli were presented to 11 subjects, who judged the acceptability of each word on a scale from 1 to 10. A scale was used so that artificial categoriality would not be induced by the task. Subjects then wrote how they thought the word would be spelled in ordinary English spelling.

The results provide two types of evidence that the mental representation of phonotactics reflect lexical frequency. First, a *post hoc* tabulation of the transcribed data revealed that most reanalyses were from a less frequent cluster to a more frequent cluster (409 improving reanalyses versus 147 worsening reanalyses). The rate of improving reanalyses was negatively correlated with the log probability of the actual input cluster (r^2 = .64, df = 7, p < 0.01); worse clusters were corrected more often.[2] The rate of worsening reanalyses was uncorrelated with log probability. This result indicates that lexical frequencies are active in the perception-production loop that resulted in the transcription. If reanalyses occurred entirely at random, the overall pattern of reanalyses would be towards the middle of the frequency range. Regression towards the mean would occur, because the lowest-frequency clusters can only be reanalysed upwards, and the highest-frequency clusters can only be reanalysed downwards. If reanalyses were based only on acoustic similarity, they would not correlate with cluster frequency.

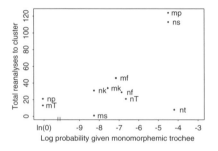

Figure 3.1 Distribution of the outcomes of reanalysis

Figure 3.1 shows the distribution of outcomes of reanalysis. The log probability of each cluster in trochaic monomorphemes is graphed against how often that cluster was the outcome of reanalysis. For example, the log probability of /mp/ is –4.5, and there were 124 cases in which a cluster other than /mp/ was reanalysed as /mp/. Note that 'T' is used to represent /θ/ in this graph. The graph contains some clusters which were not explicitly included in the experiment. For example the cluster /ns/ did not appear in the stimuli, but it appears on this graph because of the high frequency with which other clusters (such as /ms/) were reanalysed as /ns/. The upper left-hand quadrant of this graph is empty, as expected if reanalysis is a function of both acoustic similarity and lexical frequency. High-frequency clusters attract responses, but only if they are acoustically similar to the speech signal. The cluster /nt/, for example, is high frequency, but was not similar to any cluster in the stimuli. Low-frequency clusters are not outcomes of reanalysis, no matter how similar they are to the stimulus.

The well-formedness judgements also reflect the influence of lexical frequency. Excluding the unattested clusters, the mean acceptability of each cluster was highly correlated with its log frequency (r^2 = .87, df = 5, p < .003).

A gradient dependence was also found within subjects, with 10 of the 11 subjects showing $r^2 > .64$ and $p < .03$.

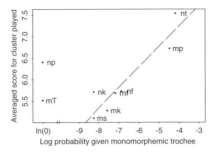

Figure 3.2 Distribution of well-formedness judgements

The two unattested clusters (/np/ and /mθ/) showed anomalous behaviour. The mean rating for /np/ was 6.41, the mean rating for /mθ/ was 5.52, whereas the mean ratings for the lowest two attested clusters were 5.28 and 5.11. The overall picture of well-formedness ratings is shown in Figure 3.2. To the right of the discontinuity in the x axis, we see the gradient relationship between log probability and well-formedness, as summarised by the regression line. The two unattested clusters are shown to the left of the discontinuity. They lie above the regression line. One hypothesis for explaining this boomerang shape might be that the unattested clusters were analysed on perception as higher-frequency clusters. But this does not fully explain their behaviour. On an analysis of the ratings of the clusters actually transcribed (not shown), the /mθ/ and /np/ clusters are still anomalous; in many instances, subjects heard and accurately transcribed the sequences, but still rated them highly.

To explain this result, we hypothesised that words transcribed with unattested clusters were interpreted as containing an internal boundary. In Experiment 3 we explore this hypothesis, and find that it explains the response pattern very well.

Experiment 2

Experiment 3 was designed to eliminate any possibility that the phonetic quality of the cross-splices was responsible for the results. Nonsense compounds were created in which the affiliation of an obstruent is ambiguous, either ending the first word or beginning the second. If the splicing is responsible for the effects observed in Experiment 1, then we expect subjects to rate both parses of the same phonetic item identically. If, however, the effects are due to gradient phonotactic well-formedness, we expect different ratings for the two parses; and this difference in ratings should be a function of the difference in probability between the two parses.

Each NO cluster was used in two stimulus types. In one type, the obstruent could be interpreted as either ending the first syllable, or providing an onset for the following syllable (e.g. *zampirshdom* may be analysed as *zamp-irshdom* or as *zam-pirshdom*). In the second type, the obstruent either ends the first syllable, or is the first phoneme in a cluster onset for the second (e.g. *zamplirshdom* may be interpreted either as *zamp-lirshdom* or as *zam-plirshdom*). Including both simple and complex onsets in the stimulus set allowed us to maximise the difference in probability between competing parses, and to ensure that for some pairs the affiliation of the obstruent to the coda was the more probable parse, and for others the onset parse was more probable. Table 3.2 shows the stimuli, with the log expected probability of the parses.[3]

Table 3.2 *Parsed stimuli for Experiment 2, with log-expected probabilities of parses*

	compound	ln(prob)	compound	ln(prob)
Type 1:	zan-sirshdom	8.79	zans-irshdom	−9.64
	zam-pirshdom	−8.97	zamp-irshdom	−8.43
	zan-tirshdom	−9.25	zant-irshdom	−8.96
	zam-firshdom	−9.50	zamf-irshdom	(−18.78)
	zan-pirshdom	−8.76	zanp-irshdom	(−18.78)
	zam-tirshdom	−9.46	zamt-irshdom	(−18.78)
Type 2:	zan-swirshdom	−11.18	zans-wirshdom	−11.51
	zam-plirshdom	−10.32	zamp-lirshdom	−8.61
	zan-twirshdom	−11.74	zant-wirshdom	−10.77
	zam-flirshdom	−10.45	zamf-lirshdom	(−18.78)
	zan-plirshdom	−10.10	zanp-lirshdom	(−18.78)
	zam-twirshdom	−12.02	zamt-wirshdom	(−18.78)

Following Coleman and Pierrehumbert (1997), the expected probability for the critical region of *zam-plirshdom* is calculated by taking the product of the probability of an /æm/ rhyme and the probability of a /pl/ onset, given our corpus of monomorphemes.

Each cross-spliced stimulus was then presented in two discourse contexts. The same token *zamplirshdom*, for example, was presented separately in each of the contexts shown in (2a,b).

(2)   a.   This is a zam, and this is a plirshdom. A plirshdom for a zam is a zam-plirshdom.

        b.   This is a zamp, and this is a lirshdom. A lirshdom for a zamp is a zamp-lirshdom.

As in experiment 1, the NO clusters were created by cross-splicing from homorganic environments. Each of the subparts in the contextual sentence was spliced out from the compound, and so represented identical phonetic material.

Subjects heard and read the stimuli in context. A written version was provided to reduce the complication of reanalysis of low-frequency forms. The compound appeared in bold, and nine subjects were asked to rate it from 1 to 7, according to 'how acceptable it would be as a word form for the English of the near future'.

The different priming conditions induced different well-formedness judgements for the same phonetic stimuli. Furthermore, the difference in judgements between competing parses is predicted by the difference in log expected probability between those two parses (r^2=.73, df = 10, p< .001). That is, the well-formedness ratings were better for the more probable parse, and the larger the difference in probability between competing parses, the larger the difference in well-formedness judgements between them. This result provides clear validation of the cross-splicing technique. Subjects' well-formedness ratings are related to the probability of the nonsense form. Even when subjects are presented with identical stimuli, well-formedness ratings shift if the probability of the form is manipulated.

Experiment 3

As discussed, the attested clusters in experiment 1 showed remarkably uniform behaviour. However the judgements for /mθ/ and /np/ were anomalously high. We hypothesised that the high ratings were due to morphology. We originally sought to explore clusters in monomorphemes, but cannot be sure that the stimuli received a monomorphemic parse. The clusters may have been perceived as preceding an affix (*ɹʌmp#eɹ*, like *camp#er*), or as bridging a boundary between morphemes (*strin#pea*, like *sweet#pea*). Experiment 3 was designed to test this hypothesis.

We included all voiceless labial and coronal NO clusters − a total of 14, including five unattested clusters.[4] We chose the three sets from Experiment 1 that received the highest ratings: /zæNOɚ/, /stɹɪNOi/ and /krɛNOɪk/. All three have lax front vowels in the strong syllable; our probability calculations take account of this fact. This reflects an attempt to use the most narrow description of our stimuli which does not render the universe of comparison so small as to make the estimates unstable, and thus to provide the most precise description of the data possible without sacrificing generalisability across the sets. Fresh cross-spliced stimuli were constructed. This gave 52 stimuli, which were presented in block randomised order three times each. Nine subjects rated the words from 1 to 7, and spelled them, using the same instructions used in Experiment 1.

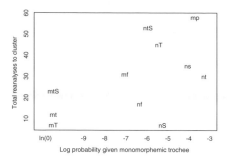

Figure 3.3 Distribution of outcomes of reanalysis

Figure 3.3, corresponding to Figure 3.1 for Experiment 1, shows the outcomes of phonemic reanalysis. The overall counts of errors are not comparable across the two experiments because of differing numbers of stimuli and subjects. This figure has the same empty upper-left quadrant, and supports the conclusion that reanalyses tend to be towards acoustically similar clusters which are more frequent in the lexicon. Note that in this, and subsequent graphs, 'S' is used for /ʃ/, and 'T' for /θ/.

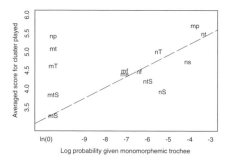

Figure 3.4 Distribution of well-formedness judgements

Figure 3.4, corresponding to Figure 3.2 for Experiment 1, shows the ratings of the new stimulus set. As in Experiment 1, the unattested clusters differ in their perceived well-formedness. Also, the best-unattested clusters are better than the worst-attested clusters. However, the careful orthogonal design of this stimulus set has not caused the responses to fall neatly on a line, but rather has produced a graph with scatter, reminiscent of the data in Coleman and Pierrehumbert (1997). The r^2 for the nonzero clusters is .49, with p < .04 (df = 7).

Plots we do not show reveal that the scatter is reduced a little by looking at the frequency of the cluster actually transcribed. Some portion of the time, low-frequency clusters were reanalysed, and the rating (which occurred before the transcription) may be based on this reanalysis. This reduces some of the scatter, but certainly not all. And there is still considerable variation in the well-formedness of the zero-frequency clusters. The data becomes much more orderly, only when we also allow for the possibility of competing morphological parses.

There are two possible parses in addition to a monomorphemic parse: a compound parse, in which the boundary splits the cluster (*krem#pick*, like *drum#pad*), and a affixed parse in which the boundary follows the cluster (*zamp#er*, like *camp#er*). We wish to explore the idea that parses such as these compete in terms of likelihood.

Table 3.3 shows the raw counts of monomorphemic and affixed trochees, and of monosyllabic words, with lax front vowels. These counts are taken from CELEX. Monosyllables are included because each syllable of a bisyllabic compound is a monosyllabic word, and we calculate compound probabilities based on the assumption that any two monosyllabic words can combine to form a compound. That is, compound probabilities are assumed to be roughly approximated by probabilities across word boundaries. Assuming the three cases in Table 3.3 exhaust the possibilities, we can translate them into probabilities, as shown in the third column.[5] This gives a rough estimate of the overall probability of each of the parses, given the first syllable is strong, and contains a lax front vowel.

Note that these are straight counts of type frequency in the CELEX lexicon. There is no attempt to model the effects of morphological productivity, and so the counts may be slightly conservative. There may be some words ending in *#er*, for example, which some subjects have in their lexicon, yet are not represented in CELEX. However, we do not want to make the assumption that subjects generalise over *all possible* words with *#er*, whether or not they have ever encountered them. That is, we are trying to approximate the results of a generalisation over an existent lexicon, not over the potentially infinite set of words which could be licensed by morphological productivity.

Table 3.3 *Raw counts and compound probabilities of monomorphemic and affixed trochees, and of monosyllabic words, with lax front vowels*

	Count	Probability
monomorphemic:	1609	.457
affixed:	866	.246
monosyllabic:	1048	.297

We can now estimate the probability of each cluster given each parse, by simply calculating the proportion of types for any given parse, which contain the relevant cluster. For example, of the 866 affixed trochees with lax front vowels, 9 contain an /mp/ cluster directly before the morpheme boundary. The probability of an /mp/ medial cluster given an affixed trochee with a lax front vowel is therefore 9/866. For each cluster, the overall probability of it occurring in a given parse can be estimated by the probability of the parse times the probability of the cluster occurring, given the parse. So the probability of encountering /mp/ in an affixed trochee with a lax front vowel is .246*9/866. These, and the analogous calculations for the other two analyses for /mp/ are summarised below. They show that, for /mp/, the best parse is as a monomorphemic trochee, with a probability of .00795276.

Monomorphemic analysis:
(zamper, like pamper)

P(*monomorphemic trochee | lax front vowel*) x
P(*/mp/ medial cluster | monomorphemic
trochee with lax front vowel*)
= .457 * (28/1609)
= 0.00795276

Analysis as a CC# suffix:
(zamp#er, like camp#er)

P(*bimorphemic trochee | lax front vowel*) x
P(*/mp/ cluster before # | bimorphemic trochee
with lax front vowel*)
= .246 * (9/866)
= 0.00256

**Analysis as a trochaic
compound:**
(krem#pick, like
drum#pad)

P(*monosyllabic word | lax front vowel*) x P(*/m/
coda | monosyllabic word with lax front vowel*
x
P(*second syll is a monosyllabic word given the
first was*) x P(*/p/ onset | monosyllabic word*)
= .297 * (44/1048) * 1 * (174/3880)
= 0.000559

We completed these three calculations for each of the 14 clusters. Figure 3.5 shows how the probabilities of bimorphemic parses compare to those of monomorphemic parses.

On the x axis is the probability of the target cluster in a monomorphemic word. On the y axis is the probability in a bimorphemic word, with open squares representing the case of words with a boundary after the cluster (as in *camp#er*), and filled squares representing the case in which the boundary splits the cluster *(as in drum#pad)*. If the cluster probabilities were the same for bimorphemic as for monomorphemic parses, the points would fall on the line x=y. But they are not the same.

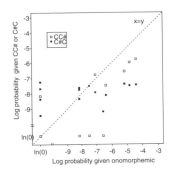

Figure 3.5 Log probability of clusters given monomorphemic versus log probability given affixed or compound parses

Across word boundaries consonants combine independently.[6] The probabilities for clusters in monomorphemes are therefore polarised compared to those in compounds (filled squares). Some clusters are less probable morpheme-internally than the most improbable cluster across a word boundary. But the most probable morpheme-internal clusters are more probable than any cluster crossing a word boundary. The parses involving an affix (open squares) fall between the monomorphemes and the compounds. The range in the y dimension is greater than for compounds (it extends to include zero probabilities), but less than for monomorphemes. The probabilities of clusters on either bimorphemic analysis are not correlated with the probability of the monomorphemic analysis. Both filled and open squares fall in a horizontal band.

The pattern in Figure 3.5 is, we would argue, a fundamental characteristic of phonology. It would be logically possible to design a language in which phonological restrictions across word boundaries were strong and pervasive. But human language is not like this. Because words have arbitrary meanings, and coherence of meaning dominates how words are combined, phoneme transitions across word boundaries are closer to being statistically independent than transitions within morphemes.

Suppose that listeners choose the most probable analysis of what they hear. If a cluster is highly probable morpheme-internally, then no bimorphemic analysis of that cluster can ever be more probable. However, if the cluster is improbable morpheme-internally, then a bimorphemic analysis might be more probable. Table 3.4 shows the probability of the winning parse for each cluster.

Table 3.4 *Probability of best parse for each consonant cluster*

Cluster	Prob. of best parse	Best parse
nt	0.0122132	(monomorphemic)
mp	0.00795276	(monomorphemic)
ns	0.00568056	(monomorphemic)
nʃ	0.00170416	(monomorphemic)
nθ	0.00142014	(monomorphemic)
ntʃ	0.00113626	(CC#)
np	0.000711707	(C#C)
nf	0.000568056	(monomorphemic)
ms	0.00048528	(C#C)
mt	0.000459572	(C#C)
mf	0.000430647	(C#C)
mʃ	0.000234679	(C#C)
mtʃ	0.000231392	(C#C)
mθ	0.000080344	(C#C)

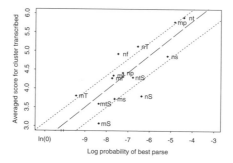

Figure 3.6 Log probability of the most likely parse for each cluster versus well-formedness judgements for clusters perceived as that cluster

Figure 3.6 shows that viewing our data in this light renders them very orderly. On the x axis is the log probability of the most likely parse for each cluster. On the y axis is the mean well-formedness judgement for stimuli (rightly or wrongly) transcribed with that cluster. Each time /np/ is transcribed as /mp/, for example, the related well-formedness score contributes to the average well-formedness of /mp/ rather than /np/. The data are now more linear than in

Figure 3.4, with the regression line for the whole data set having an r^2 of .65, df = 12, p < .0005. This gradience is also present within individual subjects. Individual r^2s range from .28 to .71, and p values from .05 to .0002.

Examination of the residuals from this regression line shows an additional factor at work. Clusters containing strident obstruents (/s/, /ʃ/ or /tʃ/) fall below the regression line, whereas those containing other obstruents fall above it. This pattern reflects an effect of the Obligatory Contour Principle (OCP). OCP-Place refers to a tendency to avoid excessively similar consonants at the same place of articulation in close proximity (see McCarthy 1986). The *striN* and *zaN* stems begin with coronal stridents, and additional coronal stridents appear to be avoided even as far away as the beginning of the next syllable. Support for this interpretation can be found by comparing overall ratings for the three stems. The stem *kreN* does not contain a strident, so we predict that judgements for this set will not show a difference between stridents and other obstruents. Indeed, the difference in average well-formedness rating between stridents and non-stridents is only 0.07 for the *kreN* set, but 1.43 for the *zaN* set, and 1.39 for the *striN* set. This is consistent with findings by Pierrehumbert (1994) and Berkley (1994) indicating that OCP-Place operates across intervening phonemes in English.

When we fit separate lines through the strident and nonstrident points of Figure 3.6, very high r^2 values are obtained. These lines are shown in dots; for stridents, r^2=.8, df=4, p<.02; for nonstridents, r^2=.93, df=6, p<.0001. The overall well-formedness reflects a cumulative effect of the local probability of the parse and the long-distance factor of the OCP.

The well-formedness ratings in Experiment 3 reflect the most probable analysis of the stimulus. There is active competition amongst multiple analyses of the same stimulus, and the listener probabilistically imputes a phonemic and morphological analysis. As a result, judgements are well behaved when plotted against the probability of the best analysis of the cluster transcribed, but poorly behaved when plotted against the morpheme-internal probability of the original cluster played.

3.3 Discussion and conclusion

This study was undertaken to evaluate the relationship between well-formedness and frequency in the lexicon. The results support a model in which well-formedness is directly related to the perceived likelihood of the form. Furthermore, this relationship is gradient rather than categorical.

In the model we would propose, lexical probabilities figure twice. First, they influence perception and reproduction of the stimuli. Second, they determine perceived well-formedness. The percept of a stimulus is a probabilistic function of its acoustic character and of the likelihood of its components. The best analysis of a stimulus may involve relabelling phonemes and/or imputing morpheme boundaries. That the same probabilities figure twice – both in perception and in judging the result of the perception – supports models in which perception, production, and well-formedness all depend on lexical frequency. That well-formedness is based on the optimal analysis supports models in which analyses of the signal compete, and in which recognising a signal as having a particular phonological form is equated with the triumph of that form in the competition with its alternatives. Models that have this property include both connectionist models (e.g. Rumelhart and McClelland 1986) and Hidden Markov models (see Rabiner and Juang 1986 for an overview).

The interaction of NO likelihood and the OCP broadly supports the claim of Coleman and Pierrehumbert (1997) that well-formedness reflects the cumulative effect of the likelihood of the subparts. However, the Coleman and Pierrehumbert model does not handle the effects we have found here. Their model provides for the probabilistic interaction of syllable onsets and rhymes as components in a metrical tree. However, the NO clusters investigated here crosscut the syllable structure, as they include the coda of one syllable and the onset of the next. That such strong results have been obtained for NO clusters indicates that not only syllabic components, but also junctures, are important cognitive elements. Contrary to Levelt (1989) and Schiller (1997), junctural configurations appear to be just as cognitively important as the onset and rhyme configurations that the junctures crosscut.

The Coleman and Pierrehumbert model also does not provide for the interaction between NO phonotactics and the OCP. Their model provides only for the interaction of independent components combined in sequence. In the present data, both the NO phonotactics and OCP-Place target the post nasal obstruent. The failure to model junctural effects and overlaid generalisations is probably one reason for the high degree of scatter in Coleman and Pierrehumbert's results. Another is that they do not model the reanalysis of stimuli as phonologically better forms.

One of the main goals of our study was to investigate the status of unattested clusters. Are these clusters categorically different from attested clusters, or can zero frequency be viewed as the limiting case of low frequency? Under the model we propose, unattested clusters do differ from attested ones in that they are not exemplified in the lexicon. Since stimuli are analysed with reference to the lexicon, unattested clusters must be coerced onto a form with non-zero probability. This coercion may involve reanalysis of phonemes, or it may involve imputing an internal boundary. This coercion is not unique to unattested clusters however. Low-frequency clusters are also probabilistically reanalysed as more probable ones, and are likely to receive a bimorphemic parse. In these respects, unattested clusters do indeed show the limiting behaviour of less and less probable clusters.

A possible objection to this model is its apparent prediction that unattested combinations can never be recognised as single words. This prediction is obviously falsified in our own experiment, since all of our stimuli were nonsense words and therefore represented combinations of 5 to 8 phonemes which are not exemplified in the lexicon. However, the results lead us to believe that subjects judged these as monomorphemic, and common experience shows that such words can be internalised readily and added to the English vocabulary. This objection rests on the assumption that probabilities are computed over large, detailed, phonological fragments. If the relevant probability for each cluster were its probability in the light of the entire phonological description up to that point in the word, then all of the clusters in our experiment would have probability zero. By the time /m/ of *strimpy* is reached, the cumulative probability of the analysis is zero. No words begin in *strim*.[7] The ability of the subjects to reliably assess differences in likelihood indicates that probabilities over large fragments are not relevant to this task. To explain knowledge of phonotactics, it is necessary to posit abstraction over the lexicon. Thus, our work broadly provides new evidence for Pitt and McQueen's claim (against Elman and McClelland) that knowledge of phonological grammar abstracts over the lexicon. Phonotactic knowledge cannot simply consist of cumulative probability calculated from the hypothesised word-onset.

We ourselves made an abstraction over the lexicon when we computed the probabilities of various parses. Were the universes we selected for computing probabilities cognitively realistic? We suggest three ways in which they were. First, the phonological descriptions we evaluated were formally simple. Second, they represented descriptions which would plausibly be recovered bottom up from the speech signal.[8] Third, they provided sets of large enough size that probabilities could be reliably estimated. Each of these factors affects the degree to which a computation is robust. And we might expect listeners to be most finely attuned to probabilistic patterns which are robust: simple descriptions, which are easily recoverable and statistically reliable. Because these factors were in confluence, we are not in a position to offer conjectures about which is most important. If they are naturally in confluence – all appearing together when examples of psychologically real probabilities are found – then this would be an important fact about cognition.

Notes

1   All probabilities reported in this paper were calculated using the CELEX Lexical Database (Baayen *et al.* 1995). Our corpus of monomorphemes includes all words coded as monomorphemic in CELEX, as well as many words coded as having 'obscure morphology' or as 'possibly containing a root'. Three linguists

independently identified words in the latter two categories which they considered to be multimorphemic. Any word identified by any of the linguists as multimorphemic was omitted from the corpus. The researchers also rejected several words coded as monomorphemic, including reduplicative forms (e.g. *tomtom*), and adjectives relating to places or ethnic groups (e.g. *Mayan*).

2   In this calculation, unattested clusters were treated as if they occurred just once in the lexicon, to avoid taking log of zero. Also note that if /nk/ was transcribed as 'nk', this was not counted as a reanalysis, even though it may well have been heard as /ŋk/, but not recorded by the English spelling. This r^2 is therefore a conservative estimate.

3   To avoid taking log of zero, the expected probabilities for zero-frequency forms was set to $\ln(0.000000007) = -18.78$. This is the probability a compound would receive if there was just one pair of words in the corpus which could combine to create a compound with the relevant characteristics.

4   Velars were eliminated because English spelling does not record the place of articulation of a nasal before a velar.

5   This is a slight over-simplification, as it omits marginal possibilities such as compounds where the cluster ends the first word (*camp#out*).

6   While external sandhi provides an exception, there is no reason to believe it is relevant to this data set.

7   Our reviewers point out that *strim* and *strimmer* are, in fact, words in British English. It is reasonably safe for us to assume, however, that these were not items in our subjects' lexicons.

8   See Shipman and Zue (1982) for evidence that major class features for consonants and major groupings of vowels can be recovered bottom up from the speech signal, and Mermelstein (1975) for evidence of syllable-count recoverability.

4

Factors of lexical competition in vowel articulation

4.1 Introduction

Understanding sources of variability in spoken language is one of the most important challenges that face speech researchers today. Traditionally, variability had been treated as noise to be controlled or ignored in studying spoken language; however, there has recently been an increasing interest in exploring lawful variability in spoken language. For example, Byrd (1994b) found that sex and to a lesser degree dialect differences resulted in between-talker differences in the degree of reduction along a number of dimensions including speech rate, stop release, flapping and quantity of central vowels. In addition to inter-talker differences which might be viewed as talker- or group-specific constants, there are many forces that act on spoken language that may change the way a word is pronounced from one utterance to the next by the same talker.

Reduced and clear speech processes represent a significant source of within talker variability, much of which has been attributed to talkers varying their pronunciation to accommodate the communicative needs of the listener (e.g., Anderson, Bard, Sotillo, Newlands and Doherty-Sneddon 1997; Bolinger 1963; Lieberman 1963; Lindblom 1990). In these studies talkers have been shown to produce more reduced speech when contextual information within the utterance or in the environment can aid the listener in recognising what is said, and to produce more careful speech when the talker is aware of conditions that may impede the listener's ability to understand what is said. When words are isolated from their spoken contexts, the speech that has been produced under conditions of high contextual predictability has a low intelligibility. Conversely the speech produced under conditions of low contextual predictability has a high intelligibility. Although most studies have concentrated on contextual and environmental factors, relatively few have examined how word-specific characteristics might affect production strategies. The purpose of this study is to examine the degree to which factors in lexical competition that are known to affect intelligibility of individual words influence the carefulness with which talkers produce words.

4.2 Reduction and sources of information

Although many studies have assumed reduction as a constant, Lindblom (1990) has proposed a more explicit model of the interaction between the forces that shape both reduced and clear speech. In his model, speech motor control is output-oriented and plastic. In this view, reduced speech and clear speech lie along a continuum of contextually determined variability. In a communicative context there is pressure on the system to maintain sufficient information in the signal for the listener to recover the intended message. With a decrease in likelihood that a listener will be able to recover the message, output constraints become more severe and the talker is forced to produce clearer speech (i.e. exaggerate contrast among lexical items). This Lindblom calls 'hyper-speech'. As output constraints become less severe, the system tends towards economy of effort becoming more system-oriented, resulting in reduced speech ('hypo-speech'). Speech perception involves discrimination among stored items – lexical access is a function of distinctiveness not invariance. Thus reduction and hyperarticulation will occur along dimensions that will increase or decrease the perceptual distance among lexical items. Reduction in speech can be measured in a number of ways; some of the better-known characteristics are shortening of vowels, increased flapping, increased consonant and vowel deletion, and acoustic vowel centralisation.

A commonly cited example of the talker modifying pronunciation to accommodate the hearer's needs is the Lombard effect (Lane and Tranel 1971; Lane, Tranel and Sisson 1970; Lombard 1911), in which the talker produces more careful and higher-intensity speech in response to increased environmental noise. More careful productions have also been observed when talkers introduce unexpected or novel information into the discourse (Bolinger 1963; Chafe 1974; Hawkins and Warren 1994). On the other hand, reduction occurs when the talker estimates that a listener will have little difficulty in identifying a word. For example, Lieberman (1963) found that words that are highly predictable from sentential context are more reduced than identical words produced in an equivalent sentence that does little to narrow the field of lexical candidates.

Similar results have been found for a variety of predictive contexts (Bard and Anderson 1983; Fowler and Housum 1987; Hunnicutt 1985).

Talkers are sensitive to a wide variety of sources of information not only from the auditory mode but also from the visual mode (and one would predict the haptic mode as well). For example, Anderson *et al.* (1997) found that a talker's performance reflects the listener's access to visual information from the talker's face. Anderson *et al.* (1997) found that when talkers estimated that listeners had access to visual information, tokens in spoken language were significantly degraded. In later intelligibility tests, the reduction of the auditory signal was offset only if subjects were given access to the accompanying video stimuli in addition to the audio stimuli. An interesting point that emerged from the study was that talkers maintained only a loose model of the information available to the listener; rather than tracking the listener's use of visual information from moment to moment, the talker adjusts the carefulness of speech in a more global fashion basing the model on talker-internal conditions. That is, talkers did not pay attention to whether or not the listener was actually looking at his/her face, but rather to whether or not the listener had the ability to look.

4.3 Lexical competition and intelligibility

In addition to the message-internal and environmental contextual factors that affect a word's intelligibility, there are lexical factors that may increase or decrease the probability of a talker identifying a word correctly. Word frequency is perhaps the best-known lexical trait that may affect a word's intelligibility. It is also a proposed factor in overall word shortening and increase in reduction processes (Balota, Boland and Shields 1989; Bybee 1994; Zipf 1935). However, overall word frequency alone has proven to be a rather poor predictor of intelligibility (Luce and Pisoni 1998; Pisoni, Nusbaum, Luce and Slowiaczek 1985) and has proven an unreliable predictor of reduction. Rather, word identification must be viewed in the context of lexical competition for the role of frequency in intelligibility to be clearly seen. In his dissertation, Luce (1986) studied patterns of auditory word confusion and found that a word's intelligibility is affected by two lexical factors: (1) *neighbourhood density*: the number of phonologically similar words in the language, and (2) *relative frequency*: the frequency of the target word relative to its nearest phonological neighbours. In calculating nearest neighbours, Luce found a reasonably close match between his confusion matrices and neighbourhood density determined using the *single phoneme substitution* method (Greenberg and Jenkins 1964) in which all words that differ from the target word by a single phoneme are considered nearest neighbours.

Luce (1986) proposed the Neighbourhood Activation Model (NAM), an activation model based on R. D. Luce's biased choice rule. In the model, acoustic-phonetic input activates a pool of word candidates drawn from a similarity neighbourhood. The probability of the listener correctly recognising the target word is a frequency-weighted function of the probability that the target word was presented versus the frequency-weighted probabilities that each of the neighbourhood competitors was presented. In this model, while frequency will determine the probability of correct identification, a word with few neighbours is also likely to be identified even if its usage frequency is low. It is worth noting that the strong frequency bias in the model allows it to deal with the apparent top-down effects without positing explicit bi-directional pathways. Based on intelligibility properties, words from high-density neighbourhoods and with low relative frequency have been termed 'hard' and those from low density similarity neighbourhoods and with high relative frequency have been termed 'easy' (Luce and Pisoni 1998; Pisoni *et al.* 1985).

A preliminary study of the effect of neighbourhood density on voice-onset time or VOT (one of the main indicators of stop-consonant voicing) was conducted by Goldinger and Van Summers (1989). In their study, they had talkers read minimal pairs of CVC words in which the word-initial stop consonant was either a voiced or a voiceless stop. The pairs were chosen so that both were from sparse neighbourhoods or both were from dense neighbourhoods. Each talker read each pair of words four times. Overall the VOT was more exaggerated in minimal pairs from dense neighbourhoods than in minimal pairs from sparse neighbourhoods. Moreover, across repetitions the difference in VOT between the dense pairs increased dramatically while the VOT difference between the sparse pairs increased slightly.

A potential flaw in the study was the method of presenting the words in minimal pairs. This presentation technique attracts the talker's attention to the contrast being studied and is generally thought to result in an exaggeration of the contrast; it may heighten the talker's sensitivity to lexical factors. Nevertheless, the fact that the sparse and dense neighbourhoods predicted differences in talkers' behaviour over repetitions is a preliminary indication that neighbourhood density is a factor in variability of spoken language. Interestingly, the fact that all the words in the study showed the effect indicates that neighbourhood density appears to have an effect on all phonemes in a word, at least in monosyllabic words, because the majority of lexical competitors would not have been confusable on the first phoneme. That is, although some of the words may have had neighbours that were close because they differed only in voicing of the initial phoneme, the single-phoneme substitution method that the authors employed to calculate neighbourhood density implies that roughly two thirds of the neighbours are based on the second or third phonemes in the words. The apparent whole-word effect implies that talkers use only a loose sense of sources of neighbourhood density rather than using fine positional information in making adjustments. This last point is similar to the observation in Anderson *et al.* that talkers maintain only a crude estimation of what visual information listeners may be using.

The current study was designed with these preliminary VOT findings in mind. Because of the interaction between neighbourhood density and relative frequency in the intelligibility studies mentioned above, it was decided that the first place to look for an effect was in 'easy' versus 'hard' words. This choice was further driven by the existence of a publicly available pre-recorded database of 'easy' and 'hard' tokens. The main prediction of this study is that factors in lexical competition should affect the degree of reduction in production of rhythmically strong vowels just as contextual factors do. That is, 'easy' words should show a greater degree of reduction than 'hard' words (or conversely that 'hard' words should show a greater degree of hyperarticulation). Because differences in acoustic vowel centralisation have been shown to differentiate clear from casual speech (e.g. Byrd 1994; Lindblom 1990; Moon and Lindblom 1994) and because increased vowel dispersion is an established correlate of intelligibility (Bond and Moore 1994; Bradlow, Torretta and Pisoni 1996; Picheny, Durlach and Braida 1985), 'hard' words are predicted to have vowels that are at the more dispersed end of the reduction–hyperarticulation continuum than 'easy' words. Increased dispersion is characterised by an expanded vowel space or by overall increased acoustic distances between vowels from different categories.

4.4 Method

4.4.1 Recording materials

Tokens in the study were all monosyllabic CVC words drawn from a pre-recorded database of words spoken in isolation (Torretta 1995). All words were of equally high familiarity, being between 6.8 and 7.0 on the 1–7 point Hoosier Mental Lexicon scale (Nusbaum, Pisoni and Davis 1984), but varied crucially in their similarity neighbourhood density and in relative-usage frequency. One set of words, termed 'easy', came from sparse-similarity neighbourhoods and had usage frequencies that were high relative to their neighbours. A second set of words, termed 'hard', came from dense-similarity neighbourhoods and had usage frequencies that were low relative to their neighbours. The words were chosen to provide a balanced segmental context for the vowel; consonantal contexts that could result in vowel colouring were avoided while maintaining similar contexts in 'easy' and 'hard' words. For example, postvocalic /r/ and /l/ were avoided altogether for both types of words, and nasal codas, when unavoidable, were balanced in both sets. The full set of tokens is listed in Appendix 1. Overall, there are 34 'easy' and 34 'hard' words spoken by 10 talkers (5 male and 5 female) of General American English resulting in 680 tokens total. Although a variety of neighbouring dialects were represented, all the dialects had the same vowel-quality categories in all of the stimuli. The sound files in the database are digital recordings of monosyllabic words presented singly in pseudo-random order on a CRT monitor and read once in isolation. The talkers were instructed to say each word at a 'medium' rate (the database also includes recordings at other speech rates). The utterances were antialias filtered and digitised directly to disk at 22050 Hz.

4.4.2 Measurement

As the file names in the database included lexical neighbourhood information, the files were renamed (to the word contained in the file) and randomised prior to measurement. The first and second formants (F1 and F2) of each vowel were measured at the point of maximal displacement on all 680 tokens. The initial and final 50 ms of the vowel were excluded to minimise the effect of flanking consonants on the measurement. Because these words were spoken in isolation at a medium speaking rate, the vowels' durations were all long enough to permit excluding the initial and final 50 ms. The point of maximal displacement occurs when F1 and F2 are the most characteristic for that particular vowel. For example, for the vowel /i/ it is the point where F1 is lowest and F2 is highest and for /a/ it is the point where F1 is highest and F2 is lowest. Where F1 and F2 were not in agreement, F1 was taken as the point of reference and F2 was measured at that point. This measure is equivalent to what has typically been described in the literature as the 'steady state' but takes into account the dynamic character of vowels which often results in the absence of a clear steady state. For diphthongs the measure was taken in the primary portion of the vowel (e.g. for /aɪ/ the measure was for the /a/ portion). Formant values were measured from a twelfth order LPC with a 25 ms window overlaid on a simultaneous 512 point FFT. A wideband spectrogram was used to locate the measurement point and for reference during the formant measures. The formant values were converted into the Bark scale (an auditory transform) using the formula given in (1) (Zwicker and Terhardt 1980) where Z is bark and f is frequency in Hertz.

(1) $$Z = \left[\frac{26.81f}{(1960+f)} \right] - 0.53$$

The degree of dispersion was measured using a technique applied in Bradlow *et al.'s* (1996) study of talker intelligibility: the Euclidean distance from the centre of a talker's F1 by F2 vowel space. Using this measure, Bradlow *et al.* found that one of the best correlates of talker intelligibility was the degree of vowel dispersion. Differences in dispersion were submitted to an analysis of variance with dispersion as the dependent variable and lexical category (easy/hard), vowel category, and talker as the independent variables.

4.5 Results and discussion

Overall, the hypothesis was borne out; there was a reliable effect of lexical category ('easy' versus 'hard') on dispersion (the Euclidean distance from the centre of the vowel space). With an alpha level of .01 the analysis revealed a significant main effect of lexical category, $F(1,480) = 130.92$, $p < .0001$. As expected, there were also significant effects for talker and vowel category. There was also a significant interaction between lexical category and vowel type, $F(9,480) = 15.22$, $p < .0001$. Figure 4.1 shows the overall dispersion in Bark (vertical axis) in the height of the bars for 'easy' versus 'hard' words collapsing across talker and vowel type. There is a clear difference in the degree of dispersion with the vowels from 'hard' words being more dispersed on average than the vowels from 'easy' words. This difference in dispersion represents an overall expansion of the vowel space for 'hard' words. Figure 4.2 is an F1 by F2 plot of the mean values for each vowel: vowels from 'hard' words are plotted using darker, slightly larger symbols and vowels from 'easy' words are plotted with the lighter symbols. This plot illustrates two characteristics of the data: the overall expansion of the 'hard' vowel space, and the tendency for certain vowels to show greater expansion than others.

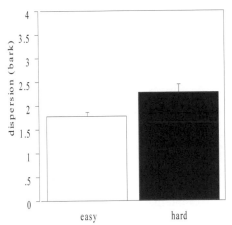

Figure 4.1 Vowel dispersion for 'easy' and 'hard' words averaged across talker and vowel; error bars indicate 95% confidence intervals

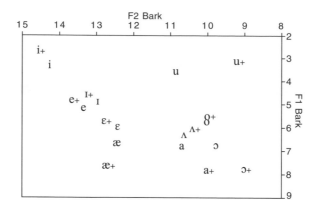

Figure 4.2 A traditional F1 by F2 vowel plot with F1 on the vertical axis and F2 on the horizontal axis. Vowel category means are plotted using symbols followed by '+' for vowels from 'hard' words and plain symbols for vowels from 'easy' words

When the data are analysed by vowel using post-hoc t-tests, the differences between vowel types become clear: the vowels /i, æ, a, ɔ, u/ (referred to as 'point vowels' henceforth) show the greatest difference between 'easy' and 'hard' words whereas the remainder of the vowels are only slightly expanded or not expanded at all. For some of the vowels /ɪ, ɛ, o, ʌ/ the difference between the two conditions was not reliable. Figure 4.3 illustrates the latter point. It is a plot of dispersion that splits 'easy' versus 'hard' by vowel category. There is a marked difference in the height of the dispersion bars between the point vowels and the remainder of the vowels.

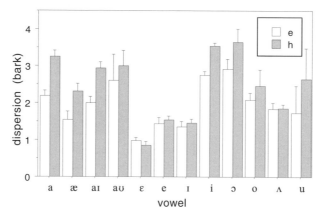

Figure 4.3 Vowel dispersion for 'easy' and 'hard' words by vowel type averaged across talker; error bars indicate 95% confidence intervals

The difference in dispersion across conditions between the point vowels and the rest of the vowels is in one sense unsurprising. Given the physiological limitations in producing vowels, and given that vowels contrast with each other rather than with the Euclidean centre of the space, moving the point vowels while leaving the other vowels fixed maximises the acoustic distance between vowels of different categories. This stretching of the acoustic space should make the vowel contrasts more salient by increasing the perceptual distance between vowels of differing categories. This finding for English mirrors a cross-linguistic simulation conducted by Liljencrants and Lindblom (1972) that explored the relationship between the number of vowels in a system and the shape of vowel spaces. Their simulation, which took into account the physiological limitations of the vocal tract aimed to find the vowel spaces which maximised the distance between vowels in a two dimensional F1 by F2 space. Their distance formula, given in (2), calculates the repulsive force in a system of vowels using the inverse sum of the squared distances between vowels. In the formula i and j represent all pairs of vowels in the system. With this measure, the closer the different items are the greater the repulsive force.

(2) $$E = \sum_{i=1}^{n-1} \sum_{j=0}^{i-1} 1/r^2{}_{ij}$$

where $r^2{}_{ij}$ is $\sqrt{(F1_i - F1_j)^2 + (F2_i - F2_j)^2}$

This measure of distance was applied to the set of data excluding the diphthongs /aɪ/ and /aʊ/ and resulted in a clear difference in repulsive force between the vowel systems from 'easy' and 'hard' words. Across talkers the 'easy' system showed dramatically more repulsive force than the 'hard' system, indicating a more expanded vowel space for 'hard' words.[1] In looking at individual talkers, this measure reveals striking individual differences. Figure 4.4 plots repulsive force on the vertical axis by talker (greater repulsive force indicates less overall distance between vowels). Although the 'hard' vowel space showed less repulsive force for all the individuals, some of the individuals exhibited a much greater magnitude of difference between the 'easy' and the 'hard' vowel spaces. For example, the magnitude of talker M9's difference is several times that of talker F1. It is interesting to note that there is a much greater difference in the height of the 'easy' force bars than the height of 'hard' force bars. This indicates that the differences in the magnitude of effect of lexical factors are based primarily on the degree to which different individuals permit centralisation of vowels in 'easy' words.

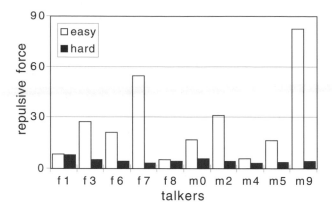

Figure 4.4 Repulsive force in vowel systems from 'easy' and 'hard' words. Greater force indicates an overall more compact vowel system with less distance between vowels tokens from different categories

4.6 Conclusion

The data support the hypothesis that vowels from 'hard' words are more hyper-articulated than vowels from 'easy' words. The expansion of the vowel space occurs in such a way that overall distances between vowels are maximised; only the point vowels, which can move without diminishing the vowel contrasts, become more dispersed while the others remain relatively unchanged across conditions. This finding replicates previous studies' findings that talkers adjust the degree of hyperarticulation to compensate for factors that may impede the intelligibility of a message. This study is novel in that it finds compensatory hyperarticulation for lexical characteristics of individual words. This finding has implications for speech recognition research because it represents a potentially significant reduction in the amount of *random* variability which must be dealt with in an *ad hoc* fashion. It also has implications for linguistics, sociolinguistics and historical linguistics in that processes that refer to reduction should take into account lexical properties of words.

Although tested only in monosyllabic tokens in this study, this effect is predicted to carry over to rhythmically strong vowels in polysyllabic words. The nuclei of weak syllables are not expected to change since their reduction is an indicator of prosodic structure. If this finding generalises to other conditions, follow-up studies should show that lexical factors interact with other linguistic and paralinguistic processes that promote reduction or hyperarticulation. Such factors may include semantic or syntactic information redundancy such as that shown in Lieberman (1963) and subsequent studies, given versus new status of an utterance (e.g. Bolinger 1963), redundant visual information about the talker's articulators (Anderson *et al.* 1997), and the familiarity of a hearer with a particular talker (e.g. Nygaard and Pisoni 1995). The Lombard effect and similar compensatory behaviour in reaction to environmental noise may also show an interaction with lexical factors. It should be the case that 'hard' words will be proportionally more hyperarticulated in conditions where the hearer is expected to have greater difficulty recovering the utterance, and that 'easy' words will be proportionally more reduced in conditions where the hearer is expected to have greater ease in recovering the utterance. There has recently been renewed interest in the syllable structure effects on consonant-cue recoverability such as the weakness of place cues in syllable coda position (e.g. Ohala 1990; Ohala and Ohala 1998; Wright 1996). It is likely that words which rely on phonological contrasts that are poorly encoded in the acoustic signal will be shown to be more difficult than their raw lexical characteristics would predict for listeners to recover. This sort of finding would argue for an additional bias factor in Luce's NAM for calculating the probability of correct word identification.

An interesting and rather unexpected outcome of the study is the variability between speakers in a fairly constrained task. The differences in the force graph in particular are interesting because they appear to indicate nonuniform behaviour in the face of relatively uniform differences in factors that affect intelligibility. The individual differences might be thought to be due to differences in the individual's lexicon. Although this is a possibility, it seems unlikely considering the high familiarity of the items used. It may rather indicate differing sensitivity to the effects of lexical factors on intelligibility, different levels of willingness to take advantage of lexical factors, or differential responses to the demands of the recording set-up. It should be noted that only one dimension of reduction/hyperarticulation was studied here. It may be that one talker will reduce along one dimension (e.g. vowel dispersion), while another talker will reduce along a theoretically independent dimension (e.g. stop releases or syllable duration). It should be noted that the individual differences seen in this study must be seen as tentative because they may be attributable to subtle dialectal differences between the talkers or other sociophonetic factors. A larger study with a more and more homogeneous group of talkers, a greater number of lexical items, and a variety of tasks and measures is needed to make clear predictions about the range of individual variation.

Notes

This work was supported by NIH-NIDCD Training Grant DC0012 to Indiana University, Bloomington. The author is grateful to Ann Bradlow, Stefan Frisch, Gina Torretta and the reviewers for helpful comments during preparation of this manuscript.

1 These diphthongs cannot be included in the calculation because their formant values are expected to be nearly identical to the values for the monophthong vowel category /a/. Since the formula calculates repulsive force by category, including them would spuriously increase the repulsive value for /a/ enormously.

Appendix 1: Words used in study

'easy' token	'hard' token	vowel
job	wad	a
watch	knob	a
shop	cod	a
gas	pat	æ
jack	hack	æ
path	hash	æ
five	rhyme	aɪ
wife	white	aɪ
vice	lice	aɪ
mouth	rout	aʊ
gave	fade	eɪ
faith	dame	eɪ
shape	mace	eɪ
page	sane	eɪ
chain	wade	eɪ
death	den	ɛ
check	wed	ɛ
leg	pet	ɛ
peace	bead	i
deep	tea	i
teeth	weed	i
give	kit	ɪ
thing	hick	ɪ
ship	kin	ɪ
thick	mitt	ɪ
wash	caught	ɔ
both	goat	oʊ
vote	moat	oʊ
food	hoot	u
young	hum	ʌ
love	pup	ʌ
judge	mum	ʌ
hung	bum	ʌ
rough	bug	ʌ

5

Commentary: probability, detail and experience

JOHN COLEMAN

5.1 Introduction: word frequency and phonetic detail

The founding mothers of Laboratory Phonology have, on various occasions, been at pains to point out that Laboratory Phonology is not a theory of phonology, like say Autosegmental Phonology, but is rather a way of *doing* phonology that admits of a broad variety of different viewpoints, theories and ideas. For instance, Pierrehumbert, Beckman and Ladd (1996) suggest that 'the existence of diverse views may perhaps serve to underscore one of our main points, which is that "laboratory phonology" is not a theoretical framework but rather a research community'. As the conference series has progressed, however, a fair number of important scientific results about phonology have been demonstrated, some of them several times over. To take one instance, at the fourth Laboratory Phonology meeting, Grabe and Warren (1995) and Vogel, Bunnell and Hoskins (1995) independently demonstrated that the Iambic Reversal analysis of the English Rhythm Rule (Liberman and Prince 1977: 319) is phonetically and perceptually untenable. To the extent that such results as these are at odds with mainstream generative phonology, it is becoming increasingly unrealistic to avoid numbering them as part of a coherent theoretical standpoint. Two such results are exhibited in the three papers I have been invited to comment on: in the mental storage and processing of phonological representations, a) phonetic detail matters, and b) word-frequency matters.

Phonetic detail of the kind discussed by Hawkins and Nguyen (this volume), and Wright (this volume), and frequency of word use, are both regarded as irrelevant in mainstream phonological theory. For example, like most other phonology textbooks, Kenstowicz (1994: 58) states 'unlike the features for place of articulation and voicing, aspiration (in English) is entirely *redundant*. ... Consequently, in learning English vocabulary, the developing grammar need not list the [± spread gl] value individually for each lexical item.' The expression 'need not' is then silently interpreted as 'does not', without further discussion.

The aversion to probability in mainstream generative grammar is harder to illustrate, but it has its roots in Chomsky's early dissatisfaction with probabilistic approaches to syntax, in particular Markov models. Miller and Chomsky (1963: 430) argue that in order to train a *k*-limited Markov model on English word sequences in which a verb can exhibit agreement with a subject noun at least fifteen words distant would require the estimation of over 10^9 probabilities, an implausible feat: 'The trouble is not merely that the statistician is inconvenienced by an estimation problem. A learner would face an equally difficult task ... We cannot seriously propose that a child learns the values of 10^9 parameters in a childhood lasting only 10^8 seconds.' In phonological theory, probability has not so much been rejected as disregarded. I shall resist the temptation to speculate here on the sociological factors behind this state of affairs.

Hawkins and Nguyen (this volume) show us that syllable-initial /l/'s are darker if the syllable-final consonant is voiced than when it is voiceless, an interesting and surprising phonetic detail in the realisation of words contrasting in the voicing of the final phoneme. Hay, Pierrehumbert and Beckman (this volume) show us that the acceptability of nonsense words containing Nasal–Obstruent clusters is related to the probabilities of their phonological parses. And the central argument of Wright (this volume) was that some spectral details of vowel quality are conditioned by word frequency, thus bringing both ideas, phonetic detail and frequency, together.

To consider phonetic detail first, it should be noted that despite its avoidance of redundant features in general, in practice mainstream generative phonology is unable to work using distinctive features alone. For example, in the rules of regular plural formation in English, nasal consonants pattern with voiced obstruents in taking /z/ rather than /s/, even though voicing is held to be a redundant feature of English nasals. Broe (1993: 77–9) observes that even in lexical entries, Halle (1959) found it necessary in setting out the foundations of generative phonology to include redundant features in lexical representations, in order to keep lexical entries distinct, where one would otherwise subsume the other. Thus, in the table of Russian morphonemes given in Halle (1959: 45), /s/ is categorised as [+strident] and [+continuant], in spite of the fact that all

[+continuant] morphonemes are predictably [+strident], in order to keep /s/ distinct from /t/, which is [–strident]. Otherwise, the highly underspecified underlying representations of /s/ as [+continuant] and /t/ as [–strident] would not be distinct, since they do not contrast in any features. Similarly, /n/ is categorised as [–strident], though this follows from its being [+nasal], in order to keep /n/ distinct from /s/ and /c/, which are unspecified for the feature [nasal], but which *are* specified as [+strident]. More recently, Frisch, Broe and Pierrehumbert (MS) have argued for the necessity of counting redundant features in the evaluation of OCP-Place in Arabic. Their central finding is that in the computation of similarity, redundant features count, though, unsurprisingly, they don't count as much as distinctive features.

The kind of redundancy normally recognised as having some function in generative phonology relates solely to features which are sometimes, elsewhere, distinctive. But the kinds of detail in Hawkins and Nguyen and Wright's papers are subtler: the distinction between more and less peripheral vowel qualities in Wright's study would require at least the adoption of some new phonological feature, e.g. [± peripheral], and Hawkins and Nguyen show that a contrast in the clearness of syllable-initial /l/ can be identified that correlates with the voicing of the postvocalic obstruent. The conventional feature inventory can deal with a contrast between clear and non-clear phonemes, of course (using the vocalic feature [back], for example, to show the secondary articulation of consonants), but the problem of how to represent the small durational difference in the /l/'s would remain. Proliferation or co-optation of binary features is not the right approach here. It needs to be recognised that the phonetic interpretation of [± voice], in the one case, or of word frequency, in the other, includes subtle phonetic details on dimensions that are not transparently related to their underpinnings in the grammar.

5.2 Hawkins and Nguyen's study

Hawkins and Nguyen begin by taking up a finding by van Santen, Coleman and Randolph (1992). In that paper, van Santen, Randolph and I were interested in trying to identify the fine spectral and temporal details of the coda voicing contrast without segmentation of the signals. We took up an idea of Macchi, Spiegel and Wallace (1990), to use dynamic time warping (Sakoe and Chiba 1978) to compare the acoustics of minimal pairs of words. Using this method, samples of acoustic parameters of two phonologically distinct utterances are registered with one another such that samples of greatest similarity are paired. The resulting correspondence function ('warp path') shows which samples of one parameter are most similar to which samples of the other. Figure 5.1 (from Slater and Coleman 1996) shows a typical result of such an alignment computation.

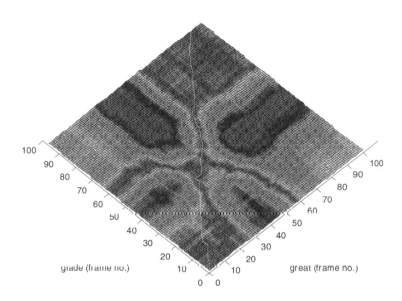

100
90
80
70
60
50
40
30
20
grade (frame no.) 10

100
90
80
70
60
50
40
30
20
great (frame no.)

0 0

Figure 5.1 Distance matrix and warp path showing the difference between the second formant frequencies of '-ter great ag-' (x-axis) versus '-ter grade ag-' (y-axis), taken from recordings of phrases of the form 'Can you utter — again?'. The greyscale represents the sample-by-sample F2 distance (dark = little difference; light = large difference). The superimposed white line shows the path of maximal similarity between samples of the two utterances

In such figures, the path of maximum similarity between the two utterances lies close to the diagonal. (If a signal is compared with itself, the warp path lies exactly on the diagonal.) Deviations of the warp path above and to the left of the diagonal show that a portion of the y-axis parameter corresponds most closely with a shorter portion of the x-axis parameter; i.e. the x-axis parameter would have to be expanded for that interval in order to be time-aligned with the y-axis parameter. Deviations of the warp path below and to the right of the diagonal indicate portions where the y-axis parameter would have to be expanded in order to follow the same time-course as the x-axis parameter. The values along the warp path indicate the magnitude of the distance between aligned samples, and show which parts of the aligned utterances are most similar and which are most different. (The dark regions far from the diagonal are correspondence between portions of accidental similarity, such as the fact that the vowel of *great* is more similar to the preceding schwa than to /gr/. Such regions can be disregarded.)

This technique is a signal-processing version of the minimal pairs test used in phonology, and can be employed for that purpose. For instance, given two words which are known to be different in meaning and which seem impressionistically to be phonetically similar except in some small phonetic detail, analysis of the warp path shows temporal differences between the words and also the region of greatest dissimilarity, that is, the location at which the phonological contrast is evident, which may be punctual or extended, and which may be different on different parameters.

For example, it is well known that vowels are longer before voiced obstruents than voiceless ones. By analysing time-warped minimal pairs such as *let* versus *led*, van Santen *et al.* (1992) found that there is much more to the temporal differences between voiced and voiceless items than vowel duration. In particular, we found that the location of maximal expansion of the voiced words, as compared with their voiceless counterparts, is rather variable. In particular, the location of maximal expansion in some words, including *meld*, *dwelled*, *canned* and *rode*, was late in the voiced portion of the word; in many cases, in the postvocalic sonorant consonant (as noted by Sweet 1877). In other cases, such as *cawed*, *spurred* and *aid*, the maximal expansion was during the vowel or diphthong. In many words containing /aɪ/, such as *hide*, *side* and *ride*, the location of maximal expansion was earlier in the diphthong. And in the odd case of *led* versus *let*, we found the location of maximal expansion to be in the initial /l/, quite remote from the final consonant.

Slater and Coleman (1996) is a similar study, on British rather than American English. We confirmed that the location of maximal expansion in voiced words varied according to the phonotactic make-up of the syllable. In some pairs (e.g. *bite* versus *bide*, *height* versus *hide* and *great* versus *grade*), maximal expansion in the 'voiced word' was found early in the sonorant portion of the syllable (i.e. during the prevocalic /r/ or the peak of the diphthong /aɪ/), in some cases even in sonorant onset consonants. In other cases, maximal expansion occurred in the vowel, either towards the beginning or the end, and in some cases in postvocalic sonorant consonants (e.g. in *meant* versus *mend* and *went* versus *wend*).

In their production study, Hawkins and Nguyen (this volume) established that /l/s in syllable onsets are longer and darker before voiced codas than voiceless ones. This finding, now firmly demonstrated, has consequences for our conception of phonological representations. Does it make any sense to continue to refer to the voicing contrast as a property of a particular obstruent, or even of the coda as a whole, if some of its phonetic exponents are to be found at such a distant remove? Even using conventional structural argumentation, we might propose that since there is only one distinctive occurrence of voicing in the onset, however big, and at most one other distinctive occurrence of voicing in the rime, the feature [±voice] is a prosodic property of onsets and rimes, as in Figure 5.2. Another reason for promoting [voice] to a prosodic position is to retain the locality of its phonetic interpretation: the interpretation of the onset is influenced by a feature of the rime, in particular the voicing of the coda.

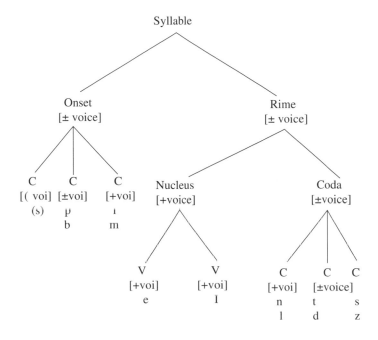

Figure 5.2 Syllable template for English, showing the distribution of values of the feature [voice] at terminal and non-terminal nodes

On this view of phonological structure, it perhaps seems less odd that the voicing of the rime might be manifest in the phonetic details of the consonants preceding it. After all, it is unobjectionable to state that the voicing of a consonant is signalled by some phonetic details of the vowel preceding it, a fact known at least since Sweet (1877). But the main lesson, I think, is that if phonology and phonetics are quite separate levels we ought not to be too fixed in our expectations about where the phonetic exponents of a particular phonological distinction may turn up. Hawkins and Nguyen have given us a contemporary example of the sometimes rather curious and arbitrary links between phonology and phonetics that are focussed on in the literature on Firthian Prosodic Phonology, such as the statement in Henderson (1949) that 'the characteristics of a long syllable are ... (3) the reduction of the possible tone alternations to tones 2 and 3 only, when the final consonant unit is accompanied by closure without plosion', or the analysis of Lhasa Tibetan in

Sprigg (1955), according to which an initial voiceless alveolar lateral or [tsh] is 'a mark of a Tone One word' (among other marks), whereas the absence of plosion, friction, and other consonantal articulations at the beginning of the word is a mark of Tone Two words.

Hawkins and Nguyen's main interest is in perception, however. They say: 'The most interesting result was that the longer /l/ is, or the lower its F2 in a nonword with a voiced coda (e.g. *larg*), the slower listeners were to identify as a real word the corresponding cross-spliced word with a voiceless coda.' But the association between duration or F2 of /l/ and the voicing of the following coda was not sufficient to outweigh other factors, such as vowel duration. In retrospect this is hardly surprising: it means that the cross-splicing method they employed was not best suited to their goal. Perhaps a gating paradigm, or independent synthetic control of just the syllable-initial durational and spectral properties of interest, might enable them to pin down the perceptual accessibility of the onset cues to coda voicing. They will need to go further yet to establish not just that a phonetic difference exists, and that it can be perceived, but also that under the right circumstances the differences in question might be a sufficient basis on which to identify the difference in meaning between the paired words. Then it would be incontrovertible that the differences are part of the ensemble of cues to the phonological distinction.

5.3 Probability

The second theme of the group of papers on which I was asked to comment is frequency of occurrence, or probability. Like fine phonetic details, probability and other statistical measures have had something of a bad press in mainstream linguistics. In *Syntactic Structures*, Chomsky (1957: 17) wrote: 'Despite the undeniable interest and importance of semantic and statistical studies of language, they have no direct relevance to the problem of determining or characterizing the set of grammatical utterances.'

Despite the recent resurrection of interest in probabilistic grammars in some areas of computational linguistics, Chomsky's attitude remains dominant in syntactic theory today. As far as the phonotactic grammaticality of words is concerned, however, his statement is demonstrably wrong. As a step towards showing this, Coleman and Pierrehumbert (1997) showed that the log likelihood of an English-like nonsense word is a better characterisation of its well-formedness, as judged by native speakers, than the likelihood of the worst part, a probabilistic variant of the orthodox view that if any part of a nonsense word is phonotactically illegal, the whole word is ill-formed. In that paper, we used a probabilistic grammar to model native-speaker judgements of the acceptability of nonsense words obtained in experiments conducted as a class project in my lab. We found that some words containing quite horrific clusters, such as *mrupation*, are regarded as better than some other words, such as *spletisark*, that break no known phonotactic rules. Our explanation of this observation was that most of *mrupation* is actually fine, especially the prosody and the *-ation* part, which is quite a high-frequency suffix.

Also, *mrupation* and its well-formed congener *mupation* were modelled on their lexical neighbour *mutation*, with which they share many parts. Whereas *spletisark*, though not specifically ill-formed in any part, happens to have low-frequency parts and low-frequency neighbours.

That study, and others like it, are open to the Chomskyan objection that acceptability is not the same as grammaticality: 'grammaticalness is only one of many factors that interact to determine acceptability' (Chomsky 1965: 11). The second experiment reported by Hay, Pierrehumbert and Beckman (this volume) sees off that objection by requiring subjects to parse *the exact same stimulus* in two different ways, in one case treating the N-O cluster as a coda, in the other case as separated by a word boundary. The only experimental factor being manipulated is thus the parse tree, so differences in acceptability must directly relate to structural properties (possibly including probabilistic properties), not 'performance factors'. They obtained different well-formedness judgements for the different parses, the magnitude of the difference being predicted from the difference in the log likelihoods of the respective parses. So, to their list of studies showing that language-specific phonotactic patterns affect perception, they add further evidence that knowledge of phonotactics has a probabilistic character.

Wright (this volume) showed that frequency is at work not just in phonotactics, but also matters in phonetic interpretation. In higher-frequency words and/or words with relatively few lexical neighbours – competitors, we might say – the vowels were produced with somewhat less peripheral qualities than the qualities found in lower-frequency words and/or words with many lexical neighbours. This result suggests that speakers pronounce less common words and/or words that might be mistaken for other similar words more distinctly.

Hawkins and Nguyen's paper identifies a confounding factor for Wright's paper, and vice-versa. If Wright is right about the way in which word frequency affects pronunciation, Hawkins and Nguyen should not have compared words with nonwords, as they can be expected to be phonetically distinct in some ways anyway, because nonwords are always less frequent than (most) actual words. But equally, Wright's words are not quite balanced for coda voicing (Table 5.1).

Table 5.1 *Numbers of words with voiced and voiceless codas in Wright's study*

	'Easy' words	'Hard' words
Voiced codas	13	17
Voiceless codas	21	17

It seems unlikely that this relatively small difference in the proportion of words with voiced and voiceless codas would by itself be sufficient to affect the difference between vowel qualities, but it might: Hawkins and Nguyen established that the differences extend to *before* the vowel, remember. The lesson we must learn from these studies is to be sensitive to word frequency and fine phonetic differences to a far greater degree than hitherto. In the design of experiments on the phonetic realisation of phonological contrasts, it should be routine to control for word frequency (or for nonwords, likelihood).

5.4 A proposal

What kind of models can take account of word-frequency effects and fine phonetic detail? If we regard frequency and detail as only contingently connected, a small extension to the kind of phonetic interpretation model instantiated by the YorkTalk synthesis by rule system (Coleman 1992; Local 1992) or its successor, IPOX (Dirksen and Coleman 1997), will suffice. Because the relationship between phonology and phonetics is viewed as an arbitrary mapping between grammar and acoustics in that system, it has no difficulty in allowing for the expression of fine-scale arbitrary phonetic details. For example, Figure 5.3 illustrates the YorkTalk rule for assigning an F2 contour to /l/ in the onset position of a strong syllable and maps a featural representation (abbreviated at left) onto a sequence of pairs of descriptions of times and descriptions of the value of F2, determined with respect to the notional duration of the onset, Dur, and the value of F2 for the up-coming vowel target, Vowtar:

$$
\text{F2(onset}_s) \Rightarrow [(50\% * \text{Dur}, 1066 + 0.2 * (\text{Vowtar} - 1066)),
$$

$$
(70\% * \text{Dur}, 1066 + 0.2 * (\text{Vowtar} - 1066)),
$$

$$
/l/ \quad (82.5\% * \text{Dur}, 1066 + 0.25 * (\text{Vowtar} - 1066)),
$$

$$
(110\% * \text{Dur}, 1066 + 0.38 * (\text{Vowtar} - 1066)),
$$

$$
(117.5\% * \text{Dur}, 1066 + 0.85 * (\text{Vowtar} - 1066)),
$$

$$
(120\% * \text{Dur}, \text{Vowtar})]
$$

Figure 5.3 YorkTalk synthesis rule for assigning an F2 contour to onset /l/

(In Figure 5.3, six data points are specified for the F2 of /l/s in strong onsets. From 50% to 70% of the way through the onset, the F2 is close to 1066 Hz, modified by the small influence (note that the coarticulation constant is only 0.2) from the up-coming vowel target.)

Hawkins and Nguyen's data present no great problems to a model of this kind. To take account of their observation that the mean F2 of onset /l/s is 16 Hz lower before voiced codas than before voiceless codas, it is sufficient to make two slightly different versions of this rule, as in Figure 5.4:

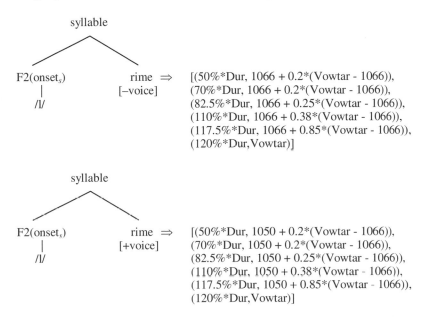

syllable

F2(onset$_s$)   rime $\Rightarrow$ [(50%*Dur, 1066 + 0.2*(Vowtar - 1066)),
| [−voice]   (70%*Dur, 1066 + 0.2*(Vowtar - 1066)),
/l/   (82.5%*Dur, 1066 + 0.25*(Vowtar - 1066)),
                              (110%*Dur, 1066 + 0.38*(Vowtar - 1066)),
                              (117.5%*Dur, 1066 + 0.85*(Vowtar - 1066)),
                              (120%*Dur,Vowtar)]

syllable

F2(onset$_s$)   rime $\Rightarrow$ [(50%*Dur, 1050 + 0.2*(Vowtar - 1066)),
| [+voice]   (70%*Dur, 1050 + 0.2*(Vowtar - 1066)),
/l/   (82.5%*Dur, 1050 + 0.25*(Vowtar - 1066)),
                              (110%*Dur, 1050 + 0.38*(Vowtar - 1066)),
                              (117.5%*Dur, 1050 + 0.85*(Vowtar - 1066)),
                              (120%*Dur,Vowtar)]

Figure 5.4 YorkTalk-type synthesis rule for assigning an F2 contour to onset /l/ in a syllable with a [−voice] coda or [+voice] coda

In case it is not obvious, all I have done in Figure 5.4 is added some appropriate context to the phonological side of the rule, and reduced 1066 by 16 Hz to 1050 in the context of a [+voice] rime. (Recall that in the analysis of Figure 5.4, the rime will be [+voice] if its coda is [+voice].)

To take account of the results of Hay, Pierrehumbert and Beckman, an additional modification is needed: probabilities must be added to the phonological grammar and then used to determine the probabilities of various phonological structures. For example, probabilistic context-free rules for primary stress feet in word-final position are given in Table 5.2, using the frequency of occurrence of final stressed feet in the Mitton (1992) dictionary as the basis for the probability estimates.

Table 5.2 *Probabilistic context-free rules for word-final primary stress feet*

(a)	$\Sigma_{sf} \rightarrow \sigma_{s1f}$,	$p \approx 0.24$
(b)	$\Sigma_{sf} \rightarrow \sigma_{s1m} \ \sigma_{wf}$,	$p \approx 0.48$
(c)	$\Sigma_{sf} \rightarrow \sigma_{s1m} \ \sigma_{wm}, \ \sigma_{wf}$,	$p \approx 0.23$
(d)	$\Sigma_{sf} \rightarrow \sigma_{s1m} \ \sigma_{wm}, \ \sigma_{wm}, \ \sigma_{wf}$,	$p \approx 0.05$
(e)	$\Sigma_{sf} \rightarrow \sigma_{s1m}, \ \sigma_{wm}, \ \sigma_{wm}, \ \sigma_{wm}, \ \sigma_{wf}$,	$p \approx 0.002$

(In these rules, Σ means 'foot' and σ means 'syllable', subscript s means 'strong' and subscript w means 'weak', as in standard metrical phonology. Following and extending upon the proposal of Coleman and Pierrehumbert (1997), subscript f means 'word final', subscript m means 'medial' and subscript 1 means 'primary stress'. Rules (a)–(c), for feet of 1–3 syllables, have been discussed at length in the theoretical phonology literature. Rules (d)–(e) allow for the possibility of words ending in several unstressed syllables, as in *administratively*.)

In combination with detailed rules of phonetic interpretation, this mechanism will also enable Wright's results to be modelled, even though Wright does not refer to parse probabilities, only word frequency (and lexical neighbourhood density). In Table 5.3, I have tabulated all of the minimal pairs of words from Wright's study, together with the log probability of each word, as determined by a stochastic context-free grammar of English words using rule probability estimates derived by training using the Mitton (1992) dictionary. As can be seen, in every case the phonotactic probability of the 'easier' word of each pair is less than the probability of the 'harder' word. That is, easy words are less probable than hard words. (I have no idea why this may be.)

Table 5.3 *Minimal pairs of words from Wright's study with log probability*

'easy' words	$\log_{10} p$	'hard' words	$\log_{10} p$
job	−5.36617	knob	−5.171
watch	−5.16995	wad	−4.86892
jack	−4.83105	hack	−4.37824
path	−5.8735	pat	−4.55823
wife	−4.80934	white	−4.31762
vice	−5.4962	lice	−4.68358
faith	−5.9129	fade	−4.64573
death	−5.38691	den	−4.7337

Table 5.3 (continued)

'easy' words	$\log_{10} p$	'hard' words	$\log_{10} p$
teeth	−5.25633	teat	−4.57639
thick	−5.39965	hick	−4.42099
wash	−4.938	wad	−4.86892
vote	−5.43341	moat	−4.77132
vote	−5.43341	goat	−4.91015
hung	−5.03829	hum	−4.78072

By augmenting standard metrical phonology with a) rule probabilities and b) detailed rules for phonetic interpretation we will have a sufficient mechanism for modelling the interesting phonetic and phonological observations of all the papers under discussion here. But according to this extension of metrical phonology, there is no linkage between phonological rule probabilities and the small phonetic variations modelled by phonetic interpretation rules.

I think this proposal can be bettered, though. There is a model in which word frequency and small phonetic details are not accidentally related: according to Bybee (1981, 2000), if lexical representations are phonetic, not phonological, it is natural for word frequency and phonetic detail to be closely linked. I find it instructive to approach this idea from a connectionist perspective. In connectionist models, every time a word is heard or produced, the weights (representing activation strengths) of all connections between that word's node or set of nodes and the other nodes to which it is connected is fractionally increased, or decreased if the connection is inhibitory (Morgan and Scofield 1991). This is how frequency and hence probability may be learned, stored and used in such an architecture.

This mechanism of encoding word-usage statistics could be applied to conventional phonological representations, as envisaged by e.g. Dell (1986), but I think other evidence stands against that idea. For example, Bybee (1981, 2000) presents data concerning the progress of lexical diffusion, arguing that it can be accounted for by a model in which the usage frequency of *phonetic* representations is invoked. Unlike Bybee, I like to think of such representations as simply memories of heard or spoken words; memories which, like others, are not encoded in some abstract system of symbols and graphs, but are at root episodic and in their form closely related to the different modalities of sensory and motor experience. This proposal is instantiated by exemplar models of lexical access (e.g. Palmeri, Goldinger and Pisoni 1993; Johnson 1997), and by Gaskell, Hare and Marslen-Wilson (1995), a connectionist model of word recognition in which phonological representations are the product of, rather than the input to, the lexical access process. Related work, in which word forms are represented as statistical trajectories in an acoustic space, has been examined for its applications to speech recognition by Goldenthal (1994).

Figure 5.5 illustrates this idea, by showing the trajectories of the first three formant frequencies of five tokens of *said* and five of *seed*, all recorded in the sentence frame 'Can you utter — again?' The two sets of tokens begin and end in the same region of the formant-frequency space, but their middle portions lie in different regions of the space, reflecting the fact that their vowels are different. There is some variation between tokens, but the distinction between the words is much greater than the inter-token variability. By plotting trajectories in a 'timeless' space (time is present only in the sequence of points that makes up each trajectory), faster and slower tokens are normalised to the same approximate path through the space. The distinction between words, shown in the figure by the shading of the trajectories, could be encoded as the association of a group of tokens to a common lemma or semantic representation.

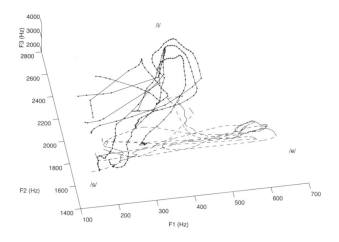

Figure 5.5 Trajectories of five tokens of *said* and *seed* plotted in an F1–F2–F3 space. Solid lines: trajectories of *seed* tokens; broken lines: trajectories of *said* tokens

Although the 'auditory memory' model is not the only possible framework for understanding the group of papers under consideration here, it is consistent with a body of neurolinguistic research, reviewed in Coleman (1998). If it is right, we should be talking not about the phonetic interpretation of phonological representations, but how people make phonological interpretations of phonetic representations.

II

Phonetic interpretation and phrasal structure

6

Release the captive coda: the foot as a domain of phonetic interpretation

6.1 Introduction

An important general goal in furthering our understanding of the phonetics–phonology interface is to determine precisely the manner in which prosodic conditions influence the phonetic interpretation of segmental information. The specific goal of this paper is to demonstrate how the set of conditioning contexts can be advantageously constrained by abandoning ambisyllabicity – the device whereby a consonantal position is granted dual membership of neighbouring syllables. The phonetic interpretation of supposedly ambisyllabic consonants can be straightforwardly detailed by reference to their location within the independently necessary domain of the foot.

The paper starts in Section 6.2 by questioning some of the fundamental assumptions that ambisyllabic analyses typically make about the nature of the phonetics–phonology interface. Section 6.3 presents specific arguments for rejecting the device in favour of a foot-centred approach. Section 6.4 introduces a range of facts involving manner and source contrasts in Danish which would submit to a standard ambisyllabic analysis but which can be quite adequately characterised in terms of the foot. Section 6.5 outlines a theory of segmental form which allows explicit statements to be made about how foot-sensitive effects map onto the acoustic signal. Section 6.6 extends the analysis to Ibibio. Section 6.7 presents the main conclusions.

6.2 A minimalist take on the phonetics–phonology interface

One widely appealed-to justification for ambisyllabicity is that it defines a conditioning site for allophonic realisation. The best-known example is surely *t*-allophony in English, where ambisyllabicity is often invoked as one of a set of conditions on the occurrence of such effects as aspiration, preglottalisation, plosive release and tapping. The analysis embraces a deviation from what is undoubtedly the universally unmarked parse, in which an intervocalic consonant belongs uniquely to the second syllable. Under a standard derivational approach, the relation between the two patterns is captured by accommodating both in the grammar, with the ambisyllabic parse emerging as a result of resyllabification. Allowing for terminological variations, we can characterise the general model of the phonetics–phonology interface within which this type of analysis is situated as in (1).

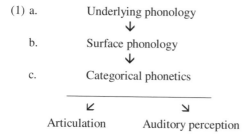

(1) a. Underlying phonology
            ↓
    b. Surface phonology
            ↓
    c. Categorical phonetics

         ↙   ↘

  Articulation   Auditory perception

In this scheme of things, resyllabification can in principle take place either between the underlying lexical level (1a) and surface representation (1b) or between (1b) and categorical phonetics (1c).

In recent years, the grammar-internal components of the model in (1) have come under fire from both top and bottom. On one side, the general shift towards output orientation in phonological theory has raised serious doubts about the validity of the underlying-surface distinction. This has led to the development of arguably more restrictive theories which either dispense with the distinction altogether, as in fully monostratal theories such as Declarative Phonology (see Scobbie, Coleman and Bird 1996 and the references there), or at least downplay its role considerably, as exemplified by the increasing reliance in Optimality Theory on constraints which evaluate correspondences between output forms (McCarthy and Prince 1995).

On the other side, there is reason to question the justification for a post-phonological level variously referred to as systematic phonetics (SPE) or categorical phonetics (Keating 1990). Much current output-oriented theory continues to take the necessity of such a level for granted (see e.g. Goldsmith

1993; McCarthy and Prince 1993: 21; Mohanan 1995). However, there is a growing awareness of the conceptual and empirical advantages of embracing the simpler alternative assumption – surely the null hypothesis – that phonology maps directly to the quantitative values of articulation and auditory perception without having to pass through some intermediate categorical level (see e.g. Pierrehumbert 1980, 1990; Flemming 1995; Kirchner 1998).

In what follows, I will take the liberty of using 'minimalist' as an inclusive label for any theory of phonology which, as depicted in (2), simultaneously subscribes to monostratalism and direct phonetic mapping.

(2)   Phonology

           ↙   ↘

    Articulation   Auditory perception

In the context of the present paper, it is pertinent to ask how allophonic regularities, such as those attributed to ambisyllabicity, are characterised in such a model. Without the luxury of a categorical phonetic level, there is perhaps a more obvious onus on the minimalist to be explicit about the articulatory, auditory and acoustic interpretation of such effects.

Actually, a moment's reflection will confirm that the very notion of allophony can have no formal status in an authentically minimalist model. How could it, when the model by definition lacks anything equivalent to the distinction between an underlying-phonemic and a surface-allophonic level? From a minimalist perspective, any given regularity formerly described as allophonic should fall into one of two types: either it is not phonological at all, in which case it is a matter for grammar-external quantitative phonetics; or it does have categorical status, in which case it is on a par with effects previously regarded as phonemic.

Assigning a given regularity to one domain or the other is an empirical issue. (It would not be too surprising if the allocation turned out to recapitulate the traditional distinction between intrinsic and extrinsic allophony.) As to how the outcome of each such decision is to be determined, the following two principles suggest themselves as reasonable yardsticks: a 'sub-phonemic' effect in a given language qualifies for categorical status if (i) it is paradigmatically contrastive in some other language and/or (ii) if it is syntagmatically informative to the extent that it delineates morphosyntactic or prosodic domains – in Firthian terms, if it has a demarcative function (see Robins 1970 for references and discussion). Aspiration in English plosives, for example, would be deemed phonological on both counts. Although not usually considered distinctive in phonemic analysis, the property indisputably has paradigmatic significance in languages such as Thai and Gujarati, where it contrasts with two or more other laryngeal terms.

Moreover, one result of its prosodically sensitive distribution in English is that it cues information about foot and morpheme structure. (Think of the familiar example of *nitrate*, with aspiration extended to the *r*, versus *night rate*.) Several of the supposedly sub-phonemic phenomena to be discussed below qualify as categorical on the same grounds.

As even this rather brief example shows, adopting a minimalist perspective on the phonetics–phonology interface forces a radical reassessment of the very nature of phonological categories. It would be surprising if familiar features, developed over a century or so of phonemic and generative research, could be neatly grafted onto a model that rejects the multistratal architecture around which they were designed. The standard SPE-derived feature set, it can be argued, has been indelibly marked by the multistratal climate within which it was conceived.

The point can be illustrated by pursuing the aspiration example. Under a conventional feature account, two-way laryngeal distinctions are universally classified in terms of [±voice] during the initial stages of derivation. The difference between languages which implement this contrast in plosives as plain versus prevoiced (French, Dutch, Polish, etc.) and those which implement it as plain versus aspirated (English, Danish, northern German, etc.) only emerges at the categorical phonetic level. Here underlyingly bivalent [voice] specifications are translated into scalar values or into different features such as [slack vocal folds] or [spread vocal folds] (SPE, Halle and Stevens 1971; Ladefoged 1971; Keating 1984, 1990).

Representing plain obstruents as [–voice] in languages such as French but as [+voice] in languages such as English fails to capture the universally unmarked nature of this series: for example, they are acquired before the prevoiced and aspirated congeners (Jakobson 1968; Kewley-Port and Preston 1974; Macken and Barton 1980); they constitute the default reflex under neutralisation; unlike prevoiced and aspirated segments, they undergo laryngeal assimilation but fail to trigger it.

This asymmetric behaviour favours an alternative categorisation of laryngeal contrasts in which cross-language phonetic differences are transparently recorded in the phonology, for example in terms of the privative features [slack] and [spread], with the plain series remaining unspecified (cf. Harris 1994; Iverson and Salmons 1995; Jessen 1997). In dispensing with the stratal distinction inherent in the use of [±voice], this account is more obviously in tune with the minimalist perspective. Moreover, the classification it sets up meets both of the criteria for phonological category-hood outlined above: (i) languages such as Thai and Gujarati utilise the full distinctive potential offered by both [slack] and [spread]; and (ii) the prosodically conditioned distribution of these categories (exemplified by neutralisation patterns such as devoicing and the suppression of aspiration after /s/ bears witness to their syntagmatically demarcative significance. These considerations lie behind the treatment of laryngeal contrasts in Danish and Ibibio to be presented below.

Another aspect to the categorial rethink required of the minimalist concerns the nature of the prosodic conditions under which segmental regularities occur. To return to the specific issue of ambisyllabicity, a reasonable first assumption would be that the device should be rejected on the grounds that the resyllabification with which it is usually associated is inextricably bound up with multistratalism. In fact, there are various ways in which the effects of resyllabification can be simulated without resort to serial derivation. One is to assume that some grammars just 'have' ambisyllabic parses of VCV and pass up the core option altogether (Local 1995b). Another is to posit grammars in which a constraint favouring the core pattern is outranked by one favouring the ambisyllabic parse (Prince and Smolensky 1993). However, the deviation from core syllabification that all of these alternatives allow, whether given a serialist or an output-oriented spin, results in a loosening of syllable theory that is neither desirable nor necessary. The main reasons for reaching this conclusion are set out in the next section.

6.3 Against ambisyllabicity

CODA CAPTURE (Kahn 1976) refers to an operation which subverts core V.CV syllabification (the point marks a syllable boundary) by moving the consonant into the first syllable, thereby violating onset maximisation. Crisp capture results when the consonant severs all connection with the onset (see e.g. Hoard 1971; Selkirk 1982; Borowsky 1986). Ambisyllabicity, in contrast, implies sloppy capture: here the consonant is allowed to retain an affiliation with the onset (see e.g. Kahn 1976; Wells 1990; Giegerich 1992; Spencer 1996).

A favourite argument for ambisyllabicity is that it coincides with native-speaker judgements about syllabification. The judgements are supposedly revealed in tasks where subjects are asked to repeat, transpose, or insert pause-breaks between syllables in polysyllabic forms (see e.g. Fallows 1981; Giegerich 1992; Rubach 1996; Hammond and Dupoux 1996 and the further references there). The results of these tests are not exactly clear cut; indeed Derwing's (1992) application of the pause-break experiment shows a clear preference for the maximal-onset parse. Nevertheless, the fact that tests of this type sometimes do elicit responses where a word such as *pity* is chunked as /pɪt/ plus /ti/ is cited as evidence that the intervocalic consonant is ambisyllabic.

However, there is good reason to suppose that these judgements often tell us more about phonological words than about syllables. It is a well-known fact that the phonological word in English, as in many other languages, consists minimally of a (bimoraic) foot (McCarthy and Prince 1986). A monosyllable with a final short vowel is sub-minimal; hence the non-occurrence of words such as */tɪ/, */bɛ/, */lʊ/, or the like. The phonological word thus constitutes the minimal utterable domain in the production of English. If this constraint is allowed to carry over into the tasks in question, it is likely to mean that the sound chunks offered by subjects are in fact words rather than syllables. Under such circumstances, it is hardly surprising that a speaker splits *pity* as /pɪt/ and /ti/, since /pɪ/ is not a possible word. It is of course perfectly possible to produce individual tokens of the /pɪ/ type – but only by switching out of English mode, in which case it is not at all clear what the judgements reveal about English syllable structure.

Another claim made for ambisyllabicity is that it accords with the observation that syllable edges are not neatly delimited in speech (see e.g. Treiman and Danis 1988). This is not a particularly convincing argument, because the observation, while undoubtedly correct, is hardly unique to syllable structure. No phonological category – feature, segment, syllable, or whatever – consistently enjoys sharp delineation in speech. Thus, rather than providing specific support for ambisyllabicity, the observation more generally accords either (i) with a radically non-segmental view of phonology, in which all categories potentially overlap (cf. Local 1992; Coleman 1994), or (ii) with some clearly articulated theory of how categorical phonological information is mapped non-linearly and non-categorically onto the speech continuum.

A third argument mounted in support of ambisyllabicity has to do with syllable weight. Coda capture is typically only invoked when the syllable preceding the target consonant is stressed. The operation, it is argued, is necessary in order to guarantee that this syllable be heavy (see e.g. Giegerich 1992). This is most pertinent in the case of stressed syllables containing a short vowel, which would remain light if not closed by the captured consonant. With ambisyllabicity, this yields the moraic configuration in (3a) or its x-slot equivalent in (3b).

(3) a. b.

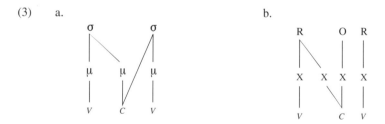

The weight-based argument for coda capture is self-serving unless there is some independent reason for believing that languages which are alleged to operate the device are indeed subject to the requirement that stressed syllables be heavy. Among languages which indisputably are subject to this constraint, one independent sign that an intervocalic consonant contributes to the weight of the preceding syllable is that it is of greater duration than one that doesn't. In other words, languages of this type have a contrast between geminates and non-geminates in this context (with a stressed vowel being necessarily long before a non-geminate, as in Italian and Norwegian). In fact, the type of representation proposed in (3), whether couched in moraic or x-slot terms, coincides exactly with that usually proposed for geminates. This naturally leads to the prediction that no language will have a contrast between geminate and ambisyllabic consonants, a claim made explicitly by Borowsky, Itô and Mester (1984). This is demonstrably false. As we will see below, Ibibio not only has short intervocalic consonants that would qualify for coda capture in any ambisyllabicist's book, but it also has authentic geminates in the same context.[1] Even if, in the absence of independent durational evidence, we were to persist with the notion that a single intervocalic consonant could behave as a covert geminate, we would have to contend with a further embarrassing fact. A fair proportion of the regularities ambisyllabicity is called on to deal with fall under the umbrella of lenition, as in the case of tapping and glottalling of /t/ in English. This is exactly the opposite of what we find with honest-to-goodness geminates, which are renowned for their ability to fend off the lenitions their non-geminate congeners often succumb to – the phenomenon of 'geminate inalterability' (Hayes 1986).

A fourth argument for ambisyllabicity is the one mentioned at the outset of this paper: the configuration supposedly defines a unique and necessary conditioning environment for phonetic realisation (see e.g. Kahn 1976; Gussenhoven 1986; Wells 1990; Giegerich 1992 and the references there). One objection to this claim relates back to the issue of stress just discussed. Stipulating that a captor syllable must be stressed amounts to saying that the VCV context forms a trochaic foot, and indeed coda capture has been explicitly formalised in just these terms by a number of researchers (e.g. Borowsky 1986: 265).[2] This immediately raises the question of why the relevant patterns of phonetic realisation couldn't be more simply characterised by referring directly to the foot, without having to call on some intermediate mechanism of resyllabification. After all, the foot has impeccably independent credentials, confirmed by the indispensable role it plays in stress and weight relations. The same cannot be said of ambisyllabicity.

Precisely this point has been made in connection with *t*-allophony in English. (4) encapsulates the well-known distributional facts pertaining to plosive, unreleased and tapped reflexes (‖ indicates utterance-finality).

(4)   Plosive: *time, boutíque*
        Unreleased stop: *get* ‖, *get Carl*
        Tap: *letter, get ón*

Broadly speaking, coda-capturing analyses of the conditions under which tapping occurs share the following main components, expressed here in terms of ambisyllabicity (see e.g. Kahn 1976; Hoard 1971; Giegerich 1992). (A similar story can be told of the contextually related pattern of glottalling; see Wells 1982.) (i) Coda capture: within a foot, the onset of the unstressed syllable is attached to the coda of the stressed syllable (e.g. *pi.ty* → *pi.t.y*, where *.t.* indicates ambisyllabicity). (ii) Onset capture: a word-final coda is attached to an unoccupied onset at the beginning of a following word (e.g. *get.a* → *ge.t. a*). (iii) Tapping: *t* taps when ambisyllabic.

There is an alternative, foot-based treatment of these facts, first proposed by Kiparsky (1979), which dispenses with coda capture. In essence, it says: prevocalic *t* taps when not foot-initial (see also Harris and Kaye 1990; Jensen 1993; Harris 1994). The relevant contexts are illustrated in (5), repeated from (4), now with foot structure indicated (by double brackets).

(5)   Plosive: [*time*], *bou*[*tíque*]
        Unreleased stop: [*get*] ‖, [*get*] *Carl*
        Tap: [*letter*], [*get*] *ón*

Amongst other things, this treatment offers a simple account of why an uphill stress configuration hosts tapping across a word boundary but not word-internally: tapping affects *t* in *get ón*, where it is foot-final, but not in *boutíque*, where it is foot-initial.

Very similar sets of facts present themselves in Danish and Ibibio. As I will try to show below, a detailed specification of the phonetic effects involved can be formulated in essentially the same foot-based terms as those just outlined for English. These cases are representative of a cross-linguistic tendency for strong distributional similarities to hold between word-final consonants (VC]) and those in prevocalic foot-internal contexts (v́Cv̆). They also illustrate a tendency for these parallels to involve neutralisation (in the English case, for example, tapping also affects *d*). That is, they reflect an unequal division of contrastive potential across different positions within the foot. The distributional spoils are evidently apportioned to the advantage of the initial CV part of the domain – the head of the foot. (In all of the cases under discussion here, the foot is trochaic, i.e. left-headed.) Thus, while the maximal system of consonantal contrasts in a language is free to appear in the onset of the foot head, it is usual to find that reduced subsystems show up in the onset of the weak or dependent syllable of v́Cv̆ forms. The fact that this curtailment of contrastive potential also afflicts a word-final consonant suggests that this position too should be deemed to fall within the weak sector of the foot. (For a detailed account of how foot-related neutralising parallels between VC] and v́Cv̆ can be established without resorting to coda capture, see Harris 1997.)

The contrastive imbalance within the foot extends to vowels. A typical scenario here is one in which the maximal inventory of vocalic contrasts is restricted to the head nucleus of the foot, while contracted subsystems show up in weak nuclei. Languages exhibiting this phenomenon include English, Bulgarian, Catalan, Neapolitan Italian and, as we will see below, Ibibio. Coda capture forces an intrinsically paradoxical treatment of this general asymmetry. With crisp capture, a consonantal position that is susceptible to reduction is moved out of the very syllable that promotes reduction in vowels. With crisp or sloppy capture, the reduction-prone consonant fetches up in the very syllable where vowels resist reduction.

The conceptual advantages that a foot-centred approach enjoys over one based on ambisyllabicity are clear: it allows us to capture prosodically conditioned distributional parallels between nuclear and non-nuclear positions in a more natural way; and it is consistent with a more restrictive theory of prosodic structure which broaches no deviation from core syllabification. The question is whether the foot-based alternative is also empirically adequate. In particular, does it allow us to nail down the conditions on regularities otherwise attributed to ambisyllabicity? The following extended example from Danish will serve to show that it does.

6.4 Danish

Danish, here represented by the regional variety of South Fyn, possesses what looks like a normal Germanic-style laryngeal contrast between voiceless aspirated and unaspirated ('plain') plosives. The distinction is robustly maintained word-initially, as in (6a), and word-internally before a stressed syllable, as in (6b) (see Fischer-Jørgensen 1968; Hutters 1985; Jessen 1997; accents mark stress).

(6) a.	*pil*	[pʰ]*il*	'arrow'	*bil*	[p]*il*	'car'	
	tale	[tʰ]*ale*	'to speak'	*dale*	[t]*ale*	'valleys'	
	ko	[kʰ]*o*	'cow'	*god*	[k]*od*	'good'	
b.	*kopi*	*ko*[pʰ]*í*	'copy'	*bebude*	*be*[p]*úde*	'to foretell'	
	atom	*a*[tʰ]*óm*	'atom'	*bedyre*	*be*[t]*ýre*	'to proclaim'	
	akut	*a*[kʰ]*út*	'acute'	*igen*	*i*[k]*én*	'again'	

The voicelessness of the plain stops is most consistently revealed utterance-initially (as in (6a)) and utterance-finally (examples below).

Outside of the contexts illustrated in (6), Danish is notorious for having laid waste to its historical stop contrasts, which are still recorded in the orthography and can be readily reconstructed on the basis of comparison with sister languages such as Norwegian. After a stressed vowel, the consonants in question have been subjected to a series of lenitions that have withered both the laryngeal and manner dimensions of the distinctions. The most damaging effect has been vocalisation (to be understood here and below as any process which weakens an obstruent to a resonant). This has resulted in one term of the original contrast being written out of the stop equation altogether. As illustrated in (7), it has affected historical coronals and velars word-finally and all three place categories intervocalically. (Here and below, *y* stands for a palatal glide.)

(7) a.   *mad*   *ma*[ð]   'food'
       lag   *la*[y]   'layer'

    b. *peber* *pe*[w]*er* 'pepper'
       modig *mo*[ð]*ig*   'brave'
       koge   *ko*[(w)]*e* 'to cook'

Vocalisation of coronals has yielded a tongue-blade approximant (traditionally, if not entirely felicitously, transcribed as *ð*). The glide reflex of historical velars generally takes its place cue from the preceding vowel – *y* after a front unround vowel (as in *læy* 'layer') or *w* after a round vowel (as in *kʰowə* 'to cook', although here the medial glide can be suppressed altogether).

The stops that survive in the otherwise leniting contexts (typically the reflexes of historical geminates) can be described as plain in the sense employed above. The voicelessness this series displays when utterance-final (see (8a)) is also evident utterance-initially (see (6a)). Before an unstressed vowel, as illustrated in (6b), the stops are subject to variable and gradient voicing, which can be interpreted as the passive interpolation of vocal-fold vibration through the VCV sequence (Hutters 1985).

(8) a. *lap*   *la*[p]   'patch'   *lab*   *la*[p]   'paw'
      sæt   *sæ*[t]   'set (imper.)'
      læk   *læ*[k]   'leak (n.)'

    b. *næppe* *næ*[b]*e* 'hardly'   *ebbe*   *e*[b]*e*   'low tide'
      sætte   *sæ*[ɾ]*e*   'to set'   *bredde* *bre*[ɾ]*e* 'width'
      frakke *fra*[g]*e*   'coat'   *lægge*   *læ*[g]*e*   'to lay'

The assault on the Danish plosive system does not stop there. As indicated in (8b), coronal stops are subject to tapping. The contextual specifics, set out in (9), are identical to those controlling tapping in English (cf. (4)).

(9)
	Stop				Tap		
	Cv́	*tale* 'speech',	*atom*		Cv̆	*sætte*	'to set'
	C]‖	*sæt*	'set'		C]v̆	*sæt og*	'set and'
	C]C	*sæt på* 'set on'			C]v́	*sæt op*	'set up'

Consistency would demand that any advocate of ambisyllabicity as a condition on tapping in English should extend the analysis to the same phenomenon in Danish. In fact, the entire set of neutralisation effects in Danish, including vocalisation and the suspension of laryngeal contrasts, might suggest a generalised ambisyllabic analysis, since the contexts involved are essentially parallel. However, for the same reasons as those outlined in Section 6.3, this parallelism can be expressed quite adequately without resorting to ambisyllabicity. As tabulated in (10), the prosodic conditions on Danish neutralisation can be captured by reference to the foot.

(10)

Danish

Foot-initial		Non-foot-initial			
[C		v́Cv̆		VC]	
pʰ	p	p	w	p	
tʰ	t	ɾ	ð	t/ɾ	ð
kʰ	k	k	w/y	k	w/y

Summarising (10), we can say that (i) aspiration is supported foot-initially but suppressed elsewhere and (ii), in the elsewhere case, tapping additionally robs coronals of the closure and accompanying release burst which are supported by other place values.[3]

We turn now to the task of identifying the phonological categories that are implicated in each of these distributional patterns.

6.5 Source and manner categories

6.5.1 Elements

This section outlines a theory of segmental categories that has been specifically tailored to the minimalist requirements described in Section 6.2. It arises out of a broad tradition initiated by Dependency Phonology (Anderson and Jones 1974), which has been developed along minimalist lines by, among others, Kaye, Lowenstamm and Vergnaud (1990) and Harris and Lindsey (1995).

The theory subscribes to the increasingly accepted view that phonological oppositions are defined privatively in terms of monovalent categories, rather than equipollently as in SPE-derived feature systems. Moreover, each monovalent category – an ELEMENT – can be phonetically expressed in isolation. In other words, some segments are 'primitive' in the sense that they represent solo interpretations of single elements. For example, on its own the element (U) is interpreted as a labial vocoid (transcribable as *u* or *w*, depending on its syllabic position). Uniting privativeness with stand-alone interpretability rids phonological representations of anything resembling redundant feature values. This in turn means that the theory dispenses with blank-filling operations and the corresponding need for separate categorical levels exhibiting differing degrees of segmental specification.

The theory takes to heart the standard Jakobsonian observation that the status of the speech signal as the shared communicative experience of speakers and listeners establishes it as the starting point for detailing the phonetic expression of phonological categories. Articulatory definitions are then framed in terms of the continuously varying neural and motoric mechanisms that speakers activate in order to achieve the signal mappings of these categories. This view is consistent with the idea that segmental categories have invariant acoustic signatures (Blumstein and Stevens 1981). (In light of Nearey's well-taken remarks (this volume), IDEA here should really read IDEAL.)

(11) lists phonetic specifications (essentially those given in Harris and Lindsey 1995) of the source and manner elements that will figure prominently in the discussion below.

(11)

Element	Acoustic interpretation	Articulatory execution
(?) 'edge'	Abrupt and sustained drop in overall amplitude	Occlusion
(h) 'noise'	Aperiodic energy	Narrowed stricture producing turbulent airflow
(H) 'high source'	Long-lag VOT	Spread vocal folds
(L) 'low source'	Long-lead VOT	Slack vocal folds

Of the two manner elements, (?) represents the closure component of oral and nasal stops, while (h) represents the steady-state noise component of fricatives and the noise burst that accompanies the release of plosives.[4] In plosives, the source elements [L] and [H] represent active prevoicing and aspiration respectively. Plain oral stops lack any independent source specification, leaving them susceptible to ambient voicing.

Although neutralisation in Danish and Ibibio specifically affects the manner and source dimensions of segments, it is necessary for the purposes of the following demonstration to say at least something about the elementary categorisation of resonance contrasts. The main exemplification can be supplied by labials, represented in terms of the element (U) mentioned above. The signal specification of this element is a target formed by a low-frequency spectral peak (representing the convergence of F1 and F2), produced by a trade-off between an expansion of the oral and pharyngeal tubes (Harris and Lindsey 1995). The pattern may manifest itself in a steady state (in rounded vowels) or as an inter-segment transition (the 'diffuse-falling' configuration of labial consonants described by Blumstein and Stevens 1981).

(12) lists the elementary expressions that characterise labial plosives and the various reflexes they adopt when lenited.

(12) a. Aspirated labial plosive   (U, ?, h, H)
      b. Prevoiced labial plosive   (U, ?, h, L)
      c. Plain labial plosive   (U, ?, h)
      d. Unreleased labial stop   (U, ?)
      e. Labial fricative   (U, h)
      f. Labial approximant   (U)
      g. Glottal stop   (?)
      h. Glottal fricative   (h)

This line-up illustrates the autonomous interpretability of elements. Any element-targeting constraint effecting lenition defines a phonological representation that can be immediately submitted to articulation/auditory perception without having to transit through some categorial component where missing phonological information is filled in. For example, the vocalisation of a plain labial plosive ((12c)) reflects the absence of (?) (stopness) and (h) (noise). The residual element, (U), is independently interpretable as a labial approximant ((12f)).

There is a clear sense in which lenition degrades the phonetic information signalled by a segment: the information-rich spectral discontinuities (abrupt amplitude shifts, rapid formant transitions, noise bursts, F_0 perturbations, etc.) associated with an unweakened consonant are partly or wholly absent from a weaker counterpart. The interpretational autonomy of elements allows this difference in informational capacity to be represented in a direct manner: an unlenited segment is elementally more complex than a lenited reflex.

Compare this with an SPE-type feature treatment of the same facts. The primary featural effect of vocalisation is the rewriting of [−continuant] as [+continuant]. On its own, however, this is not sufficient to define a phonetically interpretable segment. Supplementary adjustments have to be made at some 'later' categorial level in order to derive the required glide, including [+consonantal] → [−consonantal], [−sonorant] → [+sonorant] and [−voice] → [+voice]. Fully specifying all feature values in this way gives the misleading impression that the informational load borne by lenited and unlenited congeners is equal. This basic design flaw persists regardless of whether feature-based approaches to lenition are couched in terms of input-oriented rules or, as more recently, ranked output constraints (Kirchner 1998).

6.5.2 Signal mappings of elements: Danish

The reduction in elementary complexity that accompanies consonantal neutralisation, it can be shown, goes hand in hand with a reduction in signal complexity. The exclusion of any given element from a given context correlates directly with an absence of a particular frequency- and/or time-domain pattern from the speech signal. This can be demonstrated by detailing the elementary and signal correlates of the Danish neutralisations described in Section 6.4.

Consider first the nature of the full contrast between plain and aspirated plosives that is maintained foot-initially in Danish, illustrated by the pair *bille* and *pile* in Figures 6.1 and 6.2. Each of these figures, like all of those that follow, contains a speech-pressure waveform (top), a laryngographic trace (Lx, middle) and a broad-band spectrogram of a target word (located between cursor points), uttered in a carrier phrase.[5] The spectrograms are annotated to pick out those signal ingredients that are proposed as the exponents of particular phonological elements.

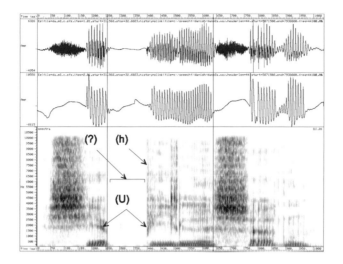

Figure 6.1 Danish *bille* (between cursor points): speech (top), Lx (middle), broad-band spectrogram (bottom)

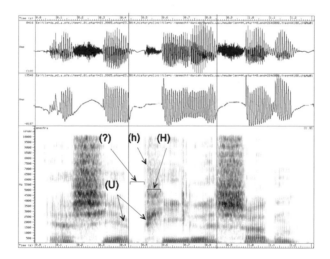

Figure 6.2 Danish **pile** (between cursor points): speech (top), Lx (middle), broad-band spectrogram (bottom)

The formant transitions in the approach and getaway phases of both labial plosives in *bille* and *pile* are directed towards the low spectral peak target

117

associated with the element (U). Both plosives exhibit the sustained amplitude drop attributable to the element (?). On release, both display the noise burst associated with the element (h). The closure phase of neither stop shows any significant presence of periodic energy, indicating an absence of vocal-fold vibration (clearly evident in the Lx traces). The main distinction between the consonants is carried by the timing of voice onset in the following vowel. In the case of *pile*, there is a long time lag between the release of closure and the onset of voicing, symptomatic of aspiration and attributable to (H). In *bille*, in contrast, the release is more or less simultaneous with voice onset, the pattern typical of a plain stop and interpretable as the absence of a source element.

Compare these patterns with what is found foot-internally, illustrated by the pair *tropisk* and *købe* in Figures 6.3 and 6.4. The medial consonant of *tropisk* shows evidence of a drop in overall amplitude and a noisy release burst, indicative of (?) and (h) respectively. It also exhibits continuous periodic vibration, an effect that can be interpreted in this context as the passive voicing of an intervocalic plain stop (see Hutters 1985). This interpretation is consistent with the conclusion that the segment lacks an independent source element. The *b* of *købe* (Figure 6.4) displays essentially the same source characteristics. In the absence of any edge or noise pattern that would be traceable to (?) or (h), the segment can be deemed to contain only (U), signalled by the expected formant transitions. This collection of effects reflects how the foot-internal contrast between historically aspirated ('fortis') and plain ('lenis') plosives in Danish has been reduced to one between plain stops and approximants. In the case of coronals, the tapping illustrated in (9) further robs the original fortis member of this distinction of its stop and noise components, exposing a bare coronal element.

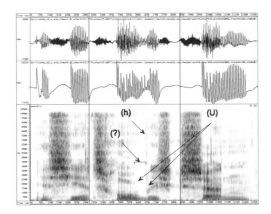

Figure 6.3. Danish *tropisk* (between cursor points): speech (top), Lx (middle), broad-band spectrogram (bottom)

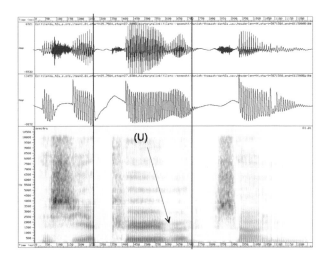

Figure 6.4 Danish *købe* (between cursor points): speech (top), Lx (middle), broad-band spectrogram (bottom)

(13) summarises the distribution of source and manner elements across different positions within the Danish foot, represented by the particular case of coronal stops and their historical reflexes.[6]

(13)   Danish coronals

	Foot-initial	Non-foot-initial	
(H)	✓	✗	
(h)	✓	✗	
(?)	✓	✗	_V

The display in (13) illustrates how the element model allows neutralisation to be uniformly expressed as the exclusion of particular segmental categories from particular positions. One immediate advantage is that the ability of a position to license segmental material is transparently reflected by the complexity of the elementary expressions it can sponsor. And this ability can be directly related to the position's place in the prosodic hierarchy: all other things being equal, a prosodic head can bear more segmental information than a dependent position. (For a detailed development of this integrated approach to neutralisation, see Harris 1997.) The following section extends this overall account to Ibibio.

6.6 Ibibio

The first thing to establish before embarking on a foot-based account of neutralisation in Ibibio is whether the language has feet at all.[7] This is perhaps not immediately obvious, since the foot is usually predicated on stress, a property that Ibibio, a language with lexical-grammatical tone, lacks (accents below mark tone).

Stress prominence is of course not the only symptom of foot-hood. As remarked on in Section 6.3, segmental and quantitative factors can also be in play, showing up in the asymmetric distribution of contrast and weight between head and dependent syllables. Both of these effects are abundantly evidenced in Ibibio, supporting the view that the foot has a vital role to play in the phonology of the language (Connell 1991; Akinlabi and Urua 1992; cf. Cook 1985 and Hyman 1990 on the cognate phenomenon in Efik).

The basic shape of the Ibibio verb, comprising a root plus an optional suffix, is circumscribed in various ways by a phonological template of the form CVXCV – a configuration that coincides with the heavy–light trochaic foot favoured by many stress languages. Amongst other things, the template places an upper bound on the size of the verb and a lower bound on certain verbal paradigms. Potentially oversized morphological material is accommodated to the trochee through segment truncation. For example, the attachment of a CV suffix to CVVC roots such as those in (14a) results either in vowel shortening, as in the forms in (14b), or consonant degemination, as in the forms in (14c) (all data from Urua 1990).

(14) a. *síít*   'block'
          fáák   'wedge'
          kɔ́ɔ́ŋ   'hang on hook'

      b. Reversive: root + Cé
          sìtté   'unblock'
          fákká   'remove wedge'
          kɔ́ŋŋɔ́   'unhook'

      c. Frequentative: root + Né
          síìŋé   'unblock (freq.)'
          fáàŋá   'remove wedge (freq.)'
          kɔ́ɔ́ŋɔ́ 'not hang on hook (freq.)'

Another weight-related function of the heavy–light trochee is to define a fixed template for certain verbal paradigms. In this case, undersized roots are subject to vowel augmentation, as in the frequentative examples in (15).

(15)   nɔ̀   'give'   nɔ̀ɔ̀-ŋɔ̀   'give (freq.)'
       k͡pá   'die'   k͡páá-ŋá   'die (freq.)'

The Ibibio foot also serves as a distributional domain, exhibiting contrastive asymmetries strongly reminiscent of those associated with trochees in stress languages. While the first syllable of the trochee sponsors the full panoply of vowel and consonant distinctions in Ibibio, the contrastive potential of the last syllable is greatly curtailed, its segmental identity being to a large extent picked up from the first. This is illustrated in the following forms by the negative suffix, the onset of which assimilates completely to the final consonant of the root, while the nucleus harmonises with the root vowel.

(16)   díp-pé   'not hide'   dóm-mó   'not bite'
       yét-té   'not wash'   màn-ná   'not give birth'
       kɔ̀k-kɔ́   'not spew'   kɔ̀ŋ-ŋɔ́   'not knock'

These distributional patterns indicate that the Ibibio foot is left-headed. This conclusion is further strengthened when we study the facts of consonantal neutralisation in more detail.

(17) summarises the distribution of oral stops and related segments in Ibibio.

(17)   Ibibio
            Foot-initial   Non-foot-initial

            [C   VCCV   VC] {‖/C}   VC(])V

k͡p	b	pp	p’	β
t	d	tt	t’	ɾ
k		kk	k’	ɣ

The initial onset of the Ibibio foot supports a two-way laryngeal contrast amongst plosives, at least in labials and coronals. Unlike Danish, the distinction manifests itself as plain versus prevoiced (Connell 1991). This is illustrated by the forms k͡pa and ba in Figures 6.5 and 6.6[8] As is to be expected, these plosives share an interval of zero or greatly reduced overall amplitude, a noise burst on release and the formant transitions associated with labiality, properties attributable to the elements (ʔ), (h) and (U) respectively. The distinction between them resides primarily in their differing VOT configurations.[9] In k͡p, periodic vibration commences more or less at the same time as the release of closure, confirming the segment as plain and therefore, in element terms, devoid of a source element.[10] In contrast, b displays uninterrupted periodic vibration throughout closure. This long-lead VOT property is also evident in utterance-initial position, indicating that the laryngeal component here has some independent phonological basis (in element terms, low-source (L)), rather than being due to the passive extension of vocal-fold vibration from the surrounding vowels.

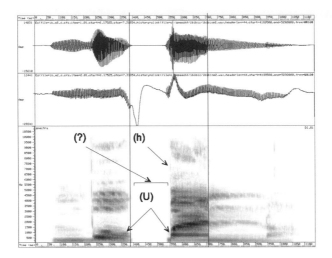

Figure 6.5 Ibibio *k͡pá* 'die' (between cursor points): speech (top), Lx (middle), broad-band spectrogram (bottom)

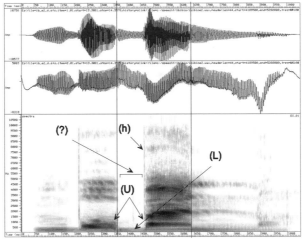

Figure 6.6 Ibibio *bá* 'exist' (between cursor points): speech (top), Lx (middle), broad-band spectrogram (bottom)

Outside of the foot-initial site, the Ibibio stop system yields to neutralising pressures in a manner similar to Danish. As shown in (17), stops are also to be found intervocalically as geminates and word-finally before a consonant or pause. In the absence of a contrast between geminate and non-geminate stops in this context, it might initially be tempting to view the segments in question as single-position Cs (see the references in Connell 1991: 47ff.). However, this would miss the clear quantitative parallel between CVCCV and CVVCV in paradigms where the heavy-light trochee defines a fixed prosodic template; see for example the forms in (14) and (15).

Irrespective of what follows, non-foot-initial consonants fail to support a laryngeal contrast. Geminate stops are plain, exemplified by the word *dáppá* in Figure 6.7. As illustrated by the word *déép* in Figure 6.8, word-final stops are unreleased and characterised by rapid decrescendo voicing from the preceding vowel (cf. Connell 1991). The signal manifestations of these consonants are consistent with the elementary representations in (12c) and (12d). That is, both can be considered to lack the source element (L) which characterises prevoiced plosives in foot-initial position, while the absence of a release burst in the word-final stop indicates a lack of (h).

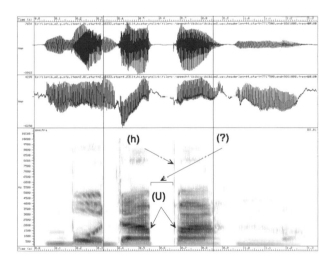

Figure 6.7 Ibibio *dáppá* 'dream (vb.)' (between cursor points): speech (top), Lx (middle), broad-band spectrogram (bottom)

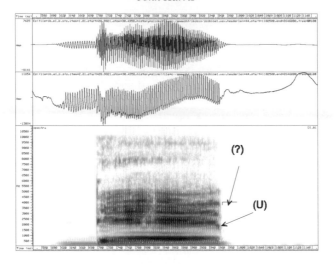

Figure 6.8 Ibibio *déép* 'scratch' (utterance-final): speech (top), Lx (middle), broad-band spectrogram (bottom)

Non-foot-initially before a vowel, non-geminate consonants are subject to lenition. This gives rise to root-final alternations such as the following:

(18) a. *díp*   'hide'   *díßé*   'hide oneself'
          déép   'scratch'   *dééßé*   'not scratching'

          bèt   'push'   *bèré*   'push oneself'
          kóót   'read/call'   *kóóró*   'not reading/calling'

          fʌ́k   'cover'   *fʌ́ɣɔ́*   'cover oneself'
          fáák   'wedge'   *fááɣá*   'not wedged'

      b. *kɔ́p*   'lock'   *kɔ́ß úsʌ́ŋ* 'lock the door'
          bèt   'push'   *bèr ówó*   'push someone'
          kʌ̀k   'shut'   *kʌ̀ɣ úsʌ́ŋ* 'shut the door'

Note that lenition occurs irrespective of whether the following vowel falls within the same word (as in (18a)) or not (as in (18b)). The weakened reflexes have been described as frictionless continuants or 'tapped approximants' (Connell 1991). (The symbols *ß* and *ɣ* are thus not being used here with their IPA fricative values.[11]) The absence of a noise component (and thus of the (h) element) from the lenited segments is confirmed by the form *díßé* in Figure 6.9. The mild degree of energy reduction observed in the intervocalic labial of this example does not match the radical amplitude drop associated with (ʔ) in the

124

stop alternant. The residue of vocalisation is thus bare resonance, in this case represented by (U).

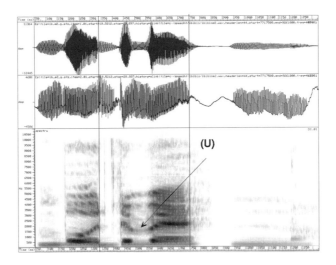

Figure 6.9 Ibibio *díßé* 'hide oneself' (between cursor points): speech (top), Lx (middle), broad-band spectrogram (bottom)

The vocalisation site in Ibibio can be specified as follows: the target segment must (i) be intervocalic and (ii) occur within the weak sector of a foot. (The second of these conditions also governs the consonantal place assimilation vowel harmony illustrated in (16).) Confirmation of the necessity of the foot-based condition is provided by the examples in (19). The forms in (19a) contain prefixes or proclitics which are not part of the verbal domain. Although the root-initial consonants here are intervocalic, they resist vocalisation because they occupy the head syllable of the foot.

(19) a *ú-[táŋ]*   *úráŋ   'plaiting'
    ú-[káp]   *úɣáp   'covering'
    í-[bàt-tá] *íβàttá '(s)he is not counting'

   b. *[séé-ɣé]*   'not look'
    [dáá-ɣá]   'not stand'

   c. *[dáppá]-ké* *dáppáɣé 'not dream'
    [fááŋá]-ké *fááŋáɣé 'not argue'

A similar result is observable when we compare the fate of the negative suffix in (19b) and (19c). In (19b), the suffix lies within the ambit of the verbal trochee, where its onset falls prey to vocalisation. In (19c), in contrast, the same suffix lies outwith the template, which is saturated by an internal trochee; as in (19a), the consonant is thus immune to vocalisation.

There are striking parallels between lenition in Ibibio on the one hand and Danish and English on the other. Aside from the obvious stress and tone differences, the contextual and segmental details of tapping, for example, are more or less identical across the three languages. Note how in all three languages tapping fails foot-initially in **bou[tíque]** (English), **a[tóm]** (Danish), *ú[táŋ]* 'plaiting' (Ibibio) but goes through foot-finally in **[get] Anne, [sæt] op** (Danish), *[bèɾ] ówó* 'push someone' (Ibibio), even though the context is intervocalic in both sets of cases.

These similarities might initially bring a gleam to the ambisyllabicist's eye, but Ibibio has a major disappointment in store. The same consideration of consistency that would require lenition in English and Danish to be treated to a unitary ambisyllabic analysis would have to be extended to Ibibio. Now recall the claim, embodied in the representations in (3), that no language will contrast single ambisyllabic consonants with geminates. Well, Ibibio clearly does. And while the single consonants in Ibibio are subject to lenition, the geminates remain inalterable. Examples are scattered throughout the data presented above; just to drive the point home, here are a few more:

(20) *áà-fìιβe*   'who sucks'   *fíppé*   'remove from mouth'
      áà-sùrè   'who blocks' *sítté*   'unblock'
      áà-fààyà   'who wedges' *fákká*   'remove wedge'

(21) presents a foot-based summary of the distribution of source and manner elements in Ibibio.

(21) Ibibio

	Foot-initial	Non-foot-initial	
(L)	✓	✗	
(h)	✓	✗	
(?)	✓	✗	(_V)

In spite of the fact that the source contrast is carried by (H) in Danish and by (L) in Ibibio, there are clear distributional parallels between the two languages, as a comparison of (21) with (13) confirms. In both cases, only the foot head is able to support the full set of source and manner elements; in the foot's weak sector, we find a total embargo on source and selective bans on manner.

6.7 Conclusion

I conclude by picking up on two general issues raised by the analyses offered above.

The first concerns the neutralising aspect of the phonological effects discussed here and the impact this has on the way we spell out their phonetic interpretation. Terms such as LENITION, WEAKENING, VOCALISATION and DEVOICING can all be understood as ways of describing the fact that certain bits of phonetic information which are available in some phonological contexts are excluded from others. Are these effects derivationally destructive? That is, is it necessary to conceive of them as involving the obliteration of lexically represented information? The descriptive terms themselves do indeed conjure up images of destruction. Their use is undeniably steeped in a derivational tradition which sets up underlying phonemes and allows them to be deleted or rewritten in various ways. Against this background, it is understandable that declarative phonologists, their eyes fixed firmly on output, have often felt uncomfortable with the very notion of neutralisation (even to the point of questioning whether it exists at all see Bird 1995).

Nevertheless, it is possible to conceive of neutralisation in non-destructive terms. Even in input-oriented derivational theory, it has long been acknowledged that static distributional regularities, including those implicated in neutralisation, can be treated in a non-procedural manner, for example by means of vacuous rule application. The real question comes down to whether it is possible to characterise dynamic phonological alternations non-destructively, without losing sight of the fact that neutralisation, like most segmental regularities, often has both static and alternating effects.

In non-derivational theory, constraints with neutralising consequences are expressed over output as bans on particular segmental categories from appearing in particular contexts. (From a vigorously minimalist viewpoint which denies the existence of an independent input level, 'output' should really just read 'phonology'.) There is no need for such constraints to refer to some underlying or canonical shape of a segment. Alternating forms of a morpheme can be linked non-derivationally and non-destructively by means of constraints which evaluate the degree of phonological correspondence between them – output-output constraints, in Optimalist parlance. With the segmental model outlined in Section 6.5, how this evaluation is performed is quite straightforward. In the case of lenition, the correspondence between an alternant containing a 'strong' segment and one containing a 'weak' counterpart takes the form of a subset relation. This is evident in (12), where we can compare the representation of full-blooded plosives with that of their lenited relatives. For instance, the elementary expression (U) representing the medial glide in Ibibio *dééβé* 'not scratching' is a proper subset of the expression (U, ?) representing the final consonant of *déép* 'scratch'.

To return to a theme struck up in Section 6.2, a second general question concerns the nature of the segmental categories invoked in the analyses presented above. From an input-oriented perspective, some of the phenomena discussed – for example, aspiration in Danish, prevoicing and vocalisation in Ibibio, plosive release in both languages – would count as sub-phonemic or 'low-level'. An output-oriented, non-phonemic theory, in contrast, gives full recognition to the information-rich potential of these effects as demarcating cues for prosodic and morphological domains. For example, the categories (L) and (h) in Ibibio consistently mark the left edge of a foot (and thus of a root); (H) marks the left edge of the Danish foot.

Moreover, by referring to different locations within the foot, it is possible to characterise the prosodic conditions on the phonetic interpretation of the regularities in question without subjecting onset consonants to coda capture.

Notes

Many thanks to Thomas Hansen, Pierre Millinge and Eno Urua for supplying and discussing the speech data presented in this paper and to Bruce Connell, Phil Harrison, Geoff Lindsey, Moira Yip and three anonymous *LabPhon* reviewers for their comments. I'm especially indebted to Eno Urua for also sharing with me her phonological insights into Ibibio.

1   The moraic status of the first part of a geminate reflects the assumption that it receives 'weight by position' (Hayes 1989). In an approach bent on asserting the formal independence of ambisyllabicity, it might seem tempting to propose that an intervocalic consonant could be captured into a coda without acquiring weight by position. That is, the resyllabified consonant would lack a mora and would instead be linked directly to the matrix node of the first syllable. Unsurprisingly, Borowsky *et al.* (1984) decline to pursue this possibility. While it would allow geminates and ambisyllabic consonants to contrast within the same language, it would also immediately undermine any weight-based argument for ambisyllabicity. Besides, any move towards allowing weight by position to be simultaneously switched on and off within the same grammar represents a bold step in the direction of unfalsifiability.

2   In principle, coda capture could be extended to supposedly iambic contexts, specifically to consonants which immediately follow the stressed nucleus of an iambic foot, yielding $[\breve{v}.C_1\acute{v}.]C_2\breve{v} \rightarrow [\breve{v}.C_1\acute{v}C_2.]\breve{v}$. (feet indicated by double brackets). I am unaware of any convincing examples of constraints on C_2 which could be exclusively attributed to this hypothetical configuration. In any event, the initial

footing assumed by such an analysis is itself open to question, given the disputed validity of iambs (see van de Vijver 1998 for discussion and references).

3   Aspiration is also supported in a word-initial unstressed syllable in Danish, as in [kʰ]*abín* 'cabin'. A unified distributional statement favours the view that the first syllable in forms with this stress configuration constitutes a degenerate foot.

4   The use of the terms HIGH and LOW as labels for source elements in consonants alludes to the well-known correlation between phonation type and fundamental frequency perturbations in the transition to a following vowel. Whether this correlation justifies representing phonation and tone contrasts in terms of the same phonological categories (as suggested by the facts of tonogenesis, for example) is not germane to the present discussion.

5   The Danish carrier phrase is *Jeg siger _ sådan* 'I say _ like this'. The figures are generated using the SFS software developed by Mark Huckvale at University College London (http://www.phon.ucl.ac.uk/resource/sfs.html).

6   The precise formulation of the constraints which deliver the distribution in (13) is not central to the discussion here. Applied to both Danish and English (see (9) and (5)), an Optimality-theoretic account might run something like this: a constraint requiring the faithful preservation of features in the foot head outranks constraints penalising the appearance of (H), (?) and (h) (cf. Kirchner 1998).

7   Ibibio, a member of the Cross River subgroup of Benue-Congo languages, is spoken primarily in Akwa Ibom State, Nigeria. This section draws on work in progress with Eno Urua (Harris and Urua 1998).

8   Except where indicated otherwise, the carrier phrase in the Ibibio figures is *ńbô _ ǹnɔ* 'I say _ for myself'.

9   In element theory, the distinction between labial and labial-velar is captured by means of differing segment-internal dependency relations.

10   The gross movement of the larynx suggested by the jump in the Lx trace during the closure phase might indicate glottalic articulation, which would be consistent with Connell's (1991) findings for the labial-velar.

11   The transcriptional tradition I am following here reflects the impression that the weakened labial typically remains phonetically distinct from |w|. In fact, the nature of the weakening varies dialectally and stylistically: besides the frictionless continuant illustrated in Figure 6.9, variants have been described as 'tapped fricatives', 'tapped stops' and 'fricated trills' (Connell 1991: 65). The dorsal articulation of [ɣ] varies between velar and uvular.

7

How many levels of phrasing? Evidence from two varieties of Italian

MARIAPAOLA D'IMPERIO AND BARBARA GILI FIVELA

7.1 Introduction

Evidence for prosodic structure above the word generally stems from two sources. On one hand, tonal phenomena, such as boundary tones and pitch accent association, have been shown to define edges and heads of prosodic domains, such as the intermediate phrase (Pierrehumbert and Beckman 1988), in a variety of languages, including English, German and Italian. On the other hand, Prosodic Phonology has mainly employed segmental sandhi phenomena at word boundaries to motivate phonological constituency. In this framework, what provides the information for the prosodic constituent to be built is surface syntactic structure (Selkirk 1984; Kaisse 1985; Nespor and Vogel 1986). At levels above the word, Prosodic Phonology posits a hierarchy of 'phrasing' levels, which are not necessarily overlapping with syntactic constituents and are domains for specific phonological rules. Independent of the specific version of the theory one adopts, the most generally assumed constituents above the word are the phonological phrase (φ) and the Intonational phrase (I).

Regardless of the specific diagnostic employed for the definition of prosodic domains, the fundamental question remains of how many levels of phrasing we need to assume in the prosodic analysis of a specific language. In Italian, while a number of proposals have been advanced regarding the metrical structure of subword constituents, such as the syllable and the mora (Repetti 1991; Nespor 1993), uncontroversial proposals regarding the status of larger units are still missing. Most research has limited its investigation to the role of external sandhi phenomena in defining some of these constituents. Our aim is to employ both sandhi and acoustic/phonetic data as evidence for prosodic structure above the word.

7.2 Syntax and phrasing

One of the phenomena that have been employed as evidence for constituency above the word is a widely studied sandhi rule of Central varieties of Italian, i.e. *Raddoppiamento (Fono-)Sintattico* or RF[1] (Bertinetto 1985; Nespor and Vogel 1986; Agostiniani 1992; Loporcaro 1997). RF lengthens the first consonant of a word 2, when immediately following a word 1, which is a finally stressed word or a strong monosyllable.[2] Moreover, word 2 cannot begin with an sC cluster or an intrinsically long segment (Loporcaro 1997). Also, in the Prosodic Phonology tradition, RF is predicted not to apply if a syntactically derived φ-boundary is present (Nespor and Vogel 1986). This is exemplified in (1).

(1) a.   *[Luca]*φ *[ha v:isto]*φ *[metá f:rate]*[3]φ
          NP   VP   NP
          Luca   has seen   half a pastry
          'Luca has seen half a pastry'

     b.   *[Luca]*φ *[ce ne ha v:isto]* φ *[metá]*φ *[fra tele]* φ *[di lino]*φ
          NP   VP   NP   PP   PP
          Luca   there of it has seen half among cloths   of linen
          'Luca has seen half of it there among linen cloths'

While RF is predicted to occur within the object NP in (1a), in (1b) it is blocked, since its target is part of the following syntactic constituent. Also, some sort of lengthening would affect the stressed vowel [a] at the edges of φ in (1b) (Nespor 1993: 204), being both the head and domain-final element of its constituent. Note that accounts based on moraic phonology invoke a relationship between RF and syllable weight. In Italian, stressed syllables are bimoraic (Repetti 1991) or 'branching' (Nespor 1993, but see also D'Imperio and Rosenthall 1999). However, word-final stressed vowels are lexically short, leaving the second mora of the stressed syllable empty. One of the accounts proposed for RF is that the newly created geminate would fill the empty mora of the final stressed syllable in word 1 (or, alternatively, make the syllable 'branching') by providing it with a coda consonant, after a resyllabification process. When RF does not occur (as in Northern varieties of Italian) the stressed vowel of word 1 must lengthen, so that spreading the vowel will fill the second mora position (Absalom and Hajek 1997).

According to Prosodic Phonology, another case in which RF is predicted not to occur is when a clause boundary break is present. Even in frameworks different from Prosodic Phonology, this type of break is very likely to be realised as a clearly definable I-boundary.

(2) a.   [[*Quando*] [*vedeva*] [*grisú b:arbablú*]]$_{S'/I}$ [[*balbettava*]] $_S$
NP
'When seeing the bluebearded Grisú, he used to falter'[4]

  b.   [[*Quando*] [*vedeva*] [*grisú*]]$_{S'/I}$ [[*Barbablú*] [*balbettava*]]$_S$
NP
'When seeing Grisú, Bluebeard used to falter'

While in (2a) word 2 is part of the direct object of the verb (within the wh-phrase) in (2b), instead, the same word is the subject of the matrix clause. This can be viewed as an example of 'attachment ambiguity' that can be resolved through the use of the appropriate I-boundary location (Nespor 1993: 188). The prediction is then that there will be a prosodic boundary between word 1 and word 2 in (2b) but not in (2a). Since I is hierarchically higher than φ, we expect absence of RF across the relevant word sequence in (2b). We also expect final lengthening to affect the final stressed vowel of word 1 in (2b) but not in (2a).

Note that RF sensitivity to syntactic structure has been recently disputed (Agostiniani 1992; Loporcaro 1997). Agostiniani (1992), for instance, reports Tuscan examples in which RF can span a φ as well as an I-boundary. Such data have led Vogel (1997) to redefine the domain for RF application for Tuscan (and another variety) to be the Prosodic Utterance. Nevertheless, we will still evaluate the impact of syntactically derived phrasing, since an effect was found in a pilot study (D'Imperio and Gili Fivela 1997). We will see that our results are, to some extent, subject-dependent, which might reflect the degree of controversy in the literature on RF. Moreover, here RF application is first transcribed, and only later is it acoustically measured. This was done for two reasons. First, we wanted to check if RF was categorical in its application. Second, we hypothesised that the complex phonetic and phonological phenomena that occur at prosodic boundary location, such as vowel lengthening (VL) and tonal disjuncture, could influence RF, both in its occurrence and its identification.

7.3 Focus and phrasing

Notions such as Focus and Topic have recently been explored in relation to their effect on Intonational phrasing (Vogel and Kenesei 1990; Frascarelli

1997). For instance, in the analysis of English and Hungarian in Vogel and Kenesei (1990), it is proposed that when a word is marked as being focussed, this triggers a restructuring rule by virtue of which a φ-boundary is imposed on the syntactic recursive side of the focussed word. More recently, Frascarelli (1997) has proposed that in Italian the boundary imposed by focus is an I-boundary.[5] The focus restructuring view predicts that a prosodic constituent (I) boundary will be inserted to coincide with the right edge of the focus constituent (Italian being right-branching). We can predict therefore that the newly created boundary will show phonetic-edge properties that are comparable to those associated with a regular I-boundary. Above all, a φ-internal rule such as RF would not apply when the word triggering it is in focus (Frascarelli 1997), as shown in (3).

(3) [[*Quando vedeva* [*GRISÚ*]F]I [*barbablú*]]S' [[*balbettava*]]S
     NP
     'When seeing the bluebearded Grisú, he used to falter'

In different frameworks, RF is claimed to be blocked by a pause or by the extreme pitch change that is often found in postfocal position (Loporcaro 1997, but see Agostiniani 1992). But does focus domain necessarily have to correspond to a specific phonological domain? We believe that this claim needs to be empirically tested. We will therefore evaluate the claim that RF is blocked by focally induced phrasing and quantify the degrees of vowel and consonant lengthening within and across focus-induced and syntactically induced boundaries.

7.4 Phonetic evidence

As mentioned above, while one approach bases the delimitation of prosodic domains on segmental sandhi phenomena, alternative views pay more attention to phonetic correlates expressing headedness and vicinity to an edge. Among these physical properties, we find tonal phenomena as well as segmental duration. While consonant lengthening is generally taken as the expression of RF occurrence and phrase-internal cohesion, VL at RF site is, on the contrary, taken as evidence for the presence of a prosodic boundary of some kind, such as an I-boundary. But vowel duration is a problematic index, in that it can also be associated with lengthening due to the expression of prominence relationships, such as stress. The two types of lengthening are often indistinguishable.

In this paper, the main questions we address are: does a deep syntactic break necessarily introduce a prosodic boundary? And what about focus: is it always correlated with phrasing? Specifically, we will investigate final lengthening at syntactically induced prosodic boundaries, as well as the orthogonal effect of focus structure on the various syntactic-prosodic constructions we will employ. We will also try to address more specific questions, such as 'what is the strength of the phrasal break?' and 'can we make claims based on phonetic evidence such as vowel and consonant duration?'. Finally, vowel duration will also be employed as a means to directly compare data from a variety of Italian that presents RF (Florentine Italian) with data from a variety in which RF does not exist (Turin Italian).

7.5 Corpus and methods

On the basis of a pilot study (D'Imperio and Gili Fivela 1997), we designed an experiment to test the effect of various boundary types and focus structure on RF occurrence and stressed vowel duration. Three speakers of Florentine Italian, an RF-variety, and three speakers of Turin Italian, a non-RF variety, participated in the experiment. The subjects read 5 repetitions of 5 paragraphs in which sentence types differing in either focus structure, syntactic structure, or a combination of the two, were embedded (Table 7.1). We thus obtained a total of 540 utterances. As in the pilot study, we decided to first transcribe RF occurrences, as well as the presence or absence of a pause or prosodic break[6] intervening between word 1 and word 2, in Florentine Italian data. We then acoustically measured, in both Florentine and Turin data, the duration of the initial consonant of word 2 in the RF sequence as well as the duration of the preceding stressed vowel.

Vowel-duration measurements followed standard procedures. However, when a strong focal accent was placed on finally stressed vowels, they presented a strong glottalised region, which manifested itself especially in terms of period-to-period irregularity at offset. This region was not included in the vowel-duration measurements. Glottalisation can in fact add significantly to vowel-duration results (Vayra 1992; van Santen and D'Imperio 1999). The potential RF-inducing word sequences in the corpus were as follows:

(4)   a.   *grisú barbablú* 'bluebearded Grisú'
      b.   *metá succo/su cose* 'half a juice', 'half on things'
      c.   *metá frate/fra tele* 'half a pastry', 'half among cloths'

The main variables of the corpus are presented in Table 7.1, with some of the target sequences that were embedded in the utterances.

Table 7.1 *Sample sequences in the corpus sentences*

FOCUS/SYNTAX			
	Cohesive	Disjoint	Clause Boundary
Broad	[*metá f:rate*]$_\varphi$	*metá*]$_{TA}$ [*fra tele*] *Grisú*]$_{SA}$ *Barbablú*
Narrow	*METÁ*]$_{FA}$ *frate*	*METÁ*]$_{F/TA}$ [*fra tele*] *GRISÚ*]$_{F/SA}$ *Barbablú*

The syntactic structure was either amenable or not amenable to RF occurrence, according to the syntax-to-prosody mapping algorithm. RF was predicted to occur in the 'cohesive' sentences (but see Absalom and Hajek 1997). Here, the RF sequence belongs to the same NP constituent, as in *metá frate* 'half a pastry' (as example (1a) above shows). Also, the fact that a clause boundary will cause an Intonational phrase break to occur is quite uncontroversial. In this case, therefore, RF is predicted not to occur at the site of the boundary, as shown in (2b) above. We will simply refer to this condition as 'clause boundary'.

Moreover, the syntactic structure could be characterised by the presence of a topicalised phrase boundary after the RF triggering word, as shown in (5). A topicalised constituent behaves like an extraposed part of the sentence, and it has been claimed that it forms an Intonational phrase of its own (Frascarelli 1997). Therefore, we expect RF not to apply in topicalised conditions and boundary strength to be very similar to clause-boundary sentences, since they should both induce an I-boundary.

(5)   *Luca ce ne ha visto metá*]$_{TA}$ [*fra tele di lino*
      'Luca has seen half of it there among linen cloths'

The claim that a topicalised structure is not amenable to RF occurrence is, like focus restructuring as well as the presence of other syntactic boundaries, in need of empirical testing. In our corpus, every prepositional phrase (PP) corresponds to a topicalised constituent. We will refer to these structures as 'disjoint'.

In addition to varying the syntactic structure of the target sentence, the paragraphs were built in such a way that the subjects could naturally produce the intended focus structures that were needed by the study. Focus was either broad over the whole sentence or narrow over the RF triggering word. Scope of focus was orthogonally manipulated in all the conditions presented above, so that we have 'broad cohesive' as opposed to 'narrow cohesive' conditions and so forth. Remember that, according to the focus-restructuring hypothesis, an I-boundary is placed at the right edge of the focused constituent (Frascarelli 1997). RF is therefore predicted not to occur in that position, and we also expect a certain degree of VL due to narrow focus placement. To sum up, according to claims in the literature, we expect RF to occur only in broad cohesive cases, while in all other cases we should find VL and no RF, due to the presence of a syntactically induced or focus-induced I-boundary.

7.6 Results

7.6.1 Auditory transcription

As in the pilot study, both authors transcribed[7] RF occurrence as well as pauses (PAU) for each sentence of the corpus (Table 7.2). The overall agreement was high, i.e. 87.96%. As expected, the highest percentage of RF was transcribed for broad cohesive sentences (78.66%). Here, both the syntax-prosody mapping and the focus structure predict a high level of cohesion, expressed by the presence of RF. On the other hand, when narrow focus was realised on the RF trigger (narrow cohesive), RF was transcribed in only 21% of cases by both transcribers, though independently transcribed in 37% of cases. Therefore, contrary to our predictions, focus restructuring might not obligatorily occur. Pauses were also transcribed in only 25% of cases in this category.

Table 7.2 *Transcription results for RF and Pause (PAU) for each sentence type and agreed upon by both transcribers. Percentages of tokens in which the event was transcribed by either transcriber are reported in parentheses. Intertranscriber Agreement (IA) scores (Pitrelli, Beckman and Hirschberg 1994) are shown to the right*

	RF%	PAU%	RF-IA%	PAU-IA%
Broad cohesive	78.66 (93)	0 (0)	85.33	100
Narrow cohesive	21.33 (37)	25.33 (36)	84	89.33
Broad disjoint	0 (40)	3.33 (20)	60	83.33
Narrow disjoint	3.33 (13)	53.33 (70)	90	83.33
Broad/clause b.	0 (0)	100 (100)	100	100
Narrow/clause b.	0 (0)	80 (93)	100	86.66

The results for broad disjoint sentences were similar to those of the pilot study, in that here both transcribers reported RF in 40% of the cases, though these cases were never agreed upon. The surprisingly high number of independently transcribed RF points to the lack of a strong barrier for RF across disjoint sentences. We must also point to the fact that the RF agreement was lowest for these sentences (60%) and generally very high for all other cases. This suggests the presence of ambiguous cues to phrasing within this category, which will be discussed below. RF was transcribed only in 3% of the cases in narrow disjoint sentences, and never in broad clause-boundary nor in narrow clause-boundary cases. Pauses were transcribed in 100% of the cases in broad clause-boundary sentences and 93% in narrow clause-boundary cases, as predicted by the presence of an I-boundary. A certain number of pauses were also transcribed in narrow disjoint tokens (53%), while pauses were never transcribed in broad cohesive sentences. We interpret these results as suggesting that a clause boundary will produce a stronger disjuncture than a topicalised boundary (disjoint cases), which contradicts our predictions.

7.6.2 Acoustic results

7.6.2.1 Florentine Italian

Our results will be presented according to the segmental context at RF location. This is to avoid the possible confound due to differences in degrees of lengthening under RF among different consonant types (Payne 2000).

All Florentine subjects - [u]...[b] contexts

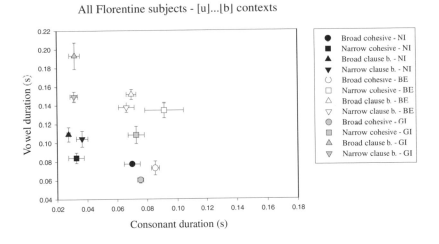

Figure 7.1 Consonant and vowel duration in all conditions for all subjects for [u]...[b] contexts. Horizontal and vertical bars indicate standard error

All Florentine subjects - [a]...[s,f] contexts

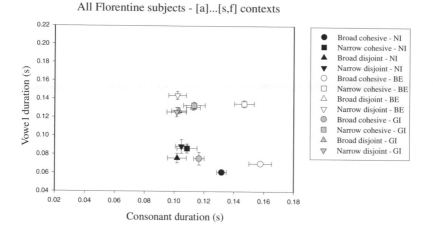

Figure 7.2 Consonant and vowel duration in all conditions for all subjects for [a]...[s,f] contexts. Horizontal and vertical bars indicate standard error

Since segmental context was not kept constant in all conditions, we will have to compare cohesive sentences with clause-boundary sentences first (which were always characterised by the word sequence in (4a)), and then with topicalised constructions (which consisted of the sequences in (4b) and (4c)). Therefore, in contrast with the auditory transcription, the comparison between topicalised and clause-boundary sentences will only be indirect. All conditions were cross-combined with either broad or narrow focus, so that we can analyse the orthogonal contribution of focus structure in both figures.

As mentioned above, PP boundaries were always accompanied by a topicalised construction (disjoint sentences), which has been claimed to produce an Intonational Phrase break. For disjoint sentences, the prediction is that some VL will be produced at the boundary location, due to the existence of a phrasal edge, and that this will be the same as VL found in focus-induced and clause-boundary phrasing. But note that, while RF was never transcribed in clause-boundary cases, it was instead transcribed (at least independently) for the other two cases (narrow cohesive and broad disjoint). This might have been caused by stronger acoustic indices of disjuncture in the first as opposed to the two latter cases. Below we show that this was indeed the case.

The results for all Florentine speakers and for [u]...[b] contexts (*Grisú Barbablú*) are shown in Figure 7.1, where mean vowel and consonant duration are plotted against each other. Subjects are differentiated by shading, while shape reflects sentence type. All the reported differences were tested by means of one-way ANOVAs for each speaker as well as by pairwise comparisons for analyses that were significant at p<0.01.

Consonant duration was similar for two out of three subjects. Note a clear separation between two categories for GI and NI, who, as expected, showed longer consonant duration in broad cohesive cases (circles), where RF was transcribed in the majority of cases, and no lengthening in clause-boundary conditions (upward and downward triangles), where RF was never transcribed. This result is at odds with the claim that RF would not be blocked by an I-boundary in Tuscan (Vogel 1997). GI and NI only differ in the behaviour for narrow cohesive sentences, in that consonants are long (as long as in broad cohesive cases) for GI (grey squares), while they are not for NI (black squares). This might explain why RF was only partially transcribed in narrow cohesive cases. We interpret this result with the idea that RF can be allowed in postfocal position and that focus restructuring is not obligatorily realised within this variety. Similarly to GI, BE showed a trend for longer consonant durations in cohesive sentences, but no difference was significant between any of the categories. Vowel duration was instead always shortest for broad cohesive sentences in all speakers. This was expected, since RF and VL have been claimed to be mutually exclusive in this variety. The additional presence of narrow focus induced longer vowel durations for BE and GI, but not for NI. All speakers, however, differentiated between broad cohesive and clause-boundary vowel duration.

Figure 7.2 shows results for [a]...[s,f] contexts. Also here two of the speakers pattern similarly. Longest consonant durations were found for broad cohesive cases (circles) for BE and NI, while the trend shown by GI was not significant. Speaker NI differentiated broad cohesive sentences from all other types, while BE only differentiated between cohesive and disjoint cases, but not between narrow and broad cohesive cases. We can account for the slightly different results from those in Figure 7.1 with the fact that fricatives appear to lengthen proportionally less than plosives under RF (Payne 2000). Topicalised sentences (upward triangles) presented longer vowel duration than broad cohesive sentences, especially when under narrow focus (downward triangles), with values that did not differ from those for narrow cohesive sentences for any of the speakers. Since final VL effect was accompanied by short consonant duration for two of the speakers, it might appear surprising that a high percentage of RF was independently transcribed for such cases. However, GI did not sufficiently maintain the consonant duration contrast between disjoint and cohesive cases, which might explain uncertainty in RF transcription.

Finally, we can indirectly compare vowel duration in clause-boundary and disjoint cases. Duration was greater (around 140 ms and up for GI and BE and around 100 ms for NI) in clause-boundary conditions than in disjoint cases (around 120 ms for BE and GI and around 80 ms for NI), despite the fact that the first were always represented by the [u] context, as opposed to [a] for disjoint sentences. We know in fact that high vowels are intrinsically shorter than low vowels. Interestingly, narrow clause-boundary sentences showed shorter vowel durations than broad clause-boundary cases, while the opposite was true for disjoint sentences. Though this is only speculative at this point, this result might be due to a higher degree of glottalisation at narrow clause-boundary location.

We interpreted these results as evidence for the existence of two separate sets of cues to structural position: (1) lack or presence of RF, to signal degree of morphosyntactic cohesion within RF sequence; (2) vowel-final lengthening, to signal vicinity to an edge and focus. These structural cues appear to be employed differently by the subjects. Narrow focus does not appear to always or consistently affect the degree of consonant lengthening. This result does not support the hypothesis that focus imposes a prosodic constituent boundary that obligatorily blocks RF in postfocal position (see also Agostiniani 1992 for a similar result). The similarity in VL between broad disjoint and narrow cohesive sentences might suggest a similarity in phrasing level. However, the degree of internal cohesion can be greater in narrow cohesive sentences because of longer consonant duration (meaning that RF applied in many instances).

7.6.2.2 Turin Italian

Since corpus and methodology were the same for the Turin Italian experiment, we will directly present the effects of the various conditions on vowel duration and consonant duration, though we do not expect to find any consonant doubling here. Again, we compare lengthening effects due to the presence of syntactic boundaries to lengthening effects due to the presence of narrow focus on the RF trigger, as we did for Florentine Italian. Figure 7.3 shows the relevant results for one of the Turin speakers, since it is very representative of the overall results for this variety. Results for both segmental contexts are here shown on a single graph. Not surprisingly, subjects showed shorter vowel durations in broad cohesive (circles) as opposed to all other cases, while they did not exploit consonant duration differences. Also according to the Turin data, vowel duration is similar in narrow cohesive and broad disjoint sentences (empty diamond and empty square).

Note also, as in Florentine, that narrow clause-boundary sentences (downward triangle, black) have shorter vowel durations than broad clause-boundary ones, while the opposite is true for disjoint sentences. In broad clause-boundary sentences (upward triangle), subjects showed longer vowel durations than in narrow cohesive sentences.

Turin subject Ba - [u]...[b] and [a]...[s,f] contexts

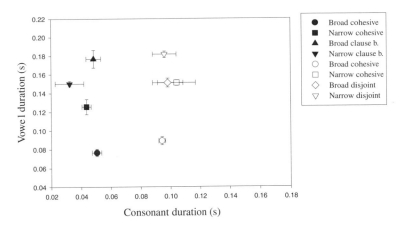

Figure 7.3 Consonant and vowel duration in all conditions for subject BA. Empty symbols represent [a]...[s,f] contexts, while filled symbols represent [u]...[b] contexts. Horizontal and vertical bars indicate standard error

Therefore, for Turin speakers, vowel duration seems to be the most stable correlate for phrasing levels: narrow focus and broad disjoint (smaller lengthening) and presence of a clause boundary (greater lengthening).

7.7 Discussion

Though an overall look at the results reveals a complex picture, we will attempt to reconcile the Florentine with the Turin results. In Florentine, longer consonant durations can be found in cohesive cases (both broad and narrow) while they are not found in disjoint and clause-boundary sentences (except for BE), i.e. the conditions in which we predicted some level of disjuncture, both from Prosodic Phonology syntax-to-prosody mapping and from our transcription. Consonants are shortest in clause-boundary conditions and disjoint sentences for two of the speakers in each segmental context (though the speakers are not the same). For instance, speaker BE did not signal the phrasing difference through consonant duration for the [b] contexts, though she did for the fricative contexts. Subjects therefore can vary in the importance they place on different phonetic factors for the realisation of contrast. A differential behaviour as to the realisation of specific phonological processes, depending on contextual variables, is also found in other languages (see Fox and Terbeek (1977) for the flapping rule in American English).

Unlike clause-boundary sentences, in which the expected I-boundary seems to be realised, narrow focus did not block consonant lengthening in cohesive cases. This result does not support the hypothesis of an obligatory 'focus restructuring' rule (Frascarelli 1997). This rule might be highly optional and subject-dependent. Also, since narrow focus is generally manifested through a strong pitch excursion in Italian (Gili Fivela and D'Imperio 1998), the consequent tonal disjuncture at postfocal position does not appear to encroach upon RF realisation, which is in line with Agostiniani (1992).

From the point of view of consonant duration, Turin results were consistent with the expectation that this variety has no RF. On the other hand, vowel duration results revealed phrasing similarity between the two varieties. In fact, we seem to discern three levels of phrasing, with the shortest vowel durations in broad cohesive sentences and the longest in (broad) clause-boundary sentences. An intermediate lengthening was found in broad disjoint and narrow cohesive sentences. The similarity in VL might suggest a similarity in prosodic phrasing in the two categories across varieties. Such a level of phrasing seems lower than I, and could correspond to the intermediate phrase (Pierrehumbert and Beckman 1988). However, tonal evidence and break indices have to be systematically investigated before we could advance such a proposal. Moreover, the VL found in broad disjoint cases was not consistently accompanied by a difference in consonant durations relative to cohesive cases in one speaker (GI). Such contradictory auditory cues to phrasing might have caused uncertainty in transcribing RF, hence the low agreement score, for this category.

Though topicalised constructions were predicted to show an I-boundary just like clause-boundary sentences, the degree of VL is not the same as in the latter cases, being instead very similar to narrow cohesive VL. Narrow cohesive cases showed also similar consonant duration relative to disjoint cases, except for subject BE (for whom consonant duration was longer in narrow cohesive cases). As a plausible account of the facts, in narrow cohesive sentences, the pressure from keeping the utterance coherent with similar morphosyntactic constructions leads to RF application (though optionally) both within and across speakers of the same variety. Focus-induced VL, instead, which is needed to render the head position prominent, is not violated. Topicalised sentences allow RF application in an optional way as well, though speaker BE kept narrow cohesive and disjoint sentences separate according to consonant lengthening. We believe that both RF and VL (as well as other phonetic and phonological events, such as tonal disjuncture) contribute in determining prosodic structure. The interplay of different constraints can often produce mixed results with conflicting cues, as in the present study. This is in line with recent constraint-based phonological theories.

7.8 Conclusions

Our study shows that RF can be blocked by an I-boundary induced by a clause boundary, both perceptually and acoustically. Narrow focus, instead, does not seem to obligatorily introduce a morphosyntactic barrier for RF, though VL is very similar to broad disjoint lengthening. This result does not support the hypothesis of an obligatory 'focus restructuring' rule.

Though differing in their use of consonant duration, due to differences in the grammar of sandhi phenomena, Turin and Florentine Italian present a similarity in exploiting vowel duration differences among various syntactic and focus structures. In both topicalised and narrow focus utterances, VL is not as strong as before a clause boundary. The similarity in VL between narrow cohesive and disjoint sentences might suggest that they induce a similar phrasing level, such as the intermediate phrase. However, it seems rather premature at this point to try to answer the question of how many levels of phrasing we can infer from the data. If we were forced to answer this question, we would say 'definitively two' (short or long consonant), when looking at consonant duration. However, we would answer 'three levels' (short, or medium or long vowel), if VL were the phonetic index singled out by our analysis. However, all phonological and phonetic exponents of phrasing should be evaluated as a whole when determining prosodic structure. Until we discover more about the relative role of competing cues, as well as their relative 'ranking' in determining the percept of a boundary, one has no way of constraining the number of potential phrasing levels that can be postulated from observing the acoustic data.

Notes

We are grateful to Mary Beckman for help in understanding the issues and for comments on an earlier version of this paper. Thanks also to Rebecca Herman for helpful suggestions and to Pier Marco Bertinetto for encouragement and advice.

1　Throughout the paper, we will refer to the rhythmic version of RF and will make no reference to 'morphological' RF, which applies in different conditions and also in Southern varieties (Agostiniani 1992; Loporcaro 1997).

2　By strong monosyllable it is meant a monosyllabic word belonging to one of the following categories: verbs, nouns, adjectives, adverbs and non-clitic pronouns.

3　We use an acute accent mark to indicate primary lexical stress, though the Italian orthography marks it as a grave accent in finally stressed words (in the majority of cases) and does not mark it at all in other positions.

4　Italian is a pro-drop language, therefore the verb can appear in absolute initial position within the matrix clause.

5   Though restructuring in not predicted in case of a prehead word (Frascarelli 1997), we did not find any differences between head and prehead behaviour (Gili and D'Imperio 1998) so we treat the two cases similarly.

6   Note that by 'pause' we refer to the percept of a prosodic break which can be produced by various acoustic indices, independently or in combination, such as a melodic or durational disjuncture, as well as silence.

7   None of the transcribers (the authors of the paper) is a native speaker of Florentine Italian (though one of them is a speaker of an RF variety and the other is not). In order to ensure the coherence of our results, we had a Florentine speaker transcribe RF and pauses for the pilot study corpus. The agreement reached between each of the authors and the Florentine speaker was high, about 80%. That is why we thought that the authors' transcription would be sufficient here.

8

Domain-initial articulatory strengthening in four languages

PATRICIA KEATING, TAEHONG CHO, CÉCILE
FOUGERON AND CHAI-SHUNE HSU

8.1 Introduction

This paper is about one way in which prosody affects individual speech segments, with segmental phonetics showing a perhaps surprising sensitivity to higher-level linguistic structure. By *prosody* we mean the phrasal and tonal organisation of speech. We will show that phonetic properties of individual segments depend on their *prosodic position*, or position in prosodic structure.

It is well known that in a monosyllabic CVC word, the initial consonant can be pronounced differently than the final consonant, the initial consonant being longer and having greater articulatory magnitude (e.g. Byrd 1994; Keating, Wright and Zhang 1999). Some interesting recent acoustic studies have extended this line of inquiry above the syllable and word level to phrasal levels. For example, at the LabPhonII conference, Pierrehumbert and Talkin (1992) presented a study in which they used acoustic measures of breathiness to show that /h/ is more consonant-like when it is phrase-initial than when it is phrase-medial ('The phrase boundary was found to shift articulation on both sides in a more consonantal direction', p. 116). Similarly, the Voice Onset Time (VOT) of /t/ is longer phrase-initially. This latter result was extended by Jun (1993), who compared the VOT of Korean /pʰ/ in three positions: initial in a small phrase, initial in a word, medial in a word; VOT varied as shown in Figure 8.1.

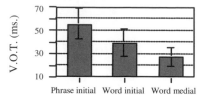

Figure 8.1.VOT of Korean /pʰ/ as a function of prosodic position. Our summary of data from Jun 1993: 235 (Figure 6.2)

Then Dilley, Shattuck-Hufnagel and Ostendorf (1996) showed that higher phrasal levels can also differ. They tabulated the presence of glottalisation of vowel-initial words in a radio-news corpus, and found that the likelihood of glottalisation depends on the prosodic position of the word. Glottalisation is most likely at the beginning of an Intonational Phrase (a large phrase), next most likely at the beginning of an Intermediate Phrase (a smaller phrase), and least likely phrase-medially.

Articulatory studies that compare positions in phrases include Stone (1981), van Lieshout, Starkweather, Hulstijn and Peters (1995), Byrd, Kaun, Narayanan and Saltzman (2000), Gordon (1996), Hsu and Jun (1997), and Byrd and Saltzman (1998). In our own earlier work (Fougeron and Keating 1997), we compared the articulation of /n/s in different prosodic positions. The speech materials consisted of arithmetic expressions as in (1).

(1)   89 x (89 + 89 + 89) = a lot

Reiterant speech was used, with most syllables replaced by the syllable /no/, as in (2).

(2)   89   times   (89   plus   89   plus   89   ) = a lot
         nonono no   (nonono no   nonono no   nonono) = a lot

The prosodic organisation of the test utterances was characterized by transcribing groupings of words into smaller phrases and larger phrases (using the ToBI conventions (Silverman, Beckman, Pitrelli, Ostendorf, Wightman, Price, Pierrehumbert and Hirschberg 1992; Beckman and Elam 1997))). Each reiterant syllable was then coded as initial, medial, or final in each of the prosodic domains Word, small Intermediate Phrase (or PP), large Intonational Phrase (or IP), and Utterance. /n/s which were not initial within a word were also coded as initial in the Syllable (S). The Utterance-initial /n/s were always and only at the beginning of the sentence, but otherwise there was no *unique* relation between prosodic position above the word and linear position in the sentence.

The relevant result here, shown in Figure 8.2a, is that in general, /n/s which were initial in higher domains had more total linguopalatal contact than /n/s which were initial only in lower domains. The effect of being in domain-initial position was generally cumulative. Each speaker showed a hierarchical pattern of peak contact, distinguishing at least three domains in this way. However, no speaker distinguished all the domains, and no distinction was reliable for all speakers. Speaker 1 distinguished IP, PP and W; Speaker 2 distinguished U, IP/PP, W and S, and Speaker 3 distinguished U, IP, PP/W, and S.

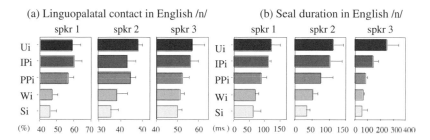

Figure 8.2 English EPG data by speaker for (a) Peak contact, based on Fougeron and Keating (1997). The horizontal bars show the %electrodes (of 96) contacted. (b) Articulatory seal duration (not in Fougeron and Keating). The horizontal bars show duration in ms. All graphs show values for consonants in initial position (indicated by small 'i' in the axis labels) in the domain indicated (U for Utterance, IP for Intonational Phrase, PP for Phonological or Intermediate Phrase, W for Word, S for Syllable)

These effects were limited to consonants in domain-initial positions. Because in this corpus there were often three or more syllables in each domain, we could test specifically whether this resulted from weakening of all non-initial syllables (that is, the first syllable's consonant is different from all others), versus final-syllable weakening (that is, the last syllable's consonant is different from all others). The results clearly showed the former. We also found no evidence for articulatory declination (global, utterance-level trends, e.g. Krakow, Bell-Berti and Wang 1994). Therefore in the present study we will focus only on domain-initial consonants.

We called the pattern seen in this study 'domain-initial strengthening' because the lingual articulations appeared to be stronger for consonants at the beginning of each prosodic domain. However, the exact nature of domain-initial strengthening is not yet clear. In Fougeron and Keating (1997), we discussed some possible mechanisms, including articulatory undershoot of shorter segments, overshoot of consonants after lengthened domain-final vowels, coarticulatory resistance by segments in initial positions and overall greater articulatory effort for initial segments. This last mechanism is explored more fully in Fougeron (1998). We also outlined how this strengthening could aid a

147

listener in prosodic parsing and feature extraction. However, no perceptual experiments have been carried out, and Fougeron (1998) argues against a primarily perceptual motivation.

The idea that longer durations allow articulatory targets to be more closely approximated, while shorter durations result in undershoot of those targets (Lindblom 1963; Moon and Lindblom 1994) can readily be related to initial strengthening. If initial segments are longer, then they would have more time to achieve more extreme articulations. For example, Soler and Romero (1999) relate duration and constriction degree in their account of Spanish stop lenition. This possibility can be explored by measuring consonant durations and testing their correlations with linguopalatal contact. A strong relation between these variables would support the hypothesis that initial strengthening and lengthening arise from a single mechanism.

Therefore articulatory duration (the duration of the stop consonant seal, from EPG data) was measured for the same tokens. These data, not reported in Fougeron and Keating (1997) but shown in Figure 8.2b, followed a similar pattern to linguopalatal contact. Speakers 1 and 3 distinguished IP, PP, and W/S; Speaker 2 distinguished IP, PP, W and S. The within-speaker correlations between articulatory duration and linguopalatal contact for domain-initial tokens above the Word level were low to modest (with r from .3 to .52, and r^2 from .09 to .27). Although domain-initial /n/s are both greater in linguopalatal contact and longer in seal duration than domain-medial ones, such weak correlations suggest that, at least for these English speakers, greater linguopalatal contact does not necessarily come from longer time given for articulation. This result weakens any articulatory undershoot hypothesis.

The present study follows up on our earlier results for English in Fougeron and Keating (1997) by comparing several languages. Not only do we want to know whether the results hold beyond English, but we want to know whether other prosodic differences among languages are reflected in any initial strengthening effect. Lehiste (1964b) showed that languages differ in how they mark word boundaries. She proposed that this depends on a language's phonology; for example, a language with phonemic vowel length would not use vowel lengthening to mark boundaries. Initial strengthening at other levels could also depend on a language's phonology. Byrd *et al.* (2000) in their LabPhonV presentation found relatively little effect of phrasal position on spatial position of articulators in Tamil, though they did find effects on duration and timing. That is, in Tamil there are temporal effects without spatial effects. Thus, although these two kinds of effects co-occur in English, the Tamil study shows that they must be distinct, and their co-occurrence must be language-particular. The Tamil results also undermine any undershoot account in which spatial variation is a necessary consequence of temporal variation. However, it is not clear that Byrd *et al.*'s Tamil corpus included a sufficient range of different prosodic domains to ensure that all possible prosodic effects were seen. Therefore our study includes three languages and clear examples of larger and smaller phrasal domains.

Since English has such prominent lexical stress and nuclear pitch accent, it might be expected that its domain edges would be phonetically less marked than edges in languages with less prominent heads. The three languages studied here, French, Korean and Taiwanese, allow such comparisons. Taiwanese is a lexical tone language, and thus, since it cannot use tones to mark domain heads, might be expected to show large edge-marking. On the other hand, Taiwanese tone sandhi is organized in a phrasal domain which does not seem to be prosodic (Hayes 1990; Hsu and Jun 1996), and for that reason prosodic domains might be expected to receive little phonetic marking. French and Korean differ from both English and Taiwanese in having neither lexical tone nor lexical stress. They are prosodically similar to each other; both have a small prosodic domain defined by phrasal tones. At the same time, it has been proposed that these two languages differ in terms of pitch, duration and amplitude variation within that phrase. Fougeron and Jun (1998) posit a H* phrasal accent at the end of the French AP, which also shows final lengthening (see also Jun and Fougeron, 2000). Unlike French, Korean has no AP-final accent (Jun 1998), and Jun (1995a) observed no AP-final lengthening; instead, the beginning of the Korean AP is marked by accent and lengthening. In addition, a French AP-final accented syllable is realised with greater amplitude (Martin 1982) while no discernible greater amplitude is found in Korean AP-final position (Jun 1995b). In sum, it can be posited that Korean reinforces the beginning of the phrase but French the end. If this is so, we might expect French not to show domain-initial articulatory strengthening like Korean.

8.2 General methods

8.2.1 Prosodic domains

We assume a hierarchical view of prosody in which smaller prosodic constituents or levels are nested within larger ones. (For a thorough review of theories of prosodic hierarchies, see Shattuck-Hufnagel and Turk (1996).) For present purposes, it does not matter whether these prosodic constituents are identical across languages. What is crucial is that each language has several domains, each with specific properties that allow it to be identified, and organised hierarchically. Where these properties seem comparable across languages we use the same name (e.g. Intonational Phrase), but no precise descriptive or theoretical claims about these languages are intended.

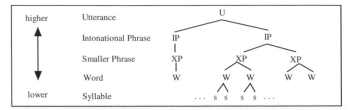

Figure 8.3 A partial Prosodic Hierarchy adopted in this study. One or more instances of each level may appear under the level above it

For each language, then, prosodic domains must be determined and defined. A schematic of a partial hierarchy of prosodic domains (mostly above the word level) is shown in Figure 8.3.

One domain that seems comparable across languages is the Intonational Phrase, or IP. An IP is marked by a complete intonational contour, and can be set off naturally by pauses. An IP can comprise a full sentence, but in our experiments it usually comprised a clause or topic phrase within a longer sentence (punctuated by a comma or semi-colon). We also tested a possible higher domain, the Utterance, corresponding to the second of two sentences (punctuated by a period), and marked by a full pause, sometimes with a breath. Whether there is a systematic difference between Utterance and Intonational Phrase is somewhat controversial. Nespor and Vogel (1986) distinguished them on the basis of where some phonological rules apply. However, in terms of intonation and pausing, they need not be different; and Wightman, Shattuck-Hufnagel, Ostendorf and Price (1992) found no difference in their amounts of final lengthening. In our Korean and Taiwanese experiments we instructed subjects not to pause within a sentence, so that the Utterance break is marked by a pause but the IP break usually is not. In our French experiment, which did not give explicit instructions, subjects were more likely to pause between IPs, as they did between Us.

A phrasal domain smaller than the IP was also sought, corresponding to the Phonological or Intermediate Phrase studied for English in Fougeron and Keating (1997). Such a phrase would be marked by less than a complete intonational contour. In French and Korean the Accentual Phrase was chosen, as it is easy to transcribe from spoken utterances. An AP usually consists of a small number of content words, plus function words, with an associated phrasal tone pattern. Following the analysis of French prosody given by Jun and Fougeron (1995) and Fougeron and Jun (1998), the French AP has an underlying phrasal tone sequence LHLH. Following the analysis of Seoul Korean prosody given by Jun (1998), the Korean AP is also marked by an underlying phrasal tone sequence LHLH. For Taiwanese, there is no phrase smaller than the Intonational Phrase which is generally accepted to be part of that language's prosodic hierarchy. The tone-sandhi group (the domain in which tone sandhi takes place, based on the Phonological Phrase, e.g. Chen 1987) would appear to be a candidate for such a domain, but this domain is not strictly layered under the IP, and Hsu and Jun (1996) concluded that the tone-sandhi group is not a prosodic domain of Taiwanese. Instead, in this study a small phrase (SP) was identified that consists of a heavy-subject Noun Phrase. This domain is not tonally marked, but is characterised by a break greater than that between words.

Finally, initial and medial positions within a Word domain were included in each experiment. What counts as a Prosodic Word in a given language is controversial. In English our Word was fairly large by some prosodic standards, being lexically complex (e.g. *eighty-nine*), but nonetheless having only one primary lexical stress; similarly, in Taiwanese the Word was a morphologically complex resultative verb comprising two verbal roots (*stepped on*). In Korean, Words were mostly inflected nouns (e.g. *man*), while in French, Words were parts of larger names (e.g. *Auntie Nadia*). The Syllable-initial consonants were all Word-medial.

8.2.2 Corpora

The test consonants in the three languages were /n/ and unaspirated /t/, which in these languages are generally laminal dental stops. For all studies, the prosodic position of test consonants was varied; by varying the text around the test syllable, the prosodic structure is varied, while the absolute position of the test syllable is kept the same. (Since it is possible that some language other than English might show articulatory declination, we control for this in all studies.) Table 8.1. shows the corpus for French /n/. The corpora for the other French consonant, /t/, and for the other languages are similar in design and are given in the appendix. The only exception is Taiwanese /n/, as described in the next section.

Table 8.1 *Corpus for French /n/. The test consonant is in bold, and the word containing it is underlined*

Positions	Test consonant /n/ in /a_a/
Ui	Paul aime Tata. <u>Na</u>dia les protège en secret.
	Paul loves Auntie. Nadia protects them in secret
IPi	La pauvre Tata, <u>Na</u>dia et Paul n'arriveront que demain.
	Poor Auntie, Nadia and Paul won't arrive until tomorrow
APi	Tonton, Tata, <u>Na</u>dia et Paul arriveront demain.
	Uncle, Auntie, Nadia and Paul will arrive tomorrow
Wi	Paul et Tata-<u>**Na**dia</u> arriveront demain matin.
	Paul and Auntie Nadia will arrive tomorrow morning
Si	Tonton et <u>A**n**abelle</u> arriveront demain matin.
	Uncle and Anabelle will arrive tomorrow morning

8.2.3 Data collection

The primary measure of strengthening reported here will be the maximum amount of contact between the tongue and the palatal surface, as recorded by electropalatography (EPG). The amount of contact is an index of tongue height at the point of contact, and thus is considered a measure of the strength of an articulation. All studies used the Kay Elemetrics Palatometer. With the Palatometer, a talker wears an individual, custom-made pseudopalate that covers the surface of the hard palate and the inner surfaces of the upper teeth with 96 contact electrodes. For French, Korean and Taiwanese speakers, the frontmost row of electrodes extends onto the back surface of the upper teeth, and two electrodes were placed at the middle of the front two incisors, so that at least some dental contact could be registered. This arrangement of electrodes is shown in Figure 8.4. The Palatometer records the pattern of tongue-pseudopalate contact every 10 ms. The audio signal was recorded with a head-mounted microphone, at 12.8 kHz, into the same data file.

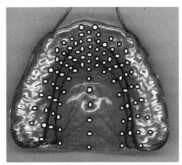

Figure 8.4 Scanned image of pseudo-palate, with special layout of the 96 contact electrodes

Subjects were not given overt instructions about the phrasing or prosody to be used in their readings of the sentences, except that Korean and Taiwanese speakers were asked to pause at a period but not pause at a comma. A native-speaker experimenter monitored subjects' productions during the recording sessions and asked for repetitions of any sentences that did not have the desired phrasing. If a subject read, for example, a sentence testing an AP boundary with a larger break, the experimenter asked the subject to read that sentence again, though still without giving any overt instructions.

Subjects produced 20 repetitions of each sentence for the French and Korean studies. Because we wanted to obtain reasonably consistent prosody for each sentence type without overt instruction, sentences were not randomised. Instead, for a given test consonant, a subject produced 5 or 6 repetitions of one sentence, then 5 or 6 repetitions of another sentence, etc. through the set of sentences for that consonant; then the same again, until all the repetitions of all the sentences for that consonant had been recorded, at which point the sentences for the other test consonant were begun. (The procedure for Taiwanese was slightly different and is described below.)

8.2.4 Data measurement

Maximum linguopalatal contact was determined by calculating, for each data frame, the percentage of contacted electrodes over the 96 electrodes. The maximum value in each test consonant was recorded as the peak contact for that token. (Additional contact measures are reported in the papers describing the studies of French and Korean: Fougeron 1998, 1999b; Cho and Keating 1999). Temporal measures were also made, including the number of frames showing a complete stop closure (articulatory seal duration), acoustic closure duration, and for voiceless stop /t/, acoustic VOT.

Reliable differences were determined by ANOVA and Fisher PLSD *posthoc* tests at the .05 level of significance. Separate ANOVAs were conducted for each consonant for each speaker, with the single factor Prosodic Position (i.e. the test sentence type). Regressions of peak contact on seal duration were calculated separately for each consonant x language x speaker condition.

8.3 Methods and results for each language

8.3.1 French

8.3.1.1 Methods
Experiments on French have been reported in Fougeron and Keating (1996), and much additional data is included in Fougeron (1998, 1999b). Two subjects participated in this study: one of the authors (female, Speaker 1) plus one other subject (male, Speaker 2). The test consonants reported on here were unaspirated /t/ and /n/. /n/ was in a /a_a/ context, /t/ in a /ɔ̃_ɔ̃ / context.

8.3.1.2 Results
EPG results are shown in Figures 8.5a–b. First, for the peak-contact data, in Figure 8.5a, there was an effect of prosodic position for both speakers, with a generally cumulative increase of contact from lowest to highest domains. More distinctions are made for /n/: both speakers distinguish all domains except IP from Utterance. For /t/, not only is the distinction between Utterance and IP unclear (in fact, it is reliably reversed for one speaker), but also the distinction between Word-initial and Syllable-initial is not made. The reliable differences, then, are those between a large phrasal domain (IP, Utterance), a small one (AP), and something smaller (Word or Syllable). Detailed analysis of contact in the front region of the palate showed that the greater contact in higher prosodic positions was mainly located in the posterior part of that anterior region. This difference is seen in the sample tokens shown in Figure 8.6, along with other differences presumably reflecting the height of the tongue body.

The duration data show fewer distinctions. The duration of the articulatory closure or seal, in Figure 8.5b, shows a large difference between U/IP and the smaller domains. Which of the further, smaller, differences are reliable varies between the speakers. However, the overall lengthening pattern is cumulative like that for contact, and indeed the two measures are well correlated (r^2 from .6 to .76). Acoustic duration of /n/ (not shown in the figure) shows lengthening at beginnings of lower domains, but IP- and U-initial /n/s are very short. Acoustic closure duration of /t/ (not shown in the figure), measured only for the lower domains because they involve no pause, patterns similarly to /n/ (and to articulatory duration, not surprisingly). For VOT of unaspirated /t/, shown in Figure 8.7a, there was little effect of prosodic position. The only difference found for both speakers was between Syllable-initial and IP-initial positions.

154

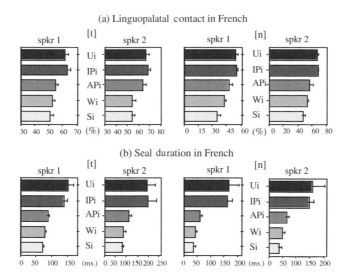

(a) Linguopalatal contact in French

(b) Seal duration in French

Figure 8.5 Data for French, displayed as in Figure 8.2. (a) Peak EPG contact for /t, n/; (b) Articulatory duration for /t, n/

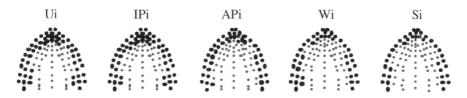

Figure 8.6 Sample French tokens for /n/ showing contact patterns across prosodic positions

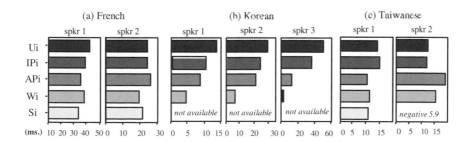

Figure 8.7 (a) French VOT, (b) Korean VOT and (c) Taiwanese VOT for /t/ across prosodic positions

8.3.2 Korean

8.3.2.1 Methods

Three subjects participated in this study, one of the authors (male, Speaker 2) and two others (one male, Speaker 1, and one female, Speaker 3). The complete study included test consonants /n t tʰ t*/ (where /t*/ refers to a fortis stop); here we report on only /t/ (the lenis stop) and /n/ as these are the consonants most comparable across the three languages. Detailed comparisons of the four test consonants, are reported elsewhere (Cho and Keating 1999). All of the domains in Figure 8.3 were included; however, two corpora were used for each consonant, one for comparison of higher-level domains, another for word-level domains. Otherwise we could not construct meaningful and grammatical sentences. In the higher-level corpus, for domains Utterance, IP, AP and Word, both /t/ and /n/ were in a /a_a/ context. In the lower-level corpus, for domains Word versus Syllable, /n/ was in a /o_ɛ/ context and /t/ was in a /a_a/ context.

8.3.2.2 Results

EPG results are shown in Figures 8.8a–b. First, in the overall contact data, shown in Figure 8.8a, all prosodic levels are generally distinguished by all the speakers for both test consonants, except that Speaker 3 does not have more contact for AP-initial than for Word-initial for either consonant and Speakers 1 and 3 do not differentiate W-initial from S-initial /t/.

Figure 8.9 shows sample tokens. Here we can see that higher domains have more front contact, as well as more back contact. Figure 8.9 also shows a shift in the nominal place of articulation (which depends on the location of the frontmost contact), due to a loss of dental contact as the stop moves from higher to lower domains. This difference is consistent for all three speakers for /n/. When this consonant has more contact, its nominal place of articulation is denti-alveolar, but when it has less contact, its place is palato-alveolar. There is a similar, but less dramatic, effect for /t/: when /t/ has less contact, its place is alveolar.

With articulatory seal duration, in Figure 8.8b, the phrasal domains are consistently distinguished by lengthening, but lower levels (AP versus Word, Word versus Syllable) are generally not distinguished. Nonetheless, articulatory duration is well-correlated with peak contact (r^2 from .77 to .91). Acoustic duration (not shown in the figure) is consistently cumulative when pooled across speakers, but the individual speaker data are not so consistent. Finally, VOT for /t/, shown above in Figure 8.7b, distinguishes all four levels tested in Korean.

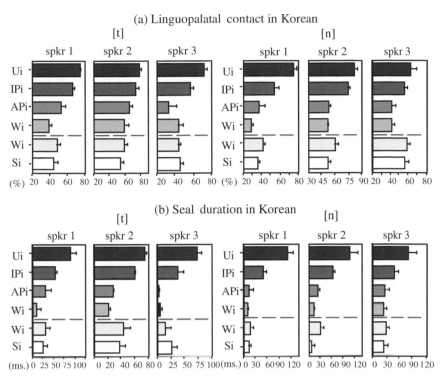

(a) Linguopalatal contact in Korean

(b) Seal duration in Korean

Figure 8.8 Data for Korean, displayed as in Figure 8.2. (a) Peak EPG contact for /t, n/; (b) Articulatory duration for /t, n/. Dashed horizontal line in each panel separates data from two different speech corpora; the two Word-initial conditions are not directly comparable.

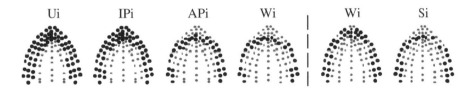

Figure 8.9 Sample Korean tokens for /n/ showing contact patterns across prosodic positions

157

8.3.3 Taiwanese

8.3.3.1 Methods

Two subjects participated in this study, reported in Hayashi *et al.* (1999): one of the authors (female, Speaker 1) plus one other subject (male, Speaker 2). The test consonants were unaspirated /t/ and /n/, followed by /a/ with a surface mid-level tone, preceded by another /a/. The corpus for /t/ consisted of sentences containing real words, as in French and Korean, but the corpus for /n/ consisted of reiterant versions of the /t/ corpus, in which all syllables in the model sentences were instead pronounced as /na/.

The sentences were presented to the subjects written in Mandarin, to be translated by the speaker. Because the speakers were reading Mandarin and translating into Taiwanese, all the repetitions of a test sentence were done in a single block. Speaker 1 read ten repetitions of each test sentence containing /t/ and six repetitions of the reiterant versions with /n/. Speaker 2 read fifteen repetitions of each test sentence containing /t/ and ten repetitions of the reiterant versions with /n/.

8.3.3.2 Results

Results are shown in Figures 8.10a–b. The overall effect of position on peak contact was highly significant for both speakers for both consonants. Differences are larger for /t/ than for /n/, but *post hoc* comparisons were generally significant at the .0001 level. Nonetheless, Speaker 1 failed to distinguish most levels for /n/ (distinguishing only one pair of domains, IP versus Small Phrase SP), and did not distinguish U from IP for /t/. In contrast, Speaker 2 distinguished all four pairs of levels for /t/ and three for /n/, SP versus W being the only exception. The effect of position on articulatory seal duration was less consistent. Both speakers made at least a two-way distinction, between higher domains (U and IP) versus lower domains, for both test consonants. Speaker 1 additionally distinguishes SP, W and S for both consonants except between W and S for /t/, while Speaker 2 distinguishes all levels but SP versus W for both consonants. In contrast, VOT for /t/, shown above in Figure 8.7c, does not vary systematically with prosodic position.

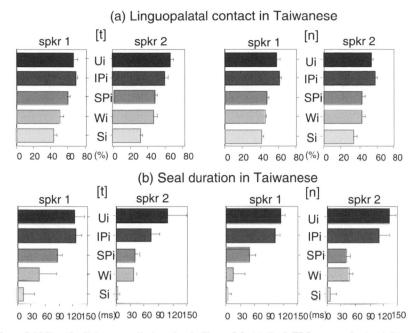

Figure 8.10 Data for Taiwanese, displayed as in Figure 8.2. (a) Peak EPG contact for /t, n/; (b) articulatory duration for /t, n/

8.4 Discussion

8.4.1 Domains

These experiments show clearly that there is phrasal/prosodic conditioning of articulation across languages: every subject makes at least one distinction (Word-internal versus Phrase-initial) and all speakers but one make at least one further distinction above the Word level, for every consonant studied. This conditioning generally affects both linguopalatal contact, which reflects overall height of the tongue, and also duration, so the total effect is on contact-over-time. At the same time, the prosodic effects can be seen to differ across speakers and consonants within a language. It differs enough that we cannot say that any single prosodic hierarchy is exhibited by all languages and speakers, or that speakers are marking every level of a hierarchy.

In general, the distinction between two phrasal levels is robust, with all speakers distinguishing between a 'high' phrasal domain and a 'low' phrasal domain. In contrast, some other differences are not so robust. Most notably, Utterance is not consistently distinguished from Intonational Phrase. A phonetic distinction was found most clearly in Korean, where the difference between Utterance and IP was specifically linked to pausing. Thus our Korean results support a break level '5' above the IP based on pausing, as posited for English by Price, Ostendorf, Shattuck-Hufnagel and Fong (1991). However, this difference was not consistently found in Taiwanese.

Also in our results, Word-initial position is not consistently distinguished from both Syllable-initial and Small Phrase-initial positions, and this is so whether our 'words' are morphologically complex (English, Taiwanese) or simpler (French, Korean).

The experiments presented here allow some comparisons of the relative sizes of different effects on linguopalatal contact. First, since results are reported for two consonants, we can ask how the prosodic effect compares with the inherent segmental effect. In general, nasals have less contact than voiceless orals. It turns out that this difference is about the same in magnitude as the difference between pairs of prosodic positions. Compare, for example, French AP-initial /t/ for Speaker 2 with both Word-initial /t/ (prosodic comparison) and AP-initial /n/ (inherent segmental comparison) in Figure 8.5a. The scales of the figures are not identical, but there is about a 10% difference in both comparisons. Another comparison is found in the two corpora for 'higher' and 'lower' domains in Korean, in Figure 8.8a. In the 'higher' corpus, the Word is the lowest domain tested, while in the 'lower' corpus it is the highest domain. The Word-initial consonants in the two corpora appear in different vowel contexts for /n/, which affect the contact location and extent. Again, this effect of vowel context turns out to be about the same as the difference between pairs of prosodic positions.

We have also presented data on articulatory and acoustic duration, and on VOT. In all of the languages, prosodic position affects consonant duration, but articulatory duration seems to reflect fewer prosodic distinctions than does peak contact. That may be in part because of the coarser grain of the duration measure (10 ms intervals) compared to % contact (96 electrodes). Similarly, our other temporal measure, VOT of /t/, is also not especially sensitive to prosodic position, varying with prosodic position in Korean but not in French or Taiwanese.

8.4.2 Languages

Despite the various predictions made about possible language differences, the languages in this study show quite similar effects of prosodic position. As noted already, the French, Korean and Taiwanese speakers all distinguished IP from the smaller phrase by the peak linguopalatal contact of the domain-initial consonants. The only systematic difference in the results from the various languages is the more consistent distinction between Utterance and Intonational Phrase in Korean compared to Taiwanese, even though the speech materials and instructions were similar in the two cases.

We had predicted differences between French and Korean because of the differences in other aspects of the realisation of their Accentual Phrases; in particular, we expected Korean to reinforce AP beginnings more than French. It is true that the Korean speakers distinguished all the prosodic domains in terms of contact more consistently than did the French speakers. However, with respect to the Accentual Phrase, the two languages are very similar, and the only lack of a distinction was by a Korean speaker. Thus our prediction was not borne out.

An intriguing difference between these two languages, though, concerns the strength of the correlations between initial consonant duration and contact across all the prosodic domains: these are higher in Korean. We interpret a strong relation between these variables as suggesting a temporal basis for strengthening, with shorter consonants undershooting the contact pattern shown by longer consonants. This relation in Korean is explored by Cho and Keating (1999), who provide support for an undershoot account. Interestingly, Korean was also the only language to show an effect of prosodic position on the VOT (a temporal measure) of /t/. So there may well be a special pairing of temporal and spatial properties in domain-initial position in Korean compared to other languages.

We had also predicted that initial strengthening could be stronger in Taiwanese than in other languages because, as a lexical tone language, it should have less recourse to pitch to mark domain edges. There is no support for such a hypothesis in these data.

In conclusion, we have shown that consonant articulation is subtly sensitive to a range of prosodic domains in similar ways in several languages. Linguistic structure is relevant for even fine phonetic detail, and prosodic constituency can be marked by details of articulation as well as by the traditional prosodic parameters.

Note

This work was supported by NSF grant #SBR 95-11118. We also thank Kay Elemetrics for making the special pseudo-palates, the subjects who participated in the experiments (including Jiyoung Yoon, Namhee Lee and Laurent Girard), Lucy Vause and Wendy Hayashi for help with measurements and manuscript preparation, and Dani Byrd for her detailed review of the manuscript.

Appendix

Table 8.2 *Corpus for French /t/*

Positions	Test consonant /t/ in /ɔ̃_ɔ̃/
Ui	J'ai vu Tonton. **Thon** lui parlait.
	I have seen Uncle. Thon was speaking to him
IPi	Le pauvre Tonton, **Thon** et Jacques sont déja partis.
	Poor Uncle, Thon and Jacques have already left
APi	Tata, Tonton, **Thon** et Jacques sont là-bas.
	Auntie,Uncle, Thon and Jaques are over there
Wi	C'est bien Tonton-**Thon** qui est là-bas.
	It's indeed Uncle Thon who is over there
Si	C'est bien ton ton<u>ton</u> qui est là-bas..
	It's indeed your uncle who is over there

Table 8.3 *Corpus for Korean /t/* *('*' refers to fortis series of obstruents)*

Positions	Test consonant /t/ in /a_a/
Ui	igosɨn patak***a. tam**biɡa jəgisə nɛrinda
	This place is the seashore. 'Sweet-rain' falls down here.
IPi	igosɨn patak***a, tam**biɡa nɛrinin koʃida
	This place the seashore, where the 'sweet-rain' falls down.
APi	idɨrin moduɡa **tam**birɨl tʃoahanda
	These people all like 'sweet-rain.'
Wi	idɨrin patak***a tam**birɨl tʃoahanda.
	These people like 'seashore sweet-rain.'
(word-level)	
Wi	idɨrin koɡjesa **ta**rirɨl tʃabat*a.
	These people held the legs of the acrobat.
Si	idɨrin koɡje sa**ta**rirɨl tʃabat*a.
	These people held the circus ladder.

Table 8.4 *Corpus for Korean /n/* (*'*' refers to fortis series of obstruents*)

Positions	Test Consonant /n/ in /a_a/ and /o_ɛ/
Ui	igosɨn patak*a. **na**mdʒuga jəgisə sanda.
	*This place is the seashore. **Namjoo** lives here.*
IPi	igosɨn patak*a, **na**mdʒue kohjaɲida.
	*This place is the seashore,(which is) **Namjoo's** hometown.*
APi	igosɨn patak*a **na**mtʃ*oge it*a
	This place is located to the south of the seashore.
Wi	igosɨn patak*a **na**mdʒaga sanɨn koʃida.
	This place is where the seashore man lives.
(word-level)	
Wi	kijədʒanɨn marimmo **ne**giɾil tʃɛanhɛt*a.
	The woman suggested betting with the parallelogram (on it)
Si	kijədʒanɨn jərim mo**ne**giɾil tʃɛanhɛt*a.
	The woman suggested fall harvest.

Table 8.5 *Corpus for Taiwanese /t/*

Positions	Test Consonant /t/ in /a_a/
Ui	wa u kʰuã-tiɤ papa⁵⁵. **ta²³ta⁵⁵** kʰai iaʔ be laiʔ?
	I can see Dad. Why isn't Tata here yet?
IPi	wa kʰuã-tiɤ a! papa⁵⁵, **ta²³ta⁵⁵** kʰai iaʔ be lai?
	I see it. Dad, why isn't Tata here yet?
APi	hit e laŋ e papa⁵⁵ **ta³¹ tiɤ³¹** tsɪt-tsɪa katsuaʔ.
	That person's dad stepped on a cockroach.
Wi	wa ka li kɥŋ, papa⁵⁵ **ta³¹⁻tiɤ³¹** tsit-tsia katsuaʔ.
	Let me tell you, Dad stepped on a cockroach.
Si	wa kina kʰuã-tiɤ **ta³³ta³³** tsim a kɤ iŋ kiã.
	Today I saw Auntie Tata and her child.

9

External sandhi as gestural overlap? Counter-evidence from Sardinian

D. ROBERT LADD AND JAMES M. SCOBBIE

9.1 Models of assimilatory external sandhi

External sandhi stands right at the heart of a number of current issues in phonology and phonetics. The traditional assumption is that such 'phonological adjustments' involve the categorical modification of the affected segment or segments, e.g. the coalescence in English of /t#j/ to /tʃ/ in *past your prime*, or the change in *that case* of /t#k/ to /k/. Hayes's (1986a) analysis of the assimilatory external sandhi of Toba Batak established that autosegmental feature spreading, the canonical mechanism for analysing assimilation (Goldsmith 1979; Clements 1976), was able to account for complex sandhi patterns just by linking and delinking autosegments. Such feature spreading, which relies crucially on the traditional assumption of categorical phonological modifications at word boundaries, has subsequently been the received analysis of external sandhi generally, including the English cases mentioned above.

More recently, however, a number of studies on English (Barry 1985; Wright and Kerswill 1989; Browman and Goldstein 1989, 1990b; Nolan 1992; Holst and Nolan 1995; Nolan, Holst and Kühnert 1996; Zsiga 1995) have cast doubt on the assumption that external sandhi assimilation involves categorical modifications of segments. Rather, the appropriate processes appear to involve language-specific rules of phonetic co-articulation,[1] usually expressed in terms of gestural overlap and gestural reduction. For example, neither the 'total'

164

assimilation of word-final /t/ to word-initial /k/ in *that case* nor the 'partial' as-similation of word-final /s/ to word-initial /j/ in *miss you* are categorical – the putative outputs (/k/ and /ʃ/ respectively) are typically not the same as underlying /k/ and /ʃ/ in similar contexts but rather may incorporate residual aspects of the apparently deleted /t/ and /s/ (Local 1992). Such behaviour has also been demonstrated in a number of languages other than English: Barry (1992) on Russian; Kühnert (1993) on German; Jun (1996) on Korean; and Zsiga (1997) on Igbo.

As a result of this instrumental research, accounts of sandhi based on phonetic co-articulation are gaining acceptance. The leading model involves gestural overlap (Browman and Goldstein 1989, 1990b), in which phonetic segments are epiphenomenal, and the categorical transformation of one segment sequence into another is not predicted. In the analysis of *that case*, for example, the gestures of velar closure overlap the weakened gestures of alveolar closure and thereby mask them perceptually. This analysis explains the percept of total /t/ to /k/ assimilation while providing an account of the residual presence of gestures related to /t/. Traditional accounts deal only with the percept of assimilation.

Hayes's original feature-spreading model of assimilation provides only two possible outcomes for *that case*: no assimilation (as shown in 1a below) or complete assimilation by means of a new association to the initial consonant /k/ and the delinking and deletion of the final consonant /t/ (as seen in 1b). Since this model is not adequate for the cases of English assimilatory external sandhi, Hayes (1992), following Nolan (1992), employs two further distinct classes of phonological representation: the complex segment (1c) and the contour segment (1d). (The complex segment has two places of articulation, while the contour segment contains a sequence of opposite values of a feature F.) Both arise when associations between word-final and word-initial segments are made but *underlying links are not broken*. This is a less radical departure from traditional analyses than the gestural overlap model. It also, arguably, less convincing: first, because it relies on a phonetic component which is not specified in any detail (Nolan 1992); and second, because the use of contour segments – seldom used in underlying representations – results in a less predictive conception of 'possible phonological representation' (Scobbie 1995).

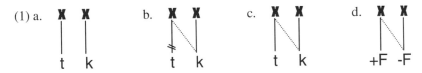

(1) a. t k   b. t k   c. t k   d. +F -F

Despite the obvious differences between the revised autosegmental approach and the gestural overlap model, it is important to note that both are intended to reflect the non-categorical nature of the English external sandhi mentioned above. They are also both intended to handle non-categorical word-internal phenomena, such as English stop epenthesis (Clements 1987; Browman and Goldstein 1990b). In general terms, therefore, these models fit rather well into the postlexical component of Lexical Phonology (e.g. Kiparsky 1985). While postlexical rules are most commonly categorical, Kiparsky (1985:110) makes it clear that some postlexical rules must be able to apply 'in gradient fashion, particularly when they contravene the lexical marking conventions'. In addition, Kiparsky notes that language-specific phonetic implementation might be responsible for such phenomena as the devoicing of sonorants. The implication to be drawn from the various laboratory studies of gradient postlexical phenomena mentioned above is that, indeed, some sort of language-specific phonetic account is required, although the exact details of are still hotly debated. For our purposes, the revised autosegmental approach and the gestural overlap approach are equivalent in the limited sense that neither predicts that the outputs of external sandhi will fall into categories already established for lexical contrasts.

It is an empirical question whether all cases of assimilatory external sandhi, under close phonetic scrutiny, turn out to be non-categorical. Our own initial assumption was that a phonetically based framework would provide the more appropriate analysis of the data discussed here, but our instrumental results suggest otherwise. This finding is relevant to conceptions of the phonetics/phonology interface and further confirms the importance of laboratory-based reinvestigations of phonological data.

9.2 Sardinian lenition and gemination

The specific empirical phenomenon with which we are concerned is the external sandhi system of Sardinian, specifically Logudorese, a dialect group spoken in the north-western quarter of the island. We begin with a brief sketch of three general aspects of Sardinian phonology: first, alternations in word-initial consonants; second, the system of oppositions in (word-medial) intervocalic position, especially the status of geminates; third, alternations among word-final consonants and the system of codas in general.[2]

9.2.1 External sandhi part 1: initial lenition

There are many synchronic alternations across word boundaries in Sardinian involving the intervocalic lenition of obstruents. ('Intervocalic' includes the context /V_rV/ despite the intervening rhotic.) Voiceless word-initial fricatives (2ab) are voiced when intervocalic (2a´b´). Voiceless word-initial stops (2cd), when intervocalic (2c´d´), are voiced with a weak closure.[3] Voiced word-initial stops (2e), when intervocalic (2e´), disappear, leaving only vowels in hiatus. There are no word-initial voiced fricatives except in loanwords.

(2)   a. ['fraɖɛ]   'brother'   a´. [su'vraɖɛ]   'the brother'
        b. ['saldu]   'Sardinian'   b´. [su'zaldu]   'the Sardinian'
        c. ['tɛra]   'land'   c´. [sa'ɖera]   'the land'
        d. ['kanɛ]   'dog'   d´. [su'ganɛ]   'the dog'
        e. ['bakːa]   'cow'   e´. [sa.'akːa]   'the cow'

Intervocalic lenition does not merely occur within closely linked phrases, but may (and often does) apply across quite major phonological boundaries. This is illustrated in (3), taken from unscripted recordings of one of our speakers.[4]

(3)   a. [azen'tezuˌgustu'entu'vritːu]
           /as entesu kustu bentu frittu/   'Did you hear that cold wind?'
    b. ['markɔva'eɖːa'bːɛnɛ'gɔmɔ]
           /marko faeddat bene komo/   'Marco speaks well now'
    c. ['markɔˌgɛrɛˌmːanɖi'garɛzu'budːu]
           /marko keret mandigare su puddu/   'Marco wants to eat the chicken'

Indeed, native speakers appear largely unaware of the effects of lenition on voiceless obstruents (2a-d), suggesting that it is a matter of 'low-level' phonetic implementation. There are a few lexical exceptions (4a), but these can be treated as exceptional underlying geminates. By contrast, the alternations between initial voiced stops and zero (2c) are readily remarked on by native speakers, and there are many lexemes which do not alternate (4b).

(4)   a. ['tia]   'aunt'   a´. [sa'tːia]   'the aunt'
        b. [du'tːɔrɛ]   'doctor'   b´. [suɖu'tːɔrɛ]   'the doctor'

9.2.2   *Word-medial contrasts of length and strength*

In word-medial position, Sardinian sonorants display a clearly audible contrast of phonetic duration (5), signalling an underlying opposition between 'long' or 'geminate' versus 'short' or 'singleton'.

(5)   a. ['bɛlːa]   'beautiful (f.sg.)'   versus   ['mɛla]   'apple'
        b. ['feru]   'iron'   versus   ['beɾu]   'true
           (m.sg.)'
        c. ['manːɔzɔ]   'big (m.pl.)'   versus   ['manɔzɔ]   'hands'

The same opposition is said to apply to obstruents as well (6).

(6)   a. ['isːu]   'he'   c. ['gatːu]   'cat'
        b. [lu'iza]   'Luisa (name)'   d. ['kadːu]   'horse'
                                e. ['naɖu]   'born'

The difficulty of establishing strictly durational correlates of gemination, however, especially for stops, is well known (cf. Contini 1987: 56; Jones 1988:

321). More generally, there is a close link between gemination and the intervocalic lenition described in the preceding section, such that 'geminate' is essentially equivalent to 'not lenited'. For fricatives there is only a two-way lexical contrast, between a long voiceless geminate fricative and a short voiced lenited one, e.g. [sː] versus [z] (6a,b). For stops, there is a three-way distinction: between voiced and voiceless 'geminates' on the one hand, which are clearly articulated as stops and may be of long duration, and a short voiced weakly articulated obstruent (a lenited stop?) on the other, e.g. [tː] versus [d̪ː] versus [ḍ] (6c–e). The weakly articulated obstruent in (6e) is apparently identical to the lenited intervocalic alternant of initial voiceless stops seen in (2c´, d´) above.

9.2.3 External sandhi part 2: word-final consonants

The close link between gemination and lenition just illustrated becomes even clearer when we consider word-final consonants. Sardinian has four such consonants, /t s n r/, but they are subject to a rich set of alternations caused by severe restrictions on codas.

9.2.3.1 Prevocalic position

When a word ending in a consonant is followed in a phrase by a vowel-initial word, intervocalic lenition of obstruents takes place (7), exactly as in (2) above. Since sonorants do not lenite, /n/ and /r/ simply appear as [n], [r].

(7)   a. ['beniḍin'dɔmɔ]   /benit in domo/   's/he comes in the house'
        b. ['trɛza'migɔzɔ]   /tres amigos/   'three friends'

Furthermore, in phrase-final position, the word-final consonant is normally followed by a so-called 'paragogic' vowel, which in quality is a copy of the immediately preceding vowel. This vowel, though it may be whispered or otherwise weakly articulated, has the effect of making the final consonant intervocalic (8), thereby leniting it if it is an obstruent (/s/ or /t/). Since citation forms are phrase-final, no citation form ends in a consonant.

(8)   a. ['beniḍi]   /benit/   's/he comes'
        b. ['benini]   /benin/   'they come'
        c. ['kanɛzɛ]   /kanes/   'dogs'

9.2.3.2   Preconsonantal position

When a word ending underlyingly in a final consonant is followed by a word which is consonant-initial, the potential for a consonant sequence arises. Some such abutting clusters are potentially 'fake geminates' (Hayes 1986a), i.e. sequences of identical consonants (9). Obstruent fake geminates (9a) are voiceless: sonorant fake geminates (9b) are impressionistically of long duration.

(9)   a. [sɔˈsːantɔzɔ]   /sos santos/   'the saints'
         b. [ɾˈnːuɔrɔ]   /in nuoro/   'in Nuoro'

Phonetic consonant sequences appear phonetically when a word-final continuant (/s/ or /r/) is followed by a non-identical consonant. Note that the contrast between /s/ and /r/ is neutralised in this context; both are realised phonetically as [s] before /p t k/ and /s/, and as [l] elsewhere (10). We introduce here the term 'variable continuant coda' to refer to neutralisable /s/ and /r/.

(10)   a. [trɛlˈmanɔzɔ]   /tres manos/   'three hands'
        b. [ˌbatːɔlˈfraɖɛzɛ]   /battor frades /   'four brothers'
        c. [sɔsˈpuɖːɔzɔ]   /sos puddos /   'the chickens'

Sequences of /n/ plus obstruent (11) are most often realised as homorganic sequences of nasal plus obstruent.

(11)   [sumˈbesːiɖɔzɔ]   /sun bessidos/   'they have gone out'

However, in some external sandhi consonant sequences, there is apparently total assimilation of the final consonant to the initial consonant, giving rise to 'geminates'. This occurs with the final /t/ of third-person-singular verb endings and to the final /n/ of the negative particle /non/. If the following word-initial consonant is a sonorant, the resulting 'geminate' is durationally long, like the lexical geminate sonorants. If it is an obstruent, the 'geminate' is of indeterminate duration, but it is voiceless and, if it is a stop, it is fully articulated as such. That is, *it is protected from lenition even though it is intervocalic*. Such cases are shown in (12). In what follows, we refer to these non-lenited apparent geminates in external sandhi contexts as 'postlexical geminates' (PLGs).

(12)   a. [amːanɖiˈgaɖu]   /at mandigadu/   's/he ate'
        b. [apːɔˌmanɖiˈgaɖu]   /appo mandigadu/   'I ate'
        c. [aˈfːatːu]   /at fattu/   's/he did'
        d. [apːɔˈvatːu]   /appo fattu/   'I did'
        e. [afːaɛˈdːaɖu]   /at faeddadu/   's/he spoke'
        f. [nɔˈfːageˈnːudːa]   /non faget nudda/ 'it doesn't matter'

The analysis of PLGs as true geminates is supported by the existence of a handful of proclitic function words apparently ending in a vowel which behave nevertheless as if they end in a consonant when they are followed by a word which itself begins with a consonant. Specifically, they protect the following word-initial consonant from lenition. This behaviour is generally analysed as the reflex of a final phantom consonant or empty skeletal slot (e.g. Bolognesi 1998), which gives rise to the gemination of the following word-initial consonant. Contrast the preposition /a^C/, which contains the phantom (13a), with the truly vowel-final preposition /dae/ (13b).

(13)   a. [apːaˈlɛrmɔ]   /a^C palermo/)   'to Palermo'
        b. [daɛɓaˈlɛrmɔ]   /dae palermo/   'from Palermo'

9.2.4 The categorical status of postlexical geminates

The facts just sketched are germane to the issues raised in the introduction. Specifically, they raise the question of whether the PLGs – the durationally long sonorants and unlenited obstruents that arise in sandhi contexts (examples 9, 12, 13) – can be identified with the word-medial lexical geminates (5, 6). A traditional analysis (e.g. Pittau 1991) would treat the total assimilation cases in (12, 13) as involving the creation of segments that are categorically identical to underlying word-medial geminates. Such an analysis is readily translated into the traditional autosegmental notation, using feature spreading and delinking (14):

(14)

a t # f a t u

V C C V C C V

The categorical-identity analysis is supported by impressionistic phonetic observations: there is a clearly perceptible difference in duration between the PLG [mː] in (12a) and the singleton [m] in (12b), just like the lexical contrast. Similarly, the PLG [fː] in (12c) – represented autosegmentally in (14) – is clearly voiceless even though it is phonetically intervocalic, while the fricative in (12d) is voiced and somewhat shorter, again like the lexical contrast.

One can equally well conceive, however, of a gestural (or revised autosegmental) account of PLGs, in which word-final and word-initial consonants overlap, producing a surface segment that is unlenited (because it is not truly intervocalic) and of relatively long duration. It would thereby resemble word-medial geminates phonetically without being the same phonologically. In some cases this analysis seems highly appropriate: we sometimes observe audible nasalisation on the vowel preceding the final /n/ of the prepositions /in/ 'in' and /kun/ 'with', although the /n/ itself has apparently assimilated to the following consonant (15). Such behaviour is typical of gestural overlap.[5]

(15)   a. [kusːuˈvɾaɖɛ] ~ [kũsːuˈvɾaɖɛ]   /kun su frade/   'with the brother'
        b. [isːaˈidːa] ~ [ˈĩsːaˈidːa]   /in sa bidda/   'in the village'

However, the negative particle /non/ (12f) never gives rise to observable residual nasalisation: is not clear how a gestural account would deal with this kind of lexical sensitivity. Other challenges for a gestural approach are: first, the final alternation involving /s/ and /r/, which does not seem reducible to gestural weakening; second, the fact that final consonants other than /n/ do not reveal any residual quality or quantity; and third, the phantom consonant (13).

The discussion so far, like much of the literature, represents the phonetic data in terms of segmental transcriptions. Yet it has been on the basis of instrumentally measurable phonetic properties, not transcription, that investigations of

English external sandhi have discovered that postlexical segments arising from assimilation are *not* the same as lexical segments. The patterns of external sandhi in Sardinian are therefore an obvious candidate for instrumental study.

9.3 The experimental study

9.3.1 Introduction

Our instrumental measurements are based on recordings of three speakers, MS, LS, and MT, of whom LS is our main experimental speaker.[6,7] Creating controlled speech materials was made difficult by the fact that there is no standard orthography for Sardinian. For MS, we wrote sentences in English, which she translated silently and then spoke aloud. This procedure worked reasonably well, though it meant that we did not always get the Sardinian forms we were anticipating. However, LS and MT do not speak English, and we did not want to elicit Sardinian by presenting sentences written in Italian, due to the potential for cross-language interference. For LS, we were able to use an Italianised version of the phonemic transcriptions given in this paper, essentially the same as the orthography used by Pittau (1991). LS had no trouble producing fluent utterances from these materials. MT found Pittau's system too abstract: if word-final *t* and *n* were present orthographically before a consonant, MT would produce a string of citation forms complete with paragogic vowels, or simply get confused. We therefore altered the orthography by removing *t* and *n* in these cases, making it more phonetically transparent. MT's results appear compatible with LS's, but we do not report them here.

Our experimental work focuses on two related questions: whether *postlexical* geminates are of comparable duration to *lexical* geminates; and whether the word-medial *contrast* between singleton and geminate is comparable to the word-initial *alternation* between lenited and 'protected' consonants. In a preliminary study (Ladd and Scobbie 1996) we reported on semi-systematic recordings of MS and LS. Our preliminary conclusion, later cited by Bolognesi (1998: 159), was that *postlexical geminates are on average rather shorter than lexical geminates*. Consequently we favoured an analysis employing gestural overlap.

However, there is a problem with this conclusion, namely that the prosodic context of the typical PLG is quite different from that of the typical lexical geminate. PLGs are word-initial and therefore by definition they precede the lexically stressed syllable. Lexical geminates, on the other hand, are most commonly encountered immediately following lexically stressed vowels. Moreover, because underlying geminates (with one or two marginal exceptions) never occur in word-initial position, they will always occur nearer to the end of the word than PLGs. Both of these factors – position relative to stress, and position in word – seemed to have substantial effects on duration in our preliminary data, especially at the end of an utterance: ceteris paribus, post-tonic consonants are longer than other consonants, and consonants at the end of a word are longer than medial ones. We also discovered that phrase-final post-tonic consonants should be subdivided into (a) those which were absolutely the last consonant in the phrase (because they were heavily lengthened in words like /manu, mannu, issu, fattu, kaddu/) and (b) all others. We do not have the space to report further details but see Tables 9.1 and 9.2 below.

In the experiments reported here we have thus tried to use materials in which the lexical geminates and the putative PLGs occur in the same prosodic context. However, there is a potentially significant dilemma here – the workings of the language make it almost impossible to design such materials. That is, our preliminary conclusion may well have been an 'artefact' of our experimental materials, yet it does nevertheless represent a valid observation about Sardinian phonetics. The statistical patterns of the language are not the same as the structural patterns. Clearly, both need to be considered as we work toward an understanding of the phonology/phonetics interface and the utility of an experimental approach to phonology (cf. Hay, Pierrehumbert and Beckman's paper in this volume).

Experiment 1 deals with postlexical geminates and lexical geminates, comparing them to each other and to the relevant singletons. Experiment 2 is a follow up in which we consider postlexical and word-medial underlying consonant sequences.

9.3.2 Experiment 1: geminates and singletons

9.3.2.1 Method

Our materials were a set of 120 sentences, read aloud twice. Alveolar nasals were chosen as representatives of the sonorants: the materials elicited singleton and geminate /n/ in word-medial position, and intervocalic word-initial /n/ in both lenited and nonlenited (PLG) alternants. Obstruents were also mostly represented by alveolars. Initial /f/ and /m/ in putative PLG environments were also included (permitting comparison with the postlexical sequences of Experiment 2). The word-final consonants which gave rise to PLGs were contained in /non/ 'not', /a^C/ 'to', /at/ 'have-3rdsg', and /as/ 'have-2ndsg'.

We were careful to provide a variety of prosodic contexts for the consonants. Specifically, consonants appeared either immediately preceding the lexically stressed vowel ('tonic onset'), immediately following it ('post-tonic') or elsewhere ('non-tonic'). Additionally, we distinguished between phrase-medial and phrase-final position. Unless mentioned, all consonants were phonetically intervocalic, and none were utterance-initial.

Consequently, we do not collapse prosodic position in reporting our results of mean consonantal duration, as we did in Ladd and Scobbie (1996). (We do, however, combine PLGs resulting from 'fake geminate' sequences like /s#s/ or /t#t/ with those resulting more clearly from assimilation, such as /t#s/.) This strategy often results in only small numbers of tokens in each cell, which makes statistical analysis inappropriate, especially given the fact, mentioned in Section 9.3.1, that the language makes it impossible to fill all the cells in a full factorial design. Nevertheless, many of our crucial conclusions are supported by t-tests on selected pairs of means. In Experiment 2 we have enough tokens in each cell to make the reporting of standard deviations appropriate. Otherwise, only the number of tokens is indicated in the tables of results along with the mean.

9.3.2.2 Results and discussion

The durational basis of medial gemination in sonorants is illustrated in Table 9.1 for /n/ versus /nn/. Singleton /n/ has approximately half the duration of /nn/, a ratio that remains stable despite the effect of prosodic position on absolute duration. The singleton/geminate contrast is comparable, in absolute and relative terms, to the word-initial alternation between intervocalic [n] and postlexical geminate [nː]: word-initial singleton /n/ is about half the duration of the postlexical geminate. [8]

Table 9.1 *Mean duration (ms) of alveolar nasals. Initial nasals are tonic onset; medial nasals are post-tonic. The number of tokens is in italics.*

Position	Init. /n/ [n]	PLG /n/ [nː]	Med. /n/ [n]	/nn/ [n̪ː]
Non-tonic	**58**, *2*	**83**, *12*		**100**, *9*
Phrase-medial, tonic	**62**, *3*	**111**, *5*	**48**, *11**	**100**, *9*
Phrase-final, tonic	**55**, *2*	**130**, *8*	**55**, *2*	**139**, *3*
Last consonant in phrase			**78**, *13*	**165**, *1*

*Also, tonic *onset* /n/ was 52ms, *n=10.*

The word-medial obstruent system is illustrated in Table 9.2.

173

Table 9.2 *Mean duration (ms) of word-medial obstruents*

Position	[ḍ]	[d̪ː]	[tː]	[z]	[sː]
Non-tonic			97, *2*		132, *5*
Phrase-medial, tonic onset		79, *18*			
Phrase-medial, post-tonic	55, *15*	79, *3*	99, *35*		138, *12*
Phrase-final, tonic onset			121, *7*		
Phrase-final, post-tonic		129, *9*	133, *14*		182, *5*
Last consonant in phrase	62, *8*	153, *9*	203, *4*	135, *8*	194, *2*

Consider the stops first. The stops [d̪ː] and [tː] have a fairly stable of duration ratio of nearly 1:1, suggesting they could both be analysed as geminate. This leaves the much shorter [ḍ] as a likely singleton, though whether it is to be analysed as /t/ or /d/ is problematic. On either analysis the putative geminate/singleton ratio is highly variable across prosodic context, being largest (and most noticeable) word- and phrase-finally, e.g. in citation versions of many words (6c-e). The medial [ḍ] (Table 9.2) is comparable in duration to lenited word-initial singleton /t/ and /d/ (Table 9.3). Table 9.3 also indicates that PLG word-initial /t/ is comparable to putative medial geminate /tt/ (Table 9.2). Consequently, our conclusion about the nasals is applicable to stops too: the contrast between medial geminate and singleton is categorically the same as the initial alternation between lenited singleton and PLG.

Table 9.3 *Mean duration (ms) of word-initial coronal stops*

Position	/t/ [ḍ]	/d/ [ḍ]	PLG /t/ [tː]
Non-tonic	46, *4*	48, *6*	100, *6*
Phrase-medial, tonic onset	49, *12*	55, *8*	
Phrase-final, tonic onset	55, *4*	56, *6*	119, *13*

We only have a small amount of data on the medial fricative contrast (Table 9.2), but rather more information on word-initial /s/ (Table 9.4). Lenited /s/ and /f/ are fairly short, while PLG [sː] is comparable to the medial geminate.

Table 9.4 *Mean duration (ms) of word-initial lenited /f/ and /s/, and of PLG [s:]*

Position	[v]	[z]	as#s	non#s	at#s	aᶜ#s
Phrase-medial, non-tonic	**75**, *5*	**87**, *43*	**143**, *8*		**140**, *6*	**122**, *7*
Phrase-medial, tonic onset	**69**, *11*			**152**, *6*	**153**, *4*	
Phrase-final, tonic onset	**95**, *2*					**156**, *8*

Our conclusion based on these data is that structurally *there is a clear durational equivalence between lexical and postlexical geminates*. Our results therefore confirm the position which Sardinian native speaker linguists have generally taken for granted (e.g. Pittau 1991; Bolognesi 1998; Molinu 1998). The PLGs resulting from external assimilation in Sardinian are not like the phonetic coarticulation cases in English discussed above. Rather, in the majority of cases there appears to be a categorical alternation word-initially between singletons and geminates, the same categories that are contrastive word-medially. Word-final consonants alternate, on the whole, with zero – they do not condition the residual extra duration which, as Browman (1995) has argued, occurs in English when extreme gestural overlap leads to the apparent deletion of the word-final consonant.

9.3.3 Experiment 2: coda-onset sequences

9.3.3.1 Introduction

As mentioned in Section 9.2, there are cases in which word-initial consonants are protected from lenition by a preceding word-final consonant that is *overtly present* phonetically. It is present as residual nasalisation in the case of final /n/, and as an (unassimilated) independent segment in the case of variable continuant codas /s/ and /r/. Recall that these final continuants surface as [l] in some cases, such as before /f/ (16a), and as [s] before a word-initial voiceless stop (16b). It is clear that a complete examination of how initial segments are protected from lenition requires that, in addition to considering postlexical geminates (16cd), we must look at the postlexical sequences and their relationship to word-medial lexical ones (cf. Molinu MS).

(16)	a. [al'fat:u]	/as fattu /	'you [sg] made'
	b. [sɔs'kad:ɔzɔ]	/sos caddos/	'the horses'
	c. [a'f:at:u]	/at fattu/	's/he made'
	d. [nɔ'f:agedɛ]	/non faget/	'it doesn't make'

Presumably postlexical sequences such as [lf] and [sk] are structurally coda-onset, with the onset being an unlenited singleton segment. In the categorical autosegmental analysis illustrated in (14), such protected singletons should be comparable in duration (all things being equal) to other singletons, and not to PLGs. This is because PLGs are formed by double linking as the result of assimilation. In the postlexical sequences there is no assimilation and no double linking, and there should therefore be no geminate duration.

9.3.3.2 Method

In the dataset prepared for Experiment 1 we were able to include only a few materials eliciting postlexical sequences. Specifically, we collected data on final /n/ before /s/, and on final /s/ before initial /f/. As with the other materials, it was not possible to get tokens in all environments. For example, *medial* [lf] sequences are very rare and are mostly loans, so were not suitable for analysis. Note also that though there is preconsonantal neutralisation of word-final /s/ and /r/, there is no such neutralisation word-medially (illustrated by the near-minimal pair [oltu] /ortu/ 'garden' versus [postu] /postu/ 'place'). Consequently we collected no materials on medial sequences at this stage. Ultimately, however, supplementary material from LS was collected to enable comparison between medial and initial consonant sequences. The sequences used were [lm] and [s] before voiceless stops, and the second consonant was always tonic onset.

9.3.3.3 Results and discussion

At the time of the oral version of this paper, the postlexical [lf] sequences were the only cases of variable continuant coda plus onset included purposely in the materials. Contrary to our expectations, the singleton fricative in /s#f/ [lf] (on the fourth row of Table 9.5) is *comparable* in duration to the PLG in /t#f/ and /non#f/, previously transcribed [fː]. One possible explanation would be that both structures conditioning word-initial [fː] (sequence and PLG) do so in the same way. Since gemination cannot be responsible for lengthening in the sequence, we considered the possibility that some sort of domain-initial strengthening of a singleton was responsible in PLGs and singletons alike. In fact, there is in fact no single source of [fː], as our results comparing initial and medial sequences, given below, make clear.

Table 9.5 *Mean duration (ms) of phrase-medial word-initial /f/, /n/, /m/ in intervocalic position and when following word-final /t/, /n/ and /s/*

context	f	non-tonic	tonic	n	non-tonic	tonic	m	non-tonic	tonic
vowel	v	**75**, *5*	**69**, *11*		**58**, *2*	**62**, *3*		**67**, *2*	**72**, *2*
/t/	fː	**127**, *7*	**137**, *4*		**112**, *3*			**96**, *5*	
/non/	fː	**142**, *2*	**125**, *8*						**104**, *5*
/s/ [l]	fː	**121**, *5*	**138**, *2*		**128**, *2*			**78**, *4*	

Before reporting the results for such comparisons, we will make use of postlexical sequences which happened to be contained in the materials prepared for Experiment 1. There were a handful of examples of two further postlexical sequences, namely /s#n/ and /s#m/. From Table 9.5 it appears that word-initial /m/ is rather different from /f/. At 78 ms, the duration of postlexical (non-tonic) [m] in a sequence is *intermediate between singleton and PLG*. These data are worth reporting, since in the supplementary materials we targeted medial [lm] sequences and both postlexical sources of [lm] (namely /s#m/ and /r#m/).

Table 9.6 confirms the result in Table 9.5 that word-initial /m/ following a variable continuant coda is intermediate in duration between intervocalic singletons (72 ms) and PLGs (104 ms). Moreover, the duration of word-medial and word-initial /m/ (and [l]) is comparable, just as was observed for PLGs and geminates. Table 9.6 and Table 9.5 make a strong case that lexical and postlexical [lm] sequences contain a singleton /m/ which has a somewhat greater duration (as measured by acoustic segmentation) than an intervocalic singleton. Since this greater duration is not domain-initial, it cannot be implicated in the external sandhi system.

Table 9.6 *Mean duration (ms) of variable continuant coda + /m/ (n=8) and word-medial /lm/ (n=9). NB, the figures in parentheses are standard deviations*

Position	[l]	[m]
Word-initial, phrase-medial, tonic onset	**70** (11)	**92** (10)
Word-medial, phrase-medial, tonic onset	**67** (11)	**89** (8)

Table 9.7 demonstrates that postlexical sequences of variable continuant coda and voiceless stop are also comparable in duration to medial sequences (of invariant /s/ and voiceless stop). Fricative duration, stop closure duration and VOT are very similar in each condition.

Table 9.7 *Mean duration (ms) of variable continuant coda + voiceless stop (n=13) and word-medial /s/ + voiceless stop (n=10). Standard deviations in parentheses*

Position	[s]	closure	VOT
Word-initial, phrase-medial, tonic onset	**81** (14)	**72** (11)	**23** (13)
Word-medial, phrase-medial, tonic onset	**85** (17)	**68** (8)	**29** (12)

Structurally, the stops are most plausibly singletons. Comparison with Table 9.3 indicates that these tonic singletons are *shorter* in duration than PLGs and the medial geminate [t:] (/tt/), and comparison with Tables 9.2 and 9.3 indicates that the singleton stops following [s] are *greater* in duration than the voiced lenited allophone of singleton /t/ (initial and medial). In other words, voiceless stops following [s] are intermediate in duration between PLGs and singletons. These results confirm that the behaviour of /m/ reported in Table 9.6 is not an aberration. In fact, it is the behaviour of /f/ (and the two tokens of /n/) in Table 9.5 which is difficult to explain. It may be that unlenited [f] is simply inherently of greater duration in all contexts, and that (if the two tokens that we have measured are representative) it is the homorganicity of the [ln] cluster which leads to a geminate-like [n:]. Clearly, these results remain problematic and require further investigation.

Note that word-final [s] (from underlying /s/ or /r/) is a great deal shorter than medial /ss/ (even non-tonic /ss/) and PLG /s/. In fact, this singleton segment is entirely comparable in duration with initial and medial [z], a final piece of evidence in favour of the analysis of [z] as the lenited allophone of singleton /s/.

Finally, we return to materials collected at the same time as Experiment 1 in order to consider the case of final /n/, present in a few words such as the prepositions /kun/ 'with' and /in/ 'in'. Final /n/ may condition residual nasalisation in some tokens, and hence is a prime candidate for a gestural overlap analysis. As far as we can tell, on the basis of a few tokens (Table 9.8), the duration of /s/ following final /n/ is intermediate between lenited singletons and PLGs. (Note also that protected /f/ following /in/ was only 89ms (*n=2*) in phrase-medial non-tonic position.) Just as in the more overt sequences [sp st sk] and [lf lm ln], the initial consonant in these /n#s/ cases seems to be a slightly lengthened singleton, though a closer analysis is clearly required.

Table 9.8 *Mean duration (ms) of word-initial /s/. Number of tokens in italics*

Prosodic position	/kun#s/	/in#s/
Phrase-medial, non-tonic	**105**, *5*	**110**, *6*
Phrase-medial, tonic onset		**130**, *2*
Phrase-final, tonic onset		**141**, *4*

In summary, in postlexical position, therefore, initial voiceless stops (following [s]) and /m/ (following [l]) are not lenited, because they are not intervocalic, and at the same time they are not geminates, because the preceding word-final consonant has not assimilated to them totally. They are unlenited singletons, which, because they are part of a cluster, are intermediate in duration between lenited singletons and geminates. The place and manner of the initial consonant appear to affect the extent of this increase in duration quite markedly. Similarly, final /n/ protects a following consonant from lenition even though /n/ is only present impressionistically in the form of a little residual nasalisation. The only information we have on a consonant following /n/ realised in this way relates to /s/: as we would now expect, it appears to be a singleton whose duration is intermediate between intervocalic singletons and postlexical geminates. We conclude that coda-onset sequences do not involve categorical postlexical assimilation.

9.4 Summary and conclusions

When prosodic context is controlled for, the absolute duration of postlexical geminates is very similar to that of lexical geminates. The ratios of medial geminate to singleton and word-initial PLG to singleton are also similar. This is true for sonorants, which have two clearly distinct durational categories, *and* for obstruents, in which the singleton category is expressed mainly through lenition, and the geminate category is not particularly long but is unlenited. The similarity between medial and initial position extends to consonant sequences.

From these results we conclude two things. First, we argue that gestural overlap is on the whole *not* a suitable model of most of the assimilatory external sandhi phenomena in Sardinian, and more generally that accounts of gestural overlap in some cases of English external sandhi cannot be carried over into all aspects of postlexical phonology. The major difference between Sardinian and

English is that Sardinian final consonants are generally lost with no residual effect on acoustic consonant duration and no observable residual effect on quality. In English assimilatory external sandhi, as noted above, some residual duration from 'deleted' word-final consonants can be detected even when there is no residual quality (Browman 1995). Such tokens have also been used as evidence that gestural overlap and reduction are not exclusively responsible for external sandhi in English (Nolan and Holst 1995; Nolan *et al.* 1996), but such examples generally appear at one extreme of a continuous spectrum of behaviour (though see Ellis and Hardcastle 1999). Phonetic variability of this type, which is so characteristic of English sandhi (cf. Browman 1992), is not seen in Sardinian.

Our second major conclusion arises from the fact that the *alternation* between postlexically lenited and postlexically protected word-initial consonants is phonetically comparable (in transcription and in acoustic segment duration) to the phonological word-medial *contrast* between singletons and geminates, in both sonorants and obstruents. We conclude that it is possible to make identifications of phonetic segment type across different positions in structure.[9] We therefore support the theory that a language has a single phonological system of recurring categories, and find against a strict interpretation of the Firthian notion of polysystematicity (e.g. Robins 1970). These categories are not, however, necessarily phonemic at every place in structure: allophonic alternations which appear in postlexical alternations may make use of the *same categories* as were established for phonological contrasts elsewhere in the system. For stops, for example, a three-term medial system has, as its phonetic exponents, certain constellations of gestures (i.e. segments) which function also to express a word-initial two-term system of contrast and the postlexical alternation between singleton and geminate arising from external sandhi.

One model of this categorical identity across different places in structure and between systems with different numbers of contrasting members is a phonological (specifically, autosegmental) one, in which feature spreading and delinking generate multiply-associated structures that are the same as underlying geminates (Hayes 1986a, and, specifically for Sardinian, Bolognesi 1998, Molinu 1998). This model, illustrated in (14), is sufficient for fake geminates, the phantom consonant and final consonants generally. The only obvious problem is the residual nasalisation resulting from 'assimilated' final /n/, which might be taken as motivating an extended autosegmental model using complex and contour segments (Hayes 1992). However, we have already reviewed briefly the arguments against such an extension (cf. Nolan 1992; Scobbie 1995; Zsiga 1997), and instead we favour a mixed analysis of external sandhi involving only simple phonological processes combined with gestural overlap. In Sardinian, gestural overlap will be *exclusively* responsible for the residual nasalisation cases. The categorical cases have a language-specific gestural component too, to account for the phonetic characteristics of intervocalic singleton obstruents and the effects of prosodic position. At heart, though, the external sandhi system of Sardinian is truly phonological.

Notes

Our first debt is to our speakers, Luisa Sorace, Monica Tarantini and Marcella Sardu. Luisa in particular has spent many hours answering questions and making recordings, well beyond the call of the family duty that results from having one of the authors (DRL) as her son-in-law. Sadly, between the completion of this paper and the publication of this volume both Luisa and Monica have died. We dedicate this paper to them and hope that it will encourage further research into Sardinian and other endangered languages about which we know so little. We are also grateful to Roberto Bolognesi and Lucia Molinu for comments, encouragement and practical assistance in creating materials, and to Steven Bird, Mike Broe, Nick Clements and Lucy Ellis for discussion at various points between 1993 and 1999. Extensive comments on a draft of this paper, from Amalia Arvaniti, Roberto Bolognesi, and an anonymous referee are gratefully acknowledged. This is a joint paper, and the authors names are listed alphabetically. We blame each other for any errors or other shortcomings in the paper.

1 Ellis and Hardcastle (1999) show that this may be over simplistic. In their study of English assimilatory external sandhi, some speakers never assimilate, while others show total assimilation in all cases. Crucially, there are also speakers who have variable output, and while some appear to vary the amount of coarticulation gradiently, others appear to vary *categorically* between no assimilation and total assimilation. The implications of Ellis and Hardcastle's study are somewhat similar to our own.

2 The phenomena addressed here have been extensively described elsewhere, in part because they pose problems for the classical conception of the phoneme (cf. Lüdtke 1953). We summarise only the most relevant aspects here. For an excellent short sketch of Sardinian in general, including the current sociolinguistic situation, see Jones (1988). The classic works on the language are by Wagner (e.g. 1941, 1951, 1960–4). Recent traditional grammars are Blasco Ferrer (1986) and Pittau (1991). A comprehensive instrumental phonetic study of Sardinian dialectology is Contini (1987). There are two recent book-length accounts, of syntax (Jones 1993) and phonology (Bolognesi 1998). A useful general resource is Mensching (12/10/1999).

3 Lenited /p/ is something like [b]~[β], /t/ is [d]~[ð], and /k/ is [ɡ]~[ɣ]. In (2c b̠–d̠) and henceforth we use the symbols [b̠ d̠ ɡ̠] to indicate the weak occlusion and phonetically variable quality of intervocalic 'stops'.

4 The retracted diacritic in [d̠ː] [n̠ː] and [n̠d̠] indicates retroflex articulations; see footnote 5. See Section 9.2.2 on the phonetic basis for our use of the length diacritic. The realisation of the sequences of underlying final /t/ and word-initial consonants in (4b) and (4c) are discussed in Section 9.2.3.2 below.

5 Further evidence against treating PLGs and lexical geminates as completely equivalent comes from the fact that lexical /dd/, /nn/ and /nd/ are retroflex or apico-alveolar while the corresponding postlexical sequences are lamino-dental (Pittau 1991). The status of retroflexion in Sardinian and various southern Italian dialects (e.g. Sicilian) is a well-known problem which is unfortunately beyond the scope of this paper.

6   Two of the speakers, LS and MT, are elderly women, sisters, from Pozzomaggiore (some 40 km south of Sassari, in the Common Logudorese dialect region) but now both living in Rome. They use Sardinian with each other in daily visits or telephone conversations but Standard Italian in the rest of their daily lives. MS is a woman in her thirties from Bosa (on the coast, west of Pozzomaggiore), but who works as an English teacher in Sassari. As with most younger speakers, her lexicon is more Italianised than LS's and MT's but she is nevertheless a fluent native speaker.

7   The experimental recordings were made on professional equipment in the Department of Theoretical and Applied Linguistics at Edinburgh University. Acoustic analysis of segment duration (using standard annotation strategies) from the digitised recordings was done using the Kay Elemetrics Multispeech system, in the Department of Speech and Language Sciences at Queen Margaret University College, Edinburgh.

8   We also have a little data on initial /m/ but not medial /m/ (or /mm/, which is rare). In phrase-medial position, non-tonic /m/ is 67 ms (n=2), while the PLG is 96 ms (n=5). Tonic onset /m/ is 72 ms (n=2) while the PLG is 115 ms (n=8). Phrase-finally, non-tonic /m/ is 71 ms (n=2) and tonic /m/ is 63 ms (n=10). The ratio of singleton to PLG is therefore smaller than for /n/, but since we have no information on medial /mm/ we do not know whether this is also true of the lexical contrast. See also Table 9.5.

9   Phonetic similarity does not necessarily indicate phonological identity, of course, and nor does phonological identity guarantee phonetic similarity. As we remarked in Section 9.3.1, the statistical and prosodic patterns of a language operate together to reduce the superficial phonetic similarity of structurally different versions of the same category. It is precisely because the prosodic contexts for initial and medial consonants are not typically comparable that, *on average*, Sardinian PLGs are shorter than lexical geminates.

10

Consonant strengthening and lengthening in various languages: comments on three papers

JONATHAN HARRINGTON

The three papers by D'Imperio and Gili Fivela (Chapter 7), Keating, Cho, Fougeron and Hsu (Chapter 8) and Ladd and Scobbie (Chapter 9) all present experimental data on lengthening or strengthening of consonants that are word- or domain-initial in a number of languages. Ladd and Scobbie's acoustic analysis is of an extensive corpus of continuous speech from the Logudorese variety of Sardinian in which they provide a strong challenge to a recent set of studies that have modelled consonant assimilation predominantly as gestural overlap. D'Imperio and Gili Fivela's analysis is of vowel and consonant lengthenings due to syntactic and prosodic boundaries and of an external sandhi effect of 'Raddoppiamento (Fono)Sintattico' that occurs in many dialects of Italian. The study by Keating *et al.* as well as their many earlier analyses, provides an impressive range of articulatory data which point to a close link between prosodic boundary strength and domain-initial consonant strengthening. The three papers are very different in their theoretical assumptions and the range of research questions that they address, but they are nevertheless interlinked by a common theme of the production of prosodic structure and its effect, in particular, on word-initial consonants.

The focus of the paper by Ladd and Scobbie is an analysis of assimilation in Sardinian and the extent to which this can be modelled as a categorical phonological modification or as the result of phonetic gradient effects. Recent experimental studies have shown that consonant assimilation is not categorical: it does not involve the substitution of one phonological segment for another, as the auditory impressions and broad transcriptions have suggested. In Nolan

(1992), for example, even the most extreme forms of alveolar-to-velar assimilation show some evidence of the supposedly deleted alveolar, either as a residual tongue-tip gesture, or else as subtle quality differences in the preceding vowel: consequently, *leg covered* and *lead covered* usually remain articulatorily and perceptually distinct. Under the interpretation that word-boundary assimilation is gradient and phonetically distinct from lexically derived segments, then lexical phonological rules that are typically couched in terms of autosegmental representations (Clements 1985) and feature delinking and relinking (Perlmutter 1995; Rubach 1995) are considered inappropriate or unable to model these kinds of non-categorical gradient phenomena that have been reported in experimental studies of assimilation in the last decade. Instead, postlexical gradient assimilation has often been modelled in terms of Browman and Goldstein's (1992) and Browman's (1995) articulatory gestural overlap model (e.g. Zsiga 1994; 1995; 1997); or else gradient assimilation is assumed to arise at a level of phonetic representation that is 'under the speaker's control' (Nolan 1992; see also Barry 1992) and which might also be an appropriate level at which to model the way in which assimilation varies between languages and dialects.

It is essentially this idea – that all assimilation and postlexical phonological processes in general are gradient – that Ladd and Scobbie challenge. Their analysis suggests that a postlexical geminate (PLG) is created at an external sandhi site when a preceding word-final consonant deletes. This PLG is shown to be more or less equivalent in duration to a *lexical* geminate in the same prosodic context. Moreover, unlike intervocalic singleton consonants which always lenite (e.g. /frade/, *brother*, but [fraḍe], *brother*), the resulting postlexical geminates are phonetically similar to lexical ones because neither of them lenite.

From these data, Ladd and Scobbie conclude that both lexical and postlexical geminates can be represented by linking a segment to two consonantal slots. The postlexical geminate would arise by breaking the link between the C slot and the word-final consonant (resulting in deletion of the unlinked consonant) and relinking it with the following word-initial consonant (as a result of which the word-initial consonant, like a lexical geminate, is doubly linked, and hence long and not lenited). This relinking and delinking in turn suggests a *categorical* change (at the postlexical level) that is not appropriately modelled by the kinds of *gradient* processes that have been found to typify assimilation in English.

It is important from the outset to be clear that Ladd and Scobbie examine two kinds of consonant sequences across word boundaries. The first category includes word-final consonants that might be present in some form underlyingly but which either never surface (/aC/, *to*, where C is what they and others refer to as a 'phantom' consonant) or which only surface preceding a vowel (e.g. /as/, *have*, second singular and /faget/ in which the consonant can surface preceding a paragogic vowel, thus [aza] and [faɣeḍe]). The second category includes words like /in/ and /sun/ in which the final consonant can surface and for which a gestural overlap analysis certainly cannot be ruled out. That is, in the absence of an acoustic analysis that goes beyond measuring duration, and without the benefit of an articulatory analysis, we cannot exclude the possibility that their example (11) /sun bessidos/ exhibits gradient assimilation effects and a gestural overlap of a similar kind to English in which the /n#b/ sequence is produced as either a heterorganic sequence, or as an overlapping sequence in which the alveolar and bilabial closures are coproduced, or with complete assimilation resulting in homorganic [m͡b]; neither can we exclude the possibility of similar gradient effects and gestural overlap between the alveolar and bilabial in [l#m] that is derived from underlying /s#m/ in (10), /tres manos/ (Ladd and Scobbie, personal communication). However, having acknowledged that this second category must await the outcome of further experimental analysis before this issue can be resolved, let us put these cases to one side and reconsider the evidence from the first category which is used to argue for the case that assimilation in Sardinian is at heart phonological.

There can probably be little doubt that the gemination phenomena in the first category are qualitatively very different from the external sandhi place assimilations that Ladd and Scobbie review in the first part of their paper. One of the salient differences is that in all the studies that Ladd and Scobbie review, the PLACE feature of a segment like /d/ that can assimilate in the context of *lead covered* must be fully specified at some stage in the representation between an autosegmental representation and a gestural score (as in the various figures in e.g. Zsiga 1995 and Holst and Nolan 1995). There is however no evidence *a priori* that this must be so in Sardinian. For example, /non/ might be represented as /noC/, where C is the same phantom consonant seen elsewhere (Ladd, personal communication). In fact, since the four possible word-final consonants in Sardinian, /t s n r/ are all alveolar/coronal, their place of articulation is entirely predictable and so the PLACE node in an autosegmental representation could be unspecified, as the shorthand notation of /noC/ and /aC/ (for the phantom consonant) correctly suggests. By definition, then, the phenomena that Ladd and Scobbie present cannot be modelled in terms of the kinds of assimilation that they describe in the introductory part of their paper ('Models of assimilatory external sandhi'), because all of these gradient assimilations presuppose that PLACE features are fully specified at the stage at which autosegments are aligned with a gestural score in the production of speech. Under this interpretation, their data are largely neutral to the matter of whether postlexical assimilation is categorical or gradient, because there is no evidence that the postlexical geminates that they describe and measure acoustically are the result of postlexical assimilation. More generally, it is perhaps questionable whether data from any Italian dialect would have much relevance to place of articulation assimilations in Germanic languages, given that, as a result of the diachronic loss of word-final consonants from Latin, the context for external place assimilation in Italian, even in those dialects like Sardinian that have retained a very small number of word-final consonants, is so rarely met.

Considerations of the diachronic loss of Latin word-final consonants and the close relationship of postlexical geminates in Sardinian to geminates triggered by *raddoppiamento sintattico* (RS) in Italian suggest instead that the Sardinian postlexical gemination may have more to do with how morae are aligned with segments. In standard Italian and various Italian dialects in Central and Southern Italy, RS causes word-initial consonant lengthening primarily if the preceding vowel is stressed (Absalom and Hajek 1997, 1998; D'Imperio and Gili Fivela, this volume; Loporcaro 1997; Vogel 1978): there is therefore lengthening in *parlò* [b:]*ene* (*he spoke well*; the final vowel is stressed; there is a lengthened [b:]) but not in 'parlo [b]ene' (*I speak well*; the final vowel is unstressed; there is no consonant lengthening – example from Absalom and Hajek 1997). Interestingly, in Logudorese/Campidanese Sardinian, RS doesn't apply, but there is consonant gemination in contexts that etymologically had a final Latin consonant (Loporcaro 1997), which are the 'phantom consonant' contexts in Ladd and Scobbie: thus, there is a postlexical geminate in [a p:eðru] (< Latin AD, *to Peter*) [e t:ot:u] (< Latin ED, *and all*) and [nɔ k:ɛreze] (< Latin NON, *you don't want*; examples from Loporcaro 1997).

Why should word-final stressed vowels provide the trigger for RS in RS-varieties of Italian? One possibility is that this has come about because of listeners' misperception (in the sense intended in Ohala 1974, 1981, 1990) of the trigger for consonant gemination. In Latin, the trigger was the word-final consonant (i.e. Latin STAT BENE might have been produced as [stat͡bene] with a doubly articulated closure), but as word-final consonants were lost, listeners might have attributed the trigger for such assimilations resulting in long consonants to the weight of the word-final syllable. Assuming that all Latin closed syllables were heavy (i.e. that they could be modelled as bimoraic), then, as Latin final consonants were lost, bimoraicity may have taken over as the trigger for gemination: hence in present-day standard Italian, RS applies principally after word-final stressed vowels which are bimoraic, even if there is no etymological word-final consonant (Absalom and Hajek 1997, 1998). In Logudorese/Campidanese Sardinian, RS never became established perhaps because these dialects have exceptionally retained many word-final consonants: that is, because word-final consonants were retained, listeners would be less likely to attribute the trigger for gemination to syllable weight *per se*, and so there would be no reason to misassociate the context for gemination with a preceding word-final stressed vowel.

How might present-day postlexical geminates in Sardinian and RS-dialects of Italian be represented phonologically? As far as RS is concerned, word-initial gemination has been modelled as a dichotomy between stressed vowels that are bimoraic but realised as phonetically short (see D'Imperio and Rosenthall 1999 for an acoustic analysis of final stressed vowels in Italian). Assuming that both morae from the vowel must also be present in the phonetic output (Vogel 1994), and assuming furthermore that the word-final stressed vowel is phonetically monomoraic (because it is short), then the second mora is attached to the following word-initial consonant which makes it long. These operations would therefore involve some form of mora delinking and relinking as shown below for the pre-boundary vowel and post-boundary consonant in *parlò* [b:]*ene* in which RS applies.

(1)

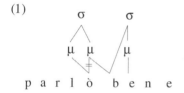

A similar kind of moraic delinking and relinking might apply at external sandhi sites in Sardinian – the difference being that moraic relinking only takes place when the second mora dominates [+cons]. Ladd and Scobbie's /aC/ (where C is a phantom consonant) could be represented as (2): the postlexically geminated /p/ in their (13) *a Palermo* would then be derived by a similar relinking of the second mora of /a/ to the following word-initial consonant. (As discussed in Absalom and Hajek 1997, Vogel 1994 has proposed exactly such a representation for word-final stressed vowels in Italian). Under this analysis, external sandhi in Sardinian is shifted away from the level at which segments give rise to overlapping gestures and becomes instead a matter of how they are prosodically parsed into morae and syllables.

(2)

σ

μ μ

| [+cons]

a

Although this seems to provide a very neat package that links at one fell swoop gemination in Sardinian, *raddoppiomento sintattico* and word-final consonant loss in Latin (but see Absalom and Hajek 1997 for a justifiably sceptical view that all diachronic and synchronic RS processes are reducible to mora relinking), D'Imperio and Gili Fivela's analysis, in which the prosodic boundary at RS sites was varied, suggests that (1) cannot adequately account for the empirical evidence. More specifically, two predictions follow from the model in (1). The first is that since the model expresses a categorical shift – a mora is either relinked or it isn't – then we might expect to find a corresponding categorical application of RS. Assuming that acoustic duration is the parameter that varies most consistently with RS application, then there is little evidence from D'Imperio and Gili Fivela's data for any such categorical change. Figure 10.1 shows individual data points from their Figure 7.1 separately for the three subjects. If RS were categorical (it does or does not apply) then we might expect to see a clear delineation on the consonant duration parameter between the broad/narrow cohesive utterances on the one hand, and the broad clause boundary ones on the other. There is some evidence that this is so for GI while for BE, the difference between the broad cohesive and clause boundary categories is very small and for both BE and NI the narrow cohesive category overlaps entirely with the other two on consonant duration.

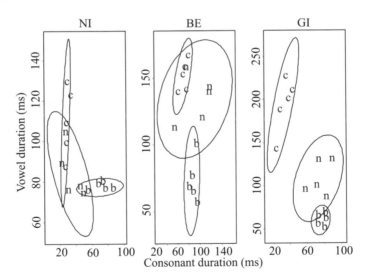

Figure 10.1   Consonant and vowel durations for broad cohesive, narrow cohesive and clause boundary (*b, n, c* respectively) corresponding to D'Imperio and Gili Fivela's Figure 7.1 (upper panel)

Another prediction from the moraic model of RS in (1) is that it should not be possible for both the pre-boundary vowel and the post-boundary consonant to be long, assuming the constraint that no additional mora can be created on the surface which is not present in the phonological representation. It is this second prediction in particular that is not compatible with the data in D'Imperio and Gili Fivela. Their data for BE and GI show that the change from a broad cohesive to a narrow cohesive utterance involves an increase in vowel duration without much change in consonant duration. The data suggest that it is not the case that a mora is attached categorically either to a word-final stressed vowel, or to a word-initial consonant, but instead that a speaker uses increased vowel length (and the associated tonal cues) to communicate the trigger as accented in parallel with increased consonant duration to signal the words are phrase-medial.

We now come back to what kind of phrase (syntactic or prosodic) is being cohered when RS applies. Earlier analyses emphasised the role of syntax in triggering gemination (Napoli and Nespor 1979) but there have been many studies prior to the analysis by D'Imperio and Gili Fivela that have called this into question, including Vogel (1994), who was one of the main protagonists of this syntactic theory of RS. If the presence of a deep syntactic break blocks RS, then we would expect to find no consonant lengthening in D'Imperio and Gili Fivela's broad disjoint utterances compared with their broad cohesive utterances. Their data show that vowel duration is greater for the disjoint compared with the cohesive utterances (significantly so for all three subjects); the same data also show that disjoint utterances have a consonant duration which is less than in cohesive utterances (significantly so for two subjects). Unfortunately, without a detailed break indices analysis of the disjoint sentences, there is simply no way to tell whether the diminished consonant duration in the disjoint sentences is the result of a prosodic or syntactic discontinuity, and the authors themselves are tentative about the degree of prosodic boundary strength in the disjoint category ('the similarity in VL between broad disjoint and narrow cohesive sentences *might suggest* a similarity in phrasing level' – emphasis added). I would suggest that the smaller consonant durations are likely to be prosodically conditioned taking into account the various analyses in the last decade that have called into question the role on syntax in conditioning RS (see in particular, Loporcaro 1997 and Vogel 1997 for whom the domain of application of RS is the phonological utterance in many dialects). My prediction, then, is that RS does not, as the authors have suggested 'signal morphosyntactic cohesion' or keep 'the utterance coherent with similar morphosyntactic constructions', but is instead one of the phonetic exponents of the prosodic boundary strength between the RS trigger and the following word.

In both Ladd and Scobbie and D'Imperio and Gili Fivela there is evidence of phrase-*medial* gemination and this seems at first sight difficult to reconcile with the electropalatographic analysis in Keating *et al.* who provide evidence for consonant strengthening (and to a certain extent lengthening) at the *onsets* of prosodic domains in four languages. The background to their research is that initial segments in a prosodic domain have been shown to be stronger than non-initial ones. This effect is cumulative: where x is a segment and P and Q are prosodic domains such that Q dominates P, then in $[[x...]_P [x ...]_P]_Q$ the leftmost x is likely to be stronger than the medial x because it also marks the onset of the prosodic domain Q. Their results showed that, although no speaker distinguished between all levels in the prosodic hierarchy, all speakers made at least one distinction between word-internal and phrase-initial segments and every speaker made at least one distinction above the word level. However, utterance-initial segments were not stronger than segments in intonational phrase-initial position and there was no reliable distinction between segments that were word-initial compared with their occurrence in the immediately lower (syllable-initial) or higher (minor phrase/accentual phrase initial) domains. Contrary to the predictions, there were also no consistent differences across the four languages in the relationship between prosodic levels and domain-initial strengthening.

The study by Keating *et al.* suggests that consonant strengthening and increased stricture at prosodic edges is analogous to vowel enhancement and increased vocal tract opening when they are in accented or nuclear accented position. As far as prosodic accent is concerned, a number of studies suggest that accented vowels are both paradigmatically and syntagmatically enhanced relative to their equivalent occurrence in unaccented positions. Paradigmatic enhancement due to accent is evident in studies by de Jong who has shown that vowel durational differences that are relevant to the voicing distinction in postvocalic stops are magnified in 'stressed' syllables (de Jong 1991) and that the back vowel [ʊ] is more retracted in nuclear accented position thereby increasing its articulatory distance from the other vowels of the language (de Jong 1995b). Syntagmatic enhancement under accent is discussed in Harrington, Fletcher and Beckman (2000): they interpreted the greater magnitude of jaw height in the transition of an accented CV syllable as evidence that speakers increase the articulatory distance between a consonant and following vowel and proposed that this has perceptual consquences of increasing the sonority rise from the C to the following tautosyllabic V. Under this interpretation, both paradigmatic and syntagmatic enhancements are listener oriented (Lindblom 1990): a greater paradigmatic contrast tends to make accented vowels acoustically more peripheral (Palethorpe *et al.* 1999; see also Wright, this volume, for analogous effects in comparing vowels in words of low and high frequency) while a steeper sonority rise may cue a sharper perceptual edge to the beginning of a syllable (Harrington *et al.*). As far as domain-initial strengthening is concerned, Hsu and Jun (1998) provide some evidence that there is a paradigmatic enhancement of the three-way voicing distinction of stops in Taiwanese, but most of the evidence seems to point to syntagmatic enhancement. As Fougeron and Keating (1997) have noted in their nasal airflow and palatographic analysis of domain-initial strengthening in French: 'these modifications [increased tongue contact in coronals, reduced velopharyngeal opening in nasals] seem to be contradictory if we looked at the effect of Prosodic Position as a "strengthening" of articulation. But from an acoustic or perceptual point of view, this increased magnitude of oral articulation and decreased magnitude of nasal articulation may contribute to the same goal: the increase of consonantality, and more generally the salience, of the consonant in "strong" prosodic positions.' In contrast to their present paper, in which Keating *et al.* are equivocal about the perceptual basis of domain-initial strengthening ('However, no perceptual experiments have been carried out, and Fougeron (1998) argues against a primarily perceptual motivation'), Fougeron and Keating's (1997) position emphasises (correctly in my view) that the domain-initial strengthening effects that they report are listener-oriented: that is, they further enhance the marked auditory modulations that characterise CV transitions (Ohala and Kawasaki 1984).

There is also some evidence that the different effects on the production of speech of phrase-final lengthening and domain-initial strengthening may be reconciled by considering their combined effects on the perception of prosodic boundaries. As is well known, the right edge of a phrase is characterised by a lengthening of the final syllable that precedes it both in English and in many other languages (e.g. Fletcher 1991 for French; Berkovits 1991 for Hebrew; Jun 1995a for Korean; Ueyama 1999 for Japanese). Moreover, the kinematic analysis of Edwards, Beckman and Fletcher (1991) and Beckman, Edwards and Fletcher (1992) shows not only no increase in articulatory movement under phrase-final lengthening, but also that most of the lengthening occurs in the rhyme's closing gesture. This elongation of the rhyme's closing gesture is likely to be precisely over the interval where the VC overlap is greatest: thus whereas domain-initial strengthening has the perceptual effect of enhancing the difference between the C and V in the body of a syllable, phrase-final lengthening has the opposite effect of increasing the auditory similarity between the V and C of a phrase-final rhyme (see also Hajek 1997 for a compatible auditory interpretation of the prevalence cross-linguistically of nasal consonant deletion and preceding vowel nasalisation in a VC context). Both these effects, then, seem to exaggerate what are intrinsic auditory properties of a syllable: phrase-initially, the body of a syllable sounds more clearly like the body of a syllable (because the auditory discontinuity is exaggerated) and phrase-finally, the rhyme sounds more clearly like a rhyme (because the auditory discontinuity is further reduced). In utterance-medial position, the sequential perception of something that sounds more distinctly like a rhyme following by something that sounds more distinctly like a CV transition at the beginning of a syllable may in combination provide listeners with the cues to parse prosodic structure to establish the boundaries between prosodic phrases.

As far as language differences are concerned, the only significant effect that was found in Keating *et al.*'s study was for Korean which, in contrast to the other languages, showed the greatest 'undershoot' effects of domain-initial consonants: that is, there was a much closer correspondence between the extent of tongue–palate contact and duration of the consonants in Korean than in the other three languages that they examined. In order to determine whether this effect is due to language-specific prosodic structure, it would be interesting to examine domain-initial effects in Japanese which is typologically similar to Korean, but different from English, French or Taiwanese, in emphasising the left edges of its prosodic constituents (Beckman 1995; Jun 1993; Pierrehumbert and Beckman 1988). Secondly, in Fougeron (1999a), domain-initial strengthening was related to the tendency for diachronic consonant weakening and change to be much more prevalent syllable-finally than medially; compatibly, as also discussed in Keating, Linker and Huffman (1983), there is a general tendency for languages to have more extensive consonant inventories in syllable-initial position. From this perspective, domain-initial strengthening might be less in evidence in indigenous Australian languages which are remarkable in showing diachronic initial consonant loss as a result of which some languages, such as Arrernte, have predominantly VC syllables (Breen and Pensalfini 1999; Evans 1995). Moreover, a typically recurring pattern in Australian languages is that there are many more consonantal contrasts word-medially than word-initially: in Warlpiri, a language spoken to the north-west of Alice Springs, all consonant phonemes are legal in medial VCV sequences, but the inventory is substantially reduced word-intially in which many apical/laminal contrasts are neutralised.

The relationship between domain-initial strengthening in Keating *et al.* and gemination in Sardinian and as a result of RS in Italian can also be briefly considered. A recent kinematic analysis by Smith (1995) suggests that (lexical) geminates in Italian are characterised by quite slow closing and opening gestures. On the other hand, if, as Keating *et al.* have shown, articulatory gestures of consonants at the onset of high prosodic domains are strengthened without duration necessarily increasing, then the opening gesture into the following vowel is likely to be quite rapid (and thus contribute to the C-V auditory salience, as suggested above). In this way, the articulatory characteristics of gemination are likely to be very different from those of domain-initial strengthening. This may provide an additional phonetic explanation for the rare occurrence of lexical geminates word-initially and hence in domain-initial position (some exceptions include Leti and Trukese, Austronesian languages that have word-initial lexical geminates – see Davis 1999 and Hume, Muller and van Engelhoven 1997; as well as Taba – see Bowden and Hajek 1996). Phonologically, the preference for word-medial geminates can been explained as an incompatibility between lexical geminates being inherently moraic on the one hand and a strong tendency for syllable-onsets to be weightless on the other. Keating *et al.*'s study points to a possible phonetic explanation: that there is an articulatory incompatibility between relatively slow gestures of geminates and rapid opening gestures that tend to characterise consonants in utterance and domain-initial position.

Note

My thanks to Mariapaola D'Imperio for providing me with the vowel and consonant duration data from their experiment and to Mary Beckman, John Hajek, Mariapaola D'Imperio, Bob Ladd, Pat Keating, Sallyanne Palethorpe and Jim Scobbie for their comments on this paper. I am especially grateful to John Hajek for many helpful discussions on sound change in Italian.

III

Phonetic interpretation and syllable structure

On the factorability of phonological units in speech perception

TERRANCE M. NEAREY

11.1 Introduction

Many key issues in speech perception revolve around two questions: first, what is the *size* of the basic phonological unit of perception (e.g. word, phoneme, feature); and, second, how *general* are the psycho-acoustic properties that are associated with those units.[1] Answers to these questions vary widely. For example, the standard distinctive feature theory of Stevens and colleagues (Stevens 1989; Stevens and Keyser 1989; Stevens and Blumstein 1981) opts for units of very small size and great generality. This theory states that the transduction from signal to symbol takes place through a universal set of small units, the distinctive features, each of which is associated with well-defined psychoacoustic properties. At the opposite end of both the size and generality scales, researchers such as Goldinger (1997; see also Johnson 1997 and Pisoni 1997) suggest that the transduction from signal to symbol is mediated by an 'episodic lexicon', involving memory traces of exemplars (i.e. individual tokens of individual words of individual speakers). In this approach the basic phonological units are large (word-sized) elements of low generality.

My own research on speech perception (Nearey 1990, 1992, 1997, in press) has focused on phoneme-sized elements as the basic units of symbolic transduction. The acoustic patterns associated with these units are relatively general, but are clearly less so (and allowably more language-specific – yet a third sense in which my position is weaker) than Stevens's universal feature set (see Nearey 1998).

The *size of units* question is primarily one of *compositionality of symbols*. Smaller symbolic units are constituents of larger ones. In the case of phonemes versus words, there is also clearly a correlation of symbol size with physical duration. Words are associated with longer temporal windows than are phonemes. A limiting case is the 'beads-on-a-string' model, where phoneme-sized elements are mapped onto non-overlapping sections of the waveform of a given word. However, if we admit overlapping time spans in the realisation of neighbouring phonemes (Nearey 1990, 1997), there will clearly be a partial dissociation of symbol size and temporal span. Finally, in the case of features versus phonemes, there exists no simple correlation with temporal span.

The *generality of units* is usually inversely correlated with their size at the symbolic level. Smaller units are typically *reusable* and are associated with more general acoustic patterns, since they are realised in a wider variety of contexts than larger units. Smaller units are typically few in number and each small unit applies to a large number of words. (There are mere dozens of distinctive features or phonemes, versus hundreds or thousands of diphones or syllables, versus hundreds of thousands of words.)

This paper reviews two streams of research relating to what I will call the 'factorability' of phonological units in speech perception. The first involves what are called *speech reception* experiments, which measure the identification of naturally produced words and pseudowords in adverse listening conditions.[2] The second involves the categorisation of parametrically synthesised speech. Evidence from both sources suggests that symbolic units of no larger than phoneme size serve as the basic elements of speech perception.

11.2 Syllable identification in noise: factorability in speech reception research

The pioneering work on factorability was done by Fletcher and colleagues at Bell Labs (see Allen 1994a, b; Fletcher 1953). Fletcher was seeking an efficient, reliable way to estimate the intelligibility of fluent speech over a telephone system. They settled on the *articulation test*, which measures correct responses to a set of phonetically balanced pseudoword CVCs. Nonsense syllables were chosen because identification of real words and connected texts was much too variable. Fletcher's research showed that the intelligibility of real words and of various kinds of texts in noise can be remarkably well predicted from articulation scores.

A key result of this research is that the rate of correct identification of nonsense syllables can be predicted from that of their constituent phonemes:

(1) $P_s = P_{C1} \, P_V \, P_{C2},$

where P_s is the probability of correct identification of entire C_1VC_2 syllables and P_{C_1}, P_V and P_{C_2} are the marginal probabilities of correctly identifying phonemes in each position in the syllable, averaged across all relevant items. Thus, if the average rate of identifying initial consonants (C_1) were 0.7, that of vowels were 0.8 and that of final consonants (C_2) were 0.6, the predicted average syllable identification rate would be 0.336 (= 0.7 $\times$ 0.8 $\times$ 0.6). For the choice of English CVCs in Fletcher's studies (and in several subsequent works), the probability of error of phonemes was found in each of the three positions, and thus $P_{C_1} \approx P_V \approx P_{C_2}$. In this case, (1) is well approximated as:

(2) $P_s \approx (P_p)^3$

where P_p is the average phoneme identification rate, $(P_{C_1} + P_V + P_{C_2})/3$.

In a later study of the identification of English CVCs at varying signal-to-noise ratios, Boothroyd and Nittrouer (1988, hereafter BN88) developed the following generalisation of Fletcher's formula (2):

(3) $P_s \approx (P_p)^j$

The exponent, j, is referred to by BN88 as the j-factor. The j-factor can be estimated empirically as $log(P_s)/ log(P_p)$. In their own experiments, for nonsense CVCs, BN88 estimated j at 3.07, but for real CVC they found a j-factor of only 2.47. In an information-theoretic interpretation consistent with that of Fletcher, BN88 interpret j as an estimate of the number of informationally independent units that compose a syllable (see also Allen 1994b). When j is exactly 3.0, equation (3) is equivalent to the approximation (2) of Fletcher's original independence formulation (1). A j-factor smaller than 3.0 for CVCs suggests that the three units are not informationally independent and syllables are recognised better than predicted by the average recognition of their constituent phonemes. The smallest attainable value of j is 1.0. This arises in the extreme case of holistic syllable perception where there are two kinds of trial: (i) the entire syllable (and, thus, each of its phonemes) is heard correctly; or , (ii) the syllable and each of its phonemes is perceived incorrectly. In this case, regardless of the overall identification rate, $P_p = P_s$, and j must equal 1.0.

While BN88 found j near 3.0 for nonsense, they found noticeably lower value, near 2.5 for real CVC words. The fact that j equals 3.0 in nonsense words suggests that phonemes are perceived independently. The reduction of the j-factor for real words is attributed by BN88 to lexical redundancy, which Allen (1994b) refers to as 'context entropy'. Allen also suggested that these findings have implications for automatic speech recognition, because they do not appear to be compatible with the use of larger units such as words or demisyllables as holistic templates in acoustic models.

Allen's comments imply that if the phonetic specification of words and pseudowords involves 'unfactorable' large units (e.g. if syllables involve *gestalt* properties that are more than the sum of their phonemic parts), then *j*-factors calculated on the basis of phonemes should be substantially smaller than 3.0. On the other hand a system that was essentially compositional, where syllables could be derived as simple functions of phonemic parts, the *j*-factor would remain high.

But what of word versus non-word differences? Both BN88 and Allen (1994b) mention Broadbent's (1967) response-bias explanation of word-frequency effects on intelligibility. Perhaps this explanation might be applied here as well, since high-frequency words are more intelligible in noise than low-frequency ones, and a nonsense syllable might be viewed as the limiting case of a low-frequency word. Broadbent provides a useful analogy illustrating how such bias effects might work. Each word is represented by a test tube. An array of test tubes, representing the lexicon, is bombarded, in effect, with informational rain. With the presentation of a particular stimulus word, the rainfall is heaviest near the 'correct' tube, and its level rises rapidly. The water level in the test tube is proportional to the (log) likelihood of its selection as a response. In the bias account, high-frequency words start out with more water in them than do low-frequency words, hence they are recognised more readily. Broadbent contrasts this with several other accounts, including one that is somewhat more like current interactive activation accounts (e.g. McClelland 1991), whereby a more frequent word has a larger funnel attached to it than does a less frequent word. Broadbent's analysis of his own experimental data bears out key predictions made by his version of a word-bias model.

Broadbent's simplifying assumptions about word activation (together with his use of a Luce choice model) allowed him to derive key predictions analytically. Unfortunately, Broadbent's approach does not apply directly to the case at hand, because it does not involve factoring words into smaller units. In the absence of suitable analytic methods, the problem can be approached using Monte Carlo simulation.

11.3 Simulation studies of factorability

Work on intelligibility in noise usually takes place in the highly abstract framework of information theory. Typically, the only 'stimulus property' discussed is signal-to-noise ratio. Although the framework of my simulations is also abstract, it represents a clear step in the direction of familiar phonetic ground. The simulations are described in detail in Nearey (in press) and are briefly summarised here.[3]

The goals of the simulations were twofold: first, to see if the *j*-factor pattern of BN88 could be replicated in a cue-space that bore at least superficial resemblance to natural speech patterns; second, to see what kinds of perturbations on underlying representations – moving roughly from segments toward holistic syllables – would have on the *j*-factors. The procedure involved construction of 'pseudo-synthetic' patterns for each of 1000 CVC syllables, the same number as in the BN88 experiments. The patterns in question could be used (though they have not been) to drive a parametric synthesiser. The consonants were based loosely on English /p t k b d g m n ŋ l /, and the vowels on / i ɪ e ɛ æ ɔ o ʊ u /. Eight cues were manipulated. Two, F1 and F2 target frequencies, related most directly to the vocalic portion. The other six related to consonantal properties. They were initial and final consonant voicing duration, initial and final 'dominant frequency' (centre of gravity of burst for stops, 'F2 steady-state' for sonorant consonants), F2 transition onset for initials, and F2 offset for finals.

11.3.1 Factorability of patterns

The baseline stimuli involved 'factorable' patterns. Here the F1 and F2 vowel cues and the consonant voicing cues were invariant targets associated with each consonant and vowel. If all cues behaved in this way, it would not be surprising that factorable behaviour could be demonstrated, since we would have essentially a 'beads on a string' phonetic system, where there were temporally distinct and invariant consonantal and vowel cues. The other four cues, those mapping place-of-articulation patterns for the consonants, are modestly more realistic, involving temporally overlapping and spectrally covarying cues. Specifically, the F2 and dominant frequency cues were (acoustic-) context dependent in that they followed patterns specified by locus-equation (Sussman, McCaffrey and Matthews 1991).

Work by Mermelstein (1978) showed that it is possible for perceptually independent phoneme-sized elements to share overlapping information in the speech signal. Nearey (1992) showed that such independent perceptual behaviour can be optimal in some simple situations. However, it was not clear how more realistic situations could be studied analytically. Accordingly, a simulation study was designed that included both a syllable-generation model and a recognition model to decode each of the syllables.

The core recogniser used a set of syllable-sized templates, which 'knew' exactly the population statistics of a set of target means for each of the 1000 syllables. It was also provided with statistical information about added noise. The core system is capable, in principle, of recognizing arbitrary patterns corresponding to irreducible (holistic) syllabic templates. It would work equally well in terms of overall correct syllable score even if the individual consonant and vowel labels are randomly scrambled among the syllables. In such a case, phoneme scores would be reduced to chance levels.

Results showed that it was easy to simulate *j*-factor patterns of BN88 if and only if the syllabic templates were constrained to be 'phoneme-factorable' by virtue of phoneme-level constraints of the type described above. However, as sketched below, even a very small departure from this situation resulted in a breakdown of phoneme factorability.

11.3.2 Simulated noise and lexical effects

Varying noise levels were simulated by adding random normal deviates to each prototype cue pattern on each virtual presentation of a stimulus to the recogniser. Higher noise conditions were simulated by adding deviates with larger variances. Arbitrarily, on each run of the simulations a random 13% of the CVCs were designated as real words (this is approximately the same proportion of real word to possible word CVCs used by BN88). A single bias parameter was selected to favour real-word responses over nonsense syllable.

The effect of this bias can be described by reference to three stages of processing similar to those described by Massaro (1989). At the *evaluation* stage, each syllable receives a score proportional to its log-likelihood based on the deviation of an input stimulus from the syllable's mean parameter values and the variance of the noise (see below). At the *integration* stage, for real words only, the log of the bias parameter is added to augment this log-likelihood score. This is analogous to the extra log-likelihood 'bilge water' in Broadbent's test tubes, and is formally equivalent to Massaro and Cohen's (1995) approach to lexical context. At the *decision* stage, a choice is made. The precise nature of the choice process has little effect on the *j*-factor results reported here (Nearey, in press).

With trial and error adjustment of the noise parameters and of the global word bias, behaviour very similar to that of BN88 could be obtained. The results are summarised in Figure 11.1. The x-axis represents average correct phoneme identification, P_p, while the y-axis represents the difference[4] between syllable identification and phoneme identification rate $(P_s - P_p)$. The lowest dashed curve represents a *j*-factor of 3.07, the empirical value found by BN88 to fit natural nonsense CVCs. The simulated nonsense syllables (circles) follow closely those of the smoothed estimates. (Each symbol represents the average identification rate of all relevant trials in a single noise condition.) The medial solid line represents a *j*-factor of 2.46, the value found for BN88 for real word CVCs. With the choice of a bias parameter favouring words by a likelihood ratio of 4.5 : 1, the simulated real-word results (triangles) are also quite close to the word value observed by BN88. The highest dotted u-shaped curve represents a *j*-factor of 2.0, corresponding to two-informationally independent units.

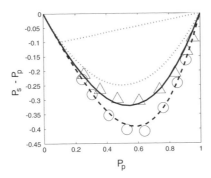

Figure 11.1 Simulations of syllable identification rates, P_s, and phoneme identification rates, P_p, using a segment-factorable model. Note the y-axis is the difference, P_s- P_p Nonsense syllables: O; real words: Δ. The lowest three curves represent (from bottom) *j*-factors of 3.07, 2.46 and 2.0

11.3.3 Addition of irreducible syllable-level stimulus effects

Figure 11.1 demonstrates that realistic *j*-factor behaviour can be achieved when syllabic patterns are phoneme-factorable. But is pure factorability a necessary condition for such behaviour, or can other relatively non-factorable patterns also approximate it? If syllabic patterns are perceived in a way that is arbitrarily (i.e. randomly) related to their phoneme 'spelling', they will have *j*-factors near 1.0 (but slightly larger because of a 'correction for guessing'). This fact does not require simulation, as it can easily be demonstrated analytically (Nearey, in press). The predicted pattern is shown as the dotted straight line near the top of Figure 11.1. But this is a 'straw' hypothesis, since probably no one believes that syllabic patterns are *totally uncorrelated* with their phonemic descriptions.

If syllables are not *fully* factorable into segments, they must contain some residue of arbitrary characteristics irreducibly associated with the syllables. Additional simulations suggested that even a small amount of irreducible syllable-level stimulus information produces *j*-factors much smaller than 3.0. These simulations involved 'syllable contaminated' production patterns. Syllable wholes that were largely, but not entirely, functions of their phoneme parts were simulated by starting with the syllable template patterns used to produce Figure 11.1, but then adding a fixed randomly chosen value to the mean of each cue for each template. After these new templates are fixed, random perturbations from the template means (simulating the effects of channel noise) were added afresh to each virtual trial. In the results shown in Figure 11.2, random normal variates with a standard deviation of 5% of the range (across the 1000 factorable seed syllables) of each cue were added to the phoneme-factorable templates used to generate Figure 11.1.

Such a model is *almost phoneme-factorable*, since each syllabic template contains only a '*soupçon* of syllabic *je ne sais quoi*' that is irreducibly non-phoneme-factorable. The cue patterns for syllable means for such mildly 'syllable contaminated' templates are still highly correlated ($r > .97$) with those of the seed templates of the factorable model. However, Figure 11.2 reveals that both the words and nonwords show j-factors much smaller than those observed by BN88. The nonwords show j-factors on average less than the 2.46 value for real words found in BN88. The real words are close to the line for a theoretical j-factor of 2.0, interpretable as two effectively independent information units. Thus, even a small admixture of irreducible syllable-level stimulus effects greatly reduces the j-factor even for nonwords.

Additional simulations were run with a larger fraction of irreducible syllabic effects. Nearey (in press) shows results with 20% syllabic contamination, where normal random deviates with a standard deviation 20% of the segment factorable cue ranges were added to the segment factorable templates. The means of the 20% syllable contaminated models are still fairly strongly correlated with those of their uncontaminated segment factorable seeds ($r > .78$ for several distinct perturbations). However, their j-factor profile is substantially deflated, with most of the points for both words and nonwords (which are no longer well separated) lying about half-way between the $j = 2.0$ curve and the arbitrary-syllable top-line in Figures 11.1 and 11.2.

Results from further simulations sketched in Nearey (in press) suggest that j-factor results are quite robust with respect to several variations in the pattern-recognition model, provided the syllable patterns are factorable. On the other hand, it was not possible to obtain j values anywhere near 3.0 for nonsense CVCs when the syllable targets were not nearly perfectly factorable. These results are also highly compatible with results reviewed below from quite a different domain in the speech perception literature.

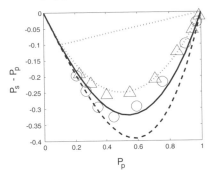

Figure 11.2 Results of simulations like those of Figure 11.1, except syllable templates contain 5% contamination with irreducible syllable-level effects. The simulated word responses (triangles) now approach a *j*-factor of 2.0, represented by the third (dotted) curve from the bottom

11.4 Factorability in parametric speech-perception experiments

Mermelstein (1978) conducted an experiment with synthetic /hVC/ syllables, where the vowel ranged over /ɛ/ and /æ/ and the consonant over /t/ and /d/. Listeners were asked to classify the syllables as the real English words, *bad, bed, bat,* or *bet.* The F1 and the duration of the vocoid were varied independently to form a two-dimensional continuum. Mermelstein's analysis indicated that *both* the F1 and duration cues affected *both* the vowel and consonant decisions. However, Mermelstein also concluded that decisions about vowel identity and consonant identity are made entirely independently of each other.

Nearey (1990 1997) has explored variations of this hypothesis using polytomous logistic models. Important aspects of these models can be illustrated with territorial maps, which show the decision regions for expected modal category response. Schematic territorial maps for possible outcomes of Mermelstein's experiment are shown in Figure 11.3.

In Figure 11.3(a), the information specifying vowel and consonant decisions is independent in every way. F1 cues vowel identity only and duration cues consonant identity only. This model illustrates several useful concepts. The irrelevance of F1 to the consonant decision is reflected by the fact that the consonant boundary is parallel to the F1 axis. If a boundary is not parallel to an axis, the opposition corresponding to that boundary is 'tuned' by the property in question. Thus, in Figure 11.3(a) vowels, but not consonants, are tuned by F1, because for a given level of vowel duration, changing F1 can cause a crossing of the /æ/ − /ɛ/ boundary.

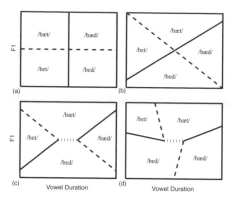

Figure 11.3 Schematic territorial maps for possible outcomes of Mermelstein's (1978) and Whalen's (1989) *bad-bet* experiments. See text for details

Figure 11.3(b) manifests a geometry that is quite different from a 'beads-on-a-string' model, in that it involves cue sharing between the consonant and vowel categories. It is also consistent with Mermelstein's hypothesis. The vowel boundary is represented by a broken line and the consonant boundary by a solid one. Neither boundary is parallel to either axis, so both the consonant boundary and the vowel boundary are tuned by both cues. Despite this, there is still potentially complete independence of the vowel and consonant decisions. A single line separates /t/ from /d/ and another line separates /ɛ/ from /æ/. We might as well have drawn two separate figures, one for the consonant and one for the vowel. Decisions could be made independently and the VC response is the simple conjunction of the two segmental decisions. This can be stated formally as:

(4) $P_r = P_V P_{C_2}$,

where P_r is the probability of a particular rhyme response consisting of a specific V and C_2 combination.

Figure 11.3(d) represents a hypothetical example of a much more complex pattern, one that involves irreducible rhyme-level stimulus properties that do not admit of factoring into segments. That is, there are characteristics of stimulus tuning that cannot be predicted from the behaviour of independent consonant- and vowel-based oppositions. In logistic models generating such a pattern, there would be no restrictions on boundary lines between any pair of categories. In fact, such models would fit equally well the results of an experiment that suffered a disastrous 'response-coding accident'; namely, one in which the four word labels were shuffled before entering the data.

Whalen (1989) describes an experiment, based on Mermelstein's, designed to test the vowel–consonant independence analysis. Whalen's analysis indicates that Mermelstein's model is not adequate to describe the fine structure of the newer results. Nearey's (1990) logistic modelling of Whalen's data confirms Whalen's claims, but it also shows that a slight modification to Mermelstein's idea does provide substantial agreement with the facts. Nearey's revised model, which can be termed a *diphone-biased segmental* model, still allows for independent, bottom-up evaluation of stimulus properties by phoneme-sized elements. However, it adds a small (stimulus-independent) bias favouring specific VC combination patterns (namely, /æt/ and /ɛd/). A schematic territorial map for this successful model is shown in Figure 11.3 (c). The stimulus-independent rhyme-bias effects serve the same role as do biases in Broadbent's (1967) models (corresponding to the standing water in his test tubes before the rain), or the real-word biases in the simulations of BN88 summarised above. Because this type of model will figure heavily in the discussion below, and since it was the kind of model selected as 'best' in Nearey (1990), it will be called the N90 model.

While the success of the N90 models is promising, it does involve the adoption of a specific modelling framework. However, we can extend non parametric *j*-factor analysis of BN88 to Whalen's (1989) data. It is convenient to extend Mermelstein's claims about independence of V and C_2 choices, given in (4), to the C_1VC_2 of (1) used for the intelligibility-in-noise experiments. This can be done by redeploying (1), repeated here as (5), with revised definitions of its factors:

(5) $P_s = P_{C_1} P_V P_{C_2}$

Here, P_s is the probability of choosing syllable *s*, P_{C_1} is the marginal probability of choosing C_1 , P_V is that of choosing V, and P_{C_2} is that of choosing C_2 on a given trial.

The application, below, of (5) to Whalen's data differs in several ways from the application of (1) to intelligibility-in-noise data . First, because of the nature of the choices, we can fix P_{C_1} at 1.0, because listeners always heard words with initial /b/. Second, while the probability values used in (1) corresponded to only 'correct' responses (where listeners responded with the actual word spoken) in the intelligibility-in-noise experiments, Mermelstein's hypothesis predicts probabilities for all response categories. Fourth, the *j*-factor calculations reported in Section 11.3 are based on average correct response over all stimuli in an experimental condition, while here we will track identification patterns for individual stimuli. In addition, *j*-factor plots require an average correct phoneme score across the three segments, P_p. Since the syllables studied by Fletcher and BN88 had approximately equal correct responses in all phoneme positions (i.e. $P_{C_1} \approx P_V \approx P_{C_2}$), it was reasonable to choose the arithmetic mean, defining $P_p = (P_{C_1} + P_V + P_{C_2}) / 3$. Under such circumstances, $(P_p)^3$ is approximately equal to the product of the three phoneme probabilities, $P_{C_1} P_V P_{C_2}$. For the Whalen data, where measures are applied to each stimulus, the assumption of equality of phoneme response probabilities is not appropriate. Instead, the 'average' phoneme probability will be defined as the *geometric mean* of phoneme response probabilities, P_p':

(6) $$P_p' = \sqrt[3]{P_{C_1} P_V P_{C_2}}$$

This ensures that (5) entails (7):

(7) $$P_s = P_p'^3$$

When these calculations are applied to the data of Whalen (1989: Appendix 1), the *j*-factor plot shown in Figure 11.4 can be constructed.

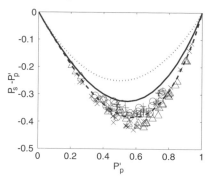

Figure 11.4 Plot of *j*-factors for the responses in Whalen's (1989) *bad-bet* experiment. The lowest dashed curve represents *j* = 3.0; the solid curve, *j* = 2.5; and the dotted curve, *j* = 2.0. *Bet* responses are shown as Δ, *bed* as +, *bat* as O, and *bad* as X

Figure 11.4 shows that *j*-factors are close to the 3.07 independence value found for nonsense syllables by BN88. Following BN88, average *j*-factors were estimated as $log(P_s)/ log(P_p')$ for each response. The results were 3.19 for *bad*, 2.83 for *bat*, 2.86 for *bed* and 3.17 for *bet*. A *j*-factor of less than 3.0 indicates that word probabilities are relatively higher than predicted from a phoneme-independence model. This suggests a bias in favour of the words *bat* and *bed*. The general pattern here is quite similar to that between real and nonsense syllables caused by lexical bias effects in the simulations. As noted above, analysis by Nearey (1990) shows that a phoneme-tuned model, supplemented by diphone biases (also favouring *bat* and *bed*), appears to be satisfactory to describe the results of Whalen's experiment.

The nature of bias effects can be characterised in terminology from the logistic regression framework of Nearey (1990), which has many points in common with the analysis of covariance. Let V indicate vowel response main effects, let C represent response main effects for the final consonant, and let $F1$ and Dur indicate the obvious stimulus dimensions. A model creating the geometry corresponding to Figure 11.3(a) is $V + C + V \times F1 + C \times Dur$. Model coefficients associated with the $V \times F1$ *interaction* can be called stimulus-tuned vowel effects, because they mediate changes in probability of vowel choice as F1 is varied. Similarly, coefficients associated with the $C \times Dur$ term can be called stimulus-tuned consonant effects. The main effect terms C and V are bias terms in the sense that coefficients associated with them contribute exactly the same constant amount to each stimulus regardless of its specific stimulus properties. The model underlying Figure 11.3(b) adds two additional terms to the previous one: $V \times Dur$ and $C \times F1$. The fact that there are no terms involving $V \times C$ response interactions entails that consonant and vowel choice is totally independent, as in Mermelstein's hypothesis. Figure 11.3(c) shows the kind of geometry that can arise when we add the $V \times C$ biases. This is the 'preferred' N90 model. Admitting $V \times C$ effect amounts to conceding that there is some aspect of the behaviour that depends simultaneously on a particular vowel and combinations that are not inherent in their segmental constituents. But such a $V \times C$ bias is not like the 'irreducible syllable-level stimulus information' discussed in the simulations. What we need to know about each VC combination is *entirely independent of stimulus properties*. Figure 11.3(d) shows what we expect from a case where we add to the previous model the stimulus-tuned rhyme terms $V \times C \times F1$ and $V \times C \times Dur$. Only now do we have irreducible rhyme-level stimulus effects. The empirical data do not require such complexity.

11.4.1 Potential sources of bias effects

But what about the diphone ($V \times C$) biases? What can they represent? There are at least four plausible sources of bias: (i) lexical frequency effects, like those discussed by Broadbent (1967); (ii) probabalistic phonotactic constraints against certain phoneme sequences, corresponding to Massaro and Cohen's (1983) 'contextual features'; (iii) more general transitional probabilities between phonemes (McQueen and Pitt 1998); (iv) classic response bias (where, perhaps, subjects may push the *bed* button more frequently if they are getting sleepy) biases. These can in principle be controlled in appropriately designed experiments. Here we can only speculate about them *post hoc*.

Since these are all common real English words (ii) cannot apply. Similarly, although response-bias effects (iv) are always possible, we have *a priori* reason to expect this particular pattern (favouring *bed* and *bat*). Lexical frequency effects (i) also appear unlikely. The Kucera and Francis (1967) word-frequency counts are: *bet* 18, *bed* 127, *bat* 20 and *bad* 142. Recall that *bat* and *bed* are favoured (smaller *j*-factor). These words rank second and fourth in frequency. Similarly, there is little support from diphone frequency. The CELEX (Brunage 1990) database shows diphone counts of /ɛt/ 9893, /ɛd/ 8274, /æt/ 38830 , and /æd/ 5339. The high count for /æt/ is likely due to the words at and that (J. McQueen, personal communication). From these values, the conditional transitional probabilities for /t/ and /d/ following /ɛ/ are .531 and .469 respectively. Following /æ/, the probabilities are more skewed (likely because of *that* and *at*), .879 for /t/ and .121 for /d/. The probabilities for the vowels conditional on the consonants is .203 for /ɛ/ and .797 for /æ/ preceding /t/ versus .620 and .380, respectively, preceding /d/. These numbers make it plausible that *bat* is a preferred response. However, we have to sift among conditional probabilities for any reason why *bed* might be preferred to *bet*.

There is fifth potential source of bias effects, (v) *essential biases*. I have called these 'essential' in the sense that hypertension is essential when it has no identifiable cause. Essential biases are quite simply fudge factors that make a pattern-recognition framework match observed behaviour more closely. In this example, the net effect of the rhyme biases is to increase the area of *bat* and *bed* at the expense of the /ɛt/ and /æd/ categories. As noted in Nearey (1997), this makes sense if production patterns are considered. Peterson and Lehiste (1960) find duration to be 40% greater for /æ/ than for /ɛ/, while vowels before /d/ are 40% to 50% longer than before /t/. Because the duration ratios associated with the consonant and vowel oppositions are comparable, the duration pattern for the rhymes is roughly /ɛt/ < /ɛd / ≅ /æt/ < /æd/. For /ɛt/ and /æd/, the duration characteristics associated with the vowels and consonants are synergistic. But they are antagonistic for /ɛd / and /æt/. An optimal decision rule must reflect some kind of correlation between consonant and vowel decisions in the middle range, where only /ɛd/ and /æt/ are likely. In such cases a simple perceptual strategy should pay off: bias decisions slightly in favour of the conflicting-cue /ɛd/ and /æt/ syllables. This rule can be applied automatically and globally, as it is unlikely to do harm in the synergistic cue situations, because expected extreme cue values achieved there can simply override the bias toward the less robustly cued choices.

It might be argued that there is little real difference between Figures 11.3(c) and 11.3(d) and their associated models. Indeed, there is only a difference of two degrees of freedom between the two in Nearey's (1990) analysis. However, the differences increase dramatically if we expand the inventory of segments and the numbers of possible diphones (Nearey 1990).

Nearey (1997) analysed an experiment with 972 stimuli involving synthetic /hVC/ stimuli where C ranges over /t/ and /d/ and V over the five central and back vowels of Canadian English. As in the Whalen experiment, F1 and duration of the vocoid are manipulated. In addition, two other factors are varied, F2 of the vocoid and duration of closure voicing during the final contoid. Considering a rhyme-biased segmental model analogous to the N90 model of Figure 11.3(c) and one with using irreducible stimulus-tuned rhymes, as in Figure 11.3(d), the difference in complexity is fairly large. There are an additional 21 degrees of freedom with the latter, yet there is only a tiny improvement of fit, with an rms (measured in percent response) of 4.18% for the large model, versus 4.53% for the smaller one.[5]

11.4.2 Nonlinear stimulus effects

Evidence from parametric speech-perception experiments show that the N90 model associated with Figure 11.3(c) performs remarkably well in a number of cases. However, there are cases where they are not adequate. Using terminology from Nearey (1990), the N90 model can be referred to as a *rhyme-biased segment-tuned logistic with linear stimulus effects*. This heavy phrase will be parsed below. *Rhyme-biases* and biases associated with other higher-level phonological objects (syllables, words) have been discussed above. *Segment-tuned* means more specifically: 'contains stimulus-related terms linked to symbolic units of no larger than phoneme size'. In the logistic framework, the predictor model can contain terms like $V \times F1$ and $C \times Dur$ but no terms like $V \times C \times F1$. The previous discussion and Figure 11.3 (d) should give some intuition about what is at stake here.

Consider now the residual phrase *with linear stimulus effects*. This property of N90 models results in boundaries between pairs of categories that are straight lines in all four panels of Figure 11.3. This is because a model term like $C \times F1$ is associated with coefficients a_t and a_d, which literally multiply F1 values and thus contribute to evaluation functions. All other things being equal, an increase in F1 of 1 Hz will affect ratio of /t/ to /d/ choices by $exp(a_t - a_d)$. Evaluation functions for individual syllables are linear equations, which will intersect in linear boundaries.

But what about the possibility of nonlinear stimulus effects? It would be possible to choose an initial nonlinear transformation of a stimulus cue, such as a Bark-or ERB-scale measurement of F1. Alternatively, we can allow for some nonlinearity in the effects of F1 by including an $F1^2$ term. This would require an additional set of coefficients associated with a new $C \times F1^2$ interaction.

Similarly, it would be possible to allow for interaction of two different stimulus factors. Consider an experiment where F2 and F3 onsets were manipulated in 'burstless' stop+vowel syllables. Stimuli with converging F2 F3 patterns might cause a perceptually relevant compact amplitude peak at onset (Stevens and Blumstein 1981). Given an explicit theory about the nature of this emergent feature, the experimenter could measure the relevant property and code it directly in the model. Alternatively, in addition to coefficients relating to $C \times F2$ and $C \times F3$, an additional quadratic $C \times F3 \times F2$ term, as well as $C \times$

$F2^2$ and $C \times F3^2$, could be included. Inclusion of all these terms would allow for certain curvilinear boundaries on territorial maps in an F2 x F3 space, and potentially for multimodal dominance regions for single categories.

Curvilinear boundaries and multimodal dominance regions may be necessary to accommodate the perception of place of articulation in stops. Nearey and Shammass (1987, see also Shammass 1985) noted that statistical patterns associated with what have since become known as locus equations (Sussman, McCaffrey and Matthews 1991) clearly entail unequal covariance patterns of the three stops /b, d, g/. This also implies quadratic rather than linear optimal class boundaries. Nearey (1991) also conjectures that quadratic logistics may be necessary to account for relations observed between burst centre-frequency and F2 in place of articulation experiments.

11.5 Reanalysis of the data of Massaro and Cohen (1983)

The question of nonlinearity also arises in a reanalysis of data from Massaro and Cohen (1983). They produced a two-dimensional continuum, manipulating F2 onsets and F3 of a glide-like element in a /C_1C_2a/ continuum spanning the syllables, /bla/, /dla/, /bra/, /dra/. The model they selected as best, involving what they term *contextual features*, can be approximated very closely by a diphone biased segmental linear logistic model (Nearey 1990: 369). However, subsequent analysis cast doubt on this interpretation (see Nearey 1998: note 6). Using raw data (read from their Figure 11.6), a simple interpolation process was used to estimate boundaries and to create a non-parametric territorial map, as shown in Figure 11.5.

The resulting pattern shows that the conditional boundaries do not appear to be parallel as required by the N90 model. The /bl/ – /br/ boundary shows tuning almost exclusively by F3 (i.e. a straight line approximating it would be roughly parallel to the F2 axis). Similarly, the /dr/ – /br/ boundary is roughly parallel to the F3 axis, showing clear tuning only on F2. However, the /dl/ – /dr/ and /dl/ – /bl/ boundaries (which under the biased segmental model should have been parallel, respectively, to the previous two boundaries) are oblique to both axes, showing tuning on both F2 and F3. This case is studied further below.

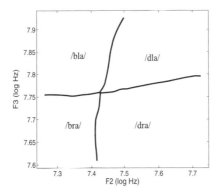

Figure 11.5 Empirical territorial map drawn for the *bla-dra* experiment of Massaro and Cohen (1983). Boundaries were estimated using simple interpolation of raw response probabilities

Following the methodology of Nearey (1990), a series of logistic models was fitted to the data of MC83. The factors involved in the analysis are outlined in Table 11.1. Table 11.2 illustrates the main effect and interaction terms of the models investigated.

Table 11.1 *Classification of effects in models studied for MC83 experiment*

Abbreviation	Description
Phonetic factors	
S	Stop (/b/ vs. /d/) main effect
G	Glide (/l/ vs. /r/) main effect
S x G	Cluster (diphone) interaction
Stimulus factors	
F2	log(F2) onset for synthetic stop
F3	log(F3) target for synthetic glide

Note. Example stimulus-tuned effects: S x F2, F2-tuned stop effect; G x F3, F3-tuned glide effect; S x G x F3, F3-tuned cluster effect; where 'x' indicates crossing of factors.

Results of tests of the relative adequacy of these models are given in Table 11.3. Tests comparing these models are based on comparing changes in the residual deviance statistic, G^2, to a heterogeneity value that is analogous to a residual mean squared error in ordinary linear regression (McCullagh and Nelder 1989). The procedure is analogous to the use of 'extra sum of squares' F-tests in stagewise regression, where a sequence of increasingly more complex models is compared with smaller ones and the increase in variance accounted for by the larger model is compared to the residual error variance of the smaller one. The data analysed here are pooled over subjects and some questions about the validity of the reported alpha levels must remain since the analysis involves approximate fixed-effects tests to repeated measures data analysis.[6] For that reason, we note that any use of the term 'significant' should implicitly be read 'nominally significant'. Table 11.3 summarises the results of several such comparisons.

Table 11.2 *Description of main models investigated for MC83 data*

Model number	Description	Terms included	Figure 11.3 panel
I	Primary cue	$S + G + S \times F2 + G \times F3$	(a)
II	Linear secondary cue	$II + G \times F3 + S \times F3$	(b)
III	Cluster-biased linear secondary cue	$II + S \times G$	(c)
IV	Full linear diphone (stimulus-tuned clusters)	$III + S \times G \times F2 + S \times G \times F3$	(d)
V	Cluster-biased quadratic secondary cue	$III + S \times F2^2 + G \times F2^2$ $+ S \times F3^2 + G \times F3^2 +$ $S \times F2 \times F3 + G \times F2 \times F3$	--
VI	Model V with linear stimulus-tuned cluster terms	$V + S \times G \times F2 + S \times G \times F3$	--
VII	Model V without cluster bias	$V - S \times G$	--

Models I–IV of Table 11.2 are consistent with the geometrical patterns illustrated in Figure 11.3 (a)–(d) respectively. The preliminary graphic investigation of MC83 data discussed in Nearey (1998) suggested that a model as complex as Model IV might be required.

As in the case of Whalen's (1989) experiments analysed in Nearey (1990), we find highly significant improvement comparing the baseline primary cue Model I to the secondary cue Model II. Interestingly, however, adding the cluster bias term in Model III hardly improves fit at all.[7] That is, there is no substantial improvement of the fit when we move from a model comparable to Figure 11.3(b) to that of Figure 11.3(c). As suggested by the preliminary discussion in Nearey (1998), there is highly significant improvement when we move to the stimulus-tuned diphone model like that of Figure 11.3(d). The relevant comparison is shown in row 4 of Table 11.3.

Table 11.3 *Comparison of selected pairs of models from Table 11.2*

Row	Models[a]	$G2$[b]	Δ df[c]	$\Delta G2$[d]	H[e]	Res.df[f]	F[g]	p	rms[h]
1	I	598.75	N/A	N/A	8.658	71	N/A	N/A	6.76
2	II/I	311.82	2	286.94	8.658	69	16.57	<.0001	4.71
3	III/II	310.18	1	1.64	4.449	68 ·	0.368	0.5463	4.74
4	IV/III	238.71	2	71.47	4.505	66	7.93	0.0008	3.99
5	V/III	182.40	6	127.78	4.505	62	4.73	0.0005	3.49
6	VI/V	167.16	2	15.24	2.970	60	2.57	0.0852	3.46
7	VI/IV	167.16	6	71.55	3.692	60	3.23	0.0081	3.46
8	V/VII	184.91	1	2.50	2.932	62	0.85	0.3590	3.49

[a] Larger model [/ smaller model, if present].
[b] G^2 (residual deviance) statistic for larger model.
[c] Number of degrees of freedom added to larger model.
[d] G^2 of smaller model minus G^2 of larger.
[e] Estimated heterogeneity (H) based on smaller model, calculated as the Pearson chi-square of the smaller model divided by its residual degrees of freedom.
[f] Residual df of the of the larger model.
[g] Calculated as $F = \lfloor \Delta G2 / \Delta df) / (H) \rfloor$ with Δdf and *Res. df* degrees of freedom.
[h] Root mean squared error of predicted and observed percent identification.

Several possible explanations should be considered. One involves phonotactic constraints. The cases studied previously (Nearey 1990, 1997) involved English CV and VC patterns, with Cs being restricted to obstruents. Under these circumstances there is relatively free occurrence of most combinations of consonants and vowels. Perhaps consonant clusters, with their highly restricted phonotactics, show different patterns.

There is, perhaps, a hint of this possibility in the literature. Fox (1992) shows large changes in slopes in identification functions of isolated front-vowel stimuli compared with similar stimuli in pre-[r] contexts. The dialect Fox investigated neutralises to two lexically contrastive vowel heights in the latter environment. In a logistic model, such changes in slope require diphone-tuned terms. This suggests a single perceptual unit interpretation for [Vr] sequences in English, which might then be represented as /V^r/, treating them parallel to 'single unit' interpretations of diphthongs. The nucleus and offset portions of a unit such as /i^r/ might bear a family resemblance to signal properties associated with the phonemes /i/ and /r/ respectively in other environments. Nevertheless, a distinct /i^r/ unit might possess links to unique stimulus properties, constituting a *'soupçon of je ne sais quoi'* that prevents its further decomposition. Such a solution receives indirect support from some phonological tests. Derwing, Dow and Nearey (1988) present evidence that [Vw] and [Vj] diphthongs are treated more like single units, /V^j/ and /V^w/ , on some psycholinguistic tasks on which [V + obstruent] sequences are treated as two. [Vr], while more variable, tends to behave more like the diphthongs. Perhaps something similar might be happening with stop + liquid onset clusters.

11.5.1 Nonlinear stimulus effects in the MC83 data

Further consideration of Figure 11.5, however, shows that the observed partition could instead be approximated by two mildly curved lines, one separating /r/ from /l/ and one separating /b/ from /d/. This geometry resembles the Mermelstein secondary model of Figure 11.3(c), except that curvilinear boundaries are admitted. Can such nonlinearities account for the observed behaviour without diphone-tuned stimulus effects?

Row 7 of Table 11.3 shows a test of two diphone-biased stimulus-tuned segment models. The smaller is Model III of Table 11.2, corresponding to the N90-type model of Figure 11.3(c). The larger model is Model V of Table 11.2. It is one that includes additional derived stimulus effects, namely the squares (F2^2 and F3^2) and cross products (F2 × F3) of the two stimulus variables. These effects are allowed to cross with segment-level terms coding stop (S) and glide (G) contrasts, but not with diphone (cluster) onset interaction contrasts (S× G). This model admits curved lines as in Figure 11.5, with boundaries restricted to quadratics.

Row 7 of Table 11.3 shows that the improvement of goodness-of-fit from the segmental linear Model III to the segmental quadratic Model V is highly significant. It is useful to use the relative reduction of the G^2 deviance statistic as a measure of improvement in moving from a smaller to a larger model. There are an additional 6 df in Model V compared to Model III, with a relative reduction of G^2 of approximately 42% (= [310.18 -182.40]/310.18). By contrast, the previously preferred cluster-tuned Model IV, with two additional degrees of freedom, shows a relative reduction of G^2 of only about 23% compared Model III (310.18 reduced to 238.76).

Models IV and V cannot be compared directly using stagewise F-tests, because models must be nested to do so (i.e. one must properly include the other). We can, however, do something akin to a partial correlation analysis by fitting a larger model, shown as Model VI in Table 11.2, that includes all the terms of both the diphone-linear Model IV and the segmental-quadratic Model V. Row 6 of Table 11.3 shows that adding quadratic segmental terms to Model IV significantly improves the fit, reducing error by about 30% (238.76 reduced to 167.16). However, as row 7 of Table 11.3 shows, comparing Model V to Model VI, which adds cluster-tuned linear terms to the segmental-quadratic model, does *not* improve fit significantly.

Figure 11.5 also suggests that diphone bias terms may not be necessary. Note in the diphone-biased case of Figure 11.3(d), there is a region where only two of four choices dominate. This results from biases that favour *bed* and *bat* over *bad* and *bet*. On the other hand, the pure segmental model of Figure 11.3(c) (with no diphone biases) leads to a 'four-corners region' near the centre, where all four response categories meet at a single point. Figure 11.5 also shows a four-corners pattern. Row 8 of Table 11.3 tests for the significance of the diphone-bias terms by comparing Model V with Model VII, which removes just the $S \times G$ terms. There is no significant change of fit. Thus, allowing for quadratic stimulus effects eliminates the need for *any* diphone terms, including $S \times G$ biases. Model VII of Table 11.2 is a pure segmental model.

The above results must be taken with a grain of salt, since we run the risk of applying 'Munchausen's statistical grid' (Martin 1984) by testing everything in sight until we find a result that suits our taste. There is a possibility that what amounts to nonlinear enrichment of the stimulus space (by including square and cross-product terms) has enabled the 'emulation' of more complex signal-to-symbol relations that in reality involve irreducible diphone tuning. Furthermore, the absence of a significant contribution of even diphone-*bias* terms is problematic to my own previous analyses in this particular case.

To improve the fit of their models, Massaro and Cohen (1983) use what they call a contextual modifier, 'not very likely', to apply to the phonotactically ill-formed */dlɑ/ Nearey (1990) argued that diphone biases could serve in this role (see also McQueen and Pitt 1998). It is difficult to accept the findings in the previous paragraph, since this appeared to be a clear case where diphone biases were very well motivated.

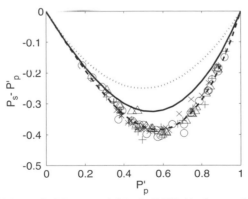

Figure 11.6 Plot of j-factors for Massaro and Cohen's (1983) *bla-dra* experiment. The lowest dashed curve represents a $j = 3.0$; the solid curve $j = 2.5$, and the dotted curve $j = 2.0$. /dlɑ/ responses are shown as Δ, /blɑ/ as +, /drɑ/ as O, and /brɑ/ as X

But there is away to look at this data more directly. Figure 11.6 presents a *j*-factor plot for MC83's *bla–dra* experiment. It was constructed in analagously to Figure 11.4 for the Whalen *bad–bet* experiment. Contrary to that case, there is no hint of a systematic bias for any of the four syllables. We might have expected, for example that */dlɑ/ would show a lower probability of response than indicated by marginal /d/ and /l/ response probabilities and hence larger *j*-factor than the legal /drɑ/. Rather, the relatively tight clustering around the *j* =3 curve shows that close adherence to non-parametric predictions of the Fletcher independence model of equations (1) or (5), suitably modified for CCVs. Empirical estimates of *j*-factors had means ranging 2.94 to 3.06 over the four syllables, with SDs ranging from 0.14 to 0.21. For this data, listeners' syllable choice probabilities are extremely well predicted from their marginal phoneme response probabilities, just as Mermelstein's (1978) hypothesis predicts. Thus, the case for the factorability of segment-sized units seems to survive this data unscathed.[8]

It should also be noted that there are empirical implications of the quadratic segment-based analysis that can be tested directly in new experiments. Namely, the curved boundaries resulting from nonlinearities in the individual segment oppositions should *generalise* to other contexts, including simple CVs. The analysis given above cannot be taken as more than suggestive until such tests are performed.

11.6 Discussion and conclusions

The pattern of evidence presented here makes an excellent *prima facie* case that, segments, i.e. factorable symbolic elements of phoneme-size, play a major role in speech perception. Furthermore, that key role is only modified by higher order elements (e.g. syllables and words) in a very limited and stylised way. Evidence from traditional intelligibility experiments involving the perception of speech in noise (Allen 1994a, b; Boothroyd and Nittrouer 1988) and data from parametric perceptual experiments (Mermelstein 1978; Massaro and Cohen 1983; Whalen 1989; Nearey 1997) are shown above to be compatible with this conclusion. Finally, results from simulations of intelligibility in noise strongly suggest that such patterns of factorability are fragile (Nearey, in press). They can be obtained relatively easily with a system based on factorable segment-sized units, but they appear to be unattainable when unique stimulus patterns are irreducibly linked to larger basic units. It seems incumbent on proponents of theories claiming that 'larger symbolic units are basic' to show how such segment-factorable behaviour can emerge from any model incorporating large basic elements.

An important question is whether factorability can be extended down to smaller sized elements. The analysis of Miller and Nicely (1955) suggests a considerable degree of independence for their ad hoc five-feature set in the perception of English consonants. An estimation of j-factor from their data suggests yields a mean value of 4.2, compared to the expected 5.0 from their five independent features. However, as noted by Miller and Nicely (229-30), there is considerable redundancy in the phoneme set, since only 16 of 24 possible feature combinations map to English consonants. This could be another form of context entropy (Allen 1994b) that could lead to a deflation of the j-factor similar to that observed for real words versus nonsense in speech-reception experiments.

This question can also be pursued more directly. Massaro and Oden (1980) investigated what amounts to the factorability of voicing and place judgements in stops. They are somewhat ambivalent in their choice of two models, one apparently compatible with a feature-tuned model with phoneme-level biases, and another involving 'featural modifiers' that would appear to imply segment-level stimulus tuning from the current perspective.

José Benki (1998) has also recently investigated feature-level factorability in the voicing and place features of stop consonants in a logistic framework explicitly linked to that used here. His preferred analyses favour a 'segment-biased feature model', where stimulus tuned effects are linked to features, while phoneme-level contributions are limited to biases. As noted by Benki, his analysis amounts to shifting the methods of Nearey (1990) down a step in the distinctive feature-phoneme-syllable phonological hierarchy.

However, preliminary analysis of data from our own laboratories suggests that English vowels will not yield to clear factorability at the distinctive feature level. While it is not clear how sensitive such an analysis is to the choice of the 'correct' feature set, the ones we have investigated so far suggest that a typical feature-based analysis leaves about twice as large a residual deviance (G^2) as one based on unfactored phonemes.

The issue of feature-factorability is an important one and should clearly be pursued in future research. From another perspective, however, once we get to the phoneme level, most of the work of factorability is done. The number of words in English is almost three orders of magnitude larger than the number of phonemes. The number of phonemes and features are of the same order of magnitude. Searching for possible phoneme-feature relations in such a space would appear to be a relatively straightforward task, especially when compared to that which would seem to await proponents of an episodic lexicon who seem (in principle, at least) prepared to allow for fractal stimulus-to-symbol mapping. It remains to be demonstrated that any exemplar model (Nosofsky 1988) based on large symbolic units can achieve (epiphenomenally – as an emergent property) the appearance of segment factorability documented here.

Notes

Thanks to Anne Cutler and the staff at Max Planck Institute for Psycholinguistics for their hospitality during the key stage of the preparation of this manuscript. Special thanks to James McQueen who kindly provided me with relevant numbers from the CELEX database. Thanks also to Roel Smits, Jose Benki, Michael Kiefte and Jont Allen for useful discussions on these general topics. (All errors are mine alone.) This work was supported by SSHRC.

1   My use of the term 'basic unit' throughout this paper is compatible with the following definition, derived from Nearey (1990). Basic phonological units are the *largest* symbolic elements that exhibit *stimulus tuning*, where stimulus-tuning entails the continuous modulation of within-category response probabilities by changes in stimulus properties. In these terms, for many (though not all) of Massaro's FLMP models, the basic phonological units are his 'features', which are elements that are differentially activated by changes in specific stimulus properties during his evaluation stage of processing (Massaro 1989).

2   In the literature of the subfield, 'intelligibility' is reserved to refer to correct response to real words and text, while *articulation (score)* is used for nonsense. The two are frequently spoken of together under the term *speech reception.* However, I will occasionally use the term *intelligibility* to cover both.

3   MATLAB programs implementing the simulations (and other software) are available at http://ualberta.ca/~tnearey/

4   The somewhat awkward choice of $(P_s.P_p)$ as the ordinate rather than P_s (as used in similar plots in BN88), was made to exploit a larger portion of the plot space. Since correct average phoneme response, P_p, must always be as great as P_s , points plotted in a P_p x P_s space are restricted to lie below diagonal $P_s = P_p$.

5   Nearey (1997) does find evidence of some statistically reliable, though very small, stimulus-tuned rhyme effects. Empirical *j*-factors show relatively slight deviation from the independence benchmark of 3.0, with values ranging from 2.83 to 3.11 over the ten response syllables (*SD*s ranged from .15 to .21).

6   Dominic Massaro and Michael Cohen kindly provided me with individual listener results from five of the subjects tested (the other data records could not be recovered). A random-coefficients-regression analysis approach, analogous to that discussed in Nearey (1997), was performed. The overall pattern was similar to that described here. However, RCR tests are not very powerful with only five subjects.

7   Indeed, the rms error value actually decreases. This is possible because the optimisation routine is a generalised linear model that is optimising G^2 values. The fitting procedure involves a weighted least-squares procedure. The weights are in general not uniform across all cells but are larger for stimuli with extreme probabilities. In practice, cases where G2 improves and rms error does not typically involve non-significant changes in G2.

8   The absence of diphone biases reflecting phonotactic constraints in this experiment remains unexplained. One factor to consider in follow-up experiments is the relatively large number of trials per stimulus each subject underwent in this

experiment. Perhaps the resultant familiarity with the stimulus set was coupled with a countervailing response bias. Such a countervailing response bias might result from a listener's tendency (conscious or otherwise) to push each of the four response buttons about equally often.

12
Articulatory correlates of ambisyllabicity in English glides and liquids

BRYAN GICK

12.1 Introduction

In a previous volume of this series, Turk (1994: 107) states that 'it is widely assumed that word-initial and word-final consonants are syllable-initial and syllable-final respectively'. However, phonological evidence abounds for complete or partial 'resyllabification' of word-final consonants across word boundaries. Examples of this include such well-known cases as alveolar 'flapping' (Kahn 1976), linking r (McMahon, Foulkes and Tollfree 1994), linking l (Gick forthcoming) and glide formation (Broadbent 1991, Harris 1994), or 'linking' (Whorf 1943). In all of these cases, when it is followed by a vowel-initial word, a final segment adopts characteristics associated either with initial allophones or with word-internal allophones of the variety often referred to as 'ambisyllabic' (Kahn 1976). Acoustic and articulatory studies of English /l/ (Bladon and Al-Bamerni 1976; Sproat and Fujimura 1993) and /r/ (Gick forthcoming) support this view of word-final consonants.

In recent years, researchers have begun using articulatory measures such as gestural timing and magnitude in an attempt to identify the general phonetic correlates of various syllable positions (Krakow 1989; Browman and Goldstein 1992, 1995; Sproat and Fujimura 1993; Wang 1995; see Turk 1994: 113 for earlier citations). The applicability of a gestural approach to the phonological modelling of the syllable would be greatly enhanced if it could be shown that these same correlates can also encompass traditional resyllabification phenomena in English. By reproducing some of the previous results for /l/

under more phonetically constrained conditions, and by additionally observing the behaviour of final offglides in this same environment, it is the goal of the present paper to attempt to identify specifically how, if at all, the spatial and dynamic properties of word-final gestures may be generally influenced by resyllabification.

12.2 Background

As mentioned above, the last decade has seen the emergence of a research programme using articulatory measures as identifying and even defining characteristics of syllable positions. While this effort has met with some success for unambiguously initial and final allophones, there has been little consensus among the few who have investigated the articulatory properties of ambiguously syllabified allophones (Krakow 1989; Sproat and Fujimura 1993; Turk 1994).

For most tokens, Krakow (1989) observes in her two subjects a bimodal pattern of syllabification, where an intervocalic /m/ appears to follow either a distinctly initial or a distinctly final pattern of intergestural timing (as with all of the previous studies cited here, the categories 'initial' and 'final' were based on lexical affiliation). Krakow's study focuses mainly on determining the syllabification of word-medial consonants (such as the /m/ in *seamy*) by comparing them with those in word-initial (*see me*) and word-final (*seem E*) positions. However, without more clearly syllabified final examples (e.g. *seem he*), it is impossible to conclude whether these lexically final allophones are syllable final or ambisyllabic. Turk's (1994) paper is directed even more toward word-internal intervocalic consonants, making it also of only indirect relevance to the present question.

Sproat and Fujimura (1993) are primarily concerned with observing and describing allophonic patterns across boundaries, including word boundaries. Theirs is therefore the only previous study with substantial relevance to the present one. Their results support the conclusion that allophonic variation in American English /l/ is not categorical, but rather that the articulatory properties of final allophones gradiently approach those of initial allophones as the strength of the following boundary decreases. This finding is consistent with the phonological phenomena cited above, suggesting that any effects of partial or complete resyllabification can potentially be elicited by the presence of a following vowel, even across word boundaries.

The following sections will outline what we should expect, based on previous findings, to find as the articulatory correlates of initial and final positions, and how we predict these will vary under conditions of resyllabification. First, a working technical definition of ambisyllabicity will be proposed within a gestural framework.

12.2.1 Toward a gestural definition of ambisyllabicity

It has been a particular challenge of the field of laboratory phonology to directly associate phonological concepts such as ambisyllabicity with phonetic properties and testable predictions. The theory of Articulatory Phonology (henceforth AP; Browman and Goldstein 1986, 1989, 1992) provides a useful means of generating such direct connections with the empirical realm. Insofar as syllables have been discussed within this framework (e.g. Krakow 1989; Browman and Goldstein 1992, 1995), it is possible to state a formal definition of ambisyllabicity in gestural terms.

Within one view of AP, many of the properties of a particular allophone are not specified directly, but rather are determined by the phasing of its component gestures to surrounding gestures. Thus, under this view, for example, the spatial displacement of an unambiguously final allophone is the result of a crucial temporal phasing with the preceding vowel gesture, while that of an unambiguously initial allophone results from phasing with the following vowel gesture. Ambisyllabicity, or partial resyllabification, traditionally describes the joint affiliation of an intervocalic consonant with two flanking vocalic peaks (with or without intervening word or other boundaries). A reformulation of ambisyllabicity in terms of AP would therefore state that certain intervocalic gestures are crucially phased to both the preceding and the following vowel gestures.

This gestural analysis of ambisyllabicity makes the specific prediction that, whatever the spatial displacement (or velocity, stiffness, etc.) of a gesture in initial and final position, its ambisyllabic allophone will display an intermediate magnitude between the two. This prediction recalls Turk's (1994: 107-8) statement that '[a]mbisyllabic consonants are predicted to share the phonetic characteristics of both syllable-initial and syllable-final consonants', as well as Sproat and Fujimura's (1993) conclusion that allophonic variation is not categorical, but gradient on the gestural level. It is this hypothesis regarding the gestural characteristics of ambisyllabicity that will be tested in the remainder of this paper.

One additional note on this point: in theory, a word-final segment described here as 'ambisyllabic' could indeed be merely 'bilexical', eliminating the need to include the notion of syllables in the discussion at all. However, this conclusion is inconsistent with the phonological evidence for 'resyllabification' phenomena (e.g. coronal flapping, or others cited in Section 12.1) occurring not only across word boundary, but also within words – both morpheme-internally and across morpheme boundaries.

12.2.2 Gestural syllable position effects

This section will set forth the two articulatory measures that will be used to test for reliable properties of initial and final allophones. Ultimately, these same properties will be observed under conditions of possible resyllabification to test for any degrees of variation between initial and final allophones.

Browman and Goldstein (1992, 1995), based on the previous findings of a number of researchers, have identified two 'gestural syllable position effects', or general effects that seem to apply to the component gestures of any consonant segment occupying a particular syllable position. These are: syllable-position-specific timing between tautosegmental[1] gestures (a property of gestural configuration) and final reduction (a property of gestural scaling).

For this discussion, it will be useful to distinguish between two types of gestures, consonant gestures and vowel gestures. In response to Smith's (1995) treatment of these as phonological categories, Ogden (1995) points out that '[t]he terms "consonant" and "vowel" in Articulatory Phonology need formal definition', going on to say that 'it is the degree of stiffness specified in the task dynamic model which determines consonantality (Browman and Goldstein 1990b: 306)'. Sproat and Fujimura (1993: 304) respond to this relative lack of definition, proposing that 'gestures can be characterised as either intrinsically *consonantal* or intrinsically *vocalic*', where 'consonantal' gestures are defined as those that 'produce an extreme obstruction in the vocal tract' (cf. the phonological feature [consonantal]), and 'vocalic' gestures as those that produce no extreme obstruction, or actively produce an opening, as in the case of the velum-lowering gesture for nasals. This definition of gestural categories will be used in the following sections.

12.2.2.1 Intergestural timing: configurational properties of gestures

Studies of the coordination of component gestures within traditional segments have revealed a patterned timing distinction between initial and final allophones (Krakow 1989; Browman and Goldstein 1992, 1995; Sproat and Fujimura 1993; Wang 1995). In terms of the two categories of gestures described above, the following generalisation can be stated based on Sproat and Fujimura's findings: In initial allophones, consonantal gestures (such as the tongue tip [TT] constriction of /l/) tend to occur earlier than, or simultaneous with, vocalic gestures; in final allophones, this generalisation is roughly reversed. Sproat and Fujimura call this coda effect 'tip delay', in reference to the fact that the TT gesture of /l/ is achieved later than the tongue dorsum (TD) gesture in final allophones.

The results of an attempt to replicate these timing results for /l/, and to further observe them in the glides, will be reported in the Experiment section below. Based on the gestural definition of ambisyllabicity proposed in Section

12.2.1, we should expect ambisyllabic gestures to show a pattern of relative timing that is between those of initial and final allophones.

12.2.2.2 Final reduction: scaling properties of gestures

'Final reduction' has also been observed to distinguish initial and final allophones in a wide variety of segments (Giles and Moll 1975; Hardcastle and Barry 1989; Browman and Goldstein 1992, 1995; Byrd 1996; Gick forthcoming). This term refers to the observation that the gestures of syllable-final allophones are smaller in magnitude (scaling) than the corresponding gestures of initial allophones. Essentially this same observation (though with some important distinctions that will not be detailed here) has also been referred to as 'initial strengthening' (see Keating *et al.*, this volume). The term 'reduction' will be adopted arbitrarily for the present purposes without implying that the initial allophone is necessarily the more 'basic' one.

Most of the gestures that have been tested for this property would be classified as consonantal under Sproat and Fujimura's definition. There is a small amount of evidence suggesting that vocalic gestures (e.g. the velum gesture of /m/ or the TD gesture of /l/) do not follow the same patterns of reduction as seen in consonantal gestures (Krakow 1989; Sproat and Fujimura 1993). This question will receive particular attention in the Experiment section.

As suggested above, in AP terms, final reduction may be analysed simply as the difference in scaling between a gesture being phased to a preceding vowel and a following vowel. Thus, we can predict that a word-final consonantal gesture will undergo less reduction when followed by a vowel-initial word than when followed by a consonant-initial word. Insufficient evidence exists upon which to form a solid hypothesis regarding vocalic gestures.

12.2.3 English liquids and glides

The articulatory properties of English liquids, particularly /l/, have been relatively well studied. The glides (both initial glides and final offglides), however, have received little attention. If the phonological evidence from 'glide formation' – the apparent 'augmentation' of final offglides when followed by a vowel-initial word or morpheme (Whorf 1943; Broadbent 1991; Harris 1995) – is any indication, investigation of these same properties in glides promises interesting results.

Glides offer the special advantage of being approximant in manner in all positions in English. American English /r/ shares this property, but cannot be included in the present study on the practical grounds that, given the current state of speech measurement technology, it is extremely difficult to collect data on the pharyngeal constriction of /r/ during speech (see Gick, forthcoming, for detailed discussion of this matter). This property of glides allows for measurement and comparison of small gradient variations in constriction degree, such as those predicted for final reduction, without the physical interference of contact surfaces such as the teeth or palate. It further enables us to categorise the component gestures of glides (the lip constriction and tongue dorsum backing of /w/ and the tongue body raising and fronting of /j/) as 'vocalic' under Sproat and Fujimura's definition. As most previous studies have concentrated on 'consonantal' gestures, such a study of glides provides a useful means for testing these gestural categories.

Certain predictions can be drawn from these properties of English glides. First, according to Sproat and Fujimura's model, the characteristic timing patterns observed in different allophones are due to their status as 'consonantal' or 'vocalic' (with vocalic gestures tending toward, and consonantal gestures away from, the syllable peak). If the component gestures of /w/ are indeed both vocalic, we must revise our hypothesis from Section 2.2.1, and predict that these timing variations will not appear in /w/. (English /j/ is generally considered to be composed of a single gesture and can therefore not be studied for internal timing – though see Keating 1988.) Rather, this view predicts that the /w/ gestures will occur simultaneously in all environments. Second, again assuming glide gestures to be vocalic, their pattern of magnitude reduction is predicted to be parallel to that of the dorsal gesture of /l/ (also a vocalic gesture).

A final note regarding English initial glides and diphthongal offglides: the phonological status of and relationship between the onset glides /w, j/ and diphthongal offglides /u̯, i̯/ have been somewhat controversial. The two have been considered distinct by many modern phonologists, with the latter considered by some to be part of the syllable nucleus. As mentioned above, however, diphthongal offglides appear to undergo at least partial resyllabification – a surprising property if they are indeed simply nuclear vowels. More importantly, purely in terms of their gestural componency, these traditionally distinct segments must be considered to be equivalent to pre- and post-vocalic allophones of other segments (e.g. /l, lʸ/). That is, they apparently involve the same gestures (lip constriction and tongue dorsum backing for /w, u̯/, tongue body raising and fronting for /j, i̯/). According to the present model, the variations between pre- and postvocalic instantiations of these gestures result from phasing relationships with flanking vowels, not from higher-level (segmental) categorisations.

12.3 Experiment

An experiment was conducted to test the predictions outlined in the previous section. Pre- and postvocalic allophones of /l/, /w/ and /j/ were measured with the goal of identifying characteristic properties of consonantal and vocalic gestures in various positions, and the effects of across-word-boundary resyllabification on these properties.

12.3.1 Method

12.3.1.1 Subjects
Three native speakers of American English were recorded: JC (female, central New Jersey, early twenties), EM (male, central Maine, early thirties) and MR (male, Southern California, mid twenties). All subjects were students or colleagues from Yale University or Haskins Laboratories. Several potential subjects were interviewed in advance of the experiment to test for vowel quality. Subjects were rejected whose dialects had incomparable vowels qualities within relevant comparison pairs (i.e. if a subject had a low, front [a] in *ha*, he or she was required to have a very similar vowel in *hall, how* and *hie*).

12.3.1.2 Stimuli
Stimuli were developed to allow for controlled comparison of ambiguously and unambiguously syllabified word-final allophones of English glides and liquids. Word-initial allophones were also collected. The strategy in constructing stimuli was to create a minimally distinct environment, always using identical words to contain the relevant final glide or liquid (changing only the presence or absence of a following word-initial consonant). /h/ was chosen as the intervening word-initial consonant to establish the following syllable boundary without in any way interfering with the movement of the oral articulators. Otherwise, the relevant glide or liquid was between low vowels. To establish this controlled phonetic environment, it was necessary to use nonsensical word combinations in a uniform carrier phrase – standard practice for experiments of this kind.

Thus, the crucial pair of words used to compare final and ambiguously syllabified allophones of /l/ was *hall hotter* versus *hall otter*; for /w/, *how hotter* versus *how otter*; and for /j/, *hie hotter* versus *hie otter*. Initial allophones were also collected, using *ha lotter, ha wadder* and *ha yotter*, respectively (for JC, minimally distinct initial allophones were not collected; initials were taken from tokens *the water* and *how'd water*). To avoid list effects, initial [p] was also used for the first word in the pair (*pa, pall, pow, pie*). Accent on the preceding vowel was effectively maintained by alternating only the first word of each pair within each block of 8 to 12 sentences. In addition, subjects were explicitly instructed to accent the first word of each pair. Within this overall structure, stimuli were presented in random order, in carrier phrases of the form: 'There was a __ in the house' (for JC and EM), or 'I say __ again' (for MR). /l/ tokens were collected for subject MR only.

228

12.3.1.3 Procedure

Subjects were instructed to read stimuli aloud from written lists of 8 to 12 tokens per page in their normal speech and at a comfortable pace.

Data were collected using EMMA (electromagnetic midsagittal articulometer – see Perkell *et al.* 1992), a three-coil transmitter system at Haskins Labs, New Haven, CT. Small receivers were attached to subjects' tongue, lips, mandible, maxilla and nose bridge, with the latter two used for correction of head movement in the midsagittal plane. Voltages induced in the receivers by three fixed electromagnets situated around the subject's head were used to determine location of the receivers in the midsagittal plane. Movement data were sampled at 625Hz for JC and EM, 500Hz for MR. The following receivers and dimensions were used in this experiment: /l/, tongue tip (TT) fronting, tongue dorsum (TD) horizontal; /w/, upper and lower lip (UL, LL) vertical, and TD horizontal; /j/, tongue body (TB) horizontal and vertical (TD was used for MR, because of a bad TB receiver).

12.3.2 Results

All subjects successfully read stimuli with the intended stress pattern and at a comfortable speaking rate. Movement data were analysed using the HADES program (Rubin 1995). Locations of closure achievement were automatically selected from velocity signals (first derivative) calculated from the relevant movement signals, by locating the point at 3 percent short of zero velocity (of the total velocity range for that articulator in that dimension). Movement trajectory maxima and minima were automatically located in movement signals. Between 8 and 12 tokens were originally collected for each condition. Due to minor design changes over the course of the experiment dictated by data-collection time limitations (receivers only stay attached to articulators for a limited time), as well as the occasional unusable token, the final number of repetitions collected and analysed for each subject and condition were:

/w/: JC initial (9), final (9), ambiguous (8); EM initial (12), final (6), ambiguous (12); MR initial (8), final (9), ambiguous (8).

/j/: JC initial (8), final (9), ambiguous (9); EM initial (8), final (8), ambiguous (8); MR initial (10), final (7), ambiguous (9).

/l/: MR initial (8), final (8), ambiguous (8).

Separate one-way analyses of variance (ANOVA) were used to compare mean durations and magnitudes for each subject's productions of each segment across the three syllable positions.

12.3.2.1 /l/: Replication of Sproat and Fujimura (1993)

As noted above, /l/ was collected for only one subject (MR). Figure 12.1 shows results for all three measures of /l/: (a) magnitude (spatial displacement) of the

TT fronting gesture, (b) magnitude of the TD backing gesture and (c) the temporal offset ('tip delay') between the two gestures.

In Figure 12.1(a), mean spatial maxima are shown for the consonantal gesture (TT fronting), with post-hoc tests revealing a significant final reduction effect (leftmost column versus rightmost column, $p < .01$). While there appears to be a tendency toward the predicted intermediate magnitude for the ambiguously syllabified case (centre column), the effect is not significant (initial versus ambiguous, $p < .25$; final versus ambiguous, $p < .12$).

Figure 12.1(b) shows the vocalic gesture (TD backing) to be unaffected by syllable position.

Figure 12.1(c) shows the mean temporal difference between achievement of TT fronting and TD retraction: a positive value indicates that the achievement of the TD gesture occurred earlier than the TT gesture, while a negative value indicates that TT preceded TD. The timing tendencies predicted for initial versus final /l/ based on Sproat and Fujimura's (1993) findings are reflected here, but are again not significant (leftmost versus rightmost column, $p < .06$). The ambiguously syllabified /l/ shows no tendency to stray from the final pattern, again showing a positive lag that is not significantly different from the negative lag of the initial /l/ (centre versus leftmost column, $p < .10$). As Figure 12.4 below will also show, MR exhibited much higher variability in timing than the other two subjects.

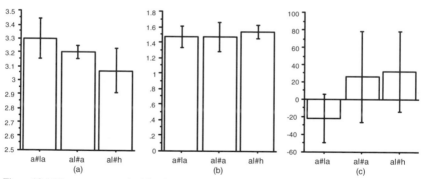

Figure 12.1 Three measures of subject MR's productions of /l/. Graphs compare: (a) mean TT fronting (in cm) for initial, ambiguous and final positions; (b) mean TD backing (in cm); (c) tip delay (in ms). Error bars indicate 95% confidence interval

12.3.2.2 /w/

Figures 12.2 to 12.5 show results for all three subjects' productions of /w/.

In Figure 12.2, despite its being an approximant (vocalic) constriction, final reduction (white columns) is present in the lip-closure gesture for all three subjects, as is the intermediate degree of constriction in ambiguously syllabified tokens (shaded columns). All differences are significant ($p < .05$).

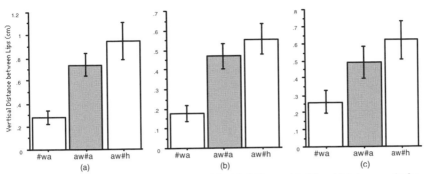

Figure 12.2 Lip aperture in initial, ambiguous and final /w/. Figures (a), (b) and (c) show results for subjects JC, EM and MR, respectively. Columns show mean vertical distance between upper and lower lip receivers (in cm). White bars show final reduction effect; shaded bars show intermediate degree of constriction. Error bars indicate a 95% confidence interval

In contrast to this, Figure 12.3 shows two different patterns: JC's and MR's patterns in (a) and (c) are statistically the same, with both exhibiting significant final reduction but with no significant intermediate magnitudes in ambiguous cases (i.e. leftmost columns are distinct from both right and centre columns, p < .05; right and centre columns do not differ significantly for all subjects). For subject EM (b), neither effect is present for TD backing (cf. Figure 12.1(b).

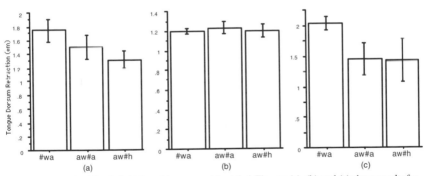

Figure 12.3 TD backing in initial, ambiguous and final /w/. Figures (a), (b) and (c) show results for subjects JC, EM and MR, respectively. Columns show mean horizontal positions of TD receiver (in cm) at maximum retraction. Error bars indicate 95% confidence interval

Figure 12.4 shows a significant effect (p < .05) of 'lip delay' distinguishing initial allophones from ambisyllabic and final allophones for all subjects. Contrary to expectations based on Sproat and Fujimura's findings, no intermediate effect is observed for timing (cf. Figure 12.3(a, c). Figure 12.5 illustrates an example comparison of lip delay from the actual movement data.

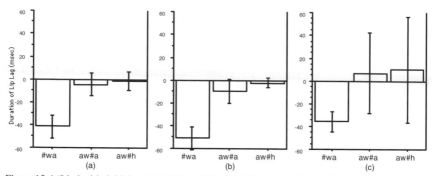

Figure 12.4 'Lip lag' in initial, ambisyllabic and final /w/. Figures (a), (b) and (c) show results for subjects JC, EM and MR, respectively. Columns show mean temporal difference between achievement of lip constriction and TD retraction (in ms). Error bars indicate a 95% confidence interval

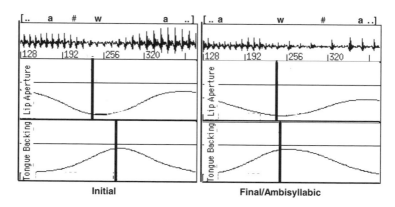

Figure 12.5 Example of intergestural timing in allophones of /w/ for subject EM. Bold vertical lines mark achievement of gestures

12.3.2.3 /j/

Figure 12.6 shows magnitude effects for the TB raising and fronting gesture (TD for subject MR) for all three subjects. The possibility of /j/ containing two distinct component gestures (e.g. tongue body and blade; Keating 1988) was pursued, but without results. It is thus tentatively concluded that /j/ indeed contains only a single gesture. Final reduction effects are significant for all three subjects ($p < .001$), but no intermediate effect can be seen in ambisyllabic cases.

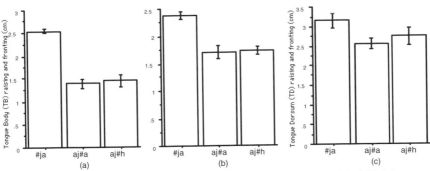

Figure 12.6 Tongue body/dorsum raising and fronting in initial, ambisyllabic and final /j/. Columns show mean Euclidian distances calculated from vertical and horizontal maxima of tongue body (tongue dorsum for MR) receiver (in cm). Error bars indicate 95% confidence interval

12.3.3 Discussion

Two gestures were measured for /l/ and /w/, and one for /j/. For most measures, /w/ and /l/ follow similar patterns in these data, though effects are less pronounced for MR's /l/ than for either the present subjects' productions of /w/, or for the /l/'s reported by Sproat and Fujimura. Some of the predicted gestural evidence for ambisyllabicity was found.

It was predicted in Section 12.2.2 that the present experiment would reveal an intermediate effect in the magnitude of, and timing between, component gestures of American English /l/ and glides. In addition to the (not statistically significant) tendency apparent in the TT gesture of /l/, the shaded bars in Figure 12.2 show evidence of resyllabification in the lip gesture of /w/ (see Gick, forthcoming, for similar results for /r/). The TD gestures of /l/ and /w/, and the TB gesture of /j/ show no evidence for a tendency to resyllabify.

The timing 'tip lag' tendency predicted for /l/ on the basis of Sproat and Fujimura's (1993) findings is also apparent in the present data, though again not significant. Similar (though significant) effects were seen in /w/: contrary to the hypothesis in Section 12.2.3, the gestures of /w/ were not found to be simultaneous. Rather, they follow a 'lip lag' pattern falling within the ranges cited for /l/ by Sproat and Fujimura (1993: 299). Not present in any of the timing effects, however, was the predicted intermediate effect in ambiguously syllabified allophones. It is unlikely that this is due to lack of resyllabification across the word boundary, as both /l/ and /w/ showed the effects of resyllabification in their magnitudes (though in only one gesture each).

12.3.3.1 C-gestures and V-gestures

One point in need of some discussion, and perhaps re-evaluation, regards Sproat and Fujimura's definition of the two categories of gestures, 'consonantal' and 'vocalic'. On the basis of their definition, it was hypothesised in Section 12.2.3 that both gestures of /w/ (because of their relatively open constriction degree) would follow typically vocalic patterns. However, while an analogy can easily be argued for between the TD gestures of /l, w/ and the TB gesture of /j/, the lip gesture of /w/, on the contrary, appears to follow closely all of the patterns predicted for consonantal gestures (final reduction, intermediate magnitude under resyllabification, and tendency away from peak vowel). This interpretation of /w/, while not the predicted one, is consistent with a number of previous findings from the phonological and perception literatures.

Anderson (1976) cites cross-linguistic evidence that, in some languages, the 'primary' articulation of labiovelars, including /w/, is the labial, while in other languages it seems to be the velar. In a recent perception study of American English glides, Lisker (1995) concludes that the primary articulation of /w/ in that dialect is indeed the lip gesture. These cases do not, however, clearly equate 'primary' with 'consonantal' articulations. Such evidence may be provided by onset cluster phonotactics.

Homorganic consonant clusters are generally banned in English onsets (Clements and Keyser 1983: 41; Harris 1994: 57, etc.). While the clusters in *twin, dwarf, quick* and *guava* present no conflict, no English words may begin with *pw-, *bw-, *fw- or *vw-. Compare this with the corresponding pattern for /l/: pl-, bl-, fl-, kl-, gl-, but *tl-, *dl-. Thus, the lip gesture of /w/ appears not only to be 'primary', but also 'consonantal', specifically conflicting with other labial (but not velar) consonants – and following a phonotactic pattern parallel to that of the coronal 'consonant' gesture of /l/.

Our experimental results, in addition to the above phonological and perception evidence, thus support the analysis of the lip gesture of /w/ as a 'consonantal' gesture. If this is true, however, then the previous definition of these categories (by constriction degree) must be amended. To eliminate this conflict, I propose the terms 'C-gesture' and 'V-gesture', designating these two gestural types as language-specific, phonologically specified categories (cf. Smith's 1995, need for specified 'consonant' and 'vowel' gestures). This analysis is consistent with Anderson's (1976) observation that the same gesture may be categorised differently in different languages or dialects.

12.3.3.2 A word on V-gestures

Under the hypotheses of the present study, the properties defining a C-gesture have been laid out: (1) final reduction, (2) intermediate magnitude under resyllabification and (3) tendency away from peak vowel. According to this framework, the TT and lip gestures of /l/ and /w/, respectively, are C-gestures, leaving the TD gestures of /w/ and /l/ and the TB gesture of /j/ as V-gestures. This, however may ultimately turn out to be an oversimplification: while there is no evidence for (2) or (3) in any of the supposed V-gestures, the final reduction effect (1) does appear in the V-gestures of both glides (except for EM's /w/). This could simply mean that final reduction is a freely varying feature of V-gestures, or it may indicate a third class of 'glide' gestures. More data will be required to differentiate between these possibilities.

A related issue regarding the glides is the fact that, in the present model, /w/ involves a C-gesture and /j/ does not. We should expect this difference in gestural composition between /w/ and /j/ to be reflected in the status of these segments in other realms (phonology, perception, development, etc.). Such a difference may be found in the phonologically based stance of numerous researchers (Clements and Keyser 1983; Davis and Hammond 1995, etc.) that /j/ – as an onglide, an offglide, or both – should be considered part of the phonological nucleus, even in cases where a corresponding /w/ would be part of the onset. Further support for this distinct categorisation of /j/ can be found in the phonological development literature, where Barlow (1995) shows that for many children, while /w/, /r/ and /l/ pattern with other consonants in onset clusters, /j/ is treated more like a vowel. Such asymmetries, not easily accounted for by previous segmental theories, are consistent with the present results.

12.4 Conclusion

This paper has proposed an analysis of syllable-based allophony in which traditional segments are composed of two types of gestures, C-gestures and V-gestures, which are phased with respect to each other, in fixed, language-particular patterns. Gestural resyllabification effects were observed, providing evidence that a gesture can be simultaneously phased to flanking syllable peaks (ambisyllabicity). The present data thus lend further support to gesture-based theories of the syllable, such as those previously proposed by Krakow (1989), Browman and Goldstein (1992, 1995), Sproat and Fujimura (1993) and others. This model of syllable structure has here and previously been shown to account for a wide variety of phonological phenomena.

Properties distinguishing initial from final allophones of /l/ and glides were found, as expected from previous results, to be twofold: compared to initials, final allophones show a reduction in magnitude of the C-gesture and a relative temporal 'lag' of the C-gesture with respect to the V-gesture. Ambisyllabic allophones (here, lexically final gestures phased across a word boundary) show a sensitivity to following context, but this is only manifest in gestural magnitude, and only in one type of gesture: the C-gesture. It is concluded that it is precisely this effect that underlies the phonetic distinction between syllable-final and ambisyllabic allophones, and that reference to gestures is necessary to account for these traditionally segment-level patterns.

Notes

The author wishes to thank Louis Goldstein and Doug Whalen for continued discussion and support, Peter Ladefoged, Diamandis Gafos, Steve Anderson, two anonymous reviewers and the volume editors for many helpful comments, and Masanobu Kumada, Dani Byrd and Vince Gracco for assistance at various points in the data collection and analysis. Work supported by NIH grants DC-02717 and HD-01994 to Haskins Labs and an NSF Graduate Fellowship to the author.

1   Although AP treats segments and other supragestural phonological categories (including syllables) as epiphenomenal, the particularly 'tight' gestural relationships within traditional segments have been recognised (Byrd 1996; Gick 1999). The present paper assumes that these gestural relationships themselves determine the higher-level categories. Whether this truly invalidates the categories as independent units, however, is controversial, and beyond the scope of the present paper. In any case, traditional terminology will be used throughout for ease of discussion.

13

Extrinsic phonetic interpretation: spectral variation in English liquids

PAUL CARTER

13.1 Introduction

Much recent phonology presupposes intrinsic phonetic interpretation, in which phonological features are effectively phonetic features. In an intrinsic model such as Bromberger and Halle (1989), the phonology organises the phonetics in the sense that features have binary values in phonology; the same features appear with scalar values in the phonetics. Phonological structure is effectively an arrangement of phonetic content.

Extrinsic Phonetic Interpretation (EPI) makes use of abstract phonological categories which are related to, but do not equate to, phonetic features (Local 1995a). EPI mechanisms are found in some contemporary frameworks, particularly in those versions of Declarative Phonology influenced by Firthian Prosodic Analysis (Local 1995a; Local and Simpson 1999; Ogden 1993, 1999a, 1999b; Ogden *et al.*, 2000). In such approaches, phonology is made up not of phonetic features but of abstract relational categories primarily concerned with contrast and not uniquely associated with phonetic events. EPI forces the analyst to recognise the need for explicit phonetic interpretation. In this paper I will argue that EPI provides for a felicitous account of phonetic variation and phonological abstraction.

This paper examines the case of secondary articulations in English liquids from a declarative phonology/EPI perspective, outlining the structure-dependent and dialect-specific aspects of their phonetic implementation, thereby extending the work of Kelly and Local (1986, 1989) to rhotic varieties

237

of English and testing the predictions made by Sproat and Fujimura (1993) against data from other varieties. The data of phonetic variation are shown to militate against a universalist interpretation of analyses such as Sproat and Fujimura (1993) and Huffman (1997) which relies on phonetic detail intrinsic to phonological representations.

13.2 Complex segments

Laterals are an often-cited case of secondary articulation, though the literature on articulatory settings (Honikman 1964) and other reports (for example in Kelly and Local 1989) suggest that secondary articulation appears with a much wider set of phonetic events than laterals and that what is secondary in a degree of stricture sense may in fact be an important part of the phonetics of any given stretch of speech.

Multiple articulations such as liquids are complex not only in a featural sense, but also temporally: there are often constraints on the relative timing of articulations which must be accounted for either in phonological representation or in phonetic implementation. Ladefoged and Maddieson (1996) suggest this may be perceptually motivated: perception may be aided by the phasing of gestures so that the transitions typical of one are found coming into an occlusion while transitions typical of another appear out of an occlusion. Their comments on secondary articulations will be discussed in Section 13.3.2.

13.3 Laterals in English

13.3.1 Allophony

The distinction between clear and dark laterals in English is well known, with comments on the subject going back at least as far as Sweet (1908). There is disagreement as to whether this clear/dark relationship should be encoded at a level of phonology (work such as Bladon and Al-Bamerni, 1976, assumes discrete allophones) or whether the observable facts can be accounted for by some sort of natural phonetic process. Sproat and Fujimura (1993) belong in this second camp.

Most work on laterals in English refers only to varieties which have a relatively clear initial lateral and a relatively dark final lateral. This is the case, for instance, in Bladon and Al-Bamerni (1976), Sproat and Fujimura (1993) and Huffman (1997). However, it is well known (Wells 1982) that there are varieties of English with noticeably clear laterals in all positions and, conversely, varieties with noticeably dark laterals in all positions. This paper examines some of this wider range of varieties.

13.3.2 A gestural account

Sproat and Fujimura's (1993) articulatory analysis of laterals in English puts forward an explanation for the allophony associated with the secondary articulation of laterals which, while not actually universalist, nevertheless claims to set out natural phonetic tendencies with which languages are predicted to comply.

They divide the articulation into two gestures: a consonantal apical gesture and a vocalic dorsal gesture compatible with Coleman's (1992) phonological analysis. Consonantal gestures are assumed to be attracted to syllable margins and assumed to be weaker syllable-finally than they are syllable-initially; vocalic gestures are assumed to be attracted to syllable nuclei and assumed to be weaker syllable-initially than they are syllable-finally (pp. 305-6). Sproat and Fujimura reach this conclusion from articulatory data which show syllable-initial laterals having a prominent apical gesture followed by a less prominent dorsal gesture whereas syllable-final laterals have a prominent dorsal gesture followed by a weaker apical gesture which may undershoot. This analysis accounts for laterals being darker in syllable-final position than they are in syllable-initial position.

Figure 13.1 gives a schematised overview of such an analysis, with vocalic gestures associated with the syllable nucleus and consonantal gestures associated with the syllable margins.

Ladefoged and Maddieson (1996: 361) dispute Sproat and Fujimura's analysis, giving the example of many speakers of American English who have dark laterals in all positions. Slow F2 transitions are identified as being indicative of the relatively slow dorsal gesture involved in 'velarisation'. A low F2 in the lateral indicates velarisation. By Sproat and Fujimura's predictions, the gradual F2 transition into a final velarised lateral should be mirrored by a gradual F2 transition out of an initial velarised lateral. Spectrographic evidence shows this not to be the case.

Sproat and Fujimura's paper is far from unusual in accounting for some well-known phenomenon in terms of a natural articulatory explanation. The present study aims to extend Sproat and Fujimura's work beyond articulatory phonetics and beyond laterals by concentrating on acoustics and by including rhotics in an attempt to see if a natural articulatory explanation is adequate to explain data which are phonologically similar but which come from a wider range of varieties of English.

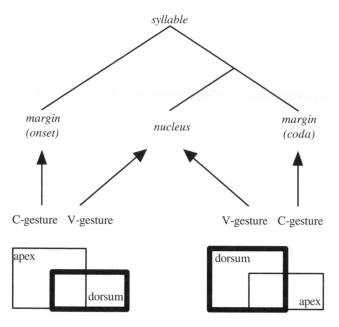

Figure 13.1 Schematic view of Sproat and Fujimura's (1993) gestural account of laterals in English. Consonantal gestures are attracted to syllable margins; vocalic gestures are attracted to syllable nuclei

13.4 Liquids in English

13.4.1 A liquid class

Evidence for a liquid class in English is primarily distributional and contrastive. That is, phonological evidence supports phonological categories. Liquids in English show certain distributional regularities, such as being the only consonantal articulations which may follow *[s] + plosive* in onset clusters.

13.4.2 Kelly and Local

Kelly and Local (1986, 1989) reported on long-domain effects of secondary articulations in laterals and rhotics. They examined (acoustically and impressionistically) two varieties of British English, focusing on the clearness or darkness of liquids and also the relative clearness or darkness of vocoids in the vicinity of liquids. They found the following polarities: speakers with a clear initial lateral had a dark initial rhotic; speakers with a dark initial lateral had a clear initial rhotic. They make no explicit predictions regarding relationships between liquids in syllable-final position, since the varieties they examined are nonrhotic. For the same reason, they do not make predictions about what patterns may be present in rhotic varieties of English.

13.4.3 Dialect typology

Kelly and Local's work, amongst others, shows that there is a spread of dialectal variation within the liquid system of English. The most well-known liquid system shibboleth for dialects of English is rhoticity, but clearness and darkness also appear to play an important part in dialectal differences. Kelly and Local are unusual in mentioning clearness and darkness in the context of [r] as well as [l] (following IPA conventions, I am using broad transcription with Roman letters rather than special characters). Most recent work on [r], such as Alwan *et al.* (1997) or Westbury *et al.* (1995), makes no reference to such patternings. A noticeable exception is Harris (1994: 259), who discusses clear and dark [r] cross-dialectally; Harris makes no connection with resonance quality in [l]. Kelly and Local, however, make no predictions regarding rhotic varieties of English. This paper examines how well their results stand up in rhotic varieties.

13.5 Overview of experiments

The data were recorded on DAT in the sound studio of the Department of Language and Linguistic Science at the University of York then resampled at 11025Hz into an SGI computer running Entropic's *ESPS* and *xwaves* analysis package.

13.5.1 Speakers

The speech of four speakers was examined. All speakers were males, between twenty and thirty years old and educated to university level. The speakers spoke with British regional varieties chosen to be representative of wider dialect groups within the language. Two variables were selected in order to classify the varieties for the purposes of this study.

Rhoticity versus nonrhoticity in the variety was an obvious candidate to use as a variable. The second variable involves clearness and darkness of syllable-initial laterals, since previous work on resonance qualities associated with liquids has tended to concentrate on laterals.

Table 13.1 shows the varieties of English examined. Sunderland (north-east England) English is a clear initial [l] nonrhotic variety; County Tyrone (Northern Ireland) English is a clear initial [l] rhotic variety; Manchester (north-west England) English is a dark initial [l] nonrhotic variety; Fife (east

Scotland) English is a dark initial [l] rhotic variety. All speakers used approximant productions of [r].

Table 13.1 *Varieties of English examined*

	Nonrhotic	Rhotic
Clear initial lateral	Sunderland	Co. Tyrone
Dark initial lateral	Manchester	Fife

13.5.2 Word lists

Sixteen representative lexemes (Table 13.2) were extracted from the full set of recorded data for the purpose of these experiments. Each lexeme is an actually-occurring English monosyllable.

Table 13.2 *Lexemes investigated in the experiment, arranged by phonological structure*

	front vowel context		back vowel context	
high vowel context	lead	reed	loot	root
	deal	deer	tool	tour
low vowel context	lap	rap	law	raw
	pal	par	all	oar

Each lexeme includes exactly one liquid in either initial or final position in the syllable. The lexemes are arranged so that there is a set of minimal contrasts which (at least for the speakers of rhotic varieties) have lateral versus rhotic articulations as their phonetic exponents.

The vocalic contexts in which the liquids were placed vary along the dimensions of phonological height and frontness versus backness ([a] and [ɑ] are conflated and counted as 'front' since they are in complementary distribution in rhotic varieties). These contrasts represent, as far as is allowable within the constraints of the English lexicon, extremes of the vocoid quality continua.

The lexemes were embedded in the frame '*Say ... again*' and recorded in blocks of ten in combination with filler words included to avoid effects of list prosody. Two tokens of each lexeme were elicited from each speaker.

13.6 Spectral analysis

Values were taken for F1, F2 and F3 in the liquid portion of each lexeme, at a relatively steady state or at the mid-point in the liquid using autocorrelation spectra with a 25ms hanning window. All measurements were checked by visual inspection of wideband spectrograms: where autocorrelation-derived values differed greatly from the spectrogram, estimates of formant frequencies were taken from DFT spectra.

Spectral analysis involved two distinct methods: firstly an examination of relationships between F2 values (chosen as an indicator of darkness) and, secondly, the statistical technique of cluster analysis.

13.6.1 F2 relationships

F2 frequencies measured in Hertz were bark-scaled. Figures 13.2 and 13.3 show the means and standard deviations of the bark transform of F2 first for nonrhotic then for rhotic varieties.

13.6.1.1 Nonrhotic varieties
Both nonrhotic varieties have laterals which are darker finally than initially, in accordance with Sproat and Fujimura's predictions. This difference is less pronounced in the dark initial [l] variety, perhaps due to some constraint on how much darker final [l] may be than initial [l], given a dark starting point. This is not unlike an interpretation given by Huffman (1997: 139) for some of her data on intervocalic [l].

Final tokens have been excluded from the data of nonrhotic speakers in Figure 13.2. This is because final liquids are not contrastive in these tokens, since syllable-final [r] is present only in juncture. In this way, a clearer picture is given of how liquids pattern within the contrastive systems employed by these speakers.

In keeping with Kelly and Local's polarities, the clear initial [l] variety has a relatively clear [l] and a relatively dark [r] whereas the dark initial [l] variety has a relatively dark [l] and a relatively clear [r]. Manchester laterals are darker than Sunderland laterals; Manchester rhotics are clearer than Sunderland rhotics.

The longer-domain effects reported by Kelly and Local are also supported in that Sunderland vocoids have a higher F2 at their mid-point after [l] than after [r] and Manchester vocoids have a lower F2 after [l] than after [r].

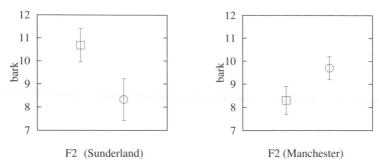

Figure 13.2 Mean bark-scaled F2 in initial liquids for nonrhotic speakers (error bars indicate standard deviation). Squares represent laterals; circles represent rhotics

13.6.1.2 Rhotic varieties

Rhotic speakers show different F2 patterns from nonrhotic speakers: despite the variation in quality of initial [l], the same pattern of relationships in resonance quality is shown in both rhotic varieties (Figure 13.3). Final liquid qualities are appropriately represented here since rhotic varieties have contrasts at that place in structure.

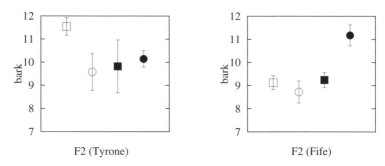

Figure 13.3 Mean bark-scaled F2 in liquids for rhotic speakers (error bars indicate standard deviation). Squares represent laterals; circles represent rhotics. Open shapes represent initial liquids; filled shapes represent final liquids

The Tyrone speaker has clearer [l] initially than finally but the Fife speaker has no significant difference between initial and final [l]. Both rhotic speakers have darker initial [r] than initial [l]. There is no evidence of the pattern Kelly and Local found for nonrhotic varieties: initial [r] in the dark initial lateral variety is not clearer than the initial [l] as it is in Manchester. Differences are minimised in the dark initial [l] variety, with the exception of final [r], which is considerably clearer than other liquids. Once again, this could be due to a putative lower limit on darkness: if initial [l] is dark, then there is not much acoustic space in which to squeeze a final [l] and an initial [r], both of which must be darker than the initial [l] if the rhotic variety pattern is to be maintained.

This rhotic pattern fits neatly with Lehiste's (1964a) data. Her speaker GEP is a good example of the distinction which must be drawn between absolute clearness or darkness on the one hand and relative clearness or darkness on the other: like the Fife speaker, his initial laterals are (in an absolute sense) dark, but they count as clear within his system since they are clearer than either his final laterals or his initial rhotics.

In post-liquid vocoids, the rhotic varieties outlined here show the same pattern as the clear initial [l] nonrhotic variety, namely that F2 is higher in vocoids which follow [l] than in those which follow [r].

13.6.1.3 Summary of F2 space analysis

There are three major results stemming from this study:

(1) Initial laterals are clearer than final laterals as Sproat and Fujimura report (Section 13.3.2);

(2) Nonrhotic varieties pattern as Kelly and Local suggest (Section 13.4.2);

(3) Rhotic varieties have a fixed pattern of resonance qualities similar to that of the clear initial [l] nonrhotic variety, not dependent on absolute values for clearness or darkness.

Two principles can be drawn from these findings.

The first principle is Extrinsic Phonetic Interpretation. Patterns of phonetic detail which interact with phonological categories in a partly absolute, partly relative, fashion demand an extrinsic interpretation function. In a dark initial [l] rhotic variety, a phonologically 'clear' [l] (clear because of the relationships it enters into with other phonological categories in the syllable) can be phonetically dark: there is no sense in which the lateral is intrinsically clear.

Secondly, there is a principle of maximal differentiation in extrinsic phonetic interpretation which may be phrased: 'differentiate categories maximally in the phonetic space.'

For nonrhotic varieties, maximal differentiation predicts that [l] will be as different as possible from [r]. There is no contrast in syllable-final position so syllable-initial liquids do not have to be differentiated from syllable-final liquids: syllable position does not therefore enter into the equation. Given that resonance qualities are available as a strategy for differentiation, one liquid will be clear and the other dark, and it does not matter which is which. Maximal differentiation thus predicts the variation in the pattern of clear and dark which is indeed found across nonrhotic varieties.

For rhotic varieties, syllable position matters since [l] and [r] contrast in both positions. If resonance quality is to be used to differentiate categories maximally in the phonetic space, then the pattern predicted will be one of the two outlined in Table 13.3.

Table 13.3 *Possible patterns of contrast in resonance predicted by maximal differentiation*

Pattern	Initial [l]	Initial [r]	Final [l]	Final [r]
(1)	clear	dark	dark	clear
(2)	dark	clear	clear	dark

If initial [l] is clear (pattern 1) then initial [r] must be dark for it to be maximally differentiated from the initial [l] (to reflect a contrast in liquid identity); final [l] must also be dark for it to be maximally differentiated from the initial [l] (to reflect a contrast in syllable position); final [r] must be clear for it to be maximally differentiated from both the initial [r] (to reflect a contrast in syllable position) and the final [l] (to reflect a contrast in liquid identity).

If initial [l] is dark (pattern 2) then the same relationships of contrast obtain, but all the values of clear and dark are reversed.

Given Sproat and Fujimura's finding that initial [l] is clearer than final [l] (ruling out pattern 2), maximal differentiation predicts that the resonance quality pattern for rhotic varieties should be pattern 1. Pattern 1 is indeed what is observed in the data.

13.6.2 Cluster analysis

Cluster analysis was performed in order to identify groups of cases within the data which have some internal similarity. It provides a principled method of sorting data where variables are not entirely independent (as is the case with formant frequencies).

If resonance quality has a noticeable effect on these data, the simple division between laterals and rhotics will be disrupted.

13.6.2.1 Distance metrics

In this study, values for F1, F2 and F3 were fed into the cluster analysis. It is essential for the difference between any one pair of formants to be comparable to the difference between any other pair of formants. The bark scale, being perceptually based, was therefore used. Distance between formants represented in bark can then be expressed in terms of simple Euclidean distance. Cluster analysis was performed using Ward's method.

13.6.2.2 Dendrograms

The sets in Figures 13.4 and 13.5 present in stylised Venn diagram form the dendrograms produced by the cluster analysis. Only stable splits in the data are portrayed in order that relatively robust clusters may be identified.

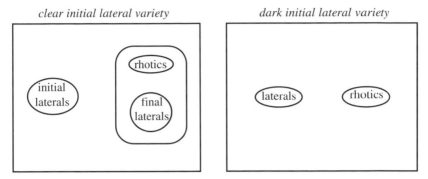

Figure 13.4 Summary of cluster analysis of bark-scaled F1 x F2 x F3 space: nonrhotic varieties

Figure 13.4 shows that in the clear initial [l] nonrhotic variety, the formant space is split into two, with initial laterals separated from other liquids. Final [l] is always dark and here patterns with [r] which, according to the F2 space analysis, is also dark. The observed split is therefore a clear/dark split, rather than the simple [l]/[r] split. The cluster analysis of the dark initial [l] variety produces the simple [l]/[r] split, but this is also a clear/dark split in this variety since laterals are dark initially as well as finally. Liquid identity ([l] versus [r]) explains one of these patterns, but resonance quality (clear versus dark) explains them both.

The clear initial [l] rhotic variety has more complex splits, although in essence the picture is similar to that found in the nonrhotic variety. Initial (clear) laterals are separated from other liquids, though some laterals found after clear (high, front) vocoids pattern with the initial laterals. Within the set containing the rest of the liquids, there is a clear/dark split with dark initial [r], dark final [l], and [r] after dark vocoids patterning together. However, in this case, an alternative analysis is equally tenable, namely that there is in fact a simple [l]/[r] split with only final [l] out of place. This simple split is what is found in the dark initial [l] rhotic variety.

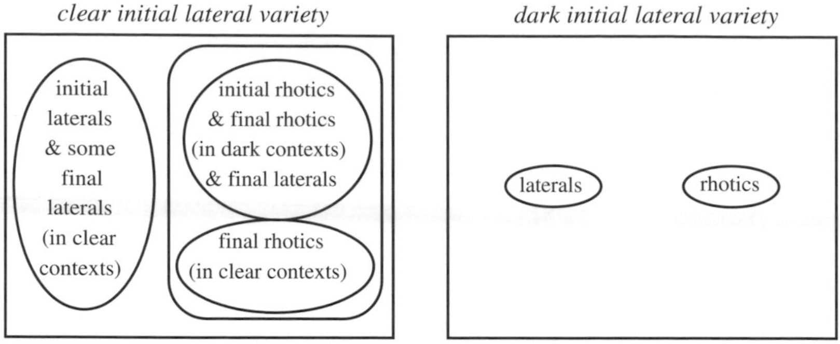

clear initial lateral variety   *dark initial lateral variety*

| initial laterals & some final laterals (in clear contexts) | initial rhotics & final rhotics (in dark contexts) & final laterals |
| | final rhotics (in clear contexts) |

laterals   rhotics

Figure 13.5 Summary of cluster analysis of bark-scaled F1 x F2 x F3 space: rhotic varieties

The cluster analysis suggests that resonance is important for nonrhotic varieties but may be less important for rhotic varieties.

13.7 Temporal analysis

13.7.1 Durational analysis

The focus of this paper is on spectral variation and indeed there appears to be no straightforward correlation in these data between duration of liquids and their identity as [l] or [r] in a given syllable position. Nevertheless, there are some durational observations worth making.

Sproat and Fujimura predict that initial laterals should be darker if they are of greater duration, since the dorsal gesture has more time to become prominent. This prediction was only in part borne out by Huffman (1997). The prediction is upheld in the clear initial [l] nonrhotic variety, but the dark initial [l] nonrhotic variety has the opposite pattern: the greater the duration of the initial lateral, the clearer that lateral becomes. This is an indication that phonetic parameters related to liquids are phased in different ways in different varieties. An opposite but less marked pattern appears in [r] in these varieties.

13.7.2 Relative timing of articulatory gestures

The data presented here support Ladefoged and Maddieson's (1996:361) criticism of Sproat and Fujimura regarding timing of F2 transitions (see Section 13.3.2), since F2 transitions in dark laterals seem to suggest dorsal gestures preceding apical gestures whether or not the lateral is in syllable-final position.

Figure 13.6 shows the duration in milliseconds of the F2 transition into and out of initial liquids in the nonrhotic varieties. The clear initial lateral variety has a longer transition into [r] than into [l]. Conversely, the dark initial lateral variety has a longer transition into [l] than into [r]. The pattern is reversed in transitions out of liquids.

Longer transitions may reflect relatively slow dorsal gestures while shorter transitions reflect relatively fast apical gestures. From Figure 13.6, it would seem that the clear initial [l] variety (Sunderland) might have a dorsal gesture timed before or at the same time as the apical gesture for [l] (since transitions into [l] are slower than transitions out of [l], though this is much more marked in the dark initial [l] variety, Manchester). The dark initial [l] variety appears to have a noticeably early dorsal gesture in [l], particularly when compared with [r]. The complete inversion of this pattern when examining the transitions out of initial liquids is evidence against the suggestion that slow transitions into dark liquids are merely an epiphenomenon related to the large displacement in F2 from the preceding vocoid in the carrier phrase (*'Say ...'*) into a portion with very low F2. These results are generally reflected in the rates of transition and may also account for the durational effect mentioned in Section 13.7.1.

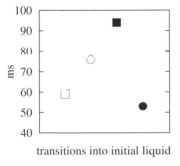 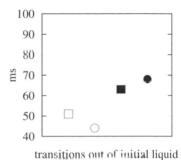

transitions into initial liquid   transitions out of initial liquid

Figure 13.6 Mean duration in milliseconds of transitions into and out of initial liquids; nonrhotic speakers. Squares represent laterals; circles represent rhotics. Open shapes represent values from the clear initial [l] variety (Sunderland); filled shapes represent values from the dark initial [l] variety (Manchester)

Sproat and Fujimura report an early dorsal gesture with final laterals and predict that initial laterals would have a relatively late (and relatively weak) dorsal gesture. This is evidently not the case for the Manchester speaker, who has noticeably dark laterals in all positions. The results presented here strongly imply that early dorsality is a marker of darkness rather than of syllable-finality.

As is the case with the F2 data presented in Section 13.6.1.2, rhotic varieties seem to pattern with the clear initial [l] nonrhotic variety, even if their laterals are phonetically dark.

13.8 Discussion

13.8.1 Gestural timing

The results outlined above suggest a model of gestural alignment closer to that in Figure 13.7 than that in Figure 13.1. Early dorsality is a marker not of syllable-finality but of darkness. The arrangement of gestures is not intrinsic to the phonology of syllable structure since it is dependent not only on position in structure but also on dialect-specific phonetic interpretation. A pan-dialectal phonology which encodes contrast thus requires an extrinsic phonetic interpretation function.

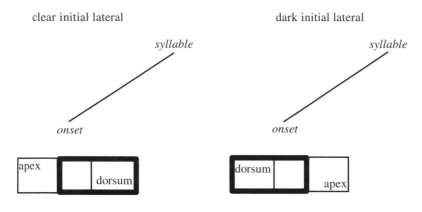

Figure 13.7 Gestural alignments for initial laterals showing dialect-specific gestural affinity

13.8.2 Feature alignment in the prosodic hierarchy

Given a (non-segmental) phonology (Local, 1992 1995a; Ogden 1992) where features or attributes are distributed across the prosodic hierarchy rather than being restricted to a terminal node or (auto-)segmental level, the issue of alignment of attributes in the hierarchy arises.

In an extrinsically-interpreted phonology, naming of attributes is arbitrary. There is nothing, aside from secondary considerations of parsimony, which prohibits the setting up of attributes relating to initial liquids which differ from those for final liquids. However, the patterning and interactions reported in this paper support the notion of a single liquid system with attributes at more than one place in the syllable. Whatever names are given to the liquid attributes, they are the same for initials as they are for finals.

If there is a single liquid system, then the phonological attributes of syllable-initial liquids must not conflict with the phonological attributes of syllable-final liquids. In practice, this means that neither of these two sets of attributes must dominate the other or occur at the same point in structure as the other. Liquid attributes may therefore not occur at syllable level since the syllable level dominates all other possible positions for the second set of attributes. The primary articulation of syllable-initial liquids precedes that of syllable-final liquids in time; the attributes of syllable-initial liquids must therefore be in onset position in order to comply with general constraints on the temporal extents of the phonetic exponents of syllable constituents (Local 1992; Ogden 1992; Coleman 1994a).

There are then three possible placements for final liquid attributes: nucleus, coda or rime. Nucleus-level attributes would threaten the generalisation that the nucleus bifurcates since liquids may follow long vowels (which can be represented as taking both nuclear places) and the association between consonantal material and the coda would be lost. On the other hand, vocalic lengthening effects such as those reported by Coleman (1994b) might suggest that laterals share some nature with vocoids, rather than being assigned, like consonants, to coda position. The historical vocalisation of rhotics and contemporary possibilities for vocalisation of laterals might suggest a compromise solution with rime liquids in nonrhotic varieties and coda liquids in rhotic varieties, but this solution would lose the generalisation of a pun-dialectal phonology.

There is yet another possibility, namely that the consonantal and vocalic attributes of liquids might be separated, with vocalic attributes at rime level and consonantal attributes at coda level. This analysis is appealing since it would result in the rime, as head of the syllable, carrying typically vocalic attributes and the coda consonantal ones. Since the phonetics of the rime begins earlier in time than the phonetics of the coda, this arrangement would make accurate predictions about phasing of gestures in syllable-final laterals, namely that the vocalic (rimal) dorsal gesture precedes the consonantal (coda) apical gesture. The lack of sub-structure in the onset analogous to the sub-structure of the rime means that no such constraints are placed on the timing of gestures in initial position, predicting variability in syllable-initial position, which is indeed what is found cross-dialectally. Moreover, this separation of vocalic attributes from consonantal attributes also predicts the sort of ambisyllabicity data reported by Gick (this volume) in that later coda gestures would have a greater affinity for the following syllable than would earlier rimal gestures, and so would vary more under conditions of ambisyllabicity.

13.9 Conclusion

The data pose problems for explanations based purely on articulatory dynamics. Sproat and Fujimura's results for laterals are generally supported here (with reservations regarding the phasing of gestures in dark initial laterals).

However, the fact that syllable-initial quality in a given variety is dependent on whether or not that variety is rhotic challenges universalist articulatory explanations since phonetic interpretation requires knowledge of nonlocal but tautosyllabic systems of contrast in addition to phonetic gestural information. Future articulatory work needs to recognise abstract phonological entities (and hence extrinsic phonetic interpretation) as well as phonetic data in order to make more accurate predictions about the constraints on phonetic interpretation.

Note

I wish to thank Peter Ladefoged, three anonymous reviewers and the phonetics and phonology research group in the University of York Department of Language and Linguistic Science for helpful comments on earlier versions of this paper. I remain solely responsible for any faults, errors or inaccuracies.

14

Temporal constraints and characterising syllable structuring

KENNETH DE JONG

14.1 Introduction: temporal constraint and the syllable

One of the most robust aspects of syntagmatic phonological patterning across languages is a strong tendency for consonants and vowels to collate with one another into structures of the size of a syllable. At the same time, an explicit and simple characterisation of the phonetics of syllables has yet to be found, leading many researchers to the conclusion that no such characterisation will ever be found. Syllabic patterning could be the result of a convergence of several different phonetic factors which each have their roots in different aspects of the speech communication process. In this paper, I will show evidence which indicates that one phonetic aspect of syllabic organisation is a tendency for gestures which inhabit particular locations in a syllable to have particular preferred intergestural timings. The evidence comes from a rate-controlled repetition experiment involving simple coda and onset structures.

The syllable has various uses in linguistic theory, many of which are reviewed in Blevins (1995). First, it acts as a foundational unit in prosodic organisation. Thus, it figures in the construction of prosodic trees and in various operations in prosodic morphology. Also, minimal words often consist of a single syllable in many languages. Second, the syllable often serves as the domain within which segmental cooccurrence restrictions are expressed. A common traditional argument for the syllable is the existence of phonotactic constraints which are easily specified in terms of syllables or syllabic constituents. Third, the syllable may serve as the domain within which a particular phonological contrast may be expressed. For example, in many languages the number of vowels in a word is in a one-to-one correspondence with the number of syllables. Zawaydeh (1998) further reports evidence of consonantal uvularisation spreading in Arabic that takes syllables as its domain, and Bosch and de Jong (1998) report categorical and subcategorical spreading effects of vocalic and secondary consonantal features at the level of the syllable in Barra Gaelic.

Based on these phonological properties, one can deduce likely phonetic characteristics of syllable structure. First, syllables are contrastive complexes which would be relatively acoustically stable in isolation and in utterance context. This means that they form 'building blocks' upon which higher-level prosodic structure can be built. Second, syllables would be complexes within which extensive acoustic coarticulation is common. This is why feature spreading and other segment-to-segment restrictions develop within a syllabic domain. Both of these properties suggest a model of syllabic structure as constraining intergestural timing in production. Consistency of intergestural timing will most likely contribute to acoustic stability both in isolation and in utterance context. Also, consistency in intergestural timing would contribute toward consistency in acoustic coarticulation. This consistency in mutual coarticulatory effects would most likely contribute to two initially separate contrasts being reinterpreted as a single contrast at the cost of one of the original contrasts.

Various experimental works also implicate a close connection between syllable structure and timing. Stetson, in his pioneering work on articulatory phonetics (reviewed in Stetson 1951) noted that coda structures become perceptually converted into onset structures at fast speech rates. Thus, according to Stetson's description, an utterance such as *eeb* when repeated at fast rates becomes *bee*. The connection between temporal rate and syllabic structure was also detected by MacKay (1974) who found that speakers, when asked to repeat syllables as fast as they could, had slower repetition rates for syllables with codas than for syllables with onsets. This connection between temporal rate and the presence of codas seems to be evident also in the phonological distinction between 'heavy' and 'light' syllables. For example, in many Arabic dialects, syllables with coda consonants pattern with phonemically long vowels in the formulation of stress rules. Thus, the presence of a coda contributes to a longer durational propensity just as the phonemic contrast between long and short vowels contributes to a longer durational propensity in long vowels.

14.2 Models of intergestural timing and syllabic organisation

Browman and Goldstein (1988) proposed a model of intergestural coordination in which gestures which bear a structural relationship with one another will have an invariant timing relationship between them. This model proposed phase rules couched within the task-dynamic speech production framework in which speech is composed of actions corresponding to underlying speech gestures described by second-order dynamic equations (Saltzman and Munhall 1989). More recently Byrd (1997) has suggested modifying this approach by encoding prosodic structure as restrictions on the amount of variability in intergestural timing.

There is some experimental evidence in favour of a constrained timing approach. Articulatory studies which examine timing relations within syllabic units often find little variability in timing relations between gestures, while studies which examine timing relations between syllables often find extreme variability. Thus, while Löfqvist and Yoshioka (1981, 1984) show a stable coordination between glottal and oral actions in /st/ onsets and Kent and Moll (1975) find consistent closure durations when the /s/ and /t/ inhabit the same syllable, Zsiga (1995) shows that the relative timing of actions which do not inhabit the same syllable is highly variable. Browman and Goldstein (1990a) also noted large timing variation in consonant sequences which gives rise to the perception of consonant cluster simplification in the often cited *perfec' memory* example.

Tuller and Kelso (1991) proposed a similar account in which syllabic structures correspond to stable modalities in articulatory coordination. As evidence for their approach, Tuller and Kelso report a replication of Stetson's (1951) findings that speakers will shift perceived coda consonants to onset consonants at fast speech rates. They model these syllabic modalities as arising out of the dynamics of motor organisation, and describe a class of nonlinear systems which exhibit the type of shifting behaviour their subjects exhibit.

14.3 A problem: highly variable timing within the syllable

De Jong (1991) investigated kinematic patterns in a corpus of X-ray microbeam data consisting of syllables with different coronal consonants (*toad, toads, toast,* etc.). Vowels were systematically shorter before voiceless consonants, before stops, and before multiple consonants. (See also similar results for American English in House and Fairbanks 1953; Peterson and Lehiste 1960; Umeda 1977; and Munhall, Fowler, Hawkins and Saltzman 1992.) If timing is fixed between the parts of the syllable, then these observed differences in vowel duration would have been due to differences in the durations of the gestures themselves rather than to differences in the timing relations between the gestures. Intergestural timing was assessed by examining the timing of peak velocities and maxima and minima of tongue-tip motions going into and out of the vowels interpreted with respect to predictions based on a task-dynamic model. While there were dynamic differences between the different consonantal gestures which accounted for part of the durational difference in the vowel, speakers also did systematically modify the timing relations between vowels and following coda consonants.

This same conclusion was reached in de Jong (1993) and de Jong (1995a), which examined tongue-dorsum and upper-lip trajectories in the same microbeam database. Tongue movement trajectories towards a retracted position for the back vowels (/o/) were reduced in shorter vowels. The lip trajectories, however, tended to remain unperturbed, introducing an asynchrony between the velar and labial constrictions. Thus, alveolar consonant activity impinged heavily on the tongue motion in shorter vowels, suggesting that the relative timing of the (lingual) consonant gestures and (lingual/labial) vowel gestures was varying considerably from token to token. De Jong (1995b) examined more specifically the effect of stress in these productions. Results also confirmed the results of de Jong (1991) that timing relations are highly variable within a syllabic unit. Using somewhat different measurement and modelling techniques, Edwards, Beckman and Fletcher (1991) and Harrington, Fletcher and Roberts (1995) similarly showed that intrasyllabic vowel-to-consonant timing varies extensively and systematically between stress categories.

These kinematic studies taken together indicate that intergestural timing does vary and varies systematically within a syllable, and thus, that a complete characterisation of syllable structure must allow for and explain these extensive patterns of variability. Particularly variable is the timing of a vocalic opening gesture and a following coda gesture. This general pattern of results conforms with expectations based on a large number of earlier acoustic studies which have found that the largest amount of durational variability in running speech is located within the vowel, the acoustic portion corresponding to the juncture between the vocalic and following consonantal gesture. (See discussions related to articulatory research in Gay 1981; Barry 1983; and de Jong 1990.)

14.4 Exploring temporal variability systematically

In order to examine the patterns of variability within various syllabic organisations, this paper presents the results of a study which sought to replicate Stetson's (and Tuller and Kelso's) effect of perceptual resyllabification. The particular approach used here pits linguistic specification in the form of visual presentation of particular words to be produced against nonlinguistic specification in the form of a metronome which controls speech rate. By systematically changing rate, I am able to examine the patterns of temporal variability associated with the linguistic specification of syllabic structure. To the extent that syllabic structuring can be modelled as constraints on intergestural coordination, syllabic structuring should appear as linguistically specified relative durational invariance in the face of systematic background variability. An additional possibility is that speakers will show discrete shifts in intergestural coordination due to categorical resyllabification.

14.4.1 Experimental methods

Four speakers (two male and two female) of a midwestern variety of American English were recorded in the Indiana University Phonetics Lab. Speakers were presented with a written list of syllables to be repeated. As in Tuller and Kelso (1991), target syllables consisted of *eep* and *pea*, and, in addition, to examine the role of phonemic voicing differences, *bee* and *eeb*. In order to control speech rate, the speakers were presented with a software-generated metronome signal over headphones. In each trial, a warning signal was given, followed by a train of clicks. Speakers were instructed to produce the appropriate 'word' once for each click. Each click was composed of a 200 Hz sinusoid with a step onset and a 1/4 sine-wave decay, and sounded roughly like a bouncing table tennis ball.

Prior to experimentation, a brief practice run of four trials was conducted; none of the speakers encountered much difficulty with the task. Following the practice, three experimental sets were run. In the first, the speakers were presented with a pulse train of 15 clicks with fixed periods ranging from 150 to 400 ms in 50 ms increments. In the second experimental set, speakers were presented with an increasing rate pulse train which began with a series of 6 clicks with a period of 400 ms. After the six clicks, the period was decremented by 12.5 ms per period until reaching a period of 150 ms. The train ended with a series of 6 more clicks at the fixed rate of 150 ms. Before the set was begun, the speakers were warned that the pacer would change rate. The third set used a decreasing rate pulse train which was the same as the second, except in reverse order.

14.4.2 Measurements and hypotheses

To examine temporal stability in the speakers' behavior, the timing of various points in each syllable were obtained using Entropics *WAVES+* implemented on a Sun Sparc 5 in the Indiana University Phonetics Lab. First, the last 12 syllables in the fixed rate condition, and all of the syllables in the variable conditions were digitised. Then, using broad band (150 Hz) spectrograms and waveform displays, the timing of consonant release, consonant closure (the time at which high-frequency energy is sharply damped, usually accompanied by a sharp fall in the second formant), and vowel onset (the time at which voicing with clear formant structure begins) were labelled.[1]

Given a timing-constraints model and assuming resyllabification of codas at fast rates, one would expect various results. First, if speakers were able to control their repetition rates in accord with the metronome, syllable-to-syllable periods should match metronome rates. If speakers find difficulty in producing a certain syllable type at a particular rate, for example producing codas at fast rates, the syllable period may be longer than the metronome period. Second, acoustic indices of consistent gestural timing should be distinct for codas and onsets at slow rates, but coda values should change to those of onsets at some critical rate. Third, Tuller and Kelso explicitly state that, once in a stable pattern, speakers will remain in that pattern. Hence, speakers might not shift out of onset patterns in the decreasing rate condition.

14.5 Results

Due to space limitations, I will present in detail only the results of one of the female speakers who exhibited all of the syllabic patterning effects, making reference to the behaviour of the other subjects where relevant.

14.5.1 Metronome entrainment

Figure 14.1 plots the latencies of acoustic events from consonant release against metronome period for the fixed period condition. One can visualise this presentation format as indicating an overlay of successive syllables running upwards, aligned at consonant release, as is illustrated to the right.

Several features of these data are of note. First, it is apparent that the speakers were quite good at producing syllables of roughly the duration of the metronome period. This is apparent in Figure 14.1 in the top functions in each panel closely approximating the diagonal, which indicates the period of the metronome. However, all of the speakers did lag behind the metronome at various rates. These lags show up here in the top function being above the diagonal. Patterns such as that with /ip/ (lower left) are particularly striking in that it was usually not the fastest rate which presented problems for the speakers, but the next-to-fastest rate. /ip/ tokens produced at the fastest rate impressionistically shift to onset structures, as will be discussed below. What is unexpected here, however, are lags which occurred for onset structures (such as at 200 ms in the upper right panel, and at 250 ms in the lower right panel).

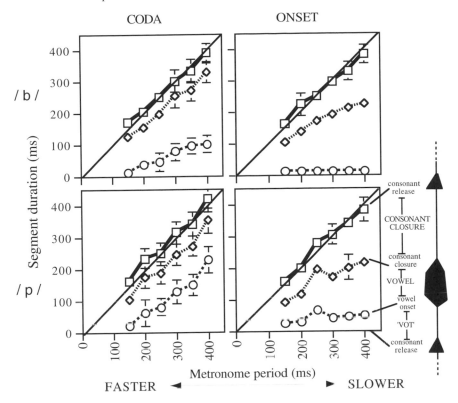

Figure 14.1 Temporal intervals plotted against metronome period for the fixed rate condition

14.5.2 Consistency of durations

Examining Figure 14.1 with an eye to identifying consistent timing across rates, one notes a pattern which conforms to our expectations in some ways, but not in others. First, the onsets (to the right) show systematic variation in durations of the vowel and the closure. However, the duration between release of consonant and onset of voicing for the vowel (which we will call VOT for convenience) remains more or less fixed in duration. In keeping with previous durational studies, the duration for voiceless onsets shows a small amount of shortening, however, considerably less than the other portions of the syllable. In addition, onset VOTs also show remarkably little variability within each rate – the error bars are shorter than the diameter of the symbols used in the figure. By contrast, the corresponding duration in codas exhibits large amounts of shortening at faster rates and far greater variability within each rate. These variable values for codas approach onset values as rates increase, until finally the values converge on the onset values for /b/ at the fastest rates. In particular, for /ip/ (lower left) the values converge on those for onsets at rates just faster than those for which the speaker was lagging behind the metronome. All of the speakers, like this one, moved from highly variable coda values to much less variable onset values.

There are, however, two other aspects of the data which should be noted. First, it is not accurate to say that /ip/ tokens shift to /pi/ at fast rates, but rather /ip/ tokens shift perceptually to /bi/ at fast rates. Figure 14.1 indicates this as well in that coda /ip/ (lower left) VOTs converge on those of /bi/ tokens (upper right), rather than those of /pi/ tokens (lower right). Second, if we examine the closure durations in greater detail, we find a similar pattern to that shown for VOT values, except that codas and onsets are switched. Closure durations remain remarkably stable, at about 50 ms, over the entire set of rates for codas (to the left). Onset closure durations shorten at faster rates to converge on values which are typical of codas. This type of behaviour was evident in three of the four speakers. This set of facts suggests an interpretation of closure durations as being a consistent characteristic of syllables with codas. Utterances at fast rates, then, incorporate consistent durations found in syllables with onsets and consistent durations found in syllables with codas at slower rates.

14.5.3 Variable rates and shifting

The patterns noted in the fixed rate conditions were also apparent in the variable rate conditions. Figure 14.2 plots VOT values against the sequence of the syllables in each utterance in which rate increased. Vertical cursors indicate an estimate of the beginning and ending of the accelerating portion of the metronome signal. In the onset conditions (to the right), one notes a similar pattern to that in the fixed-rate condition; onset /b/ shows fairly consistent durations across the rates, and onset /p/ shows a small amount of shortening. Coda /p/ and /b/ (to the left) show a pattern of extreme variability and scaling up to somewhere between the tenth and twentieth syllable, at which time the values suddenly shorten to those values found in onset /b/. This pattern was evident in each of the speakers.

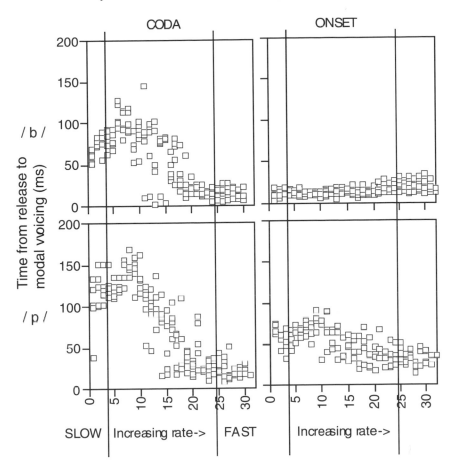

Figure 14.2 VOTs plotted against order of syllable in production train for the increasing-rate condition

Figure 14.3 plots closure durations against the sequence of syllables in the increasing-rate condition. The pattern is very similar to that in Figure 14.2, except that onsets and codas are switched. Closure durations remain essentially stable at around 50 ms for the coda /b/s and /p/s, while for onsets the values show a lot of variability at slower rates and eventually slide into consistent values of about 50 ms. This behaviour for closure durations was also evident in two other speakers.

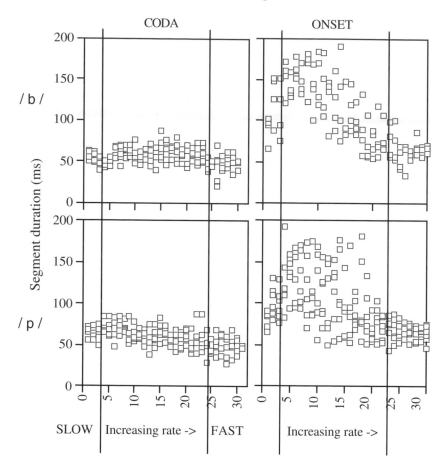

Figure 14.3 Occlusion duration plotted against order of syllable in production train for the increasing-rate condition

14.5.4 Histeresis

One additional aspect of this data set particularly supports viewing this durational behaviour as the result of stable modes in articulation, that is the occurrence of histeresis. Figure 14.4 compares coda structures in the increasing- and decreasing-rate conditions. The increasing conditions are the same as were plotted in Figure 14.2, except that the sequencing of the syllables is reversed to allow for a more direct comparison of the behaviour in the two conditions. It is quite clear that the shifting is occurring later in the decreasing-rate condition. The shift out of the 20 ms mode occurs between the eighteenth and twenty-first syllable, while it occurs between the eleventh and nineteenth for the increasing-rate mode. (See Figure 14.2 for syllable numbers.) In addition, the delayed shift in the decreasing-rate condition, when it does occur, is much larger. Thus, it appears that once they are producing a pattern, speakers tend to continue to produce that pattern.

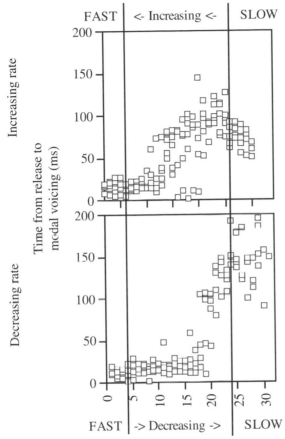

Figure 14.4 VOTs plotted against order of syllable in production train for syllables with /b/. Top panel indicates the increasing-rate condition; bottom panel indicates the decreasing-rate condition

The typical approach to understanding this sort of behaviour, as suggested by Tuller and Kelso's modelling, is to think of the articulatory patterns as the output of a system with particular types of propensities. The histeresis, then, is caused by the necessity of a greater perturbation from outside the system to get the system out of a particular mode, as it were, the injection of a certain amount of driving force from outside the system. The speakers have to 'try harder' to entrain their productions to a pacing metronome which is requiring them to leave an articulatory state, than to a metronome which is leading them into that state.

14.6 Characterizing coda and onset production

These data suggest that both onset and coda consonants do involve consistent intergestural timing patterns. This conclusion is based on several observations. (1) Some aspects of the durational patterns are consistent regardless of the speech rate. Thus, strategies for speech-rate modification respect the integrity of certain aspects of the temporal pattern but not others. The particular aspect which gets respected depends on the specification of the utterance, here whether the segments bear an onset–vowel relationship or a vowel–coda relationship. Other portions of the signal, the vowel and the interval which crosses over the juncture between the syllables, take up the rate differences and hence vary quite a bit. (2) At fast rates where the syllables are compressed together, speakers exhibit the specified temporal patterns regardless of whether they are characteristic of the specified syllabic pattern at slower rates. (3) Speakers exhibiting a stable pattern will tend to continue to exhibit it in the face of rate modification, thus giving rise to histeresis in rates at which speakers exhibit changes in durational pattern.

Although the actual articulatory behaviour which produces these acoustic patterns must be inferred, it is useful as a heuristic to consider what sorts of articulatory coordinations are likely to give rise to the acoustic intervals which remain consistent. Consistency in VOT suggests that onset stabilities involve synchronisation of glottal and oral gestures, while consistency in closure duration would involve consistency in the coordination of successive closing and opening gestures. I have attempted to illustrate these observations in the schema in Figure 14.5. These schema include the two most relevant aspects to articulation, a glottal opening and closing at the top, and an oral opening and closing at the bottom. We tentatively assume for simplicity's sake that the actual articulator used for implementing the aperture changes is irrelevant. The constrained gestural timings are indicated with arrows connecting gestures sketched with solid lines. For onsets (top), the consistent VOT durations indicate a constrained timing of glottal gestures (A) and opening-aperture gestures (B). For codas (bottom), the stable closure durations indicate stable timing between closing-aperture gestures (A) and following opening-aperture gestures (B).

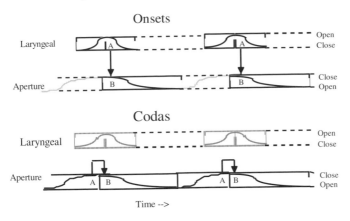

Figure 14.5 Articulatory schema for repeated onsets (top) and codas (bottom)

One thing to note from Figure 14.5 is that the temporal nature of the links for onsets and codas is quite different. Onsets involve synchronisation across articulatory structures, while codas involve asynchronous (sequential) gestures expressed by the same articulatory structures. Onsets are thus more temporally compact than codas, and are likely to allow more temporal compressibility, as MacKay (1974) found. It is tempting to also explain Stetson's resyllabification results as deriving from these differences in the temporal nature of the two structures. At fast rates, speakers abandon modes of coordination which are not temporally compact and find modes of coordination which take less time.

However, the present results do not support an account in which rate-induced resyllabification is the result of reorganisation driven by the inherent compressibility of the syllabic structures. There really is little evidence that speakers are reorganizing codas into onsets. Rather, at fast rates speakers find temporal modes at points of juncture between syllables. Eliminating unconstrained juncture in favour of specified modes allows speakers to keep up with the fastest metronome rates, while slower rates gave them difficulties. So, for example, codas (VCs) when repeated at fast rates acquire characteristics of onsets (CVs) via the abutment of a previous coda C with the initial V. Speakers repeating syllables at fast rates incorporate temporal patterns, some of which are characteristic of single syllables with onsets, and some of which are characteristic of single syllables with codas.

Figure 14.6 schematises the resulting structure. This hybrid structure could be a indicative of the situation with more linguistically natural multisyllabic phonological units (such as stress feet), or of multisyllabic words in general. My elicitation procedure had single syllable units whose timing with respect to one another was being controlled by the system-external metronome. If the

265

well-practised relative timing of multiple syllables is, instead, allowed to be determined by system-internal propensities for gestural coordination, as seems likely in normal speech, the stable linkages in Figure 14.6 are likely to be found within these multisyllabic units. One interesting aspect of this articulatory schema is that all of the gestures are linked with one another, except the sequential relationship between the opening gesture for the vowel and the closing gesture for the following consonant. As was noted in Section 14.3, this timing relationship between the vowel opening and closing gestures is that which earlier articulatory studies have found to be systematically variable in the face of stress, rate and segmental influences. Thus, the current results converge with those in earlier studies of utterances produced in more natural linguistic tasks.

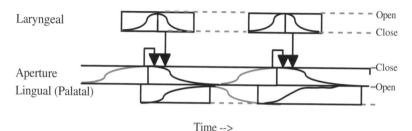

Time -->

Figure 14.6 Articulatory schema for syllable trains at fast production rates

14.7 Further questions and conclusions

The current study shows that both onsets and codas have temporal consistency, however of different types. Tuller and Kelso (1991) described onsets as involving a particular temporal alignment of glottal and oral gestures; the consistency of voice-onset times here matches this description. This also fits in well with works such as Steriade (1993) which suggest that the release of an obstruent is an extremely common temporal location for consonantal contrasts and secondary articulations. Consonantal releases provide an auditorily salient location which in addition is rich with orosensory feedback due to rapid aerodynamic changes associated with constriction and release. It thus would make sense that a basic defining characteristic of consonants in the most linguistically common syllabic locations, onsets, would be an orchestration of gestures around consonantal release.

The observation that coda consonants are characterised by stable closure durations is, I believe, new to this study. Codas would be defined by a characteristic relationship between the closure gesture and a following release gesture employing the same articulator. Thus, in terms of temporal characteristics, onsets and codas are very different kinds of coordinations.

266

Onset coordinations are basically *simultaneous* coordinations across tiers. Coda coordinations, by contrast, are basically *sequential* coordinations within various oral tiers. This characteristic difference may explain why it is that the presence of a coda reduces the temporal compressibility of an utterance. It may also explain why syllables with codas pattern phonologically with syllables with long vowels. Long vowels are incompressibly long in duration because they contrast with short vowels; codas are incompressibly long because they involve asynchronous gestures whose relative timing is tightly constrained.

This study, of course, raises many unanswered questions. One problem is the fact that /p/ in codas consistently becomes perceptually onset /b/ at fast rates, rather than onset /p/. A likely explanation for this peculiarity is that the glottal gesture for coda /p/ is considerably smaller than that for onset /p/. What counts as a stable timing relationship between glottal and oral gestures will probably depend on the type and size of the glottal gestures. In addition, the acoustic and aerodynamic results of gestures of different sizes will differ as well. Nevertheless, this aspect of the current results indicates an important caveat for discussions of the phonetics of prosodic structure. Studies such as the current one assume that prosodic structure is independent of the (segmental) content; segments in different parts of the syllable structure are the same except in syllabic position. The current results indicate that this assumption is not always right.

A second question concerns the major unexpected result of the current study, that codas exhibit temporal consistency just as onsets do. If repetitions at fast rates incorporate aspects of both codas and of onsets, why are they perceived as onsets? Although how listeners perceive syllable affiliation is not entirely clear at present, it does seem as though the type of acoustic attribute characteristic of onset stops will be much more auditorily salient than the duration of the stop-gap characteristic of the codas. This disparity in auditory salience may cause the onset percept to predominate over that of the coda in hybrid structures, hence yielding the perception of resyllabification at faster rates. With the introduction of perceptual questions comes a broader set of questions concerning temporal patterns. Just because we can identify consistent articulatory patterns in production does not mean that we understand the patterns we find. There remains the question of why a particular temporal arrangement is consistent; what kinds of articulatory and auditory factors contribute to the selection of the patterns we find?

Finally, with respect to the model of the syllable, the general model that emerges from this very preliminary work is somewhat different from the models with which we began. Temporal consistency is apparent for consonants in different locations in the syllable. Thus, the consonant's location in the prosodic structure determines the temporal pattern we find. However, the syllable itself cannot be characterised in terms of the same kind of temporal consistency. The general picture this suggests is that prosodic systems are built out of organisational tools which are afforded by speech, hearing and cognition which can be of different types and which do not apply equally to all phonological aspects of a prosodic category. Finding and characterizing these organisational tools and understanding how they are implemented in the various linguistic systems of the world is a reasonable goal for a laboratory phonology approach to prosodic theory. This experiment is but one small step in the direction of mapping out this largely uncharted territory.

Notes

This paper has benefited especially from discussions and comments by Doug Whalen, Peter Ladefoged and two anonymous reviewers. Presentation of this work was supported by the Indiana University Research and University Graduate School and the NSF under grant number SBR-9813593.

1   These measures define three intervals, vowel duration, consonant closure duration, and a period of speech without modal voicing which I will call VOT for convenience. These are shown in the lower right of Figure 14.1. The first two are straightforward measures. The third measure included combinations of release bursts, aspiration and creak or brief silence imposed by a glottal stop. None of these durations can be construed as a pause as found in the prosody literature, since boundary tones did not occur medially in the utterances. However, the juncture between syllables obviously must appear in one or another of the measures. This juncture is a period of unconstrained timing, as is discussed in Section 14.6.

15

Commentary: some thoughts on syllables – an old-fashioned interlude

PETER LADEFOGED

Two of the three papers in this group have at their centre the nature of the syllable. Gick's paper focuses on ambisyllabicity, and de Jong discusses phonetic characteristics of syllable structure. The third paper, Carter's, is more concerned with segmental characteristics, but he, too, makes extensive use of distinctions between syllable onset and coda position. Gick's and de Jong's papers assume that syllables should have universal phonetic exponents, although, as de Jong puts it, 'an explicit and simple characterisation of the phonetics of syllables has yet to be found'. Carter would probably join me in saying that it may not be possible to find universal properties of syllables, because they are local phonological constructs with no general phonetic properties.

I will begin by discussing Carter's paper on liquids. This paper is very clear and complete. As an experimentalist, I would like to have seen data from more than a single speaker from each dialect. It is possible that people who have velarised initial laterals and speak nonrhotic dialects all behave like the Mancunian speaker that Carter recorded. But, as de Jong reports in his paper discussing only four speakers, there may be differences among speakers that force one to reconsider one's previous assumptions. Nevertheless the elegance of Carter's experimental design has resulted in data that are indicative of relations among liquids that are of great interest.

Carter forces us to realise the importance of considering different dialects of English. He makes an excellent case for requiring the phonetic characteristics of different dialects to be independently noted, rather than following from some

269

universalist articulatory explanations. Stretching slightly, one can suggest that this position is within a long British tradition, going back at least to Daniel Jones, an early phonologist – to use a term that Jones would not have applied to himself, but which is nevertheless a correct term to describe his activities. Jones (1956, 1966) described forms of English by noting the sets of phonemes that were needed, and making statements about the allophones that occurred. He made it apparent that dialects differed not only in the statements that could be made about allophones of corresponding phonemes, but also in the phonetic nature (the exponents, as Carter would say) of the phonemes in the different dialects. This tradition is continued by Abercrombie (1964) in his account of the nature of phonetic transcription, which is still a textbook view (Ladefoged 1993; IPA 1999). A systematic narrow transcription can use more precise symbols in two ways. Firstly, these symbols can show different allophones; this corresponds to displaying the phonetic exponents of more phonological rules (or declarations or constraints). Alternatively, without showing any more allophones, more precise symbols can show that corresponding phonemes in different dialects have different phonetic exponents. Neither Jones nor any other phonetician noted the elegant patterning in different dialects of clear and dark, and initial and final liquids that Carter describes so well. But his observations would have delighted them all, and could have been handled, although perhaps not so elegantly, within their descriptive framework.

We must also note the importance of dialect differences when considering Gick's paper, which examines syllable-initial and ambisyllabic [w, j, l] in American English. Some of Gick's points do not apply to other forms of English, as he would no doubt recognise. The relevant dialect differences in the realisation of [w, j, l] become obvious when listening to recordings of BBC English and American Standard Newscaster English of words such as *say, yes; no, one; leaf, feel*. If these recordings are played backwards, notable differences between the two dialects become apparent.

Gick's discussion of ambisyllabicity is largely a discussion of intervocalicness. He is concerned with whether ambisyllabic allophones are distinct from other allophones; but his whole discussion could be rephrased in terms of gestures that occur before vowels, those that occur between vowels, and those that occur after vowels. He shows (again rephrasing his findings in traditional terminology) that junctural distinctions are a matter of the magnitude of the gestures involved, as well as of their relative timing. This is a point that was made some years ago by Nolan (1992), describing the varying degrees of gestural reduction of [d] before [g] in phrases such as *bad girls*.

Gick discusses ambisyllabicity in terms of the theory of Articulatory Phonology (Browman and Goldstein 1992), although he makes it clear that his results are not particularly dependent on this theoretical framework. Articulatory Phonology describes speech motor movements in terms of the blending of adjacent gestures. This is an excellent approach that allows one to describe what I have called intrinsic allophonic variation (Ladefoged 1972), such as the allophones of /k/ in *keep* and *cop*, or the allophones of /l/ in *lay* and *play*. An intrinsic allophone can be defined as one that is due to the overlapping of two adjacent gestures. Thus the variation between the fronted velar in *keep* and the more retracted velar in *cop* is due to the way a single stored tongue gesture for /k/ overlaps with the stored gestures for the different vowels. The voicelessness of the /l/ in *play* is due to the overlap of the voiceless laryngeal gesture for aspirated /p/ with the voicing gesture specified for /l/. Articulatory Phonology captures these differences in a wonderfully precise way.

Articulatory Phonology's problems come with extrinsic allophones, which require different stored gestures. The allophones of /t/ in *top* [tʰɒp] and *button* [bʌʔn] are quite distinct in this way. The glottal gesture in *button* cannot be regarded as due to the overlapping of the glottal state required for the voicing on either side of this sound and the glottal opening that occurs for initial /t/. Entirely different glottal gestures have to be specified for these two sounds. At some highly abstract level one can regard the silence during a glottal stop as equivalent to the voicelessness in an initial /t/. But this is an auditory equivalence, not due to any similarity or blending of laryngeal gestures.

When we examine the lateral allophones that Gick is investigating, similar problems arise. It is not at all clear that all the /l/ sounds have the same articulatory target, and that the observed differences are due to the blending or overlapping of adjacent articulations. This may be the case in American English, but it is clearly not the case in many varieties of British English. In my own speech, initial [l] has a closure between the tip of the tongue and the alveolar ridge, and the back of the tongue is not particularly raised. In a particular word, such as *leaf* the tongue position for [l] is a blend of the underlying target position for /l/ and that for /i/. Figure 15.1 shows estimates of the presumed targets and the result of blending them (based on unpublished palatographic and x-ray data of my own speech). In the [l] in final position, I and many other British English speakers do not have any contact between the tongue and the alveolar ridge. The tip of the tongue is down and retracted behind the lower front teeth, and the back of the tongue is raised in a back unrounded vowel position. The actual position for [l] as in *feel* must involve a different articulatory target from that for initial [l], as indicated in Figure 15.2 (also based on unpublished palatographic data and x-rays of my speech).

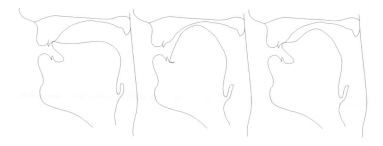

Figure 15.1 The target for initial [l] and the target for [i]. The third picture shows the actual tongue position of [l] at the beginning of *leaf*, which is a blend of the target for the initial [l] and the target for [i]

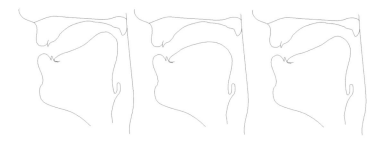

Figure 15.2 The target for final [lˠ] and the target for [ə], which might follow it. The third picture shows the tongue position of [lˠ] at the end of *feel* which can be considered to be a blend of the special target for final [lˠ] and the targets for the sounds before and after it

There is no way in which the word-final articulation can be regarded as a blend between the underlying target positions shown in Figure 15.1 for initial [l] and the preceding vowel, even taking into account the presumed target for the following silence. It is not just that the tip of the tongue is down (which could be a case of magnitude reduction of the tip gesture) but also that the back of the tongue is actively raised (which does not occur in initial [l]). The equations of Articulatory Phonology cannot create the difference between these extrinsic allophones in many forms of British English without using separate stored articulatory targets.

This makes me query the whole notion of trying to decide whether the gesture for a lateral between vowels is more like that for an initial or a final lateral. It may be all right in American English, but in British English this is not just a difference of magnitude or timing of the gesture, but a difference between gestures. For good phonological reasons we consider both the lateral in the middle of [filɪŋ] *feeling* and the approximant at the end of [filˠ] *feel* to be

272

realisations of the same phoneme. But they are not realisations of the same underlying gesture. In my pronunciation, spectrograms show that the [l] in *The feeling which stays* is virtually identical to that in *The fee linguists pay*. It is very different from that in *I feel English pays*. Thus *feeling* and *feel* involve different gestures in the same way as the glottal stop in *button* involves a different laryngeal gesture from the aspirated stop in *top*.

Articulatory phonology has not, as yet, suggested a way to account for the phonological alternations that involve different gestures, such as those in *feeling* and *feel*. This alternation is based on a reorganisation that goes beyond explanations in terms of the timing and magnitude of a given gesture. Programming an articulatory speech synthesiser to produce both *feel* and *feeling* cannot be done with a set of stored targets, one for each of the segments [f, i, l, ɪ, ŋ]. There must be an extra stored target for final [lˠ]. I like the careful work in Gick's paper that enables him to allocate some of the exponents of each segment to consonantal properties and some to vocalic properties. But I wish the excellent articulatory phonetics in the theory he is using would not masquerade as phonology. Articulatory Phonology can explain many things, but it cannot explain all the phonological properties of languages.

The final paper in this group is de Jong's discussion of syllabic properties. He begins by considering the phonological properties of syllables and from these considerations deduces likely phonetic characteristics. He suggests that the phonetic exponents are principally in the constraints that the syllable provides on intergestural timing. This is close to the textbook notion that a syllable is 'a unit in the organisation of the sounds of an utterance' (Ladefoged 1993: 248). As I am sure de Jong would agree, all these notions need refinement before they can be applied to a wide variety of syllables. He notes in his conclusions that 'phenomena associated with a syllable are liable to arise due to a variety of root causes'. We need to examine different types of syllables before we make generalisations concerning the nature of the syllable.

De Jong repeats an old experiment (Stetson 1951) with a new twist: he does it properly. He examines variations in sequences of syllables spoken at different rates. There is one point that he does not emphasise, but which may be important in considering his experiments. He is dealing not with just syllables, but with stressed syllables. We do not know what controls the organisation in sequences of seeming disyllables involving a stressed and an unstressed syllable.

This leads us back to some general considerations with regard to syllables, and to a possibility that Gick also did not consider. Can there be consonants that are neither onsets nor codas within a syllable, particularly in sequences involving a stressed syllable followed by an unstressed syllable? Such consonants could be intervocalic consonants within a single syllable. Hockett (1952: 51) used the terms onset, peak, coda and interlude in his discussion of syllable types, with an interlude being an ambisyllabic consonant. But it might be possible to define an interlude as an intervocalic consonant in a single syllable.

Phonologists think of each vowel as being dominated by a syllable node. But if we abandon the notion that there are universal phonetic characteristics of a syllable, and allow syllables to be phonologically defined units in each language, it is possible that words such as *happy* and *supper* should each be considered to be a single syllable. Alternatively, we could give up on syllables in discussions of gestural timing, and regard the timing relationships of the various gestures as properties of the foot, a metrical unit containing a single stressed syllable.

Regarding words such as *happy* and *supper* as single syllables would wreak havoc with phonological notions such as those that constrain the sequences of vowels that can occur in a single syllable. But there is ample evidence that syllables in other languages may contain intervocalic consonants. Consider, for instance, the situation in Scottish Gaelic (Ladefoged, Ladefoged, Turk, Hind and Skilton 1998).

In Scottish Gaelic there are a number of words such as *balg* /pal$^\gamma$ak / 'belly' in which the second vowel was, historically, inserted to break up a final consonant cluster that is still reflected in the spelling. These words now contrast with other words such as /pal$^\gamma$.ak/ ('skull'), which is spelled *ballag*. The difference between them can be described in phonological terms by considering the words with an epenthetic vowel as monosyllabic and the others as disyllables, although the sequence of segments is virtually identical in the two sets of words. The difference is apparent in the intonation patterns.

As exemplified in Figure 15.3, the citation form of the phonologically monosyllabic word has a rising intonation, whereas the disyllabic word generally has a rising then falling intonation. Ladefoged *et al.* (1998) note that all six of their male speakers had a rising pitch in the first word, *balg* /pal$^\gamma$ak/ ('belly'), and five of them had a fall in the second word *ballag* /pal$^\gamma$.ak/ ('skull'). The one speaker who had a slight rise in the second word had a much greater rise in the first word. Every speaker used pitch to distinguish between these two words, although sometimes the difference was small. Similar data (but analysed differently) are reported by Ellison (undated) and Bosch and de Jong (1997).

Support for an analysis in which the first word (and many similar words) are phonologically monosyllabic, whereas the second and similar words are disyllabic, is given by another set of Scottish Gaelic words. In words such as *dubhan* /tu.an/ ('hook') an intervocalic consonant has been lost. Despite this loss these words still consist of two phonological syllables and contrast with monosyllabic words such as *duan* /tuan/ ('song') with comparable sequences of segments. The contrast is manifested by pitch patterns similar to those in the contrast between *balg* /palʸak/ ('belly') and *ballag* /palʸ.ak/ ('skull').

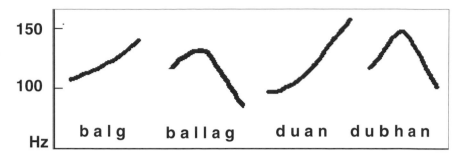

Figure 15.3 Pitch patterns of the four Scottish Gaelic words *balg* /palʸak/ ('belly'), *ballag* /palʸ.ak/ ('skull'), *duan* /tuan/ ('song'), *dubhan* /tu.an/ ('hook'), as spoken in citation form

Again as shown in Figure 15.3, the citation form of the monosyllabic word has a rising intonation, whereas the disyllabic word has a rising then falling intonation.

We can describe these intonation patterns by an analysis suggested to me by Francis Nolan on the basis of similar possibilities noted in Ladd (1996). For most speakers, all these citation forms have a LH L form, with a constraint that makes the LH obligatory. In the monosyllabic forms there is no syllable for the final L to be attached to. If this analysis is correct, other monosyllabic words should also have a similarly rising citation form, a fact that seems to be true in the limited corpus I have been able to examine.

Other cases of phonetically unusual syllables are not hard to find in other languages. As a final example in this discussion we should note words such as /s'n'm'ne/ (place for excreting) in Montana Salish. This word contains one underlying vowel at the end, as well as up to three epenthetic vowels (potentially one accompanying each glottalised nasal). But there may be no epenthetic vowels, making it not at all clear how many syllables there are. There are two lexical morphemes, and there may be a secondary stress, on some analyses (Thomason, personal communication). But asking how many syllables there are is an improper question. Syllables may be useful phonological constructs in some circumstances, but they may be totally irrelevant in others.

IV

Phonology and natural speech production: tasks, contrasts and explanations

16

The interaction of the phonetics and phonology of gutturals

BUSHRA ADNAN ZAWAYDEH

16.1 Introduction

Arabic and Interior Salish languages are distinguished from other languages in having a wide variety of consonant series that have constrictions in the back part of the vocal tract. These include pharyngeals, uvulars and uvularised segments.[1] These languages are similar in that the pharyngeals, uvulars and emphatics seem to pattern together and form a natural class with respect to a variety of phonological processes. This natural class is generally called the guttural natural class. However, these two language groups differ in that while the laryngeal consonants [ʔ] and [h] of Arabic behave as members of the guttural class, the laryngeals of Salish usually cannot be grouped with gutturals. One important question is why these language groups differ in their treatment of the laryngeal consonants.

McCarthy (1994) and Hayward and Hayward (1989) raised a more general question: why would the emphatics, uvulars, pharyngeals (and laryngeals in Arabic) be a natural class in the first place? In Feature Geometry (Halle 1995; Sagey 1986; McCarthy 1988), feature nodes, which define natural classes, are associated with active articulators. McCarthy (1994) reviews a number of phonetic studies of Arabic and concludes that the guttural class presents a problem for this view; there is no single active articulator for the gutturals. There have been two previous proposals that attempted to address this problem. The first, which is the generally accepted analysis, is to allow for 'articulatory zones' (Hayward and Hayward 1989; Vaux 1993; McCarthy 1994; Halle 1995;

Rose 1996). In Arabic, the [guttural] node can be used to represent an articulatory zone from the uvula to the larynx.

A second proposal was presented by Goldstein (1994). Goldstein proposed that the articulator that distinguishes guttural sounds from nonguttural sounds is the jaw; only nongutturals have jaw movement. Lee (1995) tested this idea but found that the evidence does not support it. For oral sounds, the jaw is raised to augment the raising of the primary articulator (the lower lip or tongue) towards the roof of the mouth for the articulation of labial, coronal and dorsal sounds. However, Lee also found that the jaw lowers during the articulation of velars and uvular stops in high vowel contexts. Furthermore, the jaw is raised for the articulation of the uvular fricative and it is lowered in pharyngeals, even though both sets pattern as gutturals. Lee proposed to solve this problem by replacing the categorical binary distinction (that the jaw does or does not participate in the articulation of oral or guttural sounds), with a continuum of degrees of participation.[2]

The research reported here presents two proposals. The first is that pharyngeal width may distinguish guttural sounds from nonguttural sounds. The pharynx can also be considered an active articulator, and thus it is not just a 'place' of articulation like the teeth or the hard palate. We can consider it an active articulator because its diameter can be changed during speech. This point has been made by Hardcastle (1976). He notes that the diameter of the pharynx can be altered by the position of the tongue root. Thus, an articulation of a front [i] would result in a large dimension, while the retracted production of an [a] would result in a narrow dimension. The anterior–posterior dimension of the pharynx can also be altered by a movement of the velum. Moreover, the lateral dimension of the pharynx could be changed considerably as well. An 'isotonic contraction of these sphincter muscles will narrow the pharynx and an isometric contraction will serve to tense the wall of the pharynx. Tensing the pharynx will affect the resonance quality of the voice, and, hence, the voice will have a "metallic" quality' (Hardcastle 1976: 125). Moreover, isometric tensing of the pharynx is important for the articulation of the 'tense' sounds of Korean. Therefore, the pharynx should be considered an articulator since it can affect the resonance and articulation of sounds.[3]

The second proposal is that guttural sounds can be grouped acoustically. They raise the first formant of sounds adjacent to them. In the X-rays of Ghazeli (1977), the pharyngeals exhibited a constriction in the lower pharynx. Moreover, uvulars and emphatics had a constriction in the upper part of the pharynx near the uvula. Such constrictions should raise F1. However, we do not know how the laryngeals are articulated. Are they articulated merely by the movement of the arytenoids which open and close the glottis? Or is there any accompanying pharyngeal constriction?

This paper is organised as follows: in Section 16.2, we will discuss how gutturals are a natural class in the phonologies of Arabic and Salish. In Section 16.3, we present an endoscopic experiment which tests the first proposal; namely that pharyngeal width could distinguish gutturals from nongutturals. In Section 16.4, we present an acoustic experiment, which tests the second proposal, namely that raised F1 is a common property of gutturals. In Section 16.5, we present the general discussion and conclusions.

16.2 Gutturals in Arabic and Salish

There is an abundance of evidence from Afro-Asiatic languages like Arabic, Tiberian Hebrew and Cushitic that gutturals form a phonological class. In addition, there is also evidence from Interior Salish languages that supports the natural class of gutturals. However, the Semitic languages and the Salish languages differ in one fact: the laryngeals are part of the guttural natural class in the Semitic languages, but they are often not so in the Salish languages. Evidence for this comes from the fact that there are co-occurence restrictions such that two gutturals do not surface in the same root. Also in both cases gutturals trigger vowel lowering. See McCarthy (1994) and Bessell (1992) for supporting evidence.

Thus, a question that one might ask is why would the laryngeals be part of the guttural natural class in some languages, but not others? Rose (1996) attempts to answer this question and proposes that in fact in language systems that have gutturals (i.e. uvulars, pharyngeals and emphatics), laryngeals are specified for place. In comparison, in languages that do not have other gutturals, laryngeals are placeless. Hence, Rose disagrees with the analysis of Bessell (1992) and Bessell and Czaykowska-Higgins (1992). Rose reanalyses the data that they presented and provides new evidence that supports her claim that laryngeals are specified for place in Interior Salish and that in fact they do pattern with the rest of the gutturals in these languages.

One of the pieces of evidence that Rose uses is the fact that the epenthetic vowel in Interior Salish is the schwa. This vowel is realised as a low vowel in the environment of pharyngeals, uvulars and also laryngeals. Rose shows that this occurs in Moses-Columbian and in Lillooet. Hence, she concludes that laryngeals should be specified with the pharyngeal node, just like the rest of the gutturals. However, Shahin (1997) does not agree with Rose (1996) that Salish laryngeals are specified. She analyses the vowel lowering case before glottal stops as being triggered by a constraint against two placeless segments (the schwa and the glottal stop, in this case). This negates any need to invoke some pharyngeal node specification for Salish laryngeals. In addition, it seems that there are more cases in which Salish laryngeals do not pattern with the other gutturals than cases where they do. They include: the morpheme structure constraints in which laryngeals in most cases co-occur with other gutturals; the patterning of high vowels; there are no roots with high vowels followed by a guttural but high vowels can be followed by a laryngeal; the retraction of vowels in the environment of uvulars, pharyngeals and uvularised segments, but not in the environment of the laryngeals (see Bessell (1992) for supporting evidence). Hence, it seems that phonologically, laryngeals in Salish are usually different from other gutturals, but it is not clear why.

Rose (1996) proposes that all guttural sounds (including laryngeals) share the node Pharyngeal. Moreover, she proposes that uvulars, pharyngeals and emphatics have the [RTR] feature. Rose justifies using the [RTR] feature by noting that all these sounds have either a retraction of the root of the tongue or a constriction in the pharynx in their articulation. Hence, laryngeals are similar to the rest of the gutturals by having the pharyngeal node, but they differ from them in not having the feature [RTR].

In Rose's analysis, the [RTR] feature refers to two different articulators. One of them is the root of the tongue, which is being retracted and raised towards the uvula as in the case of uvulars and emphatics. The second one involves the pharyngeal constriction. In this case there is a radical manner of constriction in the pharynx when the pharyngeal sounds are articulated. Thus, there is a problem with the articulatory definition of the [RTR] feature. The constriction in the pharynx that is achieved during the articulation of pharyngeal sounds is not the same as the retraction of the back of the tongue for the articulation of uvular sounds such as [q] and the emphatics.

If uvulars and emphatics have a retracted tongue back, and pharyngeals have a retracted tongue root, what do laryngeals have? How are they articulated? McCarthy (1994) says that there are no articulatory studies done about laryngeals in Arabic. There are some acoustic studies that investigate them. Klatt and Stevens (1969) found that the Arabic laryngeals do not have formant transitions at vowel onsets. However, Shahin (1997) argues that Klatt and Stevens's findings could not be generalised because the tokens that were used in their study occur in a stem-final position. She provides evidence from Palestinian Arabic that shows that laryngeals raise F1 (and lower F2 of nonlow vowels) in non-stem-final short vowels. Thus, since in Palestinian Arabic laryngeals raise the F1 of vowels following them, Shahin assumed that laryngeals are tongue-root retracted. She says that 'there is as yet no clear evidence that Arabic laryngeals are not tongue root articulated' (22). Hence, she claims that all gutturals are specified for [Tongue Root], which is an articulator feature. This would replace the zone feature [Pharyngeal]. To see if the laryngeals really have a retracted tongue root, in the next section we present an endoscopic experiment that has been conducted to study the articulation of Arabic gutturals.

16.3 An endoscopic experiment

There are two primary reasons for conducting this experiment. The first is to know if the gutturals could be grouped articulatorily by having a similar pharyngeal constriction. If they do, then this might explain why they are patterning together phonologically. The second motive is to find out if the laryngeals have a retracted tongue root, as claimed by Shahin (1997).

16.3.1 Method

16.3.1.1 Materials
A list of nonsense utterances with the form /ʔaCa/ was prepared. The consonant in all cases except one was a voiceless sound. Voiced consonants were not used, to avoid any pharyngeal tension. Table 16.1 presents the words that were used. Stress was placed on the second syllable because that vowel was produced as a long vowel (see de Jong and Zawaydeh (1999) for more on stress in this dialect).

Table 16.1 *Words used in the endoscopic experiment*

1. ʔasa	2. ʔaka	3. ʔaTa⁴	4. ʔaDa	5. ʔaXa
6. ʔaqa	7. ʔaha	8. ʔaʕa	9. ʔaha	10. ʔaʔa

16.3.1.2 Subject
Due to necessary subject discomfort, the sole subject in the experiment was the author, whose native language is the Ammani-Jordanian dialect of Arabic.

16.3.1.3 Equipment and procedure
The procedure was performed at the Indiana University Speech and Hearing Sciences Department. A fibre-optic endoscope was inserted through the nasal passage into the pharynx below the level of the uvula. Each word was repeated five times in succession by the subject. The video and audio outputs were recorded simultaneously onto a videotape.

16.3.1.4 Analysis of fiberscope images
A computer connected with a VCR allowed us to play the videotape in slow motion and to examine it in stopped modes to inspect each frame at a time. Still images were extracted at the point of maximum constriction for each consonant for three tokens of the five for a total of thirty frames.

An example of such pictures can be found in Figure 16.1 which shows the epiglottis to the left, which is crescent shaped.

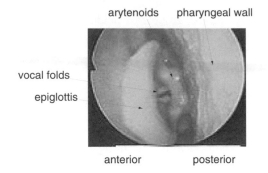

Figure 16.1 Endoscopic image showing the arytenoids, vocal folds and epiglottis

Also apparent are the domes of the arytenoids to the right, which control the opening and closing of the vocal folds. The pharyngeal wall is opposite the epiglottis. Anterior is to the left, posterior is to the right.

Laufer and Baer (1988) and Esling (1996) noted that measurements of glottal width in endoscopic images were problematic because the camera is not still, thus the lens-to-object distance is not the same in all the frames, so the apparent width of the epiglottis varied considerably. This problem can be addressed by normalizing the pharyngeal diameter to the width of the epiglottis, since the lens distance to pharyngeal constriction is mirrored by the lens distance to the epiglottis. Thus,

Normalised pharyngeal diameter = D/W

where,

D= Front–back distance from epiglottis to pharyngeal wall.
W= Width of the epiglottis in current photograph.

In Figure 16.2, the images on the left show the maximum points of constriction for [s, x, h, ʔ] and the images on the right are the maximum points of constriction for [s, q, ħ, ʕ]. The images on the right clearly show wider pharyngeal width than those on the left. This can be quantified by looking at the distance between the epiglottis and pharyngeal wall, relative to the width of the epiglottis. The normalised pharyngeal diameter measurements obtained from images such as these are illustrated graphically in Figure 16.3.

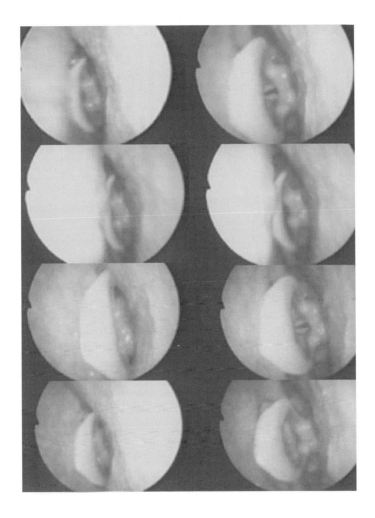

Figure 16.2 Pictures on the left show sounds that have a narrow pharyngeal diameter [ṣ, q, ħ, ʕ]. Pictures on the right show sounds that have a wide pharyngeal diameter [s, x, h, ʔ]

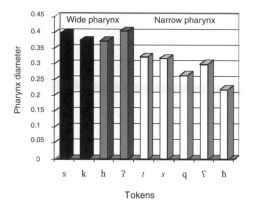

Figure 16.3 Normalised pharyngeal diameter for Arabic consonants. Orals are presented in black, laryngeals in grey and gutturals in white

16.3.1.5 Results and discussion

Figure 16.3 presents normalised pharyngeal diameter. The lower the column, the smaller the distance between the epiglottis and the pharyngeal wall. Oral sounds are presented in black, laryngeals in grey and gutturals in white. We might expect that in Arabic, since laryngeals group with gutturals phonologically, they would have a narrower pharyngeal diameter.[5] The figure shows that the [ħ] has the narrowest pharyngeal diameter, while [ʔ] has the widest pharyngeal diameter. Gutturals [*t*, s, q, ħ, ʕ] have a lower ratio than the orals [s, k] and laryngeals [h, ʔ]. An analysis of variance (ANOVA) was performed with these three groups: gutturals, orals and laryngeals as the independent variable and the normalised pharyngeal diameter as the dependent variable. The group effect was significant (F $(2, 26)= 12.536$; p=.0002). Tukey post-hoc tests were performed to determine which articulations were significantly different from each other. We found that there was a significant difference between the guttural group and the oral group. There was also a significant difference between the guttural group and the laryngeal group. There was no significant difference between the orals and the laryngeals. Thus, the laryngeals [h] and [ʔ], which behave like the other guttural sounds phonologically, do not show the degree of pharyngeal narrowing of other gutturals.

The pharyngeal narrowing which is common to the articulation of uvulars, pharyngeals and emphatics suggests that the pharynx could be considered an articulator. This preserves the original proposal of feature geometry where natural classes are associated with active articulators. However, the data also show that the tongue root is not used during the articulation of laryngeals. Hence, the implication for this with regards to feature geometry is that we cannot give these sounds the [RTR] feature, as has been proposed by Shahin (1997).

The endoscopic experiment supports the union of the emphatics, uvulars and pharyngeals under one articulator node, which is what is needed for the Salish languages. Finally, these results agree with the X-ray findings of Ghazeli (1977), which show that there is narrowing in the distance between the epiglottis and pharyngeal wall in the pharyngeals, uvulars and emphatics as opposed to nongutturals such as the coronals. However, the problem remains for the Arabic guttural class, which does unite the laryngeals with the other gutturals. This raises the question of whether a guttural zone is what unites gutturals together, or if these sounds are united acoustically. In an attempt to answer this question, an acoustic experiment was conducted.

16.4 An acoustic experiment

Before we present the design and results of the acoustic experiment, it is worthwhile to understand why we hypothesise that all gutturals, including laryngeals, have a high F1. In the acoustic theory of speech production, the vocal tract is viewed as resembling a uniform tube that is closed at one end (at the glottis) and opened at the other (the lips). If there is a constriction near the glottis this should cause the rise of F1. The F1 of the pharyngeal and uvular sounds should be high since their constriction is closer to a velocity antinode than a velocity node.

Trigo (1991: 131) says that 'according to Lindqvist (1969, 1972) there are two different kinds of laryngeal constriction: one at the level of the vocal folds and one higher up at the level of the aryepiglottic folds'. Nolan (1995) explains that the aryepiglottic folds begin from the sides of the epiglottis and end at the edges of the arytenoid cartilages. He adds that some Caucasian languages contrast these two kinds of laryngeals. Hence, he says 'It is tempting to suspect that Arabic glottals of straying in the direction of the aryepiglottals because of their phonological patterning with the pharyngeals – both sets would involve constrictions in the pharynx' (366). Thus, if Arabic laryngeals are articulated through a constriction at the level of the aryepiglottic folds, we might expect that this would raise F1. If that happens, we might be able to find that all guttural sounds could be grouped acoustically through a higher F1.[6] Below, we present the results of an acoustic analysis of the first formant frequency of the low vowel following guttural sounds.

16.4.1 Method

16.4.1.1 Material
The corpus was essentially the same that was used for the endoscopic experiment, except that we also recorded the consonant [t] and dropped [ʕ].

16.4.1.2 Subjects
We recorded five college-educated native speakers of Ammani-Jordanian Arabic; four males and one female.

16.4.1.3 Procedure
The list of words was repeated three times. The speaker spoke into a microphone and the utterance was tape recorded. SoundScope was used for digitising the data and producing individual spectrograms of each utterance. Formant values were extracted at the temporal centre of the second vowel. F1 and F2 were estimated using an LPC algorithm with 13 coefficients and a frame length of 20 ms.

16.4.1.4 Results
Mean F1 and F2 values are plotted in Figures 16.4 and 16.5, respectively. As seen in Figure 16.4, F2 does not differentiate the guttural sounds from the nonguttural sounds. Some of the gutturals, the emphatics and the [q], lower the F2. In comparison, the other gutturals [ʔ, h] do not. An ANOVA was conducted to see if there is a significant difference between the gutturals, laryngeals and orals and this was found to be the case $(F_{(2,102)}=39.105;$ $p=.0001)$. Post-hoc Tukey tests indicated that there is a significant difference between the three groups. However, this is probably due to the low F2 of the vowel following the emphatics and the [q]. Hence, the F2, as the figure illustrates, is not what distinguishes the three groups. Therefore, no further analysis will be undertaken for F2.

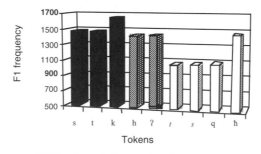

Figure 16.4 F2 of low vowels following orals, laryngeals and gutturals

288

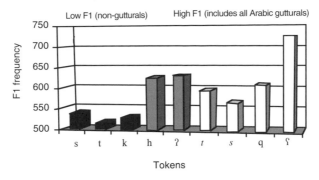

Figure 16.5 F1 of low vowels following orals, laryngeals and gutturals

If we look at the results for F1 in Figure 16.5, we will notice that it is higher for all gutturals, including the laryngeals, than the nongutturals. Each one of the columns represents the average of F1 across the five speakers. The plain sounds [s, t, k] have a lower F1 than the guttural sounds, including the laryngeals. An ANOVA indicated that there is a significant difference between the three groups: the gutturals, laryngeals and orals ($F(2, 102)= 30.020$; $p= .0001$). Post-hoc Tukey tests determined that there was a significant difference between the orals and gutturals and also the orals and the laryngeals. There is no significant difference between the gutturals and the laryngeals. This demonstrates that when the consonant is an emphatic, uvular, pharyngeal, or laryngeal, the F1 is higher than when the consonant is a nonguttural sound. Hence, all guttural sounds have a higher F1 (including the laryngeals). This acoustic grouping could explain the phonological patterning of Arabic gutturals.

However, some might argue that we should not just rely on the results of the low vowel, because in the case of the laryngeal, it is expected that laryngeals would not have formant transitions. Hence, the high F1 is the F1 of the low vowel itself. Therefore, we did another experiment and recorded the speech of two male native speakers of Ammani-Jordanian Arabic. In this case, they read words in the context of ?iCi, where the consonant was an alveolar, velar, laryngeal, emphatic, uvular, or pharyngeal. The method used was the same as the method used in the previous experiment. The results indicated that in the context of a nonguttural sound, the F1 of [i] is as low as 320 Hz. In comparison, in the context of the guttural, the F1 is between 350 Hz and 415 Hz. Hence, also in the case of an [i], the guttural sounds have higher F1 than nonguttural sounds. This was confirmed by ANOVA results which indicated that there is a significant difference between the three groups of the gutturals, laryngeals and orals ($F(2, 51)= 9.787$; $p= .0003$). Post-hoc Tukey tests indicated that the results were the same as the results for the low vowel. Laryngeals group with other pharyngeals in contrast with nongutturals.

16.4.1.5 Discussion

The above findings are supported by the results of Shahin (1997). Shahin provides acoustic evidence supporting the fact that there is what she terms 'pharyngealisation harmony' as opposed to 'uvularisation harmony'. These two harmonies are distinct harmonies in the dialect of Arabic which she focuses on, namely the Abu Shusha dialect of rural Palestinian. Most probably, these harmonies apply to all Arabic dialects as well. Pharyngealisation harmony, which is indicated by a raised F1, is triggered by laryngeals, pharyngeals, uvulars and emphatics (and also closed syllable pharyngealised vowels). In comparison, the triggers of uvularisation harmony (which is indicated by a low F2) in the dialect of Abu Shusha are the emphatics (and the [q] in the dialect of Ammani-Jordanian Arabic as found in Zawaydeh (1997)).

One might ask, do laryngeals in Salish languages also affect following vowels by raising their F1? There is evidence to indicate that Salish laryngeals do not raise the F1 of following vowels. Bessell (1992) provides acoustic measurements of the F1 and F2 values of vowels following coronals, emphatics (retracted coronals), velars, pharyngeals, uvulars and glottals from two speakers of Moses-Colombian. Her results for F1 of the nucleus indicate that the F1 means of low vowels following retracted coronals, uvulars and pharyngeals are higher than the F1 means of low vowels following coronals, velars and laryngeals. Hence, Salish languages are different from Arabic in that their laryngeals apparently do not group with gutturals acoustically.

16.5 General discussion and conclusions

The objective of this paper was to investigate why guttural sounds group together phonologically in Arabic. The proposal of McCarthy (1994) and Hayward and Hayward (1989) was that there is an articulatory guttural zone that unites these sounds. However, in this paper we presented two hypotheses. The first was that gutturals might be distinguished from nongutturals by having a narrower pharyngeal diameter. And second, that all guttural sounds have a higher F1 than do nonguttural sounds.

We presented results from two experiments on Jordanian Arabic. The experiment found narrowing for pharyngeals, uvulars and emphatics, but not for laryngeals. The second experiment found that vowels following guttural sounds, including laryngeals, have a higher F1 than vowels following oral sounds. This supports an acoustic specification of the guttural class. On the other hand, acoustic work on the Salish languages has failed to show a consistent raising of F1 by laryngeals (Bessell 1992; Shahin 1997). If we compare the different groupings of sounds found in Salish (where pharyngeals, uvulars and emphatics group together) with Semitic (where laryngeals, pharyngeals, uvulars and emphatics group together), it is possible that Salish languages exhibit grouping based on articulatory similarity. By contrast, Jordanian Arabic exhibits grouping based on acoustic similarity. This conclusion, which identifies a direct linkage between phonetic and phonological grouping, would be superior to the abstract proposal that gutturals group together phonologically because they have the same articulatory zone.

Finally, in closing, a word needs to be said about feature geometry and phonological theory in general. In the Salish guttural class, the categorisation according to the auditory feature [high F1] coincides with the articulatory feature, which we could name [Pharyngeal Diameter]. We have not done an endoscopic experiment on a native speaker of a Salish language, but we would expect that articulatorily, their pharyngeals, uvulars and emphatics will have a narrower pharyngeal width than nonguttural sounds, as we have found in Arabic. In comparison, the Arabic guttural natural class is not exclusively articulatorily based; the acoustic feature [high F1] unites the guttural sound, not the articulatory feature [Pharyngeal Diameter]. Thus, auditory/ acoustic features need to be included in phonological theory, as has been proposed by Flemming (1995). Flemming (1995) presented a number of cases where natural classes cannot be accounted for solely on articulatory-based features. Examples include the grouping of coronals and front vowels (acoustic basis = high F2), plain labials and rounded vowels (acoustic basis = low F2), and back and round (acoustic basis = low F2). The case of the Arabic guttural class seems to be one more case where a natural class is accounted for acoustically (acoustic basis = high F1).

Notes

This paper summarises portions of Zawaydeh's (1999) doctoral dissertation. I thank Kenneth de Jong, Stuart Davis, Robert Port and Karen Forrest for invaluable help and guidance. I thank the following linguists for their comments: S. Frisch, K. Iskarous, P. Keating, M. Kitahara, P. Ladefoged, J. McCarthy, J. Pierrehumbert, K. Shahin and K. Tajima. This research was supported by an Indiana University Grant in Aid of Research and a Fred Householder Grant from the Department of Linguistics.

1   Uvularised segments are commonly referred to as emphatics or pharyngealised sounds (McCarthy 1994).
2   Nolan (1995) argued that the lowering of the jaw in the cases of Arabic pharyngeals and glottals may be interpreted 'in terms of passive effects on the jaw of muscular contraction centrally involved in the articulation of those sounds' (367), and hence the lowering would not be counted as evidence against Goldstein's hypothesis.
3   There are two types of pharyngeal constriction: lower pharyngeal constriction (used for the articulation of pharyngeals) and upper pharyngeal constriction (used for the articulation of uvulars and emphatics). See Ghazeli (1977); Catford (1977) and Ladefoged and Maddieson (1996) for more on this topic.
4   Uppercase [T, D, S, Z] refer to the uvularised (emphatic) sounds in Arabic.

5 /χ/ has been dropped from this study since it was not clear whether it was articulated as an uvular or a velar. Discussion of this problem is beyond the scope of this paper.

6 It is hard to determine from the endoscopic images the role of the aryepiglottic folds, because they are often obscured by the epiglottis.

17
Pitch discrimination during breathy versus modal phonation

DANIEL SILVERMAN

17.1 Introduction

The typology of linguistic sound patterning indicates an extreme dispreference for the simultaneous implementation of contrastive tone and contrastive non-modal phonation. Accordingly, I performed a psychoacoustic experiment to investigate whether human auditory perceptual limitations may play a role in this aspect of phonological systems. The experiment consisted of subjects listening to pairs of stimuli – modally phonated pairs and breathy pairs, deriving from the natural speech of Jalapa Mazatec speakers – which differed in pitch to varying degrees. Subjects were asked to judge whether the two stimuli were the same or different in pitch. I found that, indeed, listeners are better at discerning pitch differences in complex tones implemented during modal phonation than they are discerning pitch differences implemented during breathy phonation.

17.2 Background

Moore (1989) discusses a number of relevant findings in the domain of human perception of complex tones. I summarise here the most pertinent among them.

The lowest harmonics up to the fifth seem to dominate for the purpose of pitch perception. In this harmonic range, resolution of individual overtones is possible. A pattern-recognition model of pitch perception (deriving from Terhardt's models, e.g. 1974, and studies by Ritsma 1962, 1963, 1967 and

Plomp 1967) has been offered to account for this finding, in which the values of individual harmonics are determined, and the distance between these harmonics is subsequently calculated, culminating in a pitch percept. However just-noticeable differences (JNDs) found in human pitch perception cannot be explained by this theory alone. Auditory filter bandwidths (critical bands) are too wide by a factor of about 30 compared with the JND for pitch, and therefore the pattern recognition model cannot rely solely on the individual harmonics alone. The temporal theory plays a role here since it relates the neural firings to auditory filter outputs, and thus can account for JNDs. At higher frequency levels, where individual harmonics are not resolvable, Moore argues that a temporal model – deriving from the work of Schouton (e.g. 1970) – may best account for the existence of a pitch percept: the pitch percept is ascribed to the temporal rate of repetition of the complex waveform. Moore concludes that an account of pitch perception at both lower and higher frequency ranges is best characterised by a 'spectro-temporal' model, in which both harmonic structure and pulse period are relevant.

Moore's report is based on studies in which the experimental stimuli consist of a high signal-to-noise ratio, and well as a periodic rate of repetition, thus mimicking certain qualities of normal human phonation. However, if stimuli were to depart from normal phonation in consisting of a marked lowering of signal-to-noise ratio, as well as a less periodic rate of repetition, it remains to be seen whether subjects are equally adept at perceiving and discriminating pitches.

So-called breathy phonation possesses both these qualities: lower signal-to-noise ratio, and moderate pulse period irregularity. For example, in Jalapa Mazatec (an Otomanguean language of Oaxaca, Mexico) breathy vowels involve a marked decrease in signal-to-noise ratio (Silverman, Blankenship, Kirk and Ladefoged 1995). Moreover, the glottal pulse period in breathy vowels is irregular (Kirk, Ladefoged and Ladefoged 1993). For these reasons, pitch perception during Jalapa Mazatec breathy phonation may be less accurate than pitch perception during modal phonation.

Briefly now, consider the place of Jalapa Mazatec in the typology of tonal and phonation contrasts. Some languages are tonal, such as Mandarin Chinese. Here, modally phonated vowels possess tone (although the low tone may occasionally possess a creaky quality).

Table 17.1 *Mandarin Chinese*

high level	tʰan˥	*greedy*
mid rising	tʰan˧˥	*deep*
low (-rising)	tʰan˨˩(˦)	*perturbed*
high falling	tʰan˥˩	*spy*

In contrast, some languages have contrastive breathiness while lacking tone. Gujarati is one such language (Patel and Mody 1961; Fischer-Jørgensen 1970; Taylor 1985). In such languages, breathy phonation is typically implemented for the duration of the vocalic gesture, and often into sonorant codas as well.

Table 17.2 *Gujarati (Fischer-Jørgensen 1970: no glosses provided)*

tʃir	mɔr	dṳd
bi̤	dɔ̤r̩	pɛ̤lo
sɛd͡ʒ	kɔ̤r̩	ta̤ro
mɛk	kɔ̤	wa̤li
ba̤ɪ	pɔr	kəɽi

Third, some tone languages possess non-modal phonation contrasts as well as tone. But while a full array of tonal patterns is found on modally phonated vowels, non-modally phonated vowels never contrast for tone. White Hmong exemplifies this pattern (Lyman 1974; Smalley 1976; Huffman 1987; Ratliff 1992). Breathy phonation here is reportedly implemented for the duration of the vowel.

Table 17.3 *White Hmong*

High	tau˥	*pumpkin*
Rising	tau˧˥	*to dam up (water)*
Low	tau˨˩	*axe*
Mid (normal)	tau˧	*to be able*
Falling (normal)	tau˥˩	*sp. of grass*
Creaky	ta̰ṵ˨˩	*bean*
Breathy	ta̤ṳ˥˩	*to follow*

Finally, some languages, such as Jalapa Mazatec, possess vowels in which tone and non-modal phonation fully cross-classify, that is, both tonal and phonatory contrasts may reside on a single vowel. Significantly, vowels which possess both tone and contrastive breathiness here are realised in a part-breathy/part-modal fashion. Specifically, the first portion of the vowel is breathy, while the latter portion is more or less modal. Anticipating my findings now, since pitch (tone) is more reliably distinguished during modal phonation, a portion of the vowel is given to plain voicing, where tone contrasts are presumably more salient. The remaining portion of the vowel, however, is breathy. In this way, I suggest that both phonation and tone contrasts are effectively conveyed to the listener, with tone residing on the vowel's latter, modal portion.

Table 17.4 *Jalapa Mazatec*

mmææ:˥	*wants*
nṇaa˥	*my tongue*
ɲṇaa˦	*nine*
jjææ˩	*boil*
wwọo˦	*hungry*

Indeed, throughout the Otomanguean family, tone and non-modal phonation are temporally arranged in various ways, even contrastively within a single language, as shown schematically in Table 17.5. Note that there is phonological evidence that all the patterns in Table 17.5 are treated as monosyllables (see especially Longacre 1952 and Silverman 1995, 1997). Thus Mazatec possesses vowels which may be breathy during their first portion, while contrastive tone values reside on the vowels' latter, modally phonated portion. Chinantec possesses this pattern, but also possesses a contrastive pattern in which breathy phonation *follows* modal phonation. Finally, Trique possesses both these contrastive patterns, and also possesses so-called vocalic 'interruption' in which the laryngeal intrudes upon the middle portion of the toned vowel.

Table 17.5 *Timing contrasts between tone and breathy phonation in Otomanguean*

Mazatec	CVV́		
Chinantec	CVV́	CV́h	
Trique	CVV́	CV́h	CV́ɦV́

Indeed, it is this very fact that provides the impetus for the present study. Specifically, why should breathy phonation be limited to only a portion of the vowel in these languages, whereas the canonical realisation of breathy vowels in fact involves breathiness throughout? Might there indeed be an auditory incompatibility between tone and breathiness which has led to this unusual sequencing of articulatory events? This is not to say, of course, that articulatory incompatibilities might not be playing a role here as well. That is, particular phonation-based gestures and pitch-based gestures may be difficult to simultaneously implement, or to implement in rapid succession, as they may make conflicting articulatory demands on the vocal apparatus.

The present study sets out to investigate only the issue of perceptual discriminability, however. Listeners were asked to discriminate pitch values between pairs of stimuli that were either modal or breathy in their phonatory characteristics. The stimuli themselves were derived from actual Jalapa Mazatec vowels. Results indicate that, indeed, subjects are better at distinguishing pitch values implemented during modal phonation than they are distinguishing pitch values implemented during breathy phonation. Implications for cross-linguistic tendencies in phonological structure are discussed as well.

17.3 Stimuli

Three words of Jalapa Mazatec – (a)[ᵑgi˧ᵑga̤a˥] 'he fastened', (b) [ⁿda̤a˥] 'hard' and (c) [mm̤æ̤æ˥] 'he wants' – were digitised with the Kay Computer Speech Laboratory. The first two words were spoken by normal adult male native speakers, while the third word was spoken by a normal adult female native speaker. Recordings were made in an outdoor setting in the village of Jalapa de Diaz, Oaxaca, Mexico, by Keith Johnson, Paul Kirk, Peter Ladefoged, Joyce McDonough and Donca Steriade, employing a Marantz portable cassette recorder which had a frequency response that was better than ±2 dB over the range 70 – 10,000 Hz, and had a signal-to-noise ratio of 42 dB.

Wideband and narrowband spectrograms of these source data, as well as their pitch tracks, are in Figure 17.1. Note in particular the shift in phonation during the vowel. This is best seen in the narrowband spectrograms, in which noise accompanies the harmonic structure during the early, breathy portion of the vowel, though it is significantly reduced during the latter, modal portion. Note especially the fourth harmonic, in the narrowband spectrograms, which is within what might be the most important region for the perception of pitch during speech. The third form, [mm̤æ̤æ˥], possesses a significantly less marked transition from breathy to modal phonation. This is likely due to the absence of a stop release in the transition from consonant to vowel here: oral stop releases, as opposed to sonorant releases, are aerodynamically better suited to induce a robust realisation of contrastive laryngeal states (Kingston 1985). Also note that pitch height is typically most stable on the modal portion of the vowel. Considering the results of Rosenberg (1965), who finds that when a pulse train varies, or jitters, by more than 10%, an otherwise just-noticeable pitch difference within the 300-1000 Hz range is rendered indiscriminible, the stable realisation – and/or (in the case of contours) smooth gliding realisation – of pitch is consistent with the hypothesis that tone is better conveyed during modal phonation than during breathy phonation.

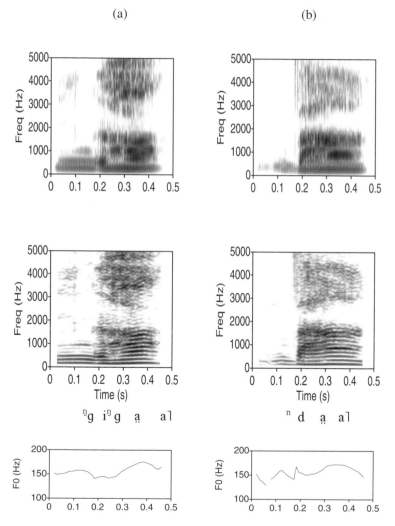

Figure 17.1(a) (b) Wideband and narrowband spectrograms, and pitch tracks of digitised speech from Jalapa Mazatec: (a) [ᵑgiᵑgạ a˥] (b) [ⁿdạa˥]

(c)

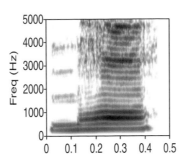

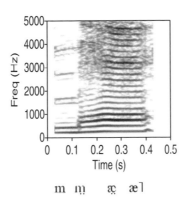

m m̥ ą̥ æ˺

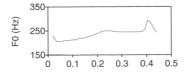

Figure 17.1 (c) Wideband and narrowband spectrograms, and pitch tracks of digitised speech from Jalapa Mazatec: [m m̥ ą̥ æ]

After digitisation, both the breathy portion and modal portion of each word were extracted. As the breathy component of Jalapa Mazatec vowels is lower in pitch than its associated modal component in the case of high tones, I lowered the pitch of modal portions to approximate the pitch of breathy portions, employing the SoundEdit17.2 'bender' feature. Pitch tracks for the base stimuli are in Figure 17.2.

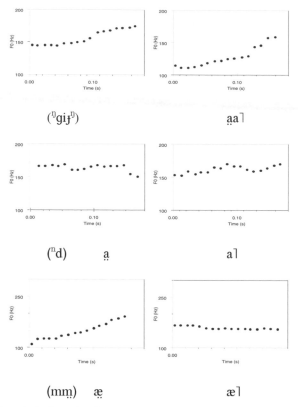

Figure 17.2 Pitch tracks for base stimuli

The peak amplitudes of the six waveforms of the stimuli were normalised, and onsets and offsets were ramped in order to avoid click artefacts. The respective fundamental frequencies of each waveform were increased in increments of approximately 3 Hz, up to 24 Hz, which resulted in six continua with nine steps each.

For the pitch shifts, the signal was simply sped up. The playback sample rate was manipulated and the sound resampled to the original sample rate. In this procedure, spectra are shifted in frequency and thus the ratios of component frequencies are preserved. Given the spectral shift involved, some slope distortion may be added to the modified signal: formants are shifted downwards in slowed-down forms, upwards in speeded-up forms. But given the very minor signal adjustments employed in this study, spectral shifts are small, and, especially important, equally present in both the modal and breathy continua. To exemplify this effect, approximate F1 values for the baseline, fourth, and final steps for the [ⁿd̪a̤aˈ] continua are presented in Table 17.6.

Table 17.6 *F1 values for baseline, fourth and final steps for the [ⁿḍạa l] continua*

	F1 modal [a]	F1 breathy [ạ]
Baseline:	841 Hz	979 Hz
Fourth step:	879	1141
Final step:	935	1187

Within-continuum increases in F1 values are a consequence of speeding up the recording, while the lower F1 values present in the modal continuum are a consequence of slowing down the baseline form to approximate the pitch of the breathy baseline form.

All forms were then converted to 200 ms in length. Every form was paired with every other form within its continuum, unless the difference between a given pair exceeded 12 Hz. This resulted in a total of 366 stimulus pairs, as schematised in Table 17.7. Thus, for example, one form possessing a fundamental frequency 21 Hz above the baseline was paired with all forms between 9 and 24 Hz above the baseline: forms between the baseline and 9 Hz above the baseline were not paired with this form, however, as their differences exceed 12 Hz.

Table 17.7 *Schematic of all paired stimuli for one of the six continua*

	0 Hz	3 Hz	6 Hz	9 Hz	12 Hz	15 Hz	18 Hz	21 Hz	24 Hz
0 Hz									
3 Hz									
6 Hz									
9 Hz									
12 Hz									
15 Hz									
18 Hz									
21 Hz									
24 Hz									

17.4 Subjects and procedure

Ten non-Jalapa Mazatec-speaking UCLA graduate students in phonetics/phonology listened (individually) in a sound booth to 1000 trials each (501 'different' pairs; 499 'same' pairs), presented in blocks of 50. The inter-stimulus interval was 300 ms, while the intertrial interval was 3 sec. Subjects were asked to judge for each pair whether the two stimuli were the same or different in pitch.

Non-Jalapa Mazatec speakers were chosen because they are readily available, but also because they might be more capable of detecting the exceedingly minor pitch differences involved, as they are less likely to be influenced by linguistically based tonal categorical perception.

17.5 Results

Subjects performed more accurately on modal vowel pairs than on breathy vowel pairs (ANOVA, $p < .05$). This is indicated by the higher error rate in breathy pairs versus corresponding modal pairs in Figure 17.3. Moreover, at the 3 Hz and 6 Hz intervals, performance was significantly worse than performance at the 9 and 12 Hz intervals (Scheffé, $< .05$; see the boxed values in Figure 17.3).

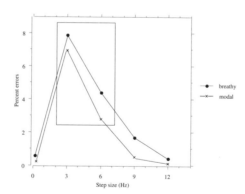

Figure 17.3 Results of same-different pitch experiment (filled circles = breathy voice ; stars = modal voice)

Thus, not only was subject performance significantly worse overall on breathy token pairs, but also, subjects performed significantly worse as the pitch interval between tokens fell to approximately 17.6 Hz and below.

In the debriefing interview, most subjects reported being unaware that the stimuli were derived from actual language, and instead assumed that they were computer-generated 'bleeps', suggesting that linguistically based categorical perception would not have been a factor, regardless of the native language of the subjects.

17.6 Discussion and conclusion

The results of this study may be seen as complementing those of Rosenberg (1965), who, recall, found that when a pulse train varies, or jitters, by more than 10%, an otherwise just-noticeable pitch difference within the 300–1000 Hz range is rendered indiscriminible. Thus whether jittered (a common acoustic correlate of vocalic 'creak') or reduced in signal-to-noise ratio (a common acoustic correlate of vocalic breathiness), or perhaps especially both, pitch perception during non-modal phonation suffers.

Of course, experimental data cannot be generalised directly to natural linguistic data. However, the results of the present study suggest that tonal and phonation contrasts have the distributions they do for good reason. Specifically, although it is only in an experimental setting, as opposed to a natural linguistic setting, that listeners may be called upon to determine just- and near-just-noticeable differences in pitch, it should not be surprising that languages might evolve to avoid less-good contrasts in favour of better ones. Such a 'sensitive dependence on initial conditions' (Gleick 1987: 8), is fully consistent with the hypothesis that minor phonetic distinctions that are never employed in phonological systems might nonetheless constitute the 'phylogenetic' origin of phonetic distinctions that *are* linguistically relevant.

There are in fact various tendencies in phonological systems that support this line of reasoning. First, trained subjects are able to discriminate minor differences in voice-onset time (VOT) that are never employed contrastively in language (see, for example, Strange 1972). Languages typically employ VOT differences that are far less effortfully noticeable; positive VOT (aspirated), zero VOT (plain), and negative VOT (voiced).

Second, nasal vowel systems tend to possess fewer quality contrasts than oral vowel systems do. For example, many American English dialects have lost the *pin–pen* contrast. The standard account of this asymmetry implicates the presence of the nasal pole and zero structure, which is superimposed on the oral formant structure. This superimposition clearly does not obliterate the *pin–pen* distinction in all dialects, but might nonetheless make it less likely that a language should exploit the oral space as fully in this context, thus possibly influencing this diachronic merger.

Third, certain low-level phonetic information may come to take a prominent phonological role as other cues undergo diachronic attrition. The pronounced English vowel-length distinction exemplifies this phenomenon, in which a difficult voicing contrast in coda stops has been displaced on to a primary vowel-length contrast (e.g. Raphael 1972). Similarly, certain cases of 'tonogenesis', in which another difficult voicing contrast evolves into a tonal one (as in Cantonese), shows that rather insignificant automatic features can come to play prominent functional roles in the system of contrasts.

While the discussed implications of the present findings – that distinctions which phonological systems never exploit might nonetheless constrain phonological patterning at a phylogenetic distance – are more speculative than both the second and third cases just discussed, they nonetheless should not be dismissed out of hand. To the extent that parallels can be observed between natural language typology and experimentally ascertained perceptual asymmetries, psychoacoustic experimentation along the present lines may constitute a potentially fruitful base for phonological theorisation.

Note

This research was supported by NIH Training Grant T32 DC 00008. Thanks to Norma Antoñanzas-Barroso, Bruce Gerratt and Jody Kreiman for their support at every stage of this study. Thanks also to Khalil Iskarous for technical assistance.

18

The phonetic interpretation of register: evidence from Yorùbá

KATRINA HAYWARD, JUSTIN WATKINS AND
AKIN OYÈTÁDÉ

18.1 Introduction

This paper is concerned with voice quality–pitch associations and their possible implications for theories of tonal register. A voice quality–pitch association is the systematic use of a particular voice quality to mark out a particular part of the phonational range or, in the case of a tone language, a particular tone. English is a possible example of a language which has a voice quality–pitch association. At least in the pronunciations with which we are familiar, the phonation type known as 'creak' may be, as it were, added to low pitches, for example in the low fall and fall–rise intonation tunes. In this way, creaky phonation (if used) is associated with the lower end of the phonational range. There is also some evidence that breathy voice may be associated with higher pitches (Pierrehumbert 1997). This is not usually commented on, but it is possible that English speakers are sensitive to it. One of the motivations of Pierrehumbert's work was to improve the quality of speech synthesis.

In some languages, an opposite type of association has been reported, with breathy voice being added to low pitches. An example is Kalam Kohistani, for which Baart (1999: 92) reports that vowels which have low tone may be pronounced with breathy voice, especially when they occur in word-initial syllables. Such examples demonstrate that the (consistent or potential) association of creaky voice with low pitch is not universal. However, the two cases are alike in that it is the bottom of the pitch range which is assigned a distinctive non-modal phonation type. There are also a number of well-known cases where a voice quality–pitch association has developed by spread of non-modal phonation from a preceding consonant. However, as our choice of examples makes clear, voice quality–pitch associations may also arise which are not explicable with reference to the consonantal environment.

Voice quality–pitch associations, so far as we know, have not received much systematic study, although many phoneticians would say that they are common. This may reflect the difficulties of separating out the systematic use of voice quality from personal quality, specific to an individual or social group, and paralinguistic uses of voice quality (cf. Laver 1994: 397-9). Nevertheless, it seems possible that voice quality might be of some relevance to the problem of how tonal contrasts should be specified in tone languages. The purpose of the present paper is to explore this possibility and to present some data on the relationship between voice quality and pitch in a tone language (Yorùbá). It should be borne in mind that our main purpose is to present the problem and outline questions for future research, and that more extensive study is needed of speech produced outside a laboratory setting. At the same time, the results, though preliminary, are not without interest.

18.2 Tonal register

Tonal 'register' is commonly understood as involving a binary division of a speaker's pitch range into upper and lower subranges. These subranges may themselves be subdivided into upper and lower portions, allowing for four distinct level tones. Registers have also provided a key to understanding the problems of tonal representation in East Asian languages with contour tones (Yip 1993, 1995). In a feature geometry, it is supposed that register will correspond to a distinct node, which may spread from one tone-bearing unit to an adjacent one (see Yip (1995) for an overview).

Different views exist as to the possible phonetic basis of the register division. According to Clements (1983: 149), 'we are dealing with subdivisions within an acoustically *homogenous* phonetic dimension, that of pitch'. This makes the division point between registers somewhat arbitrary. Because the point of division between high and low registers is rather arbitrary, the concept of 'register' has been extendable so that it may potentially refer to any 'subportion of the total range within which any speaker may produce linguistically significant tonal contrasts' (Clements 1983: 155). This is the basis of 'register' as used in the context of intonation theory (Clements 1983; Ladd 1990).

A second possible view is that upper and lower registers are defined by some particular properties in addition to F_0. Such a view of tonal register would have some affinity with 'register' as used in studies of the singing voice, where it is commonly defined as 'a phonation frequency range in which all tones are perceived as being produced in a similar way and which possess a similar voice timbre' (Sundberg 1987: 49).

Specific proposals have been made by Bao (1990: 159), Duanmu (1992), and van der Hulst (1995: 111-12). There is not space to give an account of these here. Despite some obvious differences, the three proposals are alike in that they are inspired by affinities between consonant types and tone. All three give explicit recognition to affinities between voiced/voiceless contrasts in obstruents, low versus high tone, low versus high tonal register, and non-tonal 'register' contrasts of the type well-attested in South-East Asia. Indeed, the proposals might be said to bring together the South-East Asianist's conception of 'register' and the tonologist's conception of 'register'. Van der Hulst's proposals also take account of attested affinities between glottal stops and high pitch and glottal fricatives and low pitch (Hombert 1978: 93-4). Duanmu's hypothesis – which involves an association between 'tense, clear' quality and upper register and 'lax, muddy' quality and lower register – makes very specific phonetic predictions and thus is easily falsifiable (see Yip 1995: 485).

As we have seen in Section 18.1, voice quality-pitch associations are not universal. Accordingly, there can be no universal specification of phonological tonal registers in terms of voice qualities. However, it is still necessary to ask why distinctive voice qualities should come to be associated with tones at all and whether voice quality–pitch associations might play any role in the specification of tonal register. More systematic study of tone languages spoken outside Asia will be of crucial importance here.

18.3 Phonation type, voice quality, pitch and tonal contrasts

It seems natural to assume that correlations between pitch and voice quality will have a laryngeal basis. However, it is not necessarily the case that different perceived qualities are due to laryngeal setting alone, since various supraglottal settings might also be brought into play. Accordingly, we shall refer to both 'voice quality' and 'phonation type'. 'Voice quality' will refer to a perceptually distinct quality which has (or is expected to have) identifiable acoustic correlates. 'Phonation type' will refer to a particular mode of vocal fold vibration. It is to be expected that distinctive phonation type would result in distinctive voice quality; however, a distinctive voice quality might involve other physiological mechanisms in addition to, or instead of, phonation type.

Since most discussion in the literature has centred on phonation types, we shall also concentrate on this aspect. We shall follow Ladefoged's approach (cf. Ladefoged 1971, 1973) which classifies phonation types with reference to a single dimension based on glottal constriction. Comparisons will be made in terms of more or less so that, for example, a statement that one vowel is more creaky than another implies that it is further towards the creaky end of the continuum but not necessarily that it is creaky in an absolute sense.

In many discussions of phonation types, it is stated explicitly, or at least implied that phonation contrasts are independent of pitch and can occur across the whole of a speaker's range (Ní Chasaide and Gobl 1997). Nevertheless, examples of languages in which phonation type – or, more generally, voice quality – and pitch contrast independently are rare (see Silverman (1997) for a thorough discussion).[1] At the same time, it is not uncommon to find phonation type and pitch working together in a language's system of tonal contrasts. Such associations of particular voice qualities with particular 'tones' is a well-known characteristic of tonal systems in East and South-East Asia. A simple but clear example is the so-called 'third tone' of Mandarin Chinese which falls to low pitch and may be pronounced with creaky voice at the lowest point of the contour.

In other parts of the world, it is less common to think of voice quality as a component of tonal contrasts. Phonation or voice quality features may be reported in passing and researchers may regard them as common when describing tone systems in an anecdotal way, but more formal accounts of tonal contrasts are generally based on pitch alone, represented in terms of H and L pitches. It seems clear that a more systematic study of the voice quality–pitch associations in tone languages outside of Asia would shed light on some of the questions raised in Section 18.2.

18.4 Voice quality and tone in Yorùbá

As is well known, Yorùbá is generally described as having three distinct tones, high (H), mid (M), and low (L). Pulleyblank (1986) has argued that the mid tone should be considered a default and should therefore be left unspecified in underlying representations. He also suggests that Yorùbá tones are divided into two registers, upper and lower. In his analysis, both M and L tones belong to the lower register. It has also been suggested, on the basis of alternations between L and M, that Yorùbá originally had only two tones, and that the division between M and L is the result of a historical split (Stahlke 1974).

Other descriptions of Yorùbá have called attention to similarities between the H and M tones as distinct from L. For example, Ward (1952: 33) writes that 'When one hears a word with two level tones which are not felt to be near the bottom of the speaking voice, it is usually impossible to say whether they are two high or two mid tones.' A similar view is taken by Rowlands (1955).

It has also been noted that the intonational behavior of the L tone distinguishes it from the M and H tones in that its F_0 may fall over the course of an utterance while the M and H tones remain more or less constant in pitch (Connell and Ladd 1990). This is in line with earlier studies (LaVelle 1974;

Hombert 1976; cf. Gandour 1978) which suggested that, in final position, lowered pitch level and/or a falling F_0 contour are necessary for distinguishing L from M tones. The results of perceptual experiments carried out by Harrison (1996) are also consistent with this general conclusion, insofar as none of his synthetic stimuli – all of which had flat F_0 contours – were identified by listeners as L. A final point to be made here is that, in the experience of one of us in teaching Yorùbá to speakers of European languages, students find the high and mid tones easy to produce but also easy to confuse; the low tone seems to require more effort and is the last to be acquired by learners. All of these considerations suggest, in agreement with Ward and Rowlands, that L has some special characteristics which distinguish it phonetically from M and H.

A somewhat different perspective emerges from a perceptual study by Bakare (1995). Bakare's stimuli were CV nonsense syllables pronounced by two speakers, one male and one female, with non-overlapping ranges. He conducted both identification and discrimination tests, using both Yorùbá and non-Yorùbá listeners. His conclusion was that, for the Yorùbá listeners, there was a perceptual hierarchy, H being the most distinctive, followed by L, followed by M.

Bakare's study is also interesting in that he investigated characteristics of the tones other than F_0. In his data, all three tones were distinguished by duration and intensity. As regards duration, the M tone was longer than H and L. As regards intensity, H was highest and L was lowest. He also observed differences in the frequency of the third formant (F_3), which was highest for the H tone and lowest for the L tone. Although Bakare's methodology did not make it possible to evaluate the relative contributions of these potential cues, his acoustic data suggested that intensity was likely to be of particular importance. Unfortunately, his statistical analysis included no post-hoc comparisons, so it is not possible to know whether any groupings, such as H versus M and L, might have emerged from his data.

To sum up, it has been argued on phonological grounds that H (upper register) is opposed to M and L (lower register) in Yorùbá. By contrast, discussions of the tones with a more phonetic orientation have pointed to a division L versus M and H. An exception to this generalisation is the study of Bakare, which identified H as the most distinctive, and which provided some evidence that factors other than F_0 might play a role in distinguishing between tones. The aim of the present experiment was to carry this line of research further by investigating the phonation types of the three tones.

18.4.1 Experimental procedure

The design of the experiment replicated the first experiment described in Laniran (1993: 32). It was based on a 42-item list of nonsense CV syllables, containing all possible combinations of seven vowel qualities (/i e ɛ a ɔ o u/) on three tones (H, M and L), preceded by two initial consonants (/t/ and /l/). These were placed in the frame sentence:

> So ＿＿＿ kan sí i
> /sɔ ＿＿＿ kã síi/
> *Say ＿＿＿ once more*

The recordings were of three Nigerian male speakers, aged between 30 and 45, with native competence in standard Yorùbá. None of the speakers reported abnormal speech or hearing. The materials were presented to the informants in written form with all tone marks included. Two of the subjects found the task of reading a tone-marked text somewhat difficult, and took the script away to study at home before the recording sessions. One of the authors, who is himself a native speaker of Yorùbá and a teacher of the language, was present during the sessions and checked through the recorded material afterwards. (He was the third informant.)

Simultaneous digital andio and laryngograph recordings were made in a sound-proofed booth in the recording studio of the School of Oriental and African Studies using the following: a Bruel and Kjær consenser microphone (type 4165); a Brüel and Kjær measuring amplifier (type 2609), set at 30 mV with the weighting filter set on 'fast'; a Fourcin portable laryngograph and processor (Laryngograph Ltd.); a Sony DAT Recorder (type DTC-ZE700). (The laryngograph and its use is described in Abberton, Howard and Fourcin 1989 and Howard, Lindsey and Allan 1990.) For the purposes of analysis, the laryngograph track was passed through the analogue laryngograph processor, and the recordings were converted to computer sound files using the 'SPG Analyser' programme, version 3.00. The sampling rate was set at 10 kHz.

18.4.2 Measurements

The SPG Analyser program derives Fundamental frequency (F_0) and closed quotient (CQ) from the laryngograph waveform. The closed quotient is defined as the ratio of the duration of the closed phased to the duration of the entire period of vocal fold vibration. In the algorithm used by the program, the beginning of the closed phase is defined as the positive peak of the differentiated waveform, while the end of the closed phase is a threshold fixed at 30% of the total peak-to-peak amplitude. For most of the tokens, readings were taken at the mid-point of the vowel. However, when L tokens exhibited a falling contour, average F_0 and CQ were calculated over a 100 ms portion of the vowel.[2] Other things being equal, higher values of CQ are diagnostic of creakier phonation while lower values of CQ are diagnostic of breathier phonation. However, it is also important to relate observed CQ values to the overall range of values employed by the individual speaker (see Lindsey, Hayward and Haruna 1992).

Three acoustic measures commonly used to quantify phonation type were made from narrow-band spectra (40 Hz effective bandwidth, 512-point FFT), which are also calculated and displayed by the SPG programme (see Ladefoged, Maddieson and Jackson 1988 for an overview of techniques and Watkins 1997 for a discussion of some of the problems involved). These were:

(1)   The difference in amplitude (in dB) between the first and second harmonics (H_2-H_1) (see Maddieson and Ladefoged 1985).

(2)   The difference in amplitude (in dB) between the first harmonic and the most energetic harmonic in the first formant peak (F_1-F_0) (see Kirk, Ladefoged and Ladefoged 1984; Ní Chasaide and Gobl 1997: 446). For both measure 1 and measure 2, higher values are diagnostic of creakier phonation, lower values of breathier phonation.

(3)   As a measure of spectral tilt, a simplified variant of the 'resonance balance' measure proposed by Schutte and Miller (1985). This was the difference in amplitude (in dB) between the highest harmonic peaks in the frequency ranges 0–1 kHz and 3.5–4.5 kHz. The higher-frequency value was subtracted from the lower. Lower values therefore indicate more prominent higher frequencies. Greater spectral tilt is an expected consequence of breathier phonation (see Ní Chasaide and Gobl 1997: 439). It is also associated (via phonation type) with smaller vocal effort and decreased loudness, so that spectral tilt may serve as a cue for the perception of linguistic stress (Sluijter, van Heuven and Pacilly 1997). However, it is also possible that spectral tilt may be influenced by the supraglottal configuration. The measure we have used was designed for studies of the singing voice as a measure of the strength of the 'singing formant'. In this case, the configuration of the lower pharynx is thought to play an important role (Sundberg 1987: 119-20).

Statistical analysis was carried out using the SPSS program Version 6.1. Means and standard deviations for all the measures were computed for each speaker–tone combination. A four-way analysis of variance (ANOVA) was carried out for each measure. A oneway ANOVA, with Scheffé post-hoc comparisons was also carried out for each measure, with tone as the single factor. For the purposes of the discussion below, the critical value of p (which determines the significance or non-significance of a result) is taken to be 0.05.

18.4.3 Results

Our overall impressions were that the low tone had a distinctive quality for all three speakers. However, voice quality was also influenced to some extent by vowel quality and the identity of the initial consonant. Close and close-mid vowels were breathier than open and open-mid vowels, and also tended to have longer VOT in the /t/-initial tokens.[3] The initial /t/ which appeared in half the tokens was aspirated, with the result that vowels were somewhat breathier in /t/-initial words than in /l/-initial words. It is not surprising, therefore, that we observe large standard deviations for all the measures when the data are grouped by tone and speaker.

Means and standard deviations for all the variables are presented in Table 18.1, and the results of the ANOVA tests are presented in Table 18.2. We shall not discuss the results for F_0 or for duration (which we also measured) in any detail here. As regards F_0, the three subjects were rather different as regards the extent of the ranges used in the recording. This was mainly a matter of the upper end of the range, since the lower end was very similar (roughly 120 Hz in the middle of the vowel for the low tone).

18.4.3.1 Closed quotient

The clearest result is for Subject 3, who exhibits markedly higher mean CQ for L as opposed to M and H. Subject 1 shows increasing mean CQ from H to M to L, though the overall range is smaller. In contrast, Subject 2 shows only small differences in mean CQ, and, in his case, the value for M is less than for L and H. The one-way ANOVA indicated that there was a significant difference between tones (F(2,123)= 8.5, p < 001); the Scheffé test indicated a grouping of H and M versus L.

Table 18.1 *Means and standard deviations (in italics) of measured correlates of Yorùbá tone for individual speakers and for pooled data (**in bold**)*

	F_0			CQ			H_2-H_1		
	S1	S2	S3	S1	S2	S3	S1	S2	S3
H	154.5	184.9	206.0	48	49	38	-.4	4.3	2.9
	8.4	*7.7*	*6.5*	*5.2*	*5.0*	*2.3*	*4.2*	*9.3*	*8.9*
	181.8			**45**			**2.3**		
	22.5			*6.7*			*8.1*		
M	138.5	156.6	158.7	50	46	38	5.4	0.1	3.9
	8.9	*6.3*	*6.9*	*3.2*	*13.3*	*3.1*	*3.9*	*6.7*	*4.0*
	151.3					**44.7**			**0.6**
	11.8					*9.6*			*6.3*
L	116.4	120.7	121.2	53.3	49.5	47.6	9.2	10.0	9.7
	6.9	*6.0*	*7.7*	*2.4*	*4.4*	*3.1*	*2.8*	*2.2*	*3.7*
	119.5					**50.1**			**9.7**
	7.3	*4.2*	*3.0*						

	$F1$-F_0			Spectral tilt			Duration		
	S1	S2	S3	S1	S2	S3	S1	S2	S3
H	7.1	11.0	11.0	17.1	16.0	15.8	163	207	179
	7.8	*7.3*	*8.1*	*7.8*	*6.0*	*5.7*	*28*	*35*	*21*
	10.2			**16.4**			**183**		
	8.1			*6.6*			*34*		
M	9.9	7.6	8.0	18.7	15.3	15.7	161	198	201
	5.6	*8.4*	*7.7*	*6.1*	*7.5*	*6.4*	*22*	*32*	*23*
	8.5			**16.6**			**187**		
	7.4			*6.8*			*32*		
L	9.2	10.0	9.7	15.4	14.0	15.0	24	23	28
	5.3	*4.1*	*3.7*	*6.9*	*9.5*	*6.2*	*25*	*35*	*22*
	14.9			**25.1**			**170**		
	4.5			*7.9*			*28*		

18.4.3.2 Spectral measures (1) and (2)

Our first two spectral measures, H_2-H_1 and F_1-F_0, are both concerned with the relative prominence of the fundamental component (first harmonic) in the lower part of the spectrum. Within the data for each subject, these two measures appear to be consistent with each other and also broadly in line with expectations based on the mean CQ values.

We should also note that the ANOVA results are similar for all three variables (CQ, H_2-H_1, and F_1-F_0) in that they show nearly identical patterns of two-way interactions. In all three cases, we find interactions involving the initial consonant and vowel height, though these do not always achieve significance as main effects. Given our impressionistic observations that close and close-mid vowels tend to have breathier phonation than open vowels and that phonation in /t/-initial syllables in somewhat breathier than in /l/-initial syllables, we should expect that such effects would be revealed by the quantitative analysis. The one-way ANOVA results indicated that there was a significant difference between tones for both variables (for H_2-H_1 $F(2,123)=25.4$, $p < .00005$; for F_1-F_0, $F(2,123)=9.6$; $p < .005$). The Scheffé test indicated a grouping of H and M versus L in both cases.

Table 18.2 *Results of ANOVA tests performed with SPSS software on each of the measured correlates of tone with respect to the independent variables: 2 initial consonants; 3 speakers; 3 tones; 4 vowel heights. Each test was performed on all 126 tokens with all effects entered simultaneously, using the unique sums of squares. Significant results (p < .05) are marked with an asterisk*

Source of variation	d.f.	F_0		CQ		H_2-H_1	
		F	p	F	p	F	p
Main effects	8	214.0	<.001*	39.6	<.001*	36.8	<.001*
Initial consonant	1	0.2	0.661	0.2	0.679	3.7	0.058
Speaker	2	126.9	<.001*	116.7	<.001*	2.7	0.070
Tone	2	723.9	<.001*	39.1	<.001*	74.3	<.001*
Vowel height	3	3.4	0.022*	1.0	0.420	45.6	<.001*
2-way interactions	23	7.9	<.001*	6.9	<.001*	6.8	<.001*
Initial/Speaker	2	1.5	0.239	5.2	0.007*	0.1	0.887
Initial/Tone	2	4.9	0.010*	3.3	0.042*	5.9	0.004*
Initial/Vowel height	3	0.8	0.497	0.6	0.599	0.8	0.474
Speaker/Tone	4	39.0	<.001*	14.4	<.001*	14.3	<.001*

Table 18.2 continued

Source of variation	d.f.	F_0		CQ		H_2-H_1	
		F	p	F	p	F	p
Speaker/Vowel height	6	0.8	0.587	8.1	<.001*	3.7	0.003*
Tone/Vowel height	6	1.1	0.392	6.4	<.001*	10.5	<.001*
Explained	31	66.2	<.001*	15.9	<.001*	15.2	<.001*
Residual	94						
Total 125							

Source of variation	d.f.	F1-F0		Spectral Tilt		Duration	
		F	p	F	p	F	p
Main effects	8	43.3	<.001*	5.0	<.001	23.5	<.001*
Initial consonant	1	5.1	0.027*	0.2	0.656	111.4	<.001*
Speaker	2	0.7	0.488	0.6	0.530	27.0	<.001*
Tone	2	28.8	<.001*	16.0	<.001*	8.7	<.001*
Vowel height	3	94.0	<.001*	2.3	0.086	1.9	0.142
2-way interactions	23	2.7	<.001*	0.7	0.839	3.3	<.001*
Initial/Speaker	2	1.9	0.153	2.0	0.137	3.7	0.028*
Initial/Tone	2	4.5	0.014*	0.1	0.882	0.5	0.607
Initial/Vowel height	3	0.3	0.797	1.2	0.326	10.5	<.001*
Speaker/Tone	4	4.5	0.002*	0.8	0.538	6.9	<.001*
Speaker/Vowel height	6	0.5	0.771	0.4	0.859	0.9	0.531
Tone/Vowel height	6	4.5	<.001*	0.4	0.867	0.5	0.804
Explained	31	13.5	<.001*	2.0	0.004*	9.6	<.001*
Residual	94						
Total	125						

The three phonation measures were broadly consistent with each other as regards the overall picture. Figure 18.1 shows a scatter plot of CQ (on the horizontal axis) plotted against the H_2-H_1 (on the vertical axis). There is a lot of variability in the data, particularly in the high tones. On the other hand, the low tones, all of which fall within the area enclosed by the bold lines, are more consistent. They are concentrated in the upper right-hand corner of the plot, towards the creaky end of the continuum. Thus, the data provide some evidence that L is different from H and M as regards its phonation characteristics, being somewhat creakier than the other two. A scatter plot for F_1-F_0 versus CQ is similar in appearance.

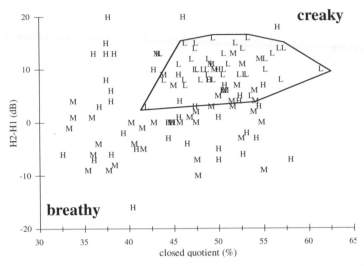

Figure 18.1 Scatter plot of closed quotient against the H_2-H_1 phonation measure. The bold outline encloses all the markers denoting Low-tone tokens

18.4.3.3 Spectral measure (3)

Our third spectral measure was a measure of spectral tilt, based on 'resonance balance'. A first observation is that it patterns differently from the other measures considered thus far. Firstly, there is much more consistency between speakers. As regards the ANOVA analysis, the spectral tilt measure shows the clearest result insofar as there are no significant two-way interactions between factors. Furthermore, in contrast to all the other measures considered thus far (including F_0), the only main effect to achieve statistical significance is tone.[4] As regards the one-way ANOVA, this indicated that there was a highly significant differences between tones (F(2,123)=20.1, p < .00005). As in the other cases, the Scheffé test indicated a grouping of H and M versus L.

A scatter plot relating spectral tilt to closed quotient is shown in Figure 18.2. Again, the points relating to the L tone are concentrated in a particular area of the chart, this time in the lower right rather than in the upper right. Unfortunately, these results are the 'wrong way round' insofar as the L tone – which, we have just concluded, is the creakiest – would appear to exhibit a steeper spectral tilt, which is more usually associated with breathier phonation. Our conclusion is that – at least for the rather limited data at hand – voice quality (as measured by spectral tilt) distinguishes L from M and H tones in

Yorùbá, but that factors other than phonation type are likely to be involved in bringing about those differences.

One obvious possibility would be to relate the greater spectral tilt of the low tone to lower intensity (noted by Hombert 1976 and Bakare 1995). Our own investigation of relative intensity for one of the speakers (Subject 3) indicated that H-toned vowels had significantly greater intensity than either M- or L-toned vowels (which were not significantly different from each other) rather than a major division between L on the one hand and M and H on the other. Accordingly, the relationship between intensity and spectral tilt needs further investigation, as does the possible role of intensity in tone perception.[5]

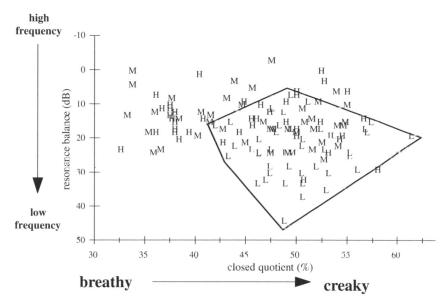

Figure 18.2 Scatter plot of closed quotient against spectral tilt. The bold outline encloses all the markers denoting Low-tone tokens

18.4.3.4 Summary

Our results provide some evidence to indicate that voice quality, as well as pitch level and pitch movement, contributes to the distinctive character of the L tone in Yorùbá. The (admittedly limited) data also suggest that the voice quality contrast is not attributable to phonation type alone. One possible reason for this is that phonation type is also influenced by vowel quality (close and half-close vowels being more breathy than open and half-open mid vowels) and so other mechanisms would need to be brought into play. Further data are needed to clarify this point.

18.5 General discussion and conclusion

In discussing our results, it is necessary first to consider the specific case of Yorùbá and then to ask what, if any, insights might be gained with regard to the general questions posed at the beginning. As regards Yorùbá, the results have provided some evidence that the low tone is marked by a distinctive voice quality, which involves both greater spectral tilt (i.e. more prominent low frequencies) and somewhat creakier phonation type. If we consider our results together with the results of Bakare's experiment, described in Section 18.4, it appears that, while the three tones are differentiated primarily by F_0, the H tone is also marked by greater intensity and the L tone by distinctive voice quality. The M tone, which has been analysed as the phonological default, appears also to be the least marked from a phonetic point of view. However, both this study and Bakare's study involved a small number of speakers recorded under laboratory conditions, and it remains to be seen to what extent the results would be corroborated in recordings of more naturally produced speech. Controlled perceptual experiments are also necessary to establish to what extent the potential cues of intensity and voice quality can be utilised by listeners for tone identification.

It must also be admitted that our results do not provide evidence for a correlation between voice quality and phonological tonal register. Rather, voice quality appears to distinguish between tones within the lower register. This suggests that, if voice quality is to play a role in the phonological specification of tone, it is more likely to be important at the subregister level. It is also possible that there are hierarchies involving the use of voice quality so that, within the lower register, the lower tone is more likely to be assigned distinctive phonation than the higher tone. Much more detailed investigation of languages with three or more level tones is needed before any suggestions can be made, and it would be particularly important to study languages with four level tones, including two in the upper register. In the case of Yorùbá, some intriguing questions arise from these speculations: if the M and L tones do indeed result from a historical split (see Section 18.4), then was L given additional phonetic marking to reflect its marked phonological status? Alternatively, did L emerge as the more marked tone phonologically partly because it was more susceptible to receiving additional marking phonetically?

It is also possible that our results simply reflect a tendency on the part of speakers and languages to mark out the bottom of the pitch range in some way. One obvious hypothesis is that higher spectral tilt (more prominent low frequencies) might enhance the overall low character of low pitches, whereas lower spectral tilt (more prominent high frequencies) might enhance the high character of high pitches.[6] In this context, it might be more appropriate to think not in terms of pitch, but in terms of a perceptual dimension of 'brightness' (Colton 1987); pitch (as measured by F_0) appears to be a major determinant of perceived brightness, but brightness is not exactly the same as pitch. The association of higher intensity with higher pitches might also be a means of increasing their perceived brightness and, in this context, it is interesting to note that correlations between F_0 and amplitude have been reported for other languages (see Whalen and Xu 1992: 45 for discussion).

An obvious mechanism of regulating spectral tilt is via phonation type since, other things being equal, breathy phonation should show a greater degree of tilt than creaky phonation. Thus, there would be some advantage for the listener in associating breathy phonation with lower pitches and creaky phonation with higher pitches. Why, then, should relatively creaky voice be assigned to low pitches? The explanation may involve associations which arise in speech production. To produce the lowest pitches of the voice, it is necessary to descend to a different 'vocal register' (in the sense of Hollien 1974). It is still considered that the mechanisms of low-pitched 'pulsed' phonation (also known as 'creak' and 'vocal fry') are not fully understood (Orlikoff and Kahane 1996: 154-5). However, it seems to involve fully adducted vocal folds and sharp vocal fold closure. These characteristics link pulsed phonation – which, by definition, cannot contrast with other phonation types – with creaky phonation, and it is interesting that (so far as we know) no language exhibits a phonological contrast based on this potential distinction.

The natural association of glottal constriction with extremely low pitches might lead to the use of a more constricted type of phonation for pitches at the bottom of an individual's range – and especially for phonologically low pitches – even when these were higher than the 70–80 Hz cut-off point established for the 'pulse' register (Hollien 1974; Keidar, Hurtig and Titze 1987). We suggest that a good example of this type of development may be found in the Punjabi low tone which has developed in syllables which historically began with breathy-released stops, and which would therefore be expected to be breathy. However, the tone is now pronounced with some glottal constriction. The Lx waveforms which we have seen for this tone (Arif Minhas, personal communication) change in shape and show increasing CQ with descending F_0, but they do not reach the extreme of pulse. Another intriguing example from this point of view is the so-called 'broken' (*ngã*) tone of Hanoi Vietnamese which is now pronounced with marked glottal constriction in the middle of the vowel, but which derives historically from syllables which one would expect to be extremely low-pitched and breathy, given that they originally began with voiced obstruents and ended in [h].[7]

In any case, if these speculations are correct, then we should expect to find either breathy voice or creaky voice associated with phonologically low pitches, and we have already seen that both types of association may occur (Section 18.1). The best of both worlds would be obtained by combining creaky voice with high spectral tilt, as we have observed in our Yorùbá data. The main conclusion of this paper, however, must be that the relationship between voice quality and F_0 is a very intriguing subject for further study, and that much more research, based on more languages, is needed.

Notes

We should like to thank the School of Oriental and African Studies for a grant to purchase the pclx software for use in this project. Special thanks are due to Bernard Howard for patient technical assistance and to Dick Hayward and Bruce Connell for comments on earlier drafts. Sadly, between the completion of this paper and the publication of this volume Katrina Hayward has died. We dedicate this paper to her.

1   Silverman (1997) suggests that it is rare for phonation type and pitch to cross-classify for two reasons. Firstly, particular pitch targets and particulatory phonatory settings might not be sufficiently compatible from an articulatory point of view. Secondly, non-modal phonation might make the identification of target pitches more difficult for the listener. We should like to suggest that the opposite kind of relationship might obtain as well – voice qualities might be more difficult to distinguish in some parts of the pitch range, most particularly if the pitch is high.

2   For our informants, the H and M tones were almost always level, though many fell slightly in the last few periods. In some cases, a slightly rising contour was observed on the H tones. In this matter, our data contrast with Laniran's (1993), whose subjects produced rising H tones and falling M tones on the syllable *ma* in this sentence context.

3   If the close and half-close vowels are [+ATR], this may account for their greater breathiness.

4   The failure of vowel height to achieve significance as a main effect, together with the lack of any significant interactions involving this variable, would seem to preclude explaining the spectral tilt results with reference to differing phonation characteristics of [+ATR] and [-ATR] vowels.

5   In this connection, it should be noted that Whalen and Xu (1992) found evidence that amplitude contours could be utilised by listeners as cues for tone identification in Mandarin.

6   If this reasoning is correct, the association of low-frequency prominence in the spectrum with low F_0 would provide a further example of 'auditory enhancement' (Diehl and Kluender 1989).

7   In Haudricourt's (1954) schema, syllables of this type first developed falling tones, which became distinctive when final [h] was lost. At the time of the tonal split associated with loss of the voicing distinction in initial obstruents, the *ngã* would have been a falling tone in the lower tonal register. However, Haudricourt's chronology has been questioned (Gregerson and Thomas 1976; Hayes 1983). Also, a development of rising tone in syllables with final [h] has been reported for the

Mon-Khmer language Jeh (Gradin 1966); since the Vietnamese *ngã* tone now rises from a middle pitch, this further calls into question the supposition that the Vietnamese syllables in question ever had low falling tone.

19

Speech rhythm in English and Japanese

KEIICHI TAJIMA AND ROBERT F. PORT

19.1 Introduction

This paper has two main objectives. First, we propose that cross-linguistic variation in speech rhythm is not phonetically manifested simply as acoustic isochrony, but rather as *relative temporal stability* of syllables – i.e. the tendency for certain syllables to occur at particular points in time despite other factors that oppose this tendency. Second, we compare two languages believed to be rhythmically distinct, English and Japanese, and demonstrate that they not only display reliable rhythmic differences, but also striking similarities in the phonetic manifestation of foot-level structure. These goals are accomplished by using speech cycling – an artificial speaking task in which subjects repeat phrases in time with periodic auditory stimuli.

19.1.1 Rhythmic typologies

There has long been an intuition that languages are spoken with different kinds of rhythm. Conventionally, languages have been classified as either 'stress-timed' or 'syllable-timed' (Jones 1918; Pike 1945; Abercrombie 1967), depending on whether it is interstress intervals or intersyllable intervals that are regular. The prediction about timing that is generally seen to follow from 'stress-timed', 'syllable-timed', or even 'mora-timed' (Port, Dalby and O'Dell 1987), is perfect isochrony (equal time intervals) of stresses, syllables or moras. Not surprisingly, however, perfect isochrony has proven to be a difficult test to satisfy, at least in naturalistic speaking styles (Lehiste 1977; Dauer 1983; Couper-Kuhlen 1993).

In generative phonology, a way of characterizing the rhythm of so-called stress-accent languages has evolved based on the quasi-periodic alternation of strong and weak syllables (Liberman and Prince 1977; Selkirk 1984). Metrical phonology uses metrical grids to formally represent the serial ordering of syllables varying in prominence. However, serially ordered steps by themselves imply nothing about their production in real time. Metrical theory can therefore offer no account of how these representations are to be phonetically interpreted. The simplest hypothesis for predicting specific time intervals would be regular timing of grid symbols (plus noise), but this is unlikely to be empirically supported. In fact, how the grid symbols are interpreted in real time was not of direct concern in many versions of metrical theory. Rather, the appeal of metrical grids stemmed from their being better able than metrical trees to explain certain rhythmic phenomena such as stress retraction (cf. Hogg and McCully 1987).

The role of metrical grids in these later versions of metrical theory is, ironically, fundamentally different from the original conception of metrical grids by Liberman (1975). In Liberman's proposal, grids were directly interpretable in real time; they partitioned time into hierarchically related intervals, much like musical notation. Liberman also made a fundamental distinction between *metrical grids*, which are hierarchically related time intervals, and *metrical patterns*, which are abstract properties of the linguistic text. The abstract patterns of strong and weak syllables in the text were interpreted in real time via alignment of the metrical patterns with the metrical grid. As will be discussed later, the conception of metre and speech presented here does better justice to Liberman's theory of metrical structure than do later versions of metrical phonology.

Rhythmic characteristics of so-called pitch-accent languages have often been investigated using verse-like texts (Lehiste 1990; Sakano 1996). In Japanese, for example, Bekku (1977) has claimed that, although the traditional *haiku* verse form employs an odd number of moras in each line (5, 7, 5), it is orally produced with a musical rest inserted at the end of each line so that the time interval between successive lines contains eight abstract mora-sized units. Homma (1991) in fact found a tendency for a longer pauses to be produced after short (5-mora) lines than after long (7-mora) lines in oral productions of *haiku*. A related claim about Japanese rhythm is that Japanese speakers tend to parse phrases into bimoraic feet, or units of two moras in length (Sakano 1996).

What seems necessary for many of these claims is phonetic evidence. To better examine how rhythmic structure is phonetically interpreted, we suspect that it will prove fruitful to study more constrained styles of speech than spontaneous speech.

19.1.2 Speech cycling

In recent years, we have been developing a method for studying speech rhythm and its variation across languages. In this general class of tasks called 'speech cycling' (Cummins 1997; Cummins and Port 1998; Tajima 1998), subjects produce a short text fragment repeatedly, in time with metronome-like stimuli. In a typical study, subjects might produce a short phrase such as *beg for a dime*, in time with a metronome adjusted to yield speech at a comfortable rate. Speakers show a strong preference for a small number of rhythmic patterns, where *beg* begins each cycle (like the first downbeat of a musical measure), and *dime* occurs on (a) the second downbeat of a two-beat measure, or on (b) the second downbeat or (c) the third downbeat of a three-beat, waltz-like measure. (Readers are encouraged to try these three patterns for themselves.) If these patterns are expressed in terms of the *phase angle* of the timing of *dime* within the cycle from the previous to the next *beg*, then the preferred pattern is to produce *dime* at phase 1/3, 1/2, or 2/3. Speakers are most stable at just these three patterns even though they are given various target phases at which to produce *dime*. These constraints on speech timing are powerful enough that it is quite difficult (without practice) to stably produce other patterns. We interpret these locations to be literally attractors of the onsets of stressed syllables on the phase circle. The phenomena invite a dynamical system interpretation in terms of coupled oscillators (Kelso 1996; Large and Jones 1999). We expect that similar effects will be observable in any language, though we should expect the details to be modulated by properties of each language.

19.1.3 Speech rhythm as temporal stability

Four hypotheses underlie the design of the experiments:

(1) Phases of the repetition cycle such as 1/3 and 2/3, called *simple harmonic phases*, are attractors of prominent syllables. That is, prominent syllables will 'want' to line up at these phases and exhibit temporal stability.
(2) An abrupt onset of acoustic energy at the beginning of vowels is a likely time point to exhibit temporal stability. It is this *beat* near vowel onsets that tends to be stably located in time (see Section 19.2.1.2 below).
(3) Changing the structure of the text, by changing segments or syllables, should cause perturbations of timing in performance of speech cycling.
(4) Languages differ in their criteria for syllable prominence. Therefore, even with comparable texts, speakers of different languages are expected to differ in the patterns they find stable in speech-cycling tasks.

19.1.4 Predictions about English and Japanese rhythm

This study uses the speech-cycling method to induce overtly rhythmic forms of speaking. By imposing a particular metrical organisation onto speech, the method allows direct evaluation of how metre is phonetically interpreted, and how it is influenced by the linguistic structure of the text.

English and Japanese were compared by using roughly comparable text materials and the identical speech-cycling task. In English, prominence is tied closely to stress. Thus, we expect stressed syllables to be regularly timed and have their onsets (their beats) located at simple harmonic fractions (e.g. 1/3 and 2/3) of the repetition cycle. In Japanese, which has no stress, predictions are more problematic. It is likely that word onsets are prominent, especially if combined with word-initial pitch accents. It is also possible that the initial moras of bimoraic feet are prominent. These moras may therefore be attracted to simple harmonic phases.

To test temporal stability, the timing of syllables was given phonological perturbations by constructing phrases that were identical except for one difference in segmental or syllabic content. The timing of corresponding syllables was then compared between these minimally contrasting phrases.

19.2 Experiment 1

19.2.1 Methods

19.2.1.1 Design of text materials
Text materials in Experiment 1 systematically varied in the duration of certain syllables, through inversion of adjacent long and short vowels. Table 19.1 gives phonemic transcriptions of some of the test phrases. The phrases contained nonexistent but phonotactically plausible words. Each phrase contained five open syllables. There were 16 phrases in each language, consisting of four sets of four phrases that followed specific patterns of durational contrasts, illustrated in the upper part of Figure 19.1. Patterns A and B constitute a 'minimal pair'; they are identical except for the underlined portion, which contains an inversion of vowels in the third and fourth syllables.[1] Since the diphthong /aj/ is inherently longer than the vowel /ə/, the third and fourth syllables are inherently long–short in A but short–long in B. Phrases C and D are analogous, except that the vowel inversion occurs in the second and third syllables. Japanese phrases were constructed in the same manner, using low versus high vowels for the long versus short contrast.

325

Table 19.1 *Phonemic transcription of sample phrases in Experiment 1. Two sets out of the four are shown for each language*

Set	Pattern	English	Japanese
I	A	/ˈgow fɔr ˈbaj.gə ˈdej/	/ku.ɾo ba.ki da/
	B	/ˈgow fɔr ˈbʌ.gaj ˈdej/	/ku.ɾo bi.ka da/
	C	/ˈgow baj ˈgʌ.nɚ ˈdej/	/ku.ba ki.ɾi da/
	D	/ˈgow.bə ˈgaj.nɚ ˈdej/	/ku.bi ka.ɾi da/
II	A	/ˈbi ðə ˈkow.bə ˈgaj/	/ta.te ka.bi da/
	B	/ˈbi ðə ˈkʌ.bow ˈgaj/	/ta.te ki.ba da/
	C	/ˈbi.kow ˈbʌ.ɾɚ ˈgaj/	/ta.ka bi.ʃa da/
	D	/ˈbi.kə ˈbow.ɾɚ ˈgaj/	/ta.ki ba.ʃa da/

Even though the vowel inversion is the same for the A-B pair and the C-D pair, the inversion was designed to cross a foot boundary in the latter pair but not in the former. The expected prosodic foot structure of the phrases is depicted in the middle part of Figure 19.1. If prominent syllables are 'attracted' toward the downbeats of the waltz rhythm, then they should show greater resistance to temporal perturbation caused by segmental manipulations. That is, the effect of vowel inversion should be smaller in the C-D pair (in which the third syllable is prominent) than in the A-B pair (in which the fourth syllable is not prominent).

In English, the prominent syllables (ó) in Figure 19.1 were stressed syllables, and the brackets corresponded to stress-feet. The brackets also corresponded to major word boundaries, so that the prominent syllables were also word-initial (e.g. [go for] [Byga] [Day]). In Japanese, the prominent syllables (ó) were morpheme-initial syllables, and the brackets corresponded to morphemes. Each Japanese phrase consisted of two unaccented bimoraic morphemes followed by the copula *da* (e.g. [naka] [niwa] [da]).[2] The prominent syllables were also the initial syllables of bimoraic feet. That is, if Japanese speakers were to show a preference toward parsing each phrase left-to-right into groups of two moras, then the test phrases would be parsed as shown by the brackets in Figure 19.1.

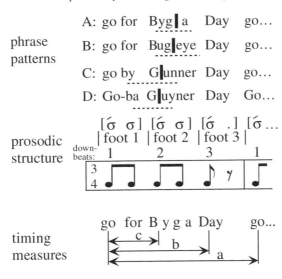

Figure 19.1 Top panel: phrase patterns A–D. Vowel inversion in the underlined portion should affect the fourth syllable beat for the A-B pair, and the third syllable beat for the C-D pair (as shown by the thick vertical lines). Middle panel: expected prosodic structure of the phrases and musical notation of the waltz rhythm. Since the third syllable is foot-initial, temporal displacement should be smaller in the C-D pair than in the A-B pair. Bottom panel: two relative measures of timing: (1) phase of a syllable relative to the cycle of successive repetition onsets (e.g. *c/a* and *b/a*), and (2) timing of a syllable relative to the first and last beats of a single repetition (e.g. *c/b*)

19.2.1.2 Procedure and measurement

Fourteen native speakers of American English and thirteen native speakers of Tokyo Japanese participated in a speech-cycling task in which they were instructed to produce the odd-numbered syllables at metrically strong positions (downbeats) of the repetition cycle. Subjects listened to an isochronous series of 50 ms, 600 Hz pure tones, presented through headphones. The metronome period was 1200 ms for English, and either 1100 ms or 1000 ms for Japanese. The following instructions were given:

> On each trial, listen to the first four beeps. Start repeating the phrase on the fifth beep, aligning the beginning of the phrase with each successive beep. Repeat the phrase rhythmically, using a waltz-like, three-beat rhythm. That is, repeat the phrase while keeping in mind the rhythm '1.. 2.. 3.. 1.. 2.. 3..', with the 1s falling on the beeps. Stop after eight repetitions. Do not insert breaths between repetitions.

Test phrases were presented using the native orthographic system of the language. Japanese phrases were written in *kanji* and *kana* in such a way that the written forms suggested the expected morphological and accentual patterns. After familiarisation with the text materials, subjects were given as much feedback and practice as necessary to perform the task before starting the test trials. The 16 phrases were presented in a random order. A total of 432 trials were analysed [16 phrases X 27 subjects].

Measurement of the recorded utterances began by first converting the speech signal into a series of *beats*, by placing a beat near the vowel onset of each syllable. This was done semi-automatically, using a 'beat extractor' that created a rectified smoothed energy profile of the formant frequency region of the speech signal, and placed a marker (beat) halfway up every local rise in this contour (see Cummins and Port 1998 for details). Visual inspection was used to correct the output of the algorithm. The series of beats over time was used to capture the timing of vowel onsets in each trial.

Measurement based on beats contrasts with conventional measures of syllable and segment durations. For example, in a CVCVCV... sequence, instead of measuring syllable durations starting from the acoustic onset of a consonant up to the offset of a vowel (i.e. [CV][CV][CV]), these beats delimit syllables from vowel onset to vowel onset (i.e. C[VC][VC]V). This measure was adopted because abrupt rises in acoustic energy (as in a vowel onset) are correlated with more activity in the auditory nerve than are less abrupt rises or acoustic offsets (as in a consonant onset) (Delgutte 1982). Also, for syllables with voiced stops and nasals, the vowel onset is roughly equal to the so-called 'perceptual moment of occurrence' or P-centre, of the syllable (e.g. Scott 1993).

Of the eight repetitions in each trial, the first two and the last were discarded to reduce transient effects. Beats from the remaining five repetitions were converted into two relative measures of timing, illustrated in the lower part of Figure 19.1. *Phase* measures the time of occurrence of a syllable relative to the cycle starting at the initial beat of the current repetition and ending at the initial beat of the following repetitions (e.g. *b/a* or *c/a* in Figure 19.1). Additionally, we measured the time of occurrence of a syllable relative to the interval between the first and last syllable beats of the current repetition (e.g. *c/b*).

19.2.2 Results

19.2.2.1 Production of waltz rhythm

To examine how well the subjects as a group maintained the three-beat waltz rhythm, Figure 19.2 plots histograms of the timing of the third and fifth syllables of each phrase. Data are collapsed across patterns A-D. Given that phase is defined in the scale {0, 100}, a perfect waltz rhythm would imply that the third and fifth syllables would begin at phases 33.3 and 66.7, as shown by the vertical lines.

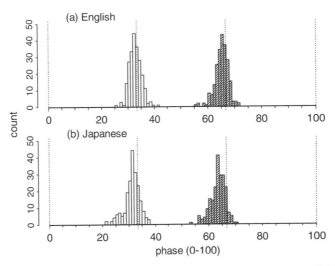

Figure 19.2 Histogram of phase of the third (unfilled bars) and fifth (filled bars) syllable beats from all trials in English (top) and Japanese (bottom)

Each cluster is based on trial means across all phrases and speakers. Trial means were calculated by averaging the observed phases of each syllable beat across the five repetitions measured in each trial. The figure shows that each cluster has a single distributional mode, with very little variability in the data. Performance was therefore highly consistent across subjects and phrases in both languages. Impressionistic judgement also suggested that speakers accurately produced the waltz rhythm.

19.2.2.2 Temporal stability of foot-initial syllables

To assess whether foot-initial and foot-internal syllables differ in temporal stability, Figure 19.3 shows the timing pattern of one matched set of English phrases, averaged across speakers. The x-axis here shows the percentage of the interval from the initial to final syllables of the phrase. This measure was adopted because the relative timing of the final syllable tended to vary across phrases. The vertical line at 50% corresponds to the second downbeat of the waltz, and is the expected phase of the third syllable. For each phrase, the vertical lines indicate the timing of the syllable beats, averaged across speakers.

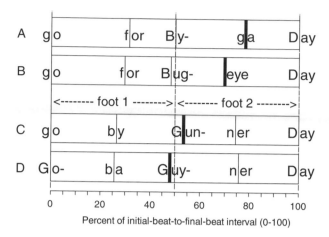

Figure 19.3 Timing of syllable beats in one matched set of English phrases. Each beat is the mean of trial means from all 14 American speakers. The x-axis shows the percentage of the interval from phrase-initial to phrase-final beats. The vertical lines at 0, 50 and 100% correspond to the three downbeats of the waltz. The thick lines are the target beats in question. Timing difference of these beats between A and B and between C and D are shown in the following figure

    The thick lines in Figure 19.3 are the target beats; duration of the vowels before and after the target beats was manipulated. In the A-B pair, the fourth syllable beat is temporally displaced as a result of the inversion of the third and fourth vowels. In the C-D pair, a similar displacement is found for the third syllable, but the displacement is smaller in magnitude in this pair than in the A-B pair, as predicted.

    Figure 19.4 directly compares the magnitude of displacement between the A-B pair and C-D pair, for all sets of phrases. Grey bars indicate displacement of the fourth syllable in the A-B pair, and black bars indicate displacement of the third syllable in the C-D pair (these syllables correspond to the thick lines in Figure 19.3). The displacement is expressed as a percentage of the interval between phrase-initial and final beats. Beat displacement in the C-D pair is smaller in magnitude than that in the A-B pair for all cases except set IV in Japanese. Overall, it appears that there are consistent differences in temporal displacement between foot-initial and foot-internal syllables. Foot-initial syllables are more resistant to temporal perturbations than are foot-internal syllables. This effect was found in both English and Japanese, contrary to previous claims that foot-level organisation is much less phonetically salient in Japanese than in English (Beckman 1994).

330

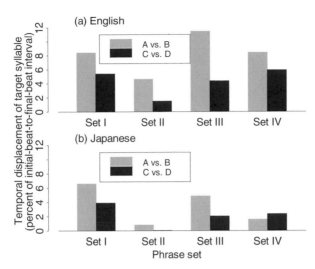

Figure 19.4 Temporal displacement of target syllables in pairs of minimally contrasting phrases. Grey bars indicate timing difference of the fourth syllable beat in the A-B pair, and black bars indicate timing difference of the third beat in the C-D pair (these syllables correspond to the thick vertical lines in the previous figure). Each bar graph shows the mean displacement across all speakers

A repeated-measures ANOVA was conducted with Syllable (foot-internal versus foot-initial) as a within-subjects factor and Language as a between-subjects factor. Results showed a highly significant main effect of Syllable $[F(1,25) = 32.78; p < .001]$, indicating that the overall difference in temporal displacement between foot-initial and foot-internal beats is statistically reliable. Also significant were the main effect of Language $[F(1,25) = 24.12; p < .001]$, and its interaction with Syllable $[F(1,25) = 7.15; p = .013]$, showing that displacement of the beats was significantly larger overall in English than in Japanese.

19.2.3 Discussion

These data demonstrate similarities in rhythmic organisation between English and Japanese. The degree of temporal displacement of a syllable beat is sensitive to the prosodic foot structure of the phrases. In particular, the beats of foot-initial syllables are more resistant to temporal perturbations – i.e. more temporally stable – than are non-initial syllables.

To express the temporal displacement in absolute terms, a simple transformation was used to convert the y-axis of Figure 19.4 into milliseconds, noting that the interval between phrase-initial and final beats is approximately two-thirds of the metronome period. On average, syllable beats in English were displaced by 66 ms, measured from the beginning of the phrase, if the target syllable was foot-internal, but only by 35 ms if the target was foot-initial. Similarly, displacement in Japanese was 24 ms for foot-internal syllables, and 14 ms for foot-initial syllables. Thus, in both languages, foot-initial beats moved roughly half as much as did foot-internal beats under similar segmental perturbations to the syllable's duration.

19.3 Experiment 2

Experiment 2 is similar to Experiment 1, but timing was perturbed through insertion of an extra syllable to a foot- or word-level unit. Text materials were made prosodically similar in English and Japanese by operationally equating English stressed syllables with Japanese accented moras. There is some limited evidence for this decision. Another speech-cycling study (Tajima 1998) compared Japanese phrases which were of the same length, but had different patterns of pitch accents and word boundaries. There was a slight tendency for word-initial accented syllables to occur at simple harmonic fractions of the phase cycle, such as 1/3 and 1/2, yielding distinct rhythmic patterns for these phrases. Thus, it is possible that both English stress and Japanese accent are attracted toward harmonic phases. However, conventional labels such as stress-timed versus mora-timed suggest that the insertion of a syllable in a phrase affects the timing of Japanese more severely than English.

19.3.1 Methods

Table 19.2 lists sample test phrases. There were 12 phrases in each language, consisting of four sets of three phrases each that followed a specified prosodic pattern, as illustrated below. The expected foot structure and downbeats of the waltz rhythm are also shown, much like the middle panel of Figure 19.1.

Pattern E:	[σ́ σ]	[σ́ σ σ]	[σ́]
Pattern F:	[σ́ σ]	[σ́ σ]	[σ́]
Pattern G:	[σ́ σ σ]	[σ́ σ]	[σ́]
Feet:	| foot 1	| foot 2	| foot 3 |
Downbeats:	1	2	3

Table 19.2 *Sample test phrases in Experiment 2*

Set	Pattern	English	Japanese
V	E	Búy the 'Dáily' for Gúy	dóno bíruma-da
	F	Búy the 'Dáy' for Gúy	dóno bíru-da
	G	Búy the 'Todáy' for Gúy	dókono bíru-da
VI	E	Gó to Báker for nów	mí-ta bíjo-mo-da
	F	Gó to Báker nów	mí-ta bíjo-da
	G	Gó to the báker nów	mí-se-ta bíjo-da

Looking at pattern F, this is a five-syllable pattern similar to the phrases in Experiment 1. Patterns E and G are six-syllable phrases that minimally contrasted with pattern F by the insertion of a syllable either to the second word-sized unit or to the first, respectively.

In English, the prominent syllables (σ́) were lexically stressed syllables, and the brackets corresponded to stress-feet. The prominent syllables were often also word-initial syllables. In Japanese, the prominent syllables were lexically pitch-accented syllables except for the phrase-final syllable which was always the unaccented copula *da*. The brackets roughly corresponded to words. Some of the words in patterns F and G were trimoraic, so the brackets shown in (1) did not correspond to bimoraic units parsed left-to-right. Thus, unlike Experiment 1, foot structure and word structure did not always coincide in the phrases used in Experiment 2.

Prosodic structure of the phrases were made reasonably comparable between English and Japanese by equating English stress-feet with short Japanese words with initial accent. In some conditions, these two units have the same intonation contour, with a high tone on the initial syllable, and relatively lower pitch elsewhere.

Despite the prosodic similarity, different predictions are made for English and Japanese. If English is stress-timed, then the stressed syllables should show relatively small temporal displacement across patterns E-G, despite the addition of an extra weak syllable in E and G. By contrast, if Japanese is mora-timed, then the addition of a mora to a word should yield a proportionate increase in word duration. This should make it difficult to keep word onsets near the downbeats of the repetition cycle.

Subjects in Experiment 2 were the same as those in Experiment 1. Two of the Americans did not participate in Experiment 2 because they had difficulty performing the task and took too much time to complete Experiment 1. Data were therefore obtained from 12 Americans and 13 Japanese. Subjects were told that some phrases were longer than others, and were instructed to maintain the waltz rhythm while repeating the phrases in a comfortable fashion. All other aspects of the experiment were the same as Experiment 1. A total of 300 trials were analysed [12 phrases X 25 speakers].

19.3.2 Results

19.3.2.1 Production of waltz rhythm

Figure 19.5 shows the same type of histograms as Figure 19.2, showing how well the subjects as a group maintained the waltz rhythm. Again, data are collapsed across patterns E–G. The unfilled and filled bar graphs are from the phrase-medial and phrase-final prominent syllables, respectively (i.e. English stressed syllables or Japanese word-initial accented moras).

The histograms in Figure 19.5 show greater variability than those in Figure 19.2. This is especially noticeable in Japanese, where the distributions for both the third and fifth syllable beats are decidedly non-Gaussian. Timing of the prominent syllables is therefore less consistent across phrases and speakers in Experiment 2 than in Experiment 1, particularly in Japanese.

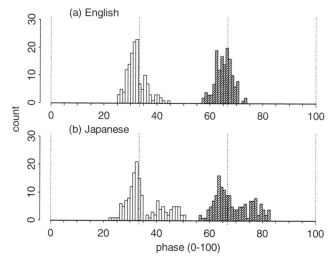

Figure 19.5 Histogram of phase of the phrase-medial (unfilled bars) and phrase-final (filled bars) prominent syllables from all trials in English (top) and Japanese (bottom). Each cluster is based on trial means from all phrases and speakers in each language

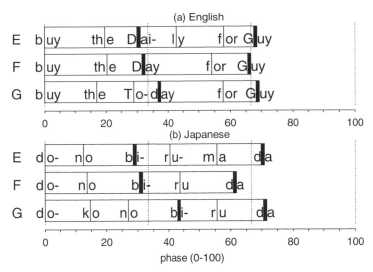

Figure 19.6 Relative timing of syllable beats in one matched set of phrases in English and Japanese. Each beat is the mean of trial means from all speakers in the language. The x-axis is phase relative to the phrase repetition cycle

19.3.2.2 Cross-linguistic differences in temporal stability

To examine how the insertion of an extra syllable affects the timing of phrases, Figure 19.6 shows the phase of syllable beats in one matched set of phrases in English and Japanese, averaged across speakers. The thick lines correspond to the prominent syllables in both languages.

Figure 19.6 shows that the prominent syllables undergo smaller temporal displacement across the phrases in English than in Japanese. English stressed syllables are produced reasonably close to the downbeats of the waltz metre. By contrast, Japanese shows a larger displacement of the word-initial accented moras. They exhibit much less tendency to occur close to the metrically strong positions. This property of Japanese is consistent with the traditional observation that moras tend to be isochronous.

Repeated-measures ANOVAs were carried out for the entire data set, with Pattern (E versus F versus G) and Language as factors. Separate tests were conducted for the phrase-medial and phrase-final prominent syllables. All main effects were significant at the .05 level, for both medial and final syllables. Importantly, Pattern-by-Language interaction was highly significant for the medial syllable [$F(2,46) = 21.69$; $p < .001$] and the final syllable [$F(2,46) = 46.91$; $p < .001$]. This indicates that the magnitude of displacement of the medial and final syllables across the three patterns was significantly different between English and Japanese.

In addition, Japanese showed more temporal variation across individual speakers than English did. It appears that all English speakers adopted a single

335

strategy for repeating the phrases, in which the stressed syllables were produced near the downbeats of the waltz. The Japanese speakers, however, showed greater inter-speaker variation. Figure 19.7 shows the mean phase of syllables from two sample speakers who apparently produced qualitatively distinct rhythmic patterns. For example, speaker 2 aligned the fifth syllable of the phrases near the third downbeat, at phase 66.6. For speaker 1, however, the sixth syllable of patterns E and G is closer to that downbeat than is the fifth syllable, perhaps suggesting that the speaker deviated from a three-beat rhythm. While the speakers differed from each other in the rhythmic patterns produced, each speaker was reasonably consistent across trials.

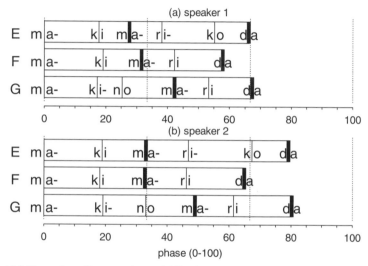

Figure 19.7 Illustration of inter-speaker variability in Japanese. Phase of syllable beats is shown for two sample speakers for one matched set of phrases

19.3.3 Discussion

Experiment 2 revealed measurable rhythmic differences between English and Japanese. English stressed syllables showed greater temporal stability across changes in foot size than Japanese word-initial accented syllables did across changes in word size. Also, compared to Experiment 1, phrases in Experiment 2 were not produced as consistently in the prescribed rhythm. This was especially true for Japanese, where individual speakers found alternative ways of aligning the text with the waltz rhythm.

Thus, the phonetic interpretation of metrical structure is highly sensitive to linguistic properties of the text. The instruction to speak in a waltz rhythm may be followed more or less accurately, and in distinct ways, depending on what language one is a native speaker of.

19.4 General discussion and conclusions

19.4.1 Toward a theory of metre in speech

As an account of what speakers do in our speech-cycling task, we propose that two distinct cognitive structures are involved. The first is a *metre system* defining a pattern of attractors at downbeats in real continuous time. It is hypothesised that this system of attractors on the phase circle draws certain events (e.g. vowel onsets in prominent syllables) toward them. The attractors may result from a system of oscillators coupled at simple ratios such as 1:2 or 1:3 (Gasser, Eck and Port 1999; Large and Jones 1999). An oscillator is a cognitive process that has an instantaneous phase cycling around from 0 to 1 (or 360 degrees). Phase zero of each oscillator seems to serve as a downbeat, or an attractor of prominent events. In a 1:3 waltz rhythm, for example, the slower cognitive oscillator entrains to the stimulus metronome period. The second, faster oscillator is phase-coupled with the slower oscillator and makes three complete cycles for each cycle of the slow one, thus generating three isochronously spaced attractors for beats in each cycle. Thus, in asking our subjects to produce phrases 'using a waltz-like pattern', it seems that we effectively invited them to activate a 1:3 metre system. A similar metre system presumably underlies the perception and production of musical waltzes as well.

The second cognitive structure is a *linguistic text* containing a sequence of syllables having varying degrees of prominence. The relative prominence is determined by language-specific factors, including: (1) lexical stress (in English, at least), (2) lexical pitch accent, (3) word-initial syllables, (4) initial syllables in bimoraic feet (for Japanese, at least), and possibly other factors.

On this view, the speaker's problem when doing speech cycling is to align the intrinsic prominence pattern – the strong and weak syllables in the text – to the periodic structure of the metre system in real time. In this process, speakers of both languages exhibit the constraint that inherently prominent syllables are attracted toward phase zeros, i.e. the downbeats of the metre system. This tendency for attraction of prominent syllables to simple harmonic phases is a possible candidate to be a universal of human speech. The universality of this attraction seems reasonable since probably all languages are occasionally spoken in rhythmical ways, whether in verse, song or chant. On the other hand, what differs between English and Japanese seems to lie in the criteria for syllable prominence.

19.4.2 Metre system versus metrical grids

The above conception of how metre relates to speech is similar to Liberman's (1975) proposal of two distinct formal structures, a *metrical pattern*, to represent the abstract prominence relations among linguistic elements, and a *metrical grid*, to represent just a pattern of nested downbeats each with some discrete degree of strength. Though our proposal clearly resembles Liberman's in many respects, the traditional notion of a metrical grid does not provide a useful framework for an account of our phenomena.

The difficulty is that metrical grids are symbol strings, and thus can only represent the division of time into identical static intervals. The attraction itself – i.e. the adjustment of vowel onsets toward harmonic phases – would need to be accounted for outside the theory. On our view, on the other hand, metre is manifested as a real-time oscillatory process that generates attractors at specific temporal locations, on the fly. This attractor structure is directly reflected in the greater temporal stability observed with syllable beats located at the downbeats of the metre.

19.4.3 Rhythmic typology revisited

This study has demonstrated the possibility of treating relative temporal stability of one syllable beat versus another as a dependent variable for exploring the prominence structures of various languages. Temporal stability therefore provides an alternative approach for describing rhythmic typology, which has for the most part relied on isochrony as the primary diagnostic. Rather than claiming that languages vary in the level at which isochrony is maintained, we claim that languages vary in what counts as prominent. On this view, we believe that it is somewhat premature to abandon the 'stress-timed'–'syllable-timed' distinction on the basis of lack of isochrony alone. Instead, our comparison of English and Japanese suggests that there is something correct about the traditional rhythmic labels, and that the problem rather lay in using isochrony as the diagnostic for rhythm.

In English, prominence seems to correlate quite straightforwardly with stress. Stressed syllables play a central role in the rhythmic organisation of phrases, and strongly tend toward metrically strong time points. In Japanese, by contrast, there is no single linguistic factor that is primarily responsible for defining prominence. Prominence seems to be determined by several factors, which sometimes compete against each other when metre is imposed. One candidate is the initial syllables of bimoraic feet, while another is word-initial syllables with accents. In Experiment 1, foot-initial moras were also word-initial moras in each phrase. This may have led to stable and consistent performance by speakers. In

Experiment 2, however, foot-initial syllables were not always word-initial syllables. This may have led to greater overall variability in the data.

As for constructing a rhythmic typology of languages, it seems premature to make such an attempt at this time. The results do suggest that English is strongly 'stress-timed'. However, whether the particular kind of temporal organisation we observe here for Japanese will prove to be a rhythmic 'type' that deserves a name seems unclear on the basis of current data.

What do the speech-cycling results tell us about English or Japanese under conditions where speakers have not been asked to speak in a waltz-like pattern? The results suggest that although both languages showed attraction of prominent syllables to harmonic phases, the factors that made syllables prominent were quite different between the languages. These differences presumably apply just as much to ordinary, unconstrained conversation as to our artificial speech task.

Furthermore, the particular kinds of temporal organisation found in each language are not some artifact of our task, but instead are closely related to other known properties of the language. For example, the results here provide further evidence for temporal correlates of bimoraic units in Japanese (cf. Tajima 1998). Bimoraic feet have been shown to play an important role in morphophonological processes (Poser 1990), and have been demonstrated to have an effect on coarticulation of segments (Kondo and Arai 1998). These units can therefore be supported on both phonetic and phonological grounds, contrary to previous scepticism about the physical salience of Japanese feet (cf. Beckman 1995). Furthermore, the phonetic interpretation of bimoraic feet – tendency toward isochrony and stability of foot-initial syllables – shows striking resemblance to how English stress-feet are phonetically manifested. Thus, it appears that speech cycling has implications for typology as well as universals of speech rhythm.

Notes

We are grateful to Ken de Jong, Mafuyu Kitahara, Richard Wright and Bushra Zawaydeh for feedback on earlier drafts of this paper. We also thank the reviewers, particularly Mary Beckman, for their helpful comments. Special thanks are due to Fred Cummins for discussion of related issues and for the beat extractor software.

1   The vowel inversion actually leads to a difference in stress pattern. The second syllable of 'Bug-eye' bears 'secondary stress' because it contains a full vowel. By contrast, the second syllable of 'Byga' is 'stressless' since it contains a reduced vowel. In the present context, however, we focus on just the difference between 'primary stress' and 'non-primary stress' syllables.

2   The morpheme structure of some phrases deviated from this, e.g. the phrase /taka biʃa da/ consisted of one morpheme [taka biʃa] followed by the copula [da].

20

Commentary: on the interpretation of speakers' performance

GERARD J. DOCHERTY

20.1 Introduction

This commentary highlights three related issues arising from the papers by Zawaydeh, Silverman, Hayward, Watkins and Oyètádé, and Tajima and Port:

(a) to what extent do these findings shed light on the characteristics of phonetic interpretation in natural speech production?

(b) how reliable are arguments which are founded on the view that the predominant influence on the vocal tract in speech production is a pressure to differentiate hypothesised contrasting phonological categories acoustically, auditorily or articulatorily?

(c) how explicit are we about how we conceive of the relationship between hypothesised features/structures and their phonetic correlates; in particular what is the burden of proof in respect of the phonetic observations which are required to postulate the existence of a particular feature, and what does the hypothesis of the existence of a particular feature predict about its phonetic correlates?

These questions are fundamental to the interpretation of the results of these papers, but are not explicitly addressed. The present investigators, however, are far from being alone in skirting around some of these areas or leaving their understanding of them implicit (and it does not seem to be that this is because the issues concerned are uncontroversial). Given the current diversification in laboratory phonology, both methodologically and in the range of theoretical perspectives which are being brought to bear in investigating the phonetic interpretation of phonological categories, it seems particularly important that underlying issues and assumptions such those in (a)–(c) are brought into view and reflected upon. My aim is to do the former in the context of this set of papers, and I hope the latter will ensue.

20.2 Phonetic interpretation in natural speech production

The first issue to be highlighted relates to the extent to which this work leads us to an understanding of phonetic interpretation within naturalistic speech production. I reflect on this primarily in the context of Tajima and Port's paper.

Speech cycling (see Cummins and Port 1998 for a comprehensive account of this technique) is used in a design of great ingenuity to demonstrate some aspects of speech timing which seem to apply across languages (or at least two languages), and others which appear to be language-specific. The context for the study is the perennial problem of trying to find a phonetic basis for clear perceptions that languages have different rhythmic structures, and Tajima and Port's perception that linguistic accounts of metrical structure and prominence have tended to maintain an unwelcome distance from what they refer to as 'real time' (323). Their principal findings are:

(a) most speakers of both languages produce remarkably stable patterns of 'beat-phasing' within the individual speech cycle when asked to cycle a prosodically identical phrase to a waltz rhythm, although less consistency is evident in the results of Experiment 2 when the prosodic structures speakers are asked to produce are more complex. Nonetheless, the cross-language consistencies are striking.

(b) Japanese and English differ in respect of the stability of certain prosodic structures in the face of local perturbations caused by either segmental inversions (Experiment 1) or the addition of unstressed syllables (Experiment 2). For the English speakers it appears that timing is adjusted so that foot-initial syllables are lined up approximately with the down-beats of the waltz rhythm. The picture for Japanese speakers is less clear, with Experiment 1 showing a degree of stability for what Tajima and Port refer to as foot- or word-initial syllables (which are also pitch-accented), but Experiment 2 showing much less of a propensity for alignment of pitch-accented syllables with stable positions in the harmonic cycle, and the beat-phasing showing a sensitivity to the number of syllables in what Tajima and Port refer to as a word-level unit.

In accounting for their findings, Tajima and Port posit two 'different kinds of cognitive structures'. *Metre* – a 'system of attractors on the phase circle' (337) – underlying the rhythmic features of speech and music (and presumably of other cyclic motor activity too). To this is coupled what Tajima and Port refer to as *linguistic text* for which they seem to have in mind a fairly familiar language-specific representation of the prosodic structure of an utterance. A key source of differences across languages resides in which elements of *linguistic text* are stably aligned with the strong positions of the metre. Thus, in the present study, for example, English stressed syllables have a strong tendency to coincide with the 1/3 and 2/3 harmonic fractions within the metrical cycle.

Whilst the experimental results do not lead inexorably to the postulation of these cognitive structures, the proposed framework is broadly in tune with the findings that speakers of different languages can be induced to behave extremely consistently in accordance with a particular imposed metre, whilst at the same time be shown to respond differentially in a manner which appears to correspond to some extent to theories of prosodic structure applying to those languages.

Space prevents discussion of a number of interesting issues raised by this work; for example, how does this account relate to existing theories of the prosodic structure of English and Japanese (Pierrehumbert and Beckman 1988; Beckman 1995)? How does it relate to the task-dynamic model of motor control which predicts language-general and language-specific aspects of cyclic articulatory kinematics without appeal to any special cognitive structure to govern the timing separate to the phonological representation (Kelso, Vatikiotis-Bateson, Saltzman and Kay 1985; Vatikiotis-Bateson and Kelso 1993)? What is the effect of speeding up or slowing down the metronome,[1] or of not insisting on the waltz beat? However, given the first area identified in the introduction, the following comments focus on the extent to which the findings of the study amplify our understanding of the rhythmic structure of natural speech.

First, looking positively, speech cycling does seem like an innovative and potentially insightful method for testing out theories of prosodic representation, particularly if it is possible to relax the constraints on linguistic structure put in place for the present study because of its comparative basis. It is possible to envisage a whole set of further experiments looking at different languages and testing out the role of different prosodic domains in accounting for the resistance or otherwise to local perturbations of the sort described in this paper.

On the other hand, given Tajima and Port's claim that *metre* (i.e. the proposed cognitive structure) is universally available, and common to both speech and music, the question arises why it is apparently so hard to get evidence of this in normal unconstrained speech tasks. Speakers were given extensive training and a severely constrained metrical environment in these experiments, and even under these conditions, some of the speakers found it difficult to produce the consistent patterns of phasing which are taken as the evidence for this underlying timing mechanism (two of the English speakers were excluded from the second experiment 'because they had difficulty in performing the task' (333), i.e. consistently producing the waltz rhythm in

Experiment 1, and the stability of the basic waltz rhythm for the Japanese speakers in the second experiment was considerably degraded by comparison to the first).

Abercrombie (1967: 98) has suggested that speakers' rhythmic performance in metrically constrained tasks such as verse (and presumably speech cycling would fall into a similar category) has its basis in the rhythmic structures of natural speech, but Tajima and Port appear to take a more radical stance suggesting that the rhythmic basis of speech (i.e. the interaction of their proposed cognitive structure of metre and linguistic structure) can only really be observed within an extraordinarily unnatural task such as speech cycling. This would seem to leave open the question of what it is that leads listeners to perceive the different rhythmic structures shown by languages, and it begs the question of how infants learn the underlying rhythmic basis of their native language, if they are only exposed to it indirectly. Overall I think it is legitimate to ask the question to what extent this task can help us understand the phonetic bases of the rhythmic features of natural speech.

This abstraction away from natural speech is also a feature of the other papers: Silverman's study is based around what he refers to as non-speech-like stimuli generated from three single-word utterances one from each of three speakers of Jalapa Mazatec; Hayward *et al.* looked at nonsense CV syllables which two of the subjects took away to practise before the recording session because they found the task difficult (the third subject was one of the authors); Zawaydeh's study has herself as the subject in the articulatory study (using a mix of real and nonsense words) and uses the same material in her acoustic study (with four additional subjects). Of course there are serious practical issues applying to some of these cases (it is not easy to get volunteers to be laryngoscoped for example), and I fully appreciate the need for controlled data in many experimental studies. However, there is no doubt that to a disinterested observer, it would seem that this group of investigators (and, indeed, a significant amount of the work which falls into the category of laboratory phonology) is not too uncomfortable with quite a wide gulf between the material they are working with and natural speech production.

There are various dimensions to this, with potentially different degrees of importance. I would like to highlight three of these. One is the use of a small number of subjects often including the investigator him/herself; this is virtually routine within this line of research and is rarely questioned (although see Vogel 1992), and yet in quantitative behavioural research, including areas which are very closely related to laboratory phonology (e.g. psycholinguistics), a design of this sort would be seen by many as being deeply flawed. Second, is the extent to which rehearsal is required in performing the experimental task; normal speech production is a fundamentally unrehearsed task and there must inevitably be a trade-off between the amount of rehearsal required of speakers to carry out a task as required and the naturalness of that task. Third, is the extensive use which is made of nonsense material in both production and perception tasks; a particular issue here is the extent to which processing of such material is equivalent to that which happens with real lexical material.

Of course, studies which have incorporated many or all of the features just described have been very prominent in experimental phonetic research for many years. The point is not that these studies are invalid – indeed, they have been the foundation for our understanding of many of the key principles of speech production and perception – however, the concerns which I have raised are symptomatic of a more general question relating to the validity of experimental findings and about the extent to which they can be generalised. It is especially important for this line of criticism to be addressed when experimental findings are being readily invoked in support of models which purport to have a lot to say about natural speech production and perception.

20.3 On contrast enhancement and preservation

I now turn to the second of the overarching issues that are raised by the papers in this section; namely, the assumptions made by investigators about the extent to which the vocal tract is driven by a requirement to differentiate contrasting phonological categories in either auditory, acoustic or articulatory space. With this in mind, I focus on papers by Silverman and Hayward *et al.* who appeal to the maintenance of sufficiently distinct contrast as a driving force in explaining synchronic and diachronic patterns of interaction between tone and phonatory activity.

Silverman presents data which is claimed to support an auditory-perceptual basis for a typological feature, namely a dispreference for simultaneous contrastive tones and contrastive non-modal phonation. Two key assumptions here are (i) that the domain of both is the same (i.e. the segment),[2] and (ii) a model of pitch perception which predicts degraded perceptual performance in signals with greater noise and greater jitter, both of which are assumed to be features of breathy voice.

A key starting point is evidence that Jalapa Mazatec seems to show a sequential phonatory change when there is a simultaneous tone/phonation contrast such that underlyingly breathy vowels are realised as breathy-modal. A clear example of this switch in mode of phonation is shown in Silverman (1997: 240). In the tokens used as the basis for the present experiment the transition from breathy to modal voice is much more gradual, to the extent that it is difficult to identify where the line could be drawn between the two.[3] Using these tokens, Silverman created a set of stimuli to use in a pitch-discrimination task, with subjects asked to identify whether pairs of stimuli have the same pitch or not. The results showed a small statistically significant difference;

suggesting that pitch discrimination is less reliable on breathy than on modal stimuli.

Given these results, Silverman constructs an argument calling on the principles of Lindblom's H and H theory (Lindblom 1990). According to the assumed model of pitch perception, pitch and non-modal phonation are not well-adapted auditorily, therefore they are dispreferred. Silverman also refers to articulatory incompatibility as a possible factor (i.e. between the greater laryngeal tension associated with higher pitch and the lower tension which is a feature of breathy voice). This latter line of argument is a key point of contact between this paper and that of Hayward *et al.*'s to which I will now turn before advancing to the main point of this section of the commentary.

The main thrust of Hayward *et al.*'s study is also to investigate the interaction of tone and phonation type in the context of there being considerable variance in accounts of the phonetic basis of tonal register. The background to their study includes some typological observations and some well-attested diachronic changes, together with the notion that there may be an articulatory and/or perceptual incompatibility between some tone and phonation features. They look at tone and phonation within Yorùbá as a case study, given that there are clearly differing accounts in the literature in respect of the mapping between tone and register. The results are not entirely clear-cut (with a good deal of cross-speaker variability, and some interaction between phonatory characteristics and vowel quality) but there is a suggestion that L tone has a distinctive creaky voice quality and that M and H tones should be grouped together in any register division applied to Yorùbá. Much of Hayward *et al.*'s discussion around the interaction of tone and phonation is hinged on the view that in general languages will prefer combinations which enhance and/or preserve and/or maintain lexical constrasts (although, as they acknowledge, it is not always clear what the predictions might be in this respect; e.g. there might be an *auditory* advantage in associating breathy phonation with low pitch and creaky with high, but on the other hand, in *articulatory* terms, glottal constriction seems to be most naturally associated with low pitch and there is some evidence of breathier vowels at high pitch).

An assumption which is explicitly present in both papers, but not explored in depth by either, is that the speech production mechanism will 'go out of its way' in order to maintain, enhance or preserve lexical contrast (in these cases at the level of tone or register, but presumably the same principle would be considered to apply to segmental contrast). So, for example, in Jalapa Mazatec, it is claimed speakers produce a complex phonatory pattern to ensure more reliable perception of the tonal contrast on a vowel which is canonically breathy (even though Silverman's study showed a difference in reliability in pitch perception of only a few percent at best); likewise Hayward *et al.* suggest that breathy voice might become associated with low tones so that the higher spectral tilt associated with breathy voice enhances the 'low character of low pitches'.

In evaluating this line of argument, it is interesting to look at how well phonological contrasts actually are maintained within natural speech production. At one level, they are clearly maintained very well; breakdown of communication between native speakers is not a regularly occurring situation. However, it is not difficult to think of cases where critically contrasting phonetic parameters show considerable phonetic overlap (i.e. where, on the face of it, speakers do not appear to be too constrained to maintain the phonetic differences between contrasting categories); e.g. VOT continua or vowel quality (where even within an individual speaker there can be significant cross-category overlap). The key insight here is obviously that of Lindblom (1990) that a parameter or group of parameters should function to keep words *sufficiently distinct* for a particular context, with sufficiency being evaluated from moment-to-moment on the basis of signal-dependent and signal-independent information. Thus, speakers do not always necessarily need to maintain, enhance and preserve particular contrasts in the way which appears to be suggested by the line of argumentation present in these two papers.

Pursuing this line, it is informative to look at the notion of sufficient distinctiveness in view of the huge amount of variability produced by speakers in everyday conversation. There is evidence from studies of corpora of natural speech which suggests that the role of contrast maintenance as a factor in explaining patterns of speech production may apparently be much less predominant than other tasks being fulfilled simultaneously by the speech production mechanism.

Table 20.1 presents a sample of results from Watt's (1998) study of phonological variation in the production of vowels of Tyneside English. It shows the usage made by different categories of Tyneside English speaker of different qualities of vowel for words which are in the NURSE category in English (i.e. words like *nurse, purse, curse, bird;* I am adopting Wells's (1982) practice of referring to a group of lexical items sharing a particular vowel quality by an exemplar from that group given in small capitals). This vowel has for a number of years been moving from a retracted quality (allegedly merged with NORSE) to a range of central and anterior qualities. Table 20.1 shows immense synchronic variability in vowel usage (although the data are pooled across different speaker categories, a similar pattern of variability is found for individuals). Statistical analysis reveals strong effects from social factors; particularly gender ($p < 0.001$) and age (and their interaction).

Findings such as this lead Watt to suggest that the huge amount of redundancy in the speech signal, in combination with speakers' and listeners' ability to normalise across wide variation in vowel quality, means that the surface variability of vowels is free to be exploited by speakers for the purposes of distinguishing themselves socially by means of subtle, or not so subtle, differences. Maintaining acoustic contrasts between vowels for communicative reasons might not actually be as important as some would have it, at least in the case of English, as contextual and coarticulatory cues do a large part of the work of disambiguation. Watt suggests that this might explain why vowels are more prone to synchronic and diachronic variation than are consonants.

Table 20.1 *Variants of NURSE vowels in groups of Tyneside English speakers: O = old, MC = middle class, WC = working class, M/F = male/female. Figures are raw token counts based on an analysis of 4 speakers per cell*

Group	Fronted	Central	Retracted	Total
	[ø]	[əː]	[ɔː]	
OMC M	38	98	19	155
YMC M	34	110	12	156
OMC F	40	105	4	149
YMC F	144	30	1	175
OWC M	20	39	36	95
YWC M	9	130	6	145
OWC F	76	72	5	153
YWC F	105	23	0	128

But similar patterns of variation can be found in the production of consonants. Table 20.2 shows the percentage realisation of five different variants of /t/ in word-final pre-vowel position by 32 speakers of Tyneside English (four per group). In accounting for this pattern of variation, lexical and social factors are as important as phonological ones (Docherty, Foulkes, Milroy, Milroy and Walshaw 1997). Note too that two of the variants used [ɹ t̞] are phonetically identical or very similar to other members of the class of English consonants, and that another two [ʔ ʔt] are phonetically similar to each other in many respects (i.e. the relationship between the variants in the table is extremely nonlinear). The question arises how communicatively efficient it is to have this range of variation of the same 'underlying form'. At one level, that of maintenance of a contrastive phonemic system, it is not at all efficient, but this does not prevent speakers performing in this way, and indeed, it does not stop them making use of this variation as a social marker.

Data such as these reflect the fact that the speech production mechanism is readily harnessed in systematic fashion to fulfil a set overlaid functions (lexical contrast, social marking, pragmatic functions), and that these may exert different degrees of influence on speaker performance at different times and in different contexts. It might also be relevant to emphasise that these overlaid functions all appear to emerge simultaneously along with phonological acquisition; it does not appear to be the case the parallel functions are grafted on to a pre-existing phonology (Roberts 1997; Foulkes, Docherty and Watt 1999), thus reinforcing the point that it is not easy to pull these apart, or to look at one in isolation from the others (Strand 1999; papers in Johnson and Mullenix 1997).

Table 20.2 *Percentage realisations of /t/ in word-final pre-vowel position, by speaker group, Tyneside corpus (WC = working class, MC = middle class, n = number of tokens analysed); from Docherty et al. (1997)*

	Variant					
	ɹ	t̪	t	ʔt	ʔ	*n*
older WC females	40	18	27	12	2	404
older WC males	15	35	7	42	2	178
young WC females	21	39	5	20	13	402
young WC males	3	59	4	23	12	230
older MC females	12	27	39	20	2	366
older MC males	6	32	5	53	4	398
young MC females	2	42	5	17	34	383
young MC males	1	48	4	27	23	305

As well as appealing to auditory enhancement of contrast, Silverman and Hayward *et al.* appeal to another aspect of Lindblom's H and H theory, namely the tendency of the vocal tract to show a skewing towards low-cost activity when the communicative context permits, and that patterns of articulation which are closer to the low-cost end of the continuum are more 'natural' (there are transparent links here of course to the notion of markedness as invoked by phonologists).

Whilst low-cost vocal tract activity is clearly an influential factor (and does appear to have had its impact on phonological typology) its explanatory power in a particular case needs to be evaluated in the context of at least two other key features of speech production: (a) on the one hand there is abundant evidence that different speakers can adopt different strategies to achieve the same goal; a very relevant example of this comes from Löfqvist, Koenig and McGowan (1995) who, in a study of voice source variation associated with tonal contrasts in Mandarin, found that individuals used different laryngeal strategies in the production of the same F_0 contour; (b) there is also evidence that speakers can quite readily make sounds which are not necessarily particularly 'natural' but are what it is that native speakers of that particular language do; e.g. voiced stops or fricatives, or, to take a different type of example, whilst it may be easier for a speaker to produce lower pitch with a breathy voice quality, it is no great effort to span a considerable F_0 range whilst retaining that phonation type; whilst I am not aware of any direct evidence on this, speakers of tone languages with a habitual breathy voice presumably do this as a matter of routine and are not communicatively disadvantaged as a result.

I do not wish to suggest that articulatory naturalness cannot be invoked (it clearly can to some extent, and there are obvious limits to the range of sounds which a normal vocal tract can generate) but, in general, I suggest that there is a need for caution in invoking contrast-enhancement as *the* unique driving force behind what it is that speakers do with their vocal tracts, especially when as is the case with DS's results, the evidence suggests only a very mild improvement in auditory enhancement may be achievable by a particular articulatory strategy and the overall error rate remains quite low.

20.4 Phonetic interpretation and feature representations

I now turn to the third area highlighted at the start of this commentary: how explicit is our conception of the relationship between hypothesised phonological features and their phonetic correlates; in particular what burden of proof is required to postulate the existence of a particular feature, and what does the hypothesis of the existence of a particular feature predict about its phonetic correlates?

In carrying out an instrumental study of the phonetics and phonology of gutturals, Zawaydeh picks up a recurrent laboratory phonology theme, and illustrates a number of the dimensions of this question. The general thrust of her study is to look for a phonetic explanation for what appear to be natural groupings of guttural sounds. Existing accounts seem to be unsatisfactory either because they violate the requirement that features should be associated with specific active articulators, or because there is dispute about the data. Zawaydeh broaches this area with a confounding problem which is that in Arabic and Interior Salish, it appears that membership of the guttural group is different, with the laryngeals patterning with the other gutturals in Arabic, but not in Interior Salish.

Zawaydeh's laryngoscopic analysis suggests that pharyngeal constriction appears to be the characteristic which unites the gutturals to the exclusion of the orals and glottals. This appears to match well with the grouping found in Interior Salish, and is a particularly attractive solution in that the pharynx can be considered to be an active articulator and hence seems to fulfil one of the main requirements of a feature (although, in light of comments made above, note that no instrumental data is presented in respect of Interior Salish).

This however leaves the problem that an articulatory feature will not account for the grouping found in Arabic. Zawaydeh suggests an acoustic basis for this instead, reporting that Arabic gutturals (including glottals) raise F1 in an adjacent V (and pointing to reported data which suggest that the same is not found in Interior Salish). Zawaydeh suggests that this acoustic grouping might explain the phonological patterning of Arabic gutturals, leading to the conclusion that acoustic/auditory and articulatory features are needed to account for the distinct natural classes of guttural sounds. I have three major comments on this work.

The first relates to the interpretation of the laryngoscopic images, and reiterates the general line taken by Nolan (1995) in his commentary on Lee's (1995) Laboratory Phonology paper on the phonetic basis of the class of gutturals. Any attempt to link pharyngeal constriction as an independent point of vocal tract constriction to a node in feature geometry has to address the fact that pharyngeal constriction is intimately and anatomically tied up with other movements and configurations of the vocal tract.

The results of Zawaydeh's articulatory study are said to support the union of the emphatics, uvulars and pharyngeals under one [pharyngeal] articulator node in the feature-geometric representation. One question that could be asked here is to what extent the pharyngeal constriction observed for the uvulars and possibly for emphatics is a secondary characteristic arising from tongue retraction (and raising in the case of uvulars), as opposed to a defining characteristic as in the case of the pharyngeals (with emphatics, this would depend on whether the secondary articulation was uvularisation or pharyngealisation; Laufer and Baer 1988 present evidence in favour of the latter, whilst Catford 1977 suggests there is evidence for both). The results of Zawaydeh's acoustic experiment may be relevant here showing that the pharyngeal consonant has a much greater effect on the quality of an adjacent vowel than the uvulars or emphatics. One explanation for this might be Laufer and Baer's finding that more extreme pharyngeal constriction is found for pharyngeal sounds with a primary as opposed to secondary pharyngeal constriction, but this would beg the question how much pharyngeal constriction is necessary for a sound to be included under the same [pharyngeal] node as the pharyngeals. Thus, there is a possibility that pharyngeal constriction might be found as a result of primary articulatory activity elsewhere in the vocal tract, and presumably, where this is found to be the case, it is questionable whether such activity can be construed as evidence for a sound being attached to the [pharyngeal] node.

Likewise, there is a strand in the literature in this area which suggests that pharyngeal constriction might also be induced by an articulatory mechanism located below the apparent locus of constriction.

Esling (1996) suggests that the aryepiglottic folds are the prime active articulator in the production of 'pharyngeal' sounds. According to Esling this single mechanism would seem to unite in articulatory grounds what are conventionally referred to and symbolised as glottals and pharyngeals (with the status of the emphatics uncertain, depending on whether they are considered to be uvularised or pharyngealised); i.e. instead of a pharyngeal sphincter, Esling claims that the main protagonist in this class of sounds is an aryepiglottic sphincter. This would suggest that the pharyngeal constriction observed in the images presented in Zawaydeh's paper may be the consequence of some other primary mechanism.

If Esling's account is accurate, this might suggest a natural articulatory grouping of gutturals and laryngeals, as found in Arabic, based around a single articulatory mechanism, particularly, if as Zawaydeh suggests, there is an aryepiglottic component to the Arabic glottals. It would of course leave the problem of what do with the Interior Salish glottals which do not group with the gutturals, but perhaps the answer there would be that these glottals may not have the aryepiglottic component and are more like the glottal stop as found in other languages involving either some simple constriction of the true vocal folds, or maybe just an interval of laryngealised voice quality.

The general point here, then, is that before assuming that a particular observation common to a group of sounds can be abstracted to play the role of a [feature], it is presumably critical to assess the extent to which its presence in the instrumental results may be interacting with or a function of other simultaneous articulatory activity. For fairly straightforward anatomical reasons, this may be a particular factor in relation to pharyngeal articulations.

My second comment relates to Zawaydeh's acoustic analysis. It is suggested that all gutturals should induce a higher F1 on an adjacent vowel as a coarticulatory result of the presence of a constriction near the glottis. It is further argued that Arabic laryngeals should have the same feature because of the possibility (raised by Nolan 1995) that they have an aryepiglottic constriction (i.e. slightly above the glottis). The prediction then is that Arabic gutturals and laryngeals might be grouped together on acoustic grounds in that they should all induce a relatively high F1 in a following V, and indeed Zawaydeh's results seem to point in this direction.

This conclusion of an acoustic-based grouping in Arabic arises from the results which show that F1 is statistically significantly higher in vowels adjacent to laryngeals and gutturals.[4] However, to judge from Zawaydeh's Figure 16.5, it also appears that within the guttural class there is a difference between the pharyngeal consonant and the others of at least the same order as that which proves to be significant between the gutturals/laryngeals and the orals. It would be interesting to see if this difference is statistically significant too. If so, applying the same principle as Zawaydeh does in order to reach the primary conclusion, this would presumably require the pharyngeal set to be split off into a separate group in acoustic terms, or at least the identification of some independent principle dictating that this should not happen.

My third area of comment considers the nature of the explanation Zawaydeh's findings provide. The starting point for this is her statement in relation to the acoustic analysis that 'this acoustic grouping could explain the phonological patterning of Arabic gutturals' (289).

It is possible to reconstruct Zawaydeh's overall argument as follows (hopefully without misrepresenting it): given a group of sounds that in some interesting respects behave in similar fashion, the theoretical framework within which this work is embedded demands that they have some feature in common; instrumental studies find commonalities in the two languages (articulatory in one and acoustic in the other) and this leads to the conclusion that auditory and/or articulatory features are needed in phonological theory, and that apparently either will do.

In studies of this sort, I think there is a danger of overstating the extent to which an explanation has been provided. What is shown is that sounds which appear to behave as a group may have some phonetic characteristic in common (as well as many that are different of course), but the conclusion that this shared characteristic can constitute evidence for a phonological feature (which is, according to at least some proponents of phonological theory, universal and presumably innate) is a supposition which does not arise from the data; it is the theory which provides the question (and clearly, from the point of view of the theory it *is* an interesting question), and the theory which determines the interpretation of the data, but, critically, the theory itself is not in question, and there is nothing intrinsic to the data that forces the theoretical conclusion.

The sceptic might be entitled to wonder what it would take for the theoretical assumptions to actually be questioned (i.e. at what point do we start to wonder about whether we are asking the right question, as opposed to seeking out another way of determining a phonetic basis for this particular group of sounds).

A key issue here is the relatively unconstrained way in which phonetic observations can apparently be assigned the status of phonological features. Problems relating to Zawaydeh's analysis of her data as supporting the existence of a [pharyngeal] feature have already been mentioned in this commentary. The same applies to the hypothesised [High F1] feature. It is not clear on what principled basis this particular acoustic feature of an adjacent vowel is assigned a phonological role *vis-à-vis* the guttural consonant.

It is also unclear what is being implied in this reasoning about the reciprocity of the relationship between phonological representation and phonetic realisation. The implication here seems to be that whatever feature underlies this natural class is mapped directly onto a phonetic realisation (e.g. [pharyngeal] corresponds to a pharyngeal constriction, [High F1] maps onto a corresponding acoustic/auditory characteristic) and this claim has certainly been made in the past for feature geometric representations (Clements 1992; Clements and Hume 1995). This runs counter to the findings of other investigators (e.g. Keating 1984; Kingston and Diehl 1994; Docherty *et al.* 1997) that a phonological representation (such as a feature geometry) is patently not a sufficient representation of what it is that speakers do in producing an utterance.

Returning to the questions I outlined at the start of this section: how explicit are we about how we conceptualise the relationship between hypothesised features/structures and their phonetic correlates? – not very in this case. What is the burden of evidence necessary to postulate the existence of a particular feature? – whatever it is, it does not appear to be very demanding. What does the hypothesis of the existence of a [feature] predict about its phonetic correlates? – this is not overtly discussed by Zawaydeh, but is surely a key component of understanding the nature of the exercise of which Zawaydeh's paper is an example.

20.5 Conclusion

An underlying theme of this commentary is that our understanding of the relationship between phonetics and phonology would be enhanced by our being more inquisitive about the characteristics of natural speech production. This is especially important if natural speech is to be conceived of as the primary stimulus which determines phonological knowledge (Beckman, this volume), and if, as Coleman (this volume) suggests, the phonetic interpretation strand of laboratory phonology is to be recast as one of phonological interpretation of phonetic substance. In pursuing this, it would be advantageous to show sensitivity to the fact that speech production is shaped simultaneously by a number of different types of constraints and functions, only some of which would correspond to what most people would want to call 'phonology' (although therein lies another debate). However, even if we adhere to the more 'traditional' aims of pursuing the phonetic interpretation of phonological categories and representations, it seems there is a need for much greater clarity in respect of the nature of that relationship, and of how we set about investigating it.

Notes

I would like to thank a number of people who have helped me in the preparation of this commentary: Janet Beck, John Esling, Paul Foulkes, Jane Stuart-Smith and Dom Watt; Bushra Zawaydeh, Katrina Hayward and Justin Watkins who kindly sent me copies of material that was difficult to access; two anonymous reviewers who provided some very helpful comments.

1   In relation to this it would also be interesting to consider the implications of the fact that Tajima and Port found it necessary to set the metronome to cycle at slightly different periods for the English and Japanese subjects (see their note 2). This could be interpreted as evidence of a language-specific dimension to their proposed 'metre'.

2   There is a suggestion in the literature (Kirk, Ladefoged and Ladefoged 1994) that the domain of phonation contrast in Jalapa Mazatec may be considered to be the syllable rather than the segment, which, if true, may weaken Silverman's analysis that tone and phonation type are fully cross-classsifying in this language.

3   It is not obvious that there is much jitter in these tokens, as assumed by Silverman, which may not be too surprising because breathy voice does not *necessarily* have any more cycle-to-cycle variation than modal voice

4   There is a confounding factor in relation to Zawaydeh's F1-raising hypothesis. For many speakers it seems likely that pharyngealisation is associated with raising of the larynx (Esling 1996; Nolan 1995; Laver 1980). Whilst the phonetic correlates of raising of the larynx are not well documented, shortening of the vocal tract should in theory lead to relatively higher formants all round, and there is some evidence that this is in fact the case (Sundberg and Nordstrom 1976). Therefore F1-raising may not be exclusively attributable to the presence of a pharyngeal constriction.

References

Abberton, E., D. Howard & A. Fourcin. 1989. Laryngographic assessment of normal voice: a tutorial. *Clinical Linguistics and Phonetics* 3: 281–96.

Abercrombie, D. 1964. *English Phonetic Texts*. London: Faber and Faber.

Abercrombie, D, 1967 *Elements of General Phonetics*. Edinburgh: Edinburgh University Press.

Absalom, M. & J. Hajek. 1998. Review of Loporcaro (1997). *L'origine del raddoppiamento fonosintattico: saggio di fonologia diacronica romanza*. Basel and Tübingen: Francke Verlag. *Phonology* 15: 272–7.

Absalom, M. & J. Hajek. 1997. Raddoppiamento Sintattico: what happens when the theory is on too tight? In P. M. Bertinetto, L. Gaeta, G. Jetchev & D. Michaels (eds.), *Certamen Phonologicum III: Papers from the 3rd Cortona Phonology Meeting*. Turin: Rosenberg and Sellier, 159–79.

Agostiniani, L. 1992. Su alcuni aspetti del 'rafforzamento sintattico' in Toscana e sulla loro importanza per la qualificazione del fenomeno in generale. *Quaderni del dipartimento di linguistica, Università di Firenze* III, 1–28.

Akinlabi, A. & E-A. E. Urua. 1992. Prosodic target and vocalic specification in the Ibibio verb. In J. Mead (ed.), *WCCFL11: Proceedings of the 11th West Coast Conference on Formal Linguistics*. Stanford, CA: CSLI, 1–14.

Allen, J. 1994a. Harvey Fletcher 1884–1981. In J. Allen (ed.), *The ASA Edition of Speech and Hearing in Communication*. New York: Acoustical Society of America

Allen, J. 1994b. How do humans process and recognize speech? *IEEE Transactions on Speech and Audio Processing* 2: 567–77.

Alwan, A. A., S. S. Narayanan & K. Haker. 1997. Toward articulatory-acoustic models for liquid approximants based on MRI and EPG data. Part II. The rhotics. *Journal of the Acoustical Society of America* 101: 1078–89.

Anderson, A. H., E. G. Bard, C. Sotillo, A. Newlands & G. Doherty-Sneddon. 1997. Limited visual control of the intelligibility of speech in face-to-face dialogue. *Perception & Psychophysics* 39: 580–92.

Anderson, J. M. & C. Jones. 1974. Three theses concerning phonological representations. *Journal of Linguistics* 10: 1–26.

Anderson, S. R. 1976. On the description of multiply-articulated consonants. *Journal of Phonetics* 4:17–27.

Baart, J. L. G. 1999. Tone rules in Kalam Kohistani (Garwi, Bashkarik). *Bulletin of the School of Oriental and African Studies* 62: 88–104.

Baayen, R. H., R. Piepenbrock & L. Gulikers. 1995. The CELEX Lexical Database (Release 2) [CD-ROM]. Philadelphia, PA: Linguistic Data Consortium, University of Pennsylvania.

Bakare, C. A. 1995. Discrimination and identification of Yorùbá tones: perception experiments and acoustic analysis. In K. Owolabi (ed.), *Language in Nigeria.* Ibadan: Group Publishers.

Balota, D. A., J. E. Boland & L. W. Shields. 1989. Priming in pronunciation: beyond pattern recognition and onset latency. *Journal of Memory and Language* 28: 14–36.

Bao, Z. 1990. On the nature of tone. PhD dissertation, Massachusetts Institute of Technology.

Bard, E. G., & A. H. Anderson. 1983. The unintelligibility of speech to children. *Journal of Child Language* 10: 265–92.

Barlow, J. 1995. The development of on-glides in American English. In *Proceedings of the 20th Annual Boston University Conference on Language Development, Nov., 1995.* Vol. 1. Somerville, MA: Cascadilla Press, 40–51.

Barry, M. C. 1985. A palatographic study of connected speech processes. *Cambridge Papers in Phonetics and Experimental Linguistics* 4: 1–16.

Barry, M. C. 1992. Palatalisation, assimilation and gestural weakening in connected speech. *Speech Communication* 11: 393–400.

Barry, W. J. 1983. Some problems of interarticulator phasing as an index of temporal regularity in speech. *Journal of Experimental Psychology* 9: 826–8.

Beckman, M. E. 1995. On blending and the mora: comments on Kubozono. In B. Connell & A. Arvaniti (eds.), *Papers in Laboratory Phonology IV: Phonology and Phonetic Evidence.* Cambridge: Cambridge University Press, 157–67.

Beckman, M. E. & J. Edwards. 1990. Lengthenings and shortenings and the nature of prosodic constituency. In J. Kingston & M.E. Beckman (eds), *Papers in Laboratory Phonology I: Between the Grammar and Physics of Speech.* Cambridge: Cambridge University Press, 152–78.

Beckman, M., J. Edwards and J. Fletcher. 1992. Prosodic structure and tempo in a sonority model of articulatory dynamics. In G. J. Docherty and D. R. Ladd (eds.), *Papers in Laboratory Phonology II: Gesture, Segment, Prosody.* Cambridge: Cambridge University Press, 68–6.

Beckman, M. E. & G. A. Elam. 1997. Guidelines for ToBI labelling. Version 3. Unpublished, Ohio State University.

Bekku, S. 1977. *Nihongo no Rizumu (The Rhythm of Japanese).* Tokyo: Kodansha.

Benki, J. 1998. Evidence for phonological categories from speech perception. Doctoral dissertation, University of Massachusetts at Amherst.

356

References

Berkley, D. M. 1994. Variability in Obligatory Contour Principle Effects. In *Papers from the 30th Regional Meeting of the Chicago Linguistic Society, Part 1*. Vol. 2: 1–12.

Berkovits, R. 1991. The effect of speaking rate on evidence for utterance-final lenghthening. *Phonetica* 48: 57–66.

Bertinetto, P. M. 1985. A Proposito di Alcuni Recenti Contributi alla Prosodia dell'Italiano. *Annali della Scuola Normale Superiore di Pisa* XV, 2: 581–643.

Bertoncini, J., C. Floccia, T. Nazzi & J. Mehler. 1995. Morae and syllables: rhythmical basis of speech representation in neonates. *Language and Speech* 38: 311–29.

Bessell, N. J. 1992. Towards a phonetic and phonological typology of postvelar articulations. PhD dissertation, University of British Columbia.

Bessell, N. J. & E. Czaykowska-Higgins. 1992. Interior Salish evidence for placeless laryngeals. *North East Linguistic Society* 22. Amherst, MA: University of Massachusetts at Amherst, GLSA, 35–49.

Best, C. T. 1994a. Learning to perceive the sound pattern of English. In C. Rovee-Collier & L.P Lipsitt (eds.), *Advances in Infancy Research*. Norwood, NJ: Ablex Publishing Corporation, Vol. 9: 217–304.

Best, C. T. 1994b. The emergence of native-language phonological influences in infants. A perceptual assimilation model. In J. C. Goodman & H. C. Nusbaum (eds.), *The Development of Speech Perception: the Transition from Speech Sounds to Spoken Words*. Cambridge, MA: MIT Press, 167–224.

Best, C. T. 1995. A direct realist view of cross-language speech perception. In W. Strange (ed.), *Speech Perception and Linguistic Experience: Issues in Cross-Language Speech Research*. Baltimore: York Press, 171–206.

Bird, S. 1995. *Computational Phonology: a Constraint-based Approach*. Cambridge: Cambridge University Press

Bladon, R. A. W. & A. Al-Bamerni. 1976. Coarticulation resistance in English /l/. *Journal of Phonetics* 4: 137–50.

Blasco Ferrer, E. 1986. *La Lingua Sarda Contemporanea. Grammatica del Logudorese e del Campidanese. Norma e Varietà dell'uso: Sintesi Storica*. Cagliari: Edizioni della Torre.

Blevins, J. 1995. The syllable in phonological theory. In J. Goldsmith (ed.), *The Handbook of Phonological Theory*. Oxford: Blackwell, 206–44.

Blumstein, S. E. & K. N. Stevens (1981). Phonetic features and acoustic invariance in speech. *Cognition* 10: 25–32.

Bolinger, D. 1963. Length, vowel, juncture. *Linguistics* 1: 5–29.

Bolognesi, R. 1998. *The Phonology of Campidanian Sardinian: a Unitary Account of a Self-Organizing Structure*. The Hague: Holland Institute of Generative Linguistics. HIL Dissertations, no. 38.

Bond, Z. S. & T. J. Moore. 1994. A note on the acoustic-phonetic characteristics of inadvertently clear speech. *Speech Communication* 14: 325–37.

Boothroyd, A. & S. Nittrouer. 1988. Mathematical treatment of context effects in phoneme and word recognition. *Journal of the Acoustical Society of America* 84: 101–14.

Borowsky, T. J. 1986. Topics in the lexical phonology of English. PhD dissertation, University of Massachusetts. Distributed by Indiana University Club.

Borowsky, T., J. Itô & R-A. Mester. 1984. The formal representation of ambisyllabicity: evidence from Danish. *North Eastern Linguistics Society* 14: 34–48.

Bosch, A. & K. de Jong. 1997. The prosody of Barra Gaelic epenthetic vowels. *Studies in the Linguistic Sciences* 27 (1): 1–16.

Bosch, A. & K. de Jong. 1998. Syllables and super-syllables: evidence for low level phonological domains. *Texas Linguistic Forum* 41: 1–14.

Bowden, J. and J. Hajek. 1996. Taba. *Journal of the International Phonetics Association* 26: 55–7.

Bradlow, A. R., G. M. Torretta & D. B. Pisoni. 1996. Intelligibility of normal speech. I: Global and fine-grained acoustic-phonetic talker characteristics. *Speech Communication* 20: 255–72.

Breen, G. & R. Pensalfini. 1999. Arrente: a language with no syllable onsets. *Linguistic Inquiry* 30: 1–25.

Bregman, A. S. 1990. *Auditory Scene Analysis: the Perceptual Organization of Sound.* Cambridge, MA: MIT Press.

Broadbent, D. E. 1967. Word-frequency effect and response bias. *Psychological Review* 74: 1–14.

Broadbent, J. 1991. Linking and intrusive r in English. *UCL Working Papers in Linguistics* 3: 281–302.

Broe, M. 1993. Specification theory: the treatment of redundancy in generative phonology. PhD dissertation, University of Edinburgh.

Bromberger, S. & M. Halle. 1989. Why phonology is different. *Linguistic Inquiry* 20: 51–70.

Browman, C. P. 1992. comments on Chapter 10. In G. J. Docherty & D. R. Ladd (eds.), *Papers in Laboratory Phonology II: Gesture, Segment, Prosody.* Cambridge: Cambridge University Press, 287–9.

Browman, C. P. 1995. Assimilation as gestural overlap: comments on Holst and Nolan. In B. Connell and A. Arvaniti (eds.), *Papers in Laboratory Phonology IV: Phonology and Phonetic Evidence.* Cambridge: Cambridge University Press, 334–42.

Browman, C. P. & L. Goldstein. 1986. Towards an articulatory phonology. *Phonology Yearbook* 3: 219–52.

Browman, C. P. & L. Goldstein. 1988. Some notes on syllable structure in articulatory phonology. *Phonetica* 45: 140–55.

Browman, C. P. & L. Goldstein. 1989. Articulatory gestures as phonological units. *Phonology* 6: 201–51.

Browman, C. P. & L. Goldstein. 1990a. Gestural specification using dynamically defined articulatory structures. *Journal of Phonetics* 18: 299–320.

Browman, C. P., & L. Goldstein. 1990b. Tiers in articulatory phonology, with some implications for casual speech. In J. Kingston & M.E. Beckman (eds.), *Papers in Laboratory Phonology I: Between the Grammar and Physics of Speech.* Cambridge: Cambridge University Press, 341–6.

Browman, C. P. & L. Goldstein. 1992. Articulatory phonology: an overview. *Phonetica* 49:155–80.

Browman, C. P. & L. Goldstein. 1995. Gestural syllable position effects in American English. In F. Bell-Berti & L. J. Raphael (eds.), *Producing Speech: Contemporary*

Issues. For Katherine Safford Harris. Woodbury, NY: American Institute of Physics, 19–34.

Brown Corpus. http://wapsy.psy.uwa.edu.au/uwa_mrc.htm.

Brunage, G. 1990. CELEX: A guide for users, Nijmegen, The Netherlands: CELEX.

Bybee [Hooper], J. 1981. The empirical determination of phonological representations. In T. Myers, J. Laver & J. Anderson (eds.), *The Cognitive Representation of Speech*. Amsterdam: North-Holland, 347–57.

Bybee, J. 1994. A view of phonology from a cognitive perspective. *Cognitive Linguistics* 5: 285–305.

Bybee, J. 1996. Lexicalization of sound change and alternating environments. Paper presented at the Fifth Conference on Laboratory Phonology, Northwestern University, July 6–8, 1996.

Bybee. J. 2000. Lexicalization of sound change and alternating environments. In M. Broe & J. Pierrehumbert (eds.), *Papers in Laboratory Phonology V: Acquisition and the Lexicon*. Cambridge: Cambridge University Press, 250–68.

Byrd, D. 1994a. Articulatory timing in English consonant sequences. PhD dissertation, UCLA, distributed as *UCLA Working Papers in Phonetics* 86: 1–196.

Byrd, D. 1994b. Relations of sex and dialect to reduction. *Speech Communication* 15: 39–54.

Byrd, D. 1996. Influences on articulatory timing in consonant sequences. *Journal of Phonetics* 24: 209–44.

Byrd, D. 1997. A phase window framework for articulatory timing. *Phonology* 13: 139–69.

Byrd, D., A. Kaun, S. Narayanan & E. Saltzman. 2000. Phrasal signatures in articulation. In M. Broe & J. Pierrehumbert (eds.), *Papers in Laboratory Phonology V: Acquisition and the Lexicon*. Cambridge: Cambridge University Press, 70–87.

Byrd, D. & E. Saltzman. 1998. Intragestural dynamics of multiple prosodic boundaries. *Journal of Phonetics* 26: 173–200.

Carey, S. 1978. The child as word learner. In M. Halle, J. Bresnan & G. A. Miller (eds.), *Linguistic Theory and Psychological Reality*. Cambridge, MA: MIT Press, 264–93.

Catford, J. C. 1977. *Fundamental Problems in Phonetics*. Bloomington: Indiana University Press.

Chafe, W. 1974. Language and consciousness. *Language* 50: 111–33.

Charles-Luce, J. 1985. Word-final devoicing in German: effects of phonetic and sentential contexts. *Journal of Phonetics* 13: 309–24.

Chen, M. 1970. Vowel length variation as a function of the voicing of the consonant environment. *Phonetica* 22: 129–59.

Chen, M. 1987. The syntax of Xiamen tone sandhi. *Phonology Yearbook* 4: 109–49.

Cho, T. & P. Keating. 1999. Articulatory and acoustic studies of domain-initial strengthening in Korean. *UCLA Working Papers in Phonetics* 97: 100–38.

Cho, T. 1998. Domain-initial articulatory strengthening in the prosodic hierarchy in Korean: an EPG study. In *Proceedings of the 11th International Conference on Korean Linguistics (ICKL)*, 363–72.

Chomsky, N. 1957. *Syntactic Structures*. The Hague: Mouton.

Chomsky, N. 1965. *Aspects of the Theory of Syntax*. Cambridge, MA: MIT Press.

Chomsky, N. 1986. *Knowledge of Language: Its Nature, Origin and Use*. New York: Preager.

Clements, G. N. 1976. The autosegmental treatment of vowel harmony. In W. Dressler & O. E. Pfeiffer (eds.), *Phonologica 1976*, 111–19.

Clements, G. N. 1983. The hierarchical representation of tone features. In I. R. Dihoff (ed.), *Current Approaches to African Linguistics*. Dordrecht: Foris, 145–76.

Clements, G. N. 1985. The geometry of phonological features. *Phonology Yearbook* 2: 225–52.

Clements, G. N. 1987. Phonological feature representation and the description of intrusive stops. In A. Bosch, B. Need and E. Schiller (eds.), *Papers from the 23rd Annual Regional Meeting of the Chicago Linguistic Society. Part 2: Parasession on Autosegmental and Metrical Phonology*. Chicago: Chicago Linguistics Society, 29–50.

Clements, G. N. & S. J. Keyser. 1983. *CV Phonology: A Generative Theory of the Syllable*. Cambridge, MA: MIT Press.

Coleman, J. S. 1992. The phonetic interpretation of headed phonological structures containing overlapping constituents. *Phonology* 9: 1–44.

Coleman, J. S. 1994a. Polysyllabic words in the YorkTalk synthesis system. In P. A. Keating (ed.), *Papers in Laboratory Phonology III: Phonological Structure and Phonetic Form*. Cambridge: Cambridge University Press, 293–324.

Coleman, J. S. 1994b. Analysis of timing in postvocalic voicing without prior segmentation. Paper presented at the Colloquium of the British Association of Academic Phoneticians, University of Manchester, March 1994.

Coleman, J. S. 1996. The psychological reality of language-specific constraints. Paper presented at the Fourth Phonology Meeting, University of Manchester, May 1996.

Coleman, J. S. 1998. Cognitive reality and the phonological lexicon: a review. *Journal of Neurolinguistics* 11: 295–320.

Coleman, J. S. & J. Pierrehumbert. 1997. Stochastic phonological grammars and acceptability. Computational phonology. In *Computational Phonology. Third Meeting of the ACL Special Interest Group in Computational Phonology*. Somerset, NJ: Association for Computational Linguistics, 49–56.

Colton, R. H. 1987. The role of pitch in the discrimination of voice quality. *Journal of Voice* 1: 240–5.

Connell, B. 1991. Phonetic aspects of the Lower Cross languages and their implications for sound change. PhD dissertation, University of Edinburgh.

Connell, B. & D. R. Ladd. 1990. Aspects of pitch realisation in Yorùbá. *Phonology* 7: 1–29.

Contini, M. 1987. *Etude de géographie phonétique et de phonétique instrumentale du Sarde*. Alessandria: Edizioni dell'Orso.

Cook, T. L. 1985. An integrated phonology of Efik. Vol 1. PhD dissertation, Universiteit Leiden.

Couper-Kuhlen, E. 1993. *English Speech Rhythm*. Amsterdam: John Benjamins.

Cummins, F. 1997. Rhythmic coordination in English speech: an experimental study. PhD dissertation, Indiana University, Bloomington, IN.

Cummins, F. & R. Port. 1998. Rhythmic constraints on stress timing in English. *Journal of Phonetics* 26: 145–71.

References

D'Imperio, M. & B. Gili Fivela. 1997. Focus, phrasing and boundary phenomena in Italian read speech. *Esca Workshop on Intonation, Athens, Greece,* 91–4.

D'Imperio, M. & S. Rosenthall. 1999. Phonetics and phonology of main stress in Italian. *Phonology* 16: 1–27.

Dauer, R. M. 1983. Stress-timing and syllable-timing reanalyzed. *Journal of Phonetics* 11: 51–62.

Davis, S. & M. Hammond. 1995. On the status of onglides in American English. *Phonology* 12: 159–82.

Davis, S. 1999. On the representation of initial geminates. *Phonology* 16: 93–104.

de Jong, K. J. 1990. Interarticulatory timing and single-articulator velocity-displacement in English stress pairs. *Ohio State University Working Papers in Linguistics* 38: 67–87.

de Jong, K. J. 1991. An articulatory study of vowel duration changes in English. *Phonetica* 48: 1–18.

de Jong, K. J. 1993. Phonetic units and American English [ow]. *UCLA Working Papers in Phonetics* 83: 117–40.

de Jong, K. J. 1995a. On the status of redundant features: the case of backness and roundness in American English. In B. Connell & A. Arvaniti (eds.), *Papers in Laboratory Phonology IV: Phonology and Phonetic Evidence.* Cambridge: Cambridge University Press, 68–86.

de Jong, K. J. 1995b. The supraglottal articulation of prominence in English: linguistic stress as localized hyperarticulation. *Journal of the Acoustical Society of America* 97: 491–504.

de Jong, K. & B. A. Zawaydeh. 1999. Stress, duration, and intonation in Arabic word level prosody. *Journal of Phonetics* 27: 3–22.

Delgutte, B. 1982. Some correlates of phonetic distinctions at the level of the auditory nerve. In R. Carlson & B. Granström (eds.), *The Representation of Speech in the Peripheral Auditory System.* Amsterdam: Elsevier Biomedical Press, 131–49.

Dell, G. S. 1986. A spreading-activation theory of retrieval in sentence production. *Psychological Review* 93: 283–321.

Dell, G. S. 1988. The retrieval of phonological forms in production: tests of predictions from a connectionist model. *Journal of Memory and Language* 27: 124–42.

Dell, G. S. 1999. Commentary: counting, connectionism, and lexical representation. In M. Broe & J. Pierrehumbert (eds.), *Papers in Laboratory Phonology V: Acquisition and the Lexicon.* Cambridge: Cambridge University Press, 335–48.

Dell, G. S., M. F. Schwartz, N. Martine, E. M. Saffran & D. A. Gagnon. 1997. Lexical access in aphasic and nonaphasic speakers. *Psychological Review* 104: 801–38.

Denes, P. 1955. Effect of duration on the perception of voicing. *Journal of the Acoustical Society of America* 27: 761–4.

Derwing, B. L. 1992. A 'pause-break' task for eliciting syllable boundary judgments from literate and illiterate speakers: preliminary results for five diverse languages. *Language and Speech* 35: 219–35.

Derwing, B., M. Dow, and M. Nearey. 1988. Experimenting with syllable structure. In *ESCOL' 88.* Columbus, OH: The Ohio State University, 83–94.

Diehl, R. & K. Kluender. 1989. On the objects of speech perception. *Ecological Psychology* 1: 123–44.

Dilley, L., S. Shattuck-Hufnagel & M. Ostendorf. 1996. Glottalization of word-initial vowels as a function of prosodic structure. *Journal of Phonetics* 24: 423–44.

Dirksen, A. & J. S. Coleman. 1997. All-prosodic speech synthesis. In J. P. H. van Santen, R. W. Sproat, J. P. Olive and J. Hirschberg (eds.), *Progress in Speech Synthesis.* New York: Springer-Verlag, 91–108.

Docherty, G. J. & P. Foulkes. 1999. Derby and Newcastle: instrumental phonetics and variationist studies. In P. Foulkes & G. Docherty (eds.), *Urban Voices: Accent Studies in the British Isles.* London: Arnold, 47–71.

Docherty, G. J., P. Foulkes, J. Milroy, L. Milroy & D. Walshaw. 1997. Descriptive adequacy in phonology: a variationist perspective. *Journal of Linguistics* 33: 275–310.

Dressler, W. U. 1985. *Morphonology: the Dynamics of Derivation.* Ann Arbor: Karoma.

Duanmu, S. 1992. A featural analysis of some onset-vowel interactions. In M. Ratcliff & E. Schiller (eds.), *Papers from the First Annual Meeting of the South East Asian Linguistics Society.* Tempe, AZ: Program for Southeast Asian Studies, Arizona State University, 141–58.

Edwards, J. R., M. E. Beckman, & J. Fletcher. 1991. The articulatory kinematics of final lengthening. *Journal of the Acoustical Society of America* 89: 369–82.

Ellis, L & W. J. Hardcastle. 1999. Alveolar-to-velar coarticulation and assimilation in careful and fast speech: some preliminary observations. *ZIS Papers in Linguistics.* 11: 105–20.

Ellison, M. T. Undated. An instrumental study of syllable structure in Scottish Gaelic. ESRC Final project report.

Elman, J. L. 1990. Finding structure in time. *Cognitive Science* 14: 179–211.

Elman, J. L. & J. McClelland. 1988. Cognitive penetration of the mechanisms of perception: compensation for coarticulation of lexically restored phonemes. *Journal of Memory and Language* 27: 143–65.

Esling, J. 1996. Pharyngeal consonants and the aryepiglottic sphincter. *Journal of the International Phonetic Association* 26: 65–88.

Evans, N. 1995. Current issues in the phonology of Australian languages. In J. Goldsmith (ed.), *Handbook of Phonological Theory.* Oxford: Blackwell, 723–61.

Fallows, D. 1981. Experimental evidence for English syllabification and syllable structure. *Journal of Linguistics* 17: 309–17.

Ferguson, C. A. & C. B. Farwell. 1975. Words and sounds in early language acquisition: English initial consonants in the first fifty words. *Language* 51: 419–39.

Firth, J. R. 1951. Modes of Meaning. *Essays and Studies of the English Association* 4: 118–49.

Firth, J. R. 1957. Introduction. *Studies in Linguistic Analysis.* Oxford: Basil Blackwell, v–vii.

Firth, J. R. 1959. Linguistics in the Laboratory. *Zeitschrift für Phonetik und allgemeine Sprachwissenschaft.* Band 12. Heft 1–4: 27–35.

Fischer-Jørgensen, E. 1968. Voicing, tenseness, and aspiration in stop consonants, with special reference to French and Danish. *Annual Report of the Institute of Phonetics, University of Copenhagen* 3: 63–114.

Fischer-Jørgensen, E. 1970. Phonetic analyses of breathy (murmured) vowels in Gujarati. *Indian Linguistics* 28:71–140.

References

Flemming, E. 1995. Auditory representations in phonology. PhD dissertation, University of California, Los Angeles.

Fletcher, H. 1953. *Speech and Hearing in Communication.* New York: Kreiger.

Fletcher, J. 1991. Rhythm and final lengthening in French. *Journal of Phonetics* 19: 193–212.

Fougeron, C. 1998. Variations articulatoires en début de constituants prosodiques de différents niveaux en français. PhD dissertation, Université Paris III – Sorbonne Nouvelle.

Fougeron, C. 1999a. Prosodically conditioned articulatory variation: a review. *UCLA Working Papers in Phonetics* 97: 1–73.

Fougeron, C. 1999b. Articulatory properties of initial segments in several prosodic constituents in French. *UCLA Working Papers in Phonetics* 97: 74–99.

Fougeron, C. & S.-A. Jun. 1998. Rate effects on French intonation: Prosodic organization and phonetic realization. *Journal of Phonetics* 26: 45–69.

Fougeron, C. & P. Keating. 1996. Variations in velic and lingual articulation depending on prosodic position: results for two French speakers. *UCLA Working Papers in Phonetics* 92: 88–96.

Fougeron, C. & P. Keating. 1997a. Articulatory strengthening at edges of prosodic domains. *Journal of the Acoustical Society of America* 101: 3728–40.

Fougeron, C. and P. Keating. 1997b. Variations in velic and lingual articulation depending on prosodic position. *The European Student Journal of Language and Speech.*

Foulkes, P., Docherty, G. J. & D. J. L. Watt. 1999. Tracking the emergence of sociophonetic variation. In *Proceedings of the XIVth International Congress of Phonetics Sciences,* San Francisco, 1–7 August 1999, Vol. 2: 1625–28.

Fowler, C. A. 1983. Converging sources of evidence on spoken and perceived rhythms of speech: cyclic production of vowels in monosyllabic stress feet. *Journal of Experimental Psychology: General* 112: 386–412.

Fowler, C. A. 1990. Comments on the contributions by Pierrehumbert and Nearey. *Journal of Phonetics* 18: 425–34.

Fowler, C. A. & J. Housum. 1987. Talkers' signalling of 'new' and 'old' words in speech and listeners' perception and use of the distinction. *Memory and Language* 26: 489–504.

Fowler, C. A. & M. R. Smith. 1986. Speech perception as 'vector analysis': an approach to the problem of invariance and segmentation. In J. S. Perkell & D. H. Klatt (eds.), *Invariance and Variability in Speech Processes.* NJ: Lawrence Erlbaum, 123–36.

Fox, R. 1992. Perception of vowel quality in a phonologically neutralized context. In Y. Tohkura, E. Vatikiotis-Bateson & Y. Sagisaka (eds.), *Speech Perception, Production and Linguistic Structure.* Tokyo: Ohmsha, 21–42.

Fox, R. & D. Terbeek. 1977. Dental flaps, vowel duration and rule ordering in American English. *Journal of Phonetics* 5: 27–34.

Frascarelli, M. 1997. The phonology of focus and topic in Italian. *Linguistic Review* 14: 221–48.

Frauenfelder, U.H. & L.K. Tyler. 1987. *Spoken Word Recognition.* Cambridge, MA: MIT Press. (Reprinted from *Cognition: International Journal of Cognitive Science* 25, 1987.)

Frisch S. A., N. Large & D. B. Pisoni. 2000. Perception of wordlikeness: effects of segment probability and length on subjective ratings and processing of non-words. *Journal of Memory and Language* 42: 481–96.

Frisch, S. A., M. Broe & J. Pierrehumbert. MS. Similarity and phonotactics in Arabic.

Gandour, J. R. 1978. The perception of tone. In V.A. Fromkin (ed.), *Tone: a Linguistic Survey*. New York: Academic Press, 41–76.

Garfinkel, H. 1967. *Studies in Ethnomethodology*. New Jersey: Prentice-Hall Inc.

Gaskell, M. G., M. Hare & W. D. Marslen-Wilson. 1995. A connectionist model of phonological representation in speech perception. *Cognitive Science* 19: 407–39.

Gasser, M., D. Eck & R. Port. 1999. Meter as mechanism: a neural network that learns metrical patterns. *Connection Science* 11: 187–216.

Gay, T. 1981. Mechanisms in the control of speech rate. *Phonetica* 4: 353–63.

Ghazeli, S. 1977. Back consonants and backing coarticulation in Arabic. PhD dissertation, University of Texas at Austin.

Gick, B. 1999a. The organization of segment-internal gestures. In *Proceedings of the XIVth International Congress of Phonetic Sciences*. San Francisco. 1–7 August 1999, Vol. 3: 1789–92.

Gick, B. 1999b. A gesture-based account of intrusive consonants in English. *Phonology*. 16 (1): 29–54.

Giegerich, H. J. 1992. *English Phonology: an Introduction*. Cambridge: Cambridge University Press.

Giles, S. B. & K. L. Moll. 1975. Cinefluorographic study of selected allophones of English /l/. *Phonetica* 31: 206–27.

Gili Fivela, B. & M. D'Imperio. 1998. Phrasing e focalizzazione nel parlato letto. *Analisi di due varietà di italiano. Atti delle VIII Giornate di Studio del G.F.S., Pisa*, 55–66.

Gleick, J. 1987. *Chaos*. Harmondsworth: Penguin.

Goldenthal, W. D. 1994. Statistical trajectory models for phonetic recognition. PhD dissertation, Laboratory of Computer Science. M.I.T. Technical Report MIT/LCS/TR–642.

Goldinger, S. D. 1997. Words and voices: Perception and production in an episodic lexicon. In K. Johnson & J. Mullenix (eds.), *Talker Variability in Speech Processing*. New York: Academic Press, 33–66.

Goldinger, S. D., P. A. Luce & D. B. Pisoni. 1989. Priming lexical neighbors of spoken words: effects of competition and inhibition. *Journal of Memory and Language* 28: 501–18.

Goldinger, S. D. & W. V. Summers. 1989. Lexical neighborhoods in speech production: a first report. *Research on Speech Perception Progress Report. Speech Research Laboratory, Indiana University* 15: 331–42.

Goldsmith, J. A. 1979. The aims of autosegmental phonology. In D. A. Dinnsen (ed.), *Current Approaches to Phonological Theory*. Bloomington: Indiana University Press, 202–22.

Goldsmith, J. A. 1993. Harmonic phonology. In J. A. Goldsmith (ed.), *The Last Phonological Rule*. Chicago: University of Chicago Press, 21–60.

Goldstein, L. 1989. On the domain of quantal theory. *Journal of Phonetics* 17: 91–7.

Goldstein, L. 1994. Possible articulatory bases for the class of guttural consonants. Commentary on J. McCarthy 'The phonology of Arabic pharyngeals'. In P. Keating (ed.), *Papers in Laboratory Phonology III: Phonological Structure and Phonetic Form.* Cambridge: Cambridge University Press, 235–41.

Gordon, M. 1996. The effect of stress and prosodic phrasing on duration, acoustic amplitude and air flow of nasals in Estonian. *UCLA Working Papers in Phonetics* 92: 151–9.

Grabe, E., & P. Warren. 1995. Stress shift: do speakers do it or do listeners hear it? In B. Connell & A. Arvaniti (eds.), *Papers in Laboratory Phonology IV: Phonology and Phonetic Evidence.* Cambridge: Cambridge University Press, 95–110.

Gradin, D. 1966. Consonantal tone in Jeh phonemics. *Mon-Khmer Studies* 2: 41–53.

Greenberg, J. H. & J. J. Jenkins. 1964. Studies in the psychological correlates of the sound system of American English. *Word* 20: 157–77.

Gregerson, K. & D. Thomas. 1976. Vietnamese hoi and ngã tones and Mon-Khmer -h finals. *Mon-Khmer Studies* 5: 76–83.

Grosjean, F., & J. P. Gee. 1987. Prosodic structure and spoken word recognition. In U. H. Frauenfelder & L. K. Tyler (eds.), *Spoken Word Recognition.* Cambridge, MA: MIT Press, 135–55.

Grossberg, S., I. Boardman & M. Cohen. 1997. Neural dynamics of variable-rate speech categorization. *Journal of Experimental Psychology: Human Perception and Performance* 23: 481–503.

Gussenhoven, C. 1986. English plosive allophones and ambisyllabicity. *Gramma* 10. 119–41.

Hajek, J. 1997. *Universals of Sound Change in Nasalization.* Blackwell: Oxford.

Halle, M. 1959. *The Sound Pattern of Russian: a Linguistic and Acoustical Investigation.* The Hague: Mouton.

Halle, M. 1995. Feature geometry and feature spreading. *Linguistic Inquiry* 26: 1–46.

Halle, M. & K. N. Stevens. 1971. A note on laryngeal features. *Quarterly Progress Report of the Research Laboratory of Electronics (MIT)* 101: 198–213.

Hammond, M. & E. Dupoux. 1996. Psychophonology. In J. Durand & B. Laks (eds.), *Current Trends in Phonology: Models and Methods.* Vol. 1. Salford: European Studies Research Institute, University of Salford, 281–04.

Hardcastle, W. J. 1976. *Physiology of Speech Production: an Introduction for Speech Scientists.* London: Academic Press.

Hardcastle, W. J. & W. Barry 1989. Articulatory and perceptual factors in /l/ vocalisations in English. *Journal of the International Phonetics Association* 15: 3–17.

Hardcastle, W. J. and J. Laver. (eds.). 1997. *The Handbook of Phonetic Sciences.* Oxford: Blackwell Publishers Ltd.

Harrington, J., J. Fletcher and M.E. Beckman. 2000. Manner and place conflicts in the articulation of accent in Australian English. In M. Broe & J. Pierrehumbert (eds.), *Papers in Laboratory Phonology V: Acquisition and the Lexicon.* Cambridge: Cambridge University Press, 40–51.

Harrington, J., J. Fletcher & C. Roberts. 1995. Coarticulation and the accented/unaccented distinction: evidence from jaw movement data. *Journal of Phonetics* 23: 305–22

Harris, J. 1994. *English Sound Structure.* Oxford: Blackwell.

Harris, J. 1997. Licensing Inheritance: an integrated theory of neutralisation. *Phonology* 14: 315–70.

Harris, J. & J. Kaye. 1990. A tale of two cities: London glottalling and New York City tapping. *Linguistic Review* 7: 251–74.

Harris, J. & G. Lindsey. 1995. The elements of phonological representation. In J. Durand & F. Katamba (eds.), *Frontiers of Phonology: Atoms, Structures, Derivations.* London: Longman, 34–79.

Harris, J. & E-A. E. Urua. 1998. Direct phonetic interpretation: foot-based lenition in Ibibio. Paper given at Current Trends in Phonology II, Royaumont, 22–24 June 1998.

Harrison, P. 1996. An experiment with tone. *UCL Working Papers in Linguistics* 8: 575–93.

Haudricourt, A.-G. 1954. De l'origine des tons en vietnamien. *Journal asiatique* 242: 69–82.

Hawkins, S. 1995. Arguments for a nonsegmental view of speech perception. In *Proceedings of the XIIIth International Congress of Phonetic Sciences.* Stockholm. Sweden. Vol. 3: 314–17.

Hawkins, S., & Nguyen, N. Submitted. Acoustic properties of syllable-onset /l/ dependent on syllable-coda voicing. Submitted to *Journal of Phonetics.*

Hawkins, S. & A. Slater. 1994. Spread of CV and V-to-V coarticulation in British English: Implications for the intelligibility of synthetic speech. In *Proceedings of the 3rd International Conference on Spoken Language Processing* 1: 57–60.

Hawkins, S. & P. Warren. 1994. Phonetic influences on the intelligibility of conversational speech. *Journal of Phonetics* 22: 493–511.

Hay, J., J. Pierrehumbert & M. E. Beckman. This volume. Speech perception, well-formedness, and lexical frequency.

Hayashi, W., C.-S. Hsu & P. Keating. 1999. *UCLA Working Papers in Phonetics* 97: 152–6.

Hayes, B. 1986a. Assimilation as spreading in Toba Batak. *Linguistic Inquiry* 17, 467–99.

Hayes, B. 1986b. Inalterability in CV phonology. *Language* 62: 321–51.

Hayes, B. 1989. Compensatory lengthening in moraic phonology. *Linguistic Inquiry* 20: 253–306.

Hayes, B. 1990. Precompiled phrasal phonology. In S. Inkelas & D. Zec (eds.), *The Phonology-Syntax Connection.* The Center for the Study of Language and Information, Stanford CA & University of Chicago Press, 85–108.

Hayes, B. 1992. Comments on chapter 10 [i.e. Nolan (1992) – DRH & JMS]. In G. J. Docherty and D. R. Ladd (eds.), *Papers in Laboratory Phonology II: Gesture, Segment, Prosody.* Cambridge: Cambridge University Press, 280–6.

Hayes, L. H. 1983. The register system of Thavung. *Mon-Khmer Studies* 12: 91–122.

Hayward, K. & R. Hayward. 1989. 'Guttural': arguments for a new distinctive feature. *Transactions of the Philiological Society* 87: 179–93.

Henderson, E. J. A. 1949. Prosodies in Siamese. *Asia Major (New Series)* 1: 189–215. Reprinted in F. R. Palmer (ed., 1970), *Prosodic Analysis.* London: Oxford University Press, 27–53.

References

Hoard, J. 1971. Aspiration, tenseness, and syllabification in English. *Language* 47: 133–40.

Hockett, C. D. 1960. Logical considerations in the study of animal communication. In W. E. Lanyon & W. N. Tavolga (eds.), *Animal Sounds and Communication*. Washington, DC: American Institute of Biological Sciences, 392–430.

Hockett, C. F. 1955. *A Manual of Phonology*. Baltimore: Waverly Press.

Hogg, R. & C. B. McCully. 1987. *Metrical Phonology: a Coursebook*. Cambridge: Cambridge University Press.

Hollien, H. 1974. On vocal registers. *Journal of Phonetics* 2: 125–43.

Holst, T. and Nolan, F. 1995. The influence of syntactic structure on [s] to [S] assimilation. In B. Connell and A. Arvaniti (eds.), *Papers in Laboratory Phonology IV: Phonology and Phonetic Evidence*. Cambridge University Press: Cambridge, 315–33.

Hombert, J.-M. 1976. Perception of tones of bisyllabic nouns in Yorùbá. *Studies in African Linguistics* Supplement 6: 109–201.

Hombert, J.-M. 1978. Consonant types, vowel quality, and tone. In V. A. Fromkin (ed.), *Tone: a Linguistic Survey*. New York: Academic Press, 77–111.

Homma, Y. 1991. The rhythm of tanka, short Japanese poems: read in prose style and contest style. In *Proceedings of the XIIth International Congress of Phonetic Sciences*. Aix-en-Provence, France, Vol. 2: 314–17.

Honikman, B. 1964. Articulatory Settings. In D. Abercrombie, D. B. Fry, P. Λ. D. MacCarthy, N. C. Scott & J. L. M. Trim (eds.), *In Honour of Daniel Jones*. London: Longmans Green, 73–84.

House, A. S., & G. Fairbanks. 1953. The influence of consonant environment upon the secondary acoustical characteristics of vowels. *Journal of the Acoustical Society of America* 25: 105–13.

Howard, D. M., G. A. Lindsey & B. Allan. 1990. Toward the quantification of vocal efficiency. *Journal of Voice* 4: 205–12.

Hsu, C.-S. & S.-A. Jun. 1996. Is Tone Sandhi Group part of the prosodic hierarchy in Taiwanese? Poster presented at the Third Joint Meeting of the Acoustical Societies of America and Japan, Honolulu. Abstract published in *Journal of the Acoustical Society of America* 100: 2824.

Hsu, C.-S. & S.-A. Jun. 1997. Prosodic strengthening in Taiwanese: syntagmatic or paradigmatic?. MS, UCLA.

Hsu, C.-S. and S.-A. Jun. 1998. Prosodic strengthening in Taiwanese: syntagmatic or paradigmatic? *UCLA Working Papers in Phonetics* 96: 69–89.

Huffman, M. K. 1997. Phonetic variation in intervocalic onset /l/'s in English. *Journal of Phonetics* 25: 115–41.

Hulst, H. van der. 1995. Radical CV phonology: the categorical gesture. In J. Durand & F. Katamba (eds.), *Frontiers of Phonology: Atoms, Structures, Derivations*. London: Longman, 80–116.

Hume, E., J. Muller and A. van Engelhoven. 1997. Non-moraic geminates in Leti. *Phonology* 14: 371–402.

Hunnicut, S. 1985. Intelligibility vs. redundancy–conditions of dependency. *Language and Speech* 28: 47–56.

Hutters, B. 1985. Vocal fold adjustments in aspirated and unaspirated stops in Danish. *Phonetica* 42: 1–24.

Hyman, L. M. 1990. Non-exhaustive syllabification: evidence from Nigeria and Cameroon. In *Papers from the Parasession on the Syllable in Phonetics and Phonology. Chicago Linguistic Society* 26: 175–95.

International Phonetic Association. 1999. *The Handbook of the International Phonetic Association.* Cambridge: Cambridge University Press.

Iverson, G. K. & J. C. Salmons. 1995. Aspiration and laryngeal representation in Germanic. *Phonology* 12: 369–96.

Jakobson, R. 1968. *Child Language, Aphasia and Phonological Universals.* (Translated by A. Keiler.) The Hague: Mouton.

Jakobson, R., G. Fant & M. Halle. 1952. *Preliminaries to Speech Analysis: the Distinctive Features and their Correlates.* Cambridge, MA: MIT Press.

Jensen, J. T. 1993. *English Phonology.* Amsterdam: Benjamins.

Jessen, M. 1997. Tense vs. lax obstruents in German. *Arbeitspapiere des Instituts für Maschinelle Sprachverarbeitung* 3. Universität Stuttgart.

Johnson, K. 1997. Speech perception without speaker normalization: an exemplar model. In K. Johnson and J. W. Mullenix (eds.), *Talker Variability in Speech Processing.* San Diego, Academic Press, 145–65.

Johnson, K. & J. Mullenix (eds.). 1997. *Talker Variability in Speech Processing.* San Diego: Academic Press.

Jones, D. 1918. *An Outline of English Phonetics.* First edition. Cambridge: W. Heffer.

Jones, D. 1956. *An Outline of English Phonetics.* Eighth edition. New York: Dutton.

Jones, D. 1966. *The Pronunciation of English.* Cambridge: Cambridge University Press.

Jones, D. 1972. *An Outline of English Phonetics.* Ninth edition (reprinted). Cambridge: Cambridge University Press.

Jones, M. 1988. Sardinian. In M. Harris & N. Vincent (eds.), *The Romance Languages.* London: Routledge, 314–50.

Jones, M. 1993. *Sardinian Syntax.* London: Routledge.

Jun, S.-A. 1993. The phonetics and phonology of Korean prosody. PhD dissertation, Ohio State University.

Jun, S.-A. 1995a. Asymmetrical prosodic effects on the laryngeal gesture in Korean. In B. Connell & A. Arvaniti (eds.), *Papers in Laboratory Phonology IV: Phonology and Phonetic Evidence.* Cambridge: Cambridge University Press, 235–53.

Jun, S–A. 1995b. An acoustic study of Korean stress. Poster presented at the 130th meeting of Acoustical Society of America, St Louis, Missouri. Abstract published in *Journal of the Acoustical Society of America* 98: 2893.

Jun, J. 1996. Place assimilation is not the result of gestural overlap: evidence from Korean and English. *Phonology* 13: 377–407.

Jun, S.-A. 1998. The accentual phrase in the Korean prosodic hierarchy. *Phonology* 15: 189–226.

Jun, S.-A. & C. Fougeron. 1995. The Accentual Phrase and the prosodic structure of French. In *Proceedings of the XIIIth International Congress of Phonetic Sciences.* Stockholm: Sweden. Vol. 2: 722–5.

Jun, S-A. & C. Fougeron. 2000. A phonological model of French intonation. In A. Botinis (ed.), *Intonation: Analysis, Modeling and Technology*. Dordrecht: Kluwer Academic Publishers, 209–42.

Jusczyk, P. W. 1993. From general to language-specific capacities: the WRAPSA Model of how speech perception develops. *Journal of Phonetics* 21: 3–28.

Jusczyk, P. W., P. A. Luce & J. Charles-Luce. 1994. Infants' sensitivity to phonotactic patterns in the native language. *Journal of Memory and Language* 33: 630–45.

Jusczyk, P. W. & R. N. Aslin. 1995. Infants' detection of the sound patterns of words in fluent speech. *Cognitive Psychology* 29: 1–23.

Kahn, D. 1976. Syllable-based generalizations in English phonology. PhD dissertation, MIT. Published 1980, New York: Garland.

Kaisse, E. M. 1985. *Connected Speech. The Interaction of Syntax and Phonology*. New York: Academic Press.

Kaye, J., J. Lowenstamm & J.-R. Vergnaud. 1990. Constituent structure and government in phonology. *Phonology* 7: 193–231.

Keating, P. A. 1984. Phonetic and phonological representations of stop consonant voicing. *Language* 60: 286–319.

Keating, P. A. 1985. Universal phonetics and the organisation of grammars. In V.A. Fromkin (ed.), *Phonetic Linguistics: Essays in Honor of Peter Ladefoged*. Orlando, FL: Academic Press, 115–32.

Keating, P. A. 1988. Palatals as complex segments: X-ray evidence. *UCLA Working Papers in Phonetics* 69: 77–91.

Keating, P. A. 1990. Phonetic representations in a generative grammar. *Journal of Phonetics* 18: 321–34.

Keating, P. A. (ed.). 1994. *Papers in Laboratory Phonology III. Phonological Structure and Phonetic Form*. Cambridge: Cambridge University Press.

Keating, P. A. 1997. Word-initial versus word-final consonant articulation. Poster presented at 134th Meeting of the Acoustical Society of America, San Diego. Abstract published in *Journal of the Acoustical Society of America* 102: 3094.

Keating, P. A., W. Linker & M. Huffman. 1983. Patterns in allophone distribution for voiced and voiceless stops. *Journal of Phonetics* 11: 277–90.

Keating, P. A., R. Wright, & J. Zhang. 1999. Word-level asymmetries in consonant articulation. *UCLA Working Papers in Phonetics* 97: 157–73.

Keidar, A., R. R. Hurti & I. R. Titze. 1987. The perceptual nature of vocal register change. *Journal of Voice* 1: 223–33.

Kelly, J. & J. K. Local. 1986. Long-domain resonance patterns in English. In *Proceedings of the International Conference on Speech Input / Output*. London. Institute of Electronic Engineers, 304–8.

Kelly, J. & J. K. Local. 1989. *Doing Phonology*. Manchester: Manchester University Press.

Kelso, J. A. S. 1996. *Dynamic Patterns: the Self-organization of Brain and Behavior*. Cambridge, MA: Bradford Books/MIT Press.

Kelso, J. A. S., E. Vatikiotis-Bateson, E. Saltzman & B. Kay. 1985. A qualitative dynamic analysis of reiterant speech production: phase portraits, kinematics, and dynamic modeling. *Journal of the Acoustical Society of America* 77: 266–80.

Kenstowicz, M. 1994. *Phonology in Generative Grammar*. Oxford: Blackwell.

Kent, R. D. & K. Moll. 1975. Cineflourographic analyses of selected lingual consonants. *Journal of Speech and Hearing Research* 15: 453–73.

Kewley-Port, D. & M. S. Preston. 1974. Early apical stop production: a voice onset time analysis. *Journal of Phonetics* 2: 195–20.

King, R. D. 1969. *Historical Linguistics and Generative Grammar*. Englewood Cliffs, NJ: Prentice-Hall.

Kingston, J. 1985. The phonetics and phonology of the timing of oral and glottal events. PhD dissertation, University of California at Berkeley.

Kingston, J. & M. Beckman (eds.). 1990. *Papers in Laboratory Phonology 1: Between the Grammar and Physics of Speech*. Cambridge: Cambridge University Press.

Kingston, J. & R. L. Diehl. 1994. Phonetic knowledge. *Language* 70: 419–54.

Kingston, J. & R. L. Diehl. 1995. Intermediate properties in the perception of distinctive feature values. In B. Connell & A. Arvaniti (eds), *Papers in Laboratory Phonology IV: Phonology and Phonetic Evidence*. Cambridge: Cambridge University Press, 7–27.

Kiparsky, P. 1979. Metrical structure assignment is cyclic. *Linguistic Inquiry* 8. 421–42.

Kiparsky, P. 1995. The phonological basis of sound change. In J. A. Goldsmith (ed.), *The Handbook of Phonological Theory*. Oxford: Blackwell, 640–70.

Kirchner, R. M. 1998. An effort-based approach to consonant lenition. PhD dissertation, UCLA.

Kirk, P. L., P. Ladefoged & J. Ladefoged. 1984. Using a spectrograph for measures of phonation types in a natural language. *UCLA Working Papers in Phonetics* 61: 102–13.

Kirk, P. L., P. Ladefoged & J. Ladefoged. 1993. Quantifying acoustic properties of modal, breathy, and creaky vowels in Jalapa Mazatec. *American Indian Linguistics and Ethnography in Honor of Laurence C. Thompson*. University of Montana Occasional Papers in Linguistics, 10: 435–50.

Klatt, D. H. 1979. Speech perception: a model of acoustic-phonetic analysis and lexical access. *Journal of Phonetics* 7: 279–312.

Klatt, D. H. & K. Stevens. 1969. Pharyngeal consonants. *MIT Research Laboratory of Electronics Quarterly Progress Report* 2: 85–138.

Kondo, Y. & Y. Arai. 1998. Prosodic constraint on V-to-V coarticulation in Japanese: a case of bimoraic foot. *On'in Kenkyuu (Phonological Studies)*. 1: 75–82.

Krakow, R. A. 1989. The articulatory organization of syllables: a kinematic analysis of labial and velar Gestures. PhD dissertation. Yale University.

Krakow, R. A., F. Bell-Berti & Q. E. Wang. 1994. Supralaryngeal declination: evidence from the velum. In F. Bell-Berti & L. Raphael (eds.), *Producing Speech: a Festschrift for Katherine Safford Harris*. Woodbury NY: AIP Press, 333–53.

Kučera, H. & Francis, W. N. 1967. *Computational Analysis of Present-day American English*. Providence, RI: Brown University Press.

Kuhl, P. K., K. A. Williams, F. Lacerda, K. Stevens & B. Lindblom. 1992. Linguistic experience alters phonetic perception in infants by 6 months of age. *Science* 225: 606–8.

Kühnert, B. 1993. Some kinematic aspects of alveolar-velar assimilations. *Forschungsberichte des Instituts für Phonetik und Sprachliche Kommunikation der Universität München (FIPKM)* 31: 263–72.

Ladd, D. R. & J. M. Scobbie. 1996. Sardinian geminates. Paper presented at the Colloquium of the British Association of Academic Phoneticians, University of York.

Ladd, D. R. 1990. Metrical representation of pitch register. In J. Kingston & M. Beckman (eds.), *Papers in Laboratory Phonology 1: Between the Grammar and Physics of Speech.* Cambridge: Cambridge University Press, 35–57.

Ladd, D. R. 1996. *Intonational Phonology.* Cambridge: Cambridge University Press.

Ladefoged, P. 1971. *Preliminaries to Linguistic Phonetics.* Chicago, IL: University of Chicago Press.

Ladefoged, P. 1972. Phonetic prerequisites for a distinctive feature theory. In A. Valdman (ed.), *Papers in Linguistics and Phonetics to the Memory of Pierre Delattre.* The Hague: Mouton, 273–86.

Ladefoged, P. 1973. The features of the larynx. *Journal of Phonetics* 1: 73–83.

Ladefoged, P. 1993. *A Course in Phonetics.* 3rd edition. Orlando: Harcourt Brace.

Ladefoged, P., J. Ladefoged, A. Turk, K. Hind & St J. Skilton. 1999. Phonetic structures of Scottish Gaelic. *Journal of the International Phonetic Association* 28: 1–41.

Ladefoged, P. & I. Maddieson. 1996. *The Sounds of the World's Languages.* Oxford: Blackwell.

Ladefoged, P., I. Maddieson & M. Jackson. 1988. Investigating phonation types in different languages. In O. Fujimura (ed.), *Vocal Physiology: Voice Production, Mechanisms and Functions.* New York: Raven Press, 297–318.

Lane, H., & B. Tranel. 1971. The Lombard sign and the role of hearing in speech. *Journal of Speech and Hearing Research* 14: 677–709.

Lane, H., B. Tranel & C. Sisson. 1970. Regulation of voice communication by sensory dynamics. *Journal of the Acoustical Society of America* 47: 618–24.

Laniran, Y. O. 1993. *Intonation in Tone Languages: the Phonetic Implementation of Tones in Yorùbá.* Cornell University: Department of Modern Languages and Linguistics.

Large, E. W. & M. R. Jones. 1999. The dynamics of attending: how we track time varying events. *Psychological Review* 106: 119–59.

Laufer, A. & T. Baer. 1988. The emphatic and pharyngeal sounds in Hebrew and Arabic. *Language and Speech* 31: 181–204.

LaVelle, C. R. 1974. An experimental study of Yorùbá tone. *UCLA Working Papers in Phonetics* 27: 160–70.

Laver, J. 1980. *The Phonetic Description of Voice Quality.* Cambridge: Cambridge University Press

Laver, J. 1994. *Principles of Phonetics.* Cambridge: Cambridge University Press.

Lee, S.-H. 1995. Orals, gutturals, and the jaw. In B. Connell & A. Arvaniti (eds.), *Papers in Laboratory Phonology IV: Phonology and Phonetic Evidence.* Cambridge: Cambridge University Press. 343–60.

Lehiste, I. 1964a. *Acoustic Characteristics of Selected English Consonants.* The Hague: Mouton.

Lehiste, I. 1964b. Juncture. In *Proceedings of the 5th International Congress of Phonetic Sciences.* Münster, 172–200.

Lehiste, I. 1977. Isochrony reconsidered. *Journal of Phonetics* 5: 253–63.

Lehiste, I. 1990. Phonetic investigation of metrical structure in orally produced poetry. *Journal of Phonetics* 18: 123–33.

Levelt, W. J. M. 1989. *Speaking: From Intention to Articulation*. Cambridge, MA: MIT Press.

Levin, B. & M. Rapaport Hovav. 1996. Lexical semantics and syntactic structure. In S. Lappin (ed.), *The Handbook of Contemporary Semantic Theory*. Oxford: Blackwell, 487–507.

Liberman, M. 1975. *The Intonational System of English*. Bloomington: Indiana University Linguistics Club.

Lieberman, P. 1963. Some effects of semantic and grammatical context on the production and perception of speech. *Language and Speech* 6: 172–87.

Liberman, M. & A. Prince. 1977. On stress and linguistic rhythm. *Linguistic Inquiry* 8: 249–336.

Liljencrants, J., & B. Lindblom. 1972. Numerical simulation of vowel quality systems: the role of perceptual contrast. *Language* 48: 839–62.

Lindblom, B. 1963. Spectrographic study of vowel reduction. *Journal of the Acoustical Society of America* 35: 1773–82.

Lindblom, B. 1990. Explaining phonetic variation: a sketch of the H&H theory. In W. J. Hardcastle & A. Marchal (eds.), *Speech Production and Speech Modelling*. NATO ASI Series D: Behavioural and Social Sciences, Vol. 55. Dordrecht: Kluwer, 403–39.

Lindsey, G., K. Hayward & A. Haruna. 1992. Hausa glottalic consonants: a laryngographic study. *Bulletin of the School of Oriental and African Studies* 55: 511–27.

Lisker, L. 1995. English /w, j/: Frictionless approximants or vowels out of place? In F. Bell-Berti & L. Raphael (eds.), *Producing speech: contemporary issues. For Katherine Safford Harris*. Woodbury, NY: AIP Press, 129–42.

Lively, S. E., D. B. Pisoni & S. D. Goldinger. 1994. Spoken word recognition: research and theory. In M. A. Gernsbacher (ed.), *Handbook of Psycholinguistics*. New York: Academic Press, 265–301.

Local, J. K. 1992. Modeling assimilation in nonsegmental, rule-free synthesis. In G. J. Docherty & D. R. Ladd (eds.), *Papers in Laboratory Phonology II: Gesture, Segment, Prosody*. Cambridge: Cambridge University Press, 190–223.

Local, J. K. 1995a. Making sense of dynamic, non-segmental phonetics. In *Proceedings of the XIIIth International Congress of Phonetic Sciences,* Stockholm. Vol. 3: 2–9.

Local, J. K. 1995b. Syllabification and rhythm in non-segmental phonology. In J. Windsor Lewis (ed.), *Studies in General and English Phonetics: Essays in Honour of Prof. J. D. O'Connor*. London: Routledge, 360–6.

Local, J. K. 1996. Conversational phonetics: some aspects of news receipts in everyday talk. In E. Couper-Kuhlen & M. Selting (eds.), *Prosody in Conversation: Ethnomethodological Studies*. Cambridge: Cambridge University Press, 175–230.

Local, J. K. & A. P. Simpson. 1999. Phonetic Implementation of Geminates in Malayalam Nouns. In *Proceedings of the XIVth International Congress of Phonetic Sciences,* San Francisco, 1–7 August 1999, Vol. 1: 595–8.

Löfqvist, A., L. L. Koenig & R. McGowan. 1995. Voice source variation in running speech: a study of Mandarin Chinese tones. In O. Fujimura & M. Hirano (eds.),

Vocal Fold Physiology: Voice Quality Control. San Diego: Singular Publishing Group, 3–18.

Löfqvist, A. & H. Yoshioka. 1981. Interarticulator programming in obstruent production. *Phonetica* 38: 21–34.

Löfqvist, A. & H. Yoshioka.1984. Intra-segmental timing: laryngeal-oral coordination in voiceless consonant production. *Speech Communication* 3: 279–89.

Lombard, E. 1911. Le signe de l'élévation de la voix. *Annales des maladies de l'oreille, du larynx, du nez et du pharynx* 37: 101–19.

Longacre, R. 1952. Five phonemic pitch levels in Trique. *Acta Linguistica* VII: 62–82.

Loporcaro, M. 1997. *L'origine del raddoppiamento fonosintattico. Saggio di fonologia diacronica romanza.* Basel and Tübingen: Francke Verlag.

Luce, P. A. 1986. Neighborhoods of words in the mental lexicon. (Research on speech perception tech report no. 6). Bloomington: Indiana University Psychology Department, Speech Research Laboratory.

Luce, P. A. & D. B. Pisoni. 1998. Recognizing spoken words: the neighbourhood activation model. *Ear & Hearing* 19: 1–36.

Luce, R. D. 1959. *Individual Choice Behavior.* New York: Wiley.

Lüdtke, H. 1953. Il sistema consonantico del sardo logudorese. *Orbis* 2: 411–22.

Lyman, T. 1974. *Dictionary of Hmong Njua.* The Hague: Mouton.

Macchi, M. J., M. F. Spiegel & K. L. Wallace. 1990. Modeling duration adjustment with dynamic time warping. In *Proceeedings of ICASSP 90*, 333–6.

MacKay, D. G. 1974. Aspects of the syntax of behavior: syllable structure and speech rate. *Quarterly Journal of Experimental Psychology* 26: 642–57.

Macken, M. A. & D. Barton. 1980. The acquisition of the voicing contrast in English: a study of voice onset time in word-initial stop consonants. *Journal of Child Language* 7: 41–87.

MacNeilage, P. F. & B. L. Davis. 1990. Acquisition of speech production: The achievement of segmental independence. In W. J. Hardcastle & A. Marchal (eds.), *Speech Production and Speech Modelling.* Dordrecht: Kluwer, 55–68.

Maddieson, I. and P. Ladefoged. 1985. 'Tense' and 'lax' in four minority languages of China. *UCLA Working Papers in Phonetics* 60. 59–83.

Malt, B. 1996. Category coherence in cross-cultural perspective. *Cognitive Psychology* 29: 85–148.

Manaster Ramer, A. 1996. A letter from an incompletely neutral phonologist. *Journal of Phonetics* 24: 477–89.

Mann, V. A. & B. H. Repp. 1980. Influence of vocalic context on perception of the [ʃ]-[s] distinction. *Perception and Psychophysics* 28: 213–8.

Manuel, S. 1999. Cross-language studies of coarticulation. In W. Hardcastle & N. Hewlett (eds.), *Coarticulation. Theory, Data and Techniques.* Cambridge: Cambridge University Press, 179–98.

Marchman, V. A. & E. Bates. 1994. Continuity in lexical and morphological development: a test of the critical mass hypothesis. *Journal of Child Language* 21: 339–66.

Marslen-Wilson, W. 1993. Issues of process and representation in lexical access. In G. T. M. Altmann & R. Shillock (eds.), *Cognitive Models of Speech Processing: the Second Sperlonga Meeting.* Hillsdale, NJ: Lawrence Erlbaum.

Marslen-Wilson, W. & P. Warren. 1994. Levels of perceptual representation and process in lexical access: words, phonemes, and features. *Psychological Review* 101: 653–75.

Martin, G. 1984. Munchausen's statistical grid. *The Lancet*, Dec. 22–29: 1547.

Martin, P. 1982. Phonetic realizations of prosodic contours in French. *Speech Communication* 1: 283–94.

Massaro, D. 1989. Testing between the TRACE model and the fuzzy logical model of speech perception. *Cognitive Psychology* 21: 398–421.

Massaro, D. W. 1998. *Perceiving Talking Faces: From Speech Perception to a Behavioral Principle.* Cambridge, MA: MIT Press.

Massaro, D. W. & M. M. Cohen. 1983. Evaluation and integration of visual and auditory information in speech perception. *Journal of Experimental Psychology: Human Perception and Performance* 9: 753–71.

Massaro, D. W. & G. C. Cohen. 1995. Independence of lexical context and phonological information in speech perception. *Journal of Experimental Psychology, Learning Memory and Cognition* 21: 1053–1064.

Massaro, D. & G. Oden, 1980. Evaluation and integration of acoustic features in speech perception. *Journal of the Acoustical Society of America* 67: 996–1013.

McCarthy, J. J. 1986. OCP effects: gemination and antigemination. *Linguistic Inquiry* 17: 207–63.

McCarthy, J. J. 1988. Feature geometry and dependency: a review. *Phonetica* 45: 84–108.

McCarthy, J. J. 1994. The phonetics and phonology of Semitic pharyngeals. In P. Keating. (ed.), *Papers in Laboratory Phonology III: Phonological Structure and Phonetic Form.* Cambridge: Cambridge University Press, 191–234.

McCarthy, J. & A. S. Prince. 1986. Prosodic morphology. MS, University of Massachusetts.

McCarthy, J. J. & A. S. Prince. 1993. Prosodic morphology I. MS, University of Massachusetts & Rutgers University.

McCarthy, J. J. & A. S. Prince. 1995. Faithfulness and reduplicative identity. In J. N. Beckman, L. W. Dickey & S. Urbanczyk (eds.), *Papers in Optimality Theory.* Amherst: GLSA, 249–384.

McClelland, J. L. 1991. Stochastic interactive processing and the effect of context on perception. *Cognitive Psychology* 23: 1–44.

McClelland, J. L. & J. L. Elman. 1986. The TRACE model of speech perception. *Cognitive Psychology* 18: 1–86.

McCullagh, P. & J. A. Nelder. 1989. *Generalized linear models.* London: Chapman and Hall.

McMahon, A., P. Foulkes & L. Tollfree. 1994. Gestural Representation and Lexical Phonology. *Phonology* 11: 277–316.

McQueen, J. & M. Pitt. 1998. Is compensation for coarticulation mediated by the lexicon? *Journal of Memory and Language* 39: 247–370.

Mensching, G. (12/10/1999) *Limba e Curtura de sa Sardigna / Sardinian Language and Culture.* http://www.spinfo.uni-koeln.de/mensch/sardengl.html

Mensching, G. 1994. *Einführung in die Sardische Sprache.* 3rd edition.

Mermelstein, J. 1975. Automatic Segmentation of Speech. *Journal of the Acoustical Society of America* 58: 880–3.

Mermelstein, P. 1978. On the relationship between vowel and consonant identification when cued by the same acoustic information. *Perception and Psychophysics* 23: 331–5.

Miller, G. & P. Nicely. 1955. An analysis of perceptual confusions among some English consonants. *Journal of the Acoustical Society of America* 27: 338–52.

Miller, G. A. & N. Chomsky. 1963. Finitary models of language users. In R. D. Luce, R. R. Bush & E. Galanter (eds.), *Handbook of Mathematical Psychology*. Vol. II. New York: John Wiley, 419–91.

Mitton, R. 1992. A computer-usable dictionary file based on the Oxford Advanced Learner's Dictionary of Current English. ftp://ota.ox.ac.uk/pub/ota/public/dicts/710/text710.dat.

Mohanan, K. P. 1995. The organization of the grammar. In J. A. Goldsmith (ed.), *The Handbook of Phonological Theory*. Oxford: Blackwell, 24–69.

Molinu, L. 1998. La syllabe en sarde. Unpublished PhD Thesis, Université de Grenoble.

Molinu, L. MS. Il raddoppiamento fonosintattico in sardo: un esempio di analisi sperimentale e fonologica. Université de Grenoble III (1998).

Moon, S. J. & B. Lindblom. 1994. Interaction between duration, context, and speaking style in English stressed vowels. *Journal of the Acoustical Society of America* 96: 40–55.

Moore, B. C. J. 1989. *An Introduction to the Psychology of Hearing*. 3rd edition. London: Academic Press.

Moore, B. C. J. & B. Glasberg. 1987. Formulae describing frequency selectivity as a function of frequency and level and their use in calculating excitation patterns. *Hearing Research* 28: 209–25.

Morgan, D. P. & C. L. Scofield. 1991. *Neural Networks and Speech Processing*. Boston, MA: Kluwer.

Morton, J. 1969. The interaction of information in word recognition. *Psychological Review* 76. 165–78.

Munhall, K. G., C. Fowler, S. Hawkins & E. Saltzman. 1992. 'Compensatory shortening' in monosyllables of spoken English. *Journal of Phonetics* 20: 225–39.

Myung, I. J. & R. N. Shepard. 1996. Maximum entropy inference and stimulus generalization. *Journal of Mathematical Psychology* 40: 342–7.

Napoli, D. J. & M. Nespor. 1979. The syntax of word-initial consonant gemination in Italian. *Language* 55: 812–42.

Nearey, T. M. 1990. The segment as a unit of speech perception. *Journal of Phonetics* 18: 347–73.

Nearey, T. M. 1991. Perception: automatic and cognitive processes. *Proceedings of the Twelfth International Congress of Phonetic Sciences*. Vol. 1: 40–9.

Nearey, T. M. 1992. Context effects in a double-weak theory of speech perception. *Language and Speech* 35: 153–72.

Nearey, T. M. 1995. A double-weak view of trading relations: comments on Kingston and Diehl. In B. Connell & A. Arvaniti (eds.), *Papers in Laboratory Phonology IV: Phonology and Phonetic Evidence*. Cambridge: Cambridge University Press, 28–40.

Nearey, T. M. 1997. Speech perception as pattern recognition. *Journal of the Acoustic Society of America* 101: 3241–54.

Nearey, T. M. 1998. Modularity and traceability in speech perception. In *Papers from the 33rd Regional Meeting of the Chicago Linguistics Society,* 399–413.

Nearey, T. M. In press. The factorability of phonological units in speech perception. In R. Smith (ed.), *Festschrift for Bruce L. Derwing.*

Nearey, T. M. and S. Shammas. 1987. Formant transitions as partly distinctive invariant properties in the identification of voiced stops. *Canadian Acoustics* 15: 17–24.

Nespor, M. & I. Vogel. 1986. *Prosodic Phonology.* Dordrecht: Foris Publications.

Nespor, M. 1993. *Fonologia.* Bologna: Il Mulino.

Newton, D. E. 1996. The nature of resonance in English: an investigation into lateral articulations. *York Papers in Linguisics* 17: 167–90.

Nguyen, N, & S. Hawkins. 1998. Syllable-onset acoustic properties associated with syllable-coda voicing. *Proceedings of the 5th International Conference on Spoken Language Processing.* Available on CD-ROM: ICSLP-98. Paper #539.

Nguyen, N. & S. Hawkins. 1999. Implications for word recognition of phonetic dependencies between syllable onsets and codas. In *Proceedings of the XIVth International Congress of Phonetic Sciences,* San Francisco, 1–7 August 1999, Vol.1: 647–50.

Ní Chasaide, A. & C. Gobl. 1997. Voice source variation. In W. J. Hardcastle & J. Laver (eds.), *The Handbook of Phonetic Sciences.* Oxford: Blackwell, 427–61.

Nittrouer, S. 1992. Age-related differences in perceptual effects of formant transitions within syllables and across syllable boundaries. *Journal of Phonetics* 20: 351–82.

Nolan, F. 1992. The descriptive role of segments: evidence from assimilation. In G. Dochtery & R. Ladd (eds.), *Papers in Laboratory Phonology II: Gesture, segment, prosody.* Cambridge: Cambridge University Press, 261–80.

Nolan, F. 1995. The role of the jaw – active or passive? Comments on Lee. In B. Connell & A. Arvaniti (eds.), *Papers in Laboratory Phonology IV: Phonology and Phonetic Evidence.* Cambridge: Cambridge University Press, 361–7.

Nolan, F., T. Holst & B. Kühnert. 1996. Modelling [s] to [ʃ] accommodation in English. *Journal of Phonetics* 24: 113–37.

Norris, D. 1994. Shortlist: a connectionist model of continuous speech recognition. *Cognition* 52: 189–234.

Nosofsky, R. M. 1988. Exemplar-based accounts of relations between classification, recognition and typicality. *Journal of Experimental Psychology, Learning Memory and Cognition* 14: 700–8.

Nusbaum, H. C., D. B. Pisoni. & C. Davis. 1984. Sizing up the Hoosier mental lexicon, Research on Speech Perception Progress Report No. 10. Bloomington, IN: Speech Research Laboratory, Indiana University.

Nygaard, L., & D. B. Pisoni. 1995. Speech perception: new directions in research and theory. In J. L. Miller & P. D. Eimas (eds.), *Speech, Language, and Communication.* San Diego: Academic Press, 63–96.

Odden, D. 1992. Simplicity of underlying representation as motivation for underspecification. *Ohio State University Working Papers in Linguistics* 41: 83–100.

Ogden, R. A. 1992. Parametric interpretation in YorkTalk. *York Papers in Linguistics* 16: 81–99.

Ogden, R. A. 1993. What Firthian Prosodic Analysis has to say to us. *Edinburgh Working Papers in Cognitive Science* 8: 107–27.

Ogden, R. A. 1995. 'Where' is timing? Comments on Smith. In B. Connell & A. Arvaniti (eds.), *Papers in Laboratory Phonology IV: Phonology and Phonetic Evidence.* Cambridge: Cambridge University Press, 223–34.

Ogden, R. A. 1999a. A syllable level feature in Finnish. In H. van der Hulst & N. Ritter (eds.), *The Syllable: Views and Facts.* Berlin: Mouton de Gruyter, 651–72.

Ogden, R. A. 1999b. A declarative account of strong and weak auxiliaries in English. *Phonology* 16: 55–92.

Ogden, R.A., S. Hawkins, J. House, M. Huckvale, J. Local, P. Carter, J. Dancovičová & S. Heid. 2000. ProSynth: an integrated prosodic approach to device-independent, natural-sounding speech synthesis. *Computer Speech and Language* 14: 177–210.

Ohala, J. J. 1974. Phonetic explanation in phonology. In A. Bruck, R.A. Fox, and M.W. LaGaly (eds.). *Papers from the Parasession on Natural Phonology.* Chicago Linguistic Society: Chicago, 251–74.

Ohala, J. J. 1981. The listener as a source of sound change. In C. S. Masek, R.A. Hendrick and M. F. Miller (eds.), *Papers from the Parasession on Language and Behavior.* Chicago Linguistic Society: Chicago, 178–203.

Ohala, J. J. 1990. The phonetics and phonology of aspects of assimilation. In J. Kingston and M. E. Beckman (eds.), *Papers in Laboratory Phonology I: Between the Grammar and Physics of Speech.* Cambridge: Cambridge University Press, 258–75.

Ohala, J. J., A. J. Bronstein, M. G. Busà, J. A. Lewis, & W. F. Weigel. 1999. *A Guide to the History of the Phonetic Sciences in the United States.* Berkeley: University of California.

Ohala, J. J. & H. Kawasaki. 1984. Prosodic phonology and phonetics. *Phonology Yearbook* 1: 113–27.

Ohala, M. & J. J. Ohala. 1998. Correlation between consonantal VC transitions and degree of perceptual confusion of place contrast in Hindi. In *Proceedings of the 5th International Conference on Spoken Language Processing, Sydney,* 2795–8.

Öhman, S. 1966. Coarticulation in VCV utterances: spectrographic measurement. *Journal of the Acoustical Society of America* 39: 151–68.

Orlikoff, R. F. & J. C. Kahane. 1996. Structure and function of the larynx. In N. J. Lass (ed.), *Principles of Experimental Phonetics.* St Louis: Mosby, 112–81.

Otake, T., K. Yoneyama, A. Cutler & A. van der Lugt. 1996. The representation of Japanese moraic nasals. *Journal of the Acoustical Society of America,* 100: 3831–42.

Palethorpe, S., M. E. Beckman, J. Fletcher & J. Harrington. 1999. The contribution of schwa vowels to the prosodic accent contrast in Australian English. *Proceedings of the International of Phonetic Sciences,* San Francisco, 1–7 August 1999, 695–8.

Palmeri, T. J., S. D. Goldinger & D. B. Pisoni. 1993. Episodic encoding of voice attributes and recognition memory for spoken words. *Journal of Experimental Psychology: Learning, Memory and Cognition* 19: 1–20.

Patel, M.S. & J. J. Mody. 1961. *The Vowel System of Gujarati.* Faculty of Education and Psychology, Maharaja Sayajirao University of Baroda.

Payne, E. M. 2000. Consonant Gemination in Italian: evidence for a fortition continuum. PhD thesis, University of Cambridge.

Perkell, J., M. Cohen, M. Svirsky, M. Matthies, I. Garabieta & M. Jackson. 1992. Electromagnetic Midsagittal Articulometer (EMMA) Systems for Transducing Speech Articulatory Movements. *Journal of the Acoustical Society of America* 92: 3078–96.

Perlmutter, D. 1995. Phonological quantity and multiple association. In J. Goldsmith (ed.), *Handbook of Phonological Theory*. Oxford: Blackwell, 307–17.

Peterson, G.A. & I. Lehiste. 1960. Duration of syllabic nuclei in English. *Journal of the Acoustical Society of America* 32: 693–703.

Picheny, M. A., N. I. Durlach & L. D. Braida. 1985. Speaking clearly for the hard of hearing I: Intelligibility differences between clear and conversational speech. *Journal of Speech and Hearing Research* 28: 96–103.

Picheny, M. A., N. I. Durlach & L. D. Braida. 1986. Speaking clearly for the hard of hearing II: Acoustic characteristics of clear and conversational speech. *Journal of Speech and Hearing Research* 29: 434–46.

Pierrehumbert, J. 1980. The phonology and phonetics of English intonation. PhD dissertation, MIT. Distributed by Indiana Linguistics Club.

Pierrehumbert, J. 1990. Phonological and phonetic representation. *Journal of Phonetics* 18. 375–94.

Pierrehumbert, J. 1994. Syllable structure and word structure: a study of triconsonantal clusters in English. In P. Keating (ed.), *Papers in Laboratory Phonology III: Phonological Structure and Phonetic Form*. Cambridge University Press: Cambridge, 168–88.

Pierrehumbert, J. 1997. Consequences of intonation for the voice source. In S. Kiritani, H. Hirose & H. Fujisaki (eds.), *Speech Production and Language. In Honour of Osamu Fujimura*. Berlin: Mouton de Gruyter, 111–30.

Pierrehumbert, J. & M. E. Beckman. 1988. *Japanese Tone Structure*. Cambridge, MA: MIT Press.

Pierrehumbert, J., M. E. Beckman & D. R. Ladd. 1996. Laboratory Phonology. In J. Durand and B. Laks (eds.), *Current Trends in Phonology: Models and Methods*. Vol. 2. Salford: European Studies Research Institute, University of Salford. 535–48.

Pierrehumbert, J. & D. Talkin. 1992. Lenition of /h/ and glottal stop. In G. Docherty & D. R. Ladd (eds.), *Papers in Laboratory Phonology II: Gesture, Segment, Prosody*. Cambridge: Cambridge University Press, 90–117.

Pike, K. L. 1945. *The Intonation of American English*. Ann Arbor, MI: University of Michigan Press.

Pisoni, D. B. 1997. Some thoughts on 'normalization' in speech perception. In K. Johnson and J. Mullenix (eds.), *Talker Variability in Speech Processing*. New York: Academic Press, 9–32.

Pisoni, D. B., H. C. Nusbaum, P. A. Luce & L. M. Slowiaczek. 1985. Speech perception, word recognition and the structure of the lexicon. *Speech Communication* 4: 75–95.

Pisoni, D. B., S. E. Lively & J. S. Logan. 1994. Perceptual learning of nonnative speech contrasts: implications for theories of speech perception. In J. C. Goodman & H. C. Nusbaum (eds.), *The Development of Speech Perception: the Transition from Speech Sounds to Spoken Words*. Cambridge, MA: MIT Press, 121–66.

Pitrelli, J. F., M. E. Beckman & J. Hirschberg. 1994. Evaluation of Prosodic Transcription labeling reliability in the ToBI framework. *Proceedings of ICSLP '94, Yokohama, Japan*, 123–6.

Pitt, M. A. & J. M. McQueen. 1998. Is compensation for coarticulation mediated by the lexicon? *Journal of Memory and Language* 39: 347–70.

Pittau, M. 1991. *Grammatica della lingua sarda (varietà logudorese)*. Sassari: Edizioni Carlo Delfino.

Plaut, D. C. & C. T. Kello. 1999. The emergence of phonology from the interplay of speech comprehension and production: a distributed connectionist approach. In B. MacWhinney (ed.), *The Emergence of Language*. Mahwah, NJ: Erlbaum, 381–415.

Plomp, R. 1967. Pitch of complex tones. *Journal of the Acoustical Society of America* 41: 1526–33.

Port, R. F., J. Dalby & M. O'Dell. 1987. Evidence for mora timing in Japanese. *Journal of the Acoustical Society of America* 81: 1564–74.

Port, R. F. & M. O'Dell. 1985. Neutralization of syllable-final voicing in German. *Journal of Phonetics* 13: 455–71.

Poser, W. J. 1990. Evidence for foot structure in Japanese. *Language* 66: 78–105.

Price, P. J., M. Ostendorf, S. Shattuck-Hufnagel & C. Fong. 1991. The use of prosody in syntactic disambiguation. *Journal of the Acoustical Society of America* 90: 2956–70.

Prince, A. S. & P. Smolensky 1993. Optimality Theory: constraint interaction in generative grammar. Technical report # 2 of the Rutgers Center for Cognitive Science, Rutgers University.

Protopapas, A. 1999. Connectionist modeling of speech perception. *Psychological Bulletin* 125: 410–36.

Pulleyblank, D. 1986. *Tone in Lexical Phonology*. Dordrecht: D. Reidel.

Rabiner, L & B. H. Juang. 1986. An introduction to Hidden Markov Models. *IEEE ASSP Magazine* 1: 4–16.

Raphael, L. 1972. Preceding vowel duration as a cue to the perception of the voicing characteristic of word-final consonants in American English. *Journal of the Acoustical Society of America* 51: 1296–1303.

Ratliff, M. 1992. Meaningful tone: a study of tonal morphology in compounds, form classes and expressive phrases in White Hmong. Center for Southeast Asian Studies Monograph Series on Southeast Asia, Special Report 27, Northern Illinois University.

Remez, R. E., J. M. Fellowes, D. B. Pisoni, W. D. Goh & P. E. Rubin. 1998. Multimodal perceptual organization of speech: evidence from tone analogs of spoken utterances. *Speech Communication* 26: 65–73.

Repetti, L. 1991. A moraic analysis of raddoppiamento fonosintattico. *Rivista di Linguistica* 3: 307–30.

Ritsma, R. J. 1962. Existence region of the tonal residue I. *Journal of the Acoustical Society of America* 34: 1224–9.

Ritsma, R. J. 1963. Existence region of the tonal residue II. *Journal of the Acoustical Society of America* 35: 1241–5.

Ritsma, R. J. 1967. Periodicity detection. In R. Plomp & G. F. Smoorenburg (eds.), *Frequency Analysis and Periodicity Detection in Hearing*. Leiden: Sijthoff.

Roberts, J. 1997. Acquisition of variable rules: a study of (-t, d) deletion in preschool children. *Journal of Child Language* 24: 351–72.

Robins, R. H. 1970. Aspects of Prosodic Analysis. In F. R. Palmer (ed.), *Prosodic Analysis*. Oxford: Oxford University Press, 188–200.

Rose, S. 1996. Variable laryngeals and vowel lowering. *Phonology* 13: 73–117.

Rosenberg, A. E. 1965. Pitch discrimination of Jittered Pulse Trains. *Journal of the Acoustical Society of America* 39: 920–8.

Rowlands, E. C. 1955. The mid tone in Yorùbá. In J. Lukas (ed.), *Afrikanistische Studien*. Deutsche Akademie der Wissenschaften zu Berlin, Institut für Orientforschung, Veröffentlichung 26. Berlin: Akademie-Verlag.

Rubach, J. 1995. Representations and the organization of rules in Slavic phonology. In J. Goldsmith (ed.), *Handbook of Phonological Theory*. Oxford: Blackwell, 848–66.

Rubach, J. 1996. Shortening and ambisyllabicity in English. *Phonology* 13: 197–237.

Rubin, P. E. 1995. HADES: a case study of the development of a signal analysis system. In A. Syrdal, R. Bennett & S. Greenspan (eds.), *Applied Speech Technology*. Boca Raton, FL: CRC Press, 501–20.

Rumelhart, D. E., J. L. McClelland & The PDP Research Group. 1986. *Parallel Distributed Processing: Explorations in the Microstructure of Cognition*. Vol. 1: *Foundations*. Cambridge, MA: MIT Press

Saffran, J. R., R. N. Aslin & E. L. Newport. 1996a. Statistical learning by 8-month-old infants. *Science* 274: 1926–8.

Saffran, J. R., E. L. Newport & R. N. Aslin. 1996b. Word segmentation: the role of distributional cues. *Journal of Memory and Language* 35: 606–21.

Sagey, E. 1986. The representation of features and relations in nonlinear phonology. PhD dissertation, MIT.

Sakano, N. 1996. *Shichi-go-cho no Nazo wo Toku (Solving the Mystery of the Seven-Five Meter)*. Tokyo: Taishukan Shoten.

Sakoe, H. & S. Chiba. 1978. Dynamic programming algorithm optimization for spoken word recognition. *IEEE Transactions on Acoustics, Speech and Signal Processing* ASSP–26: 43–9.

Saltzman, E. L. & K. G. Munhall. 1989. A dynamical approach to gestural patterning in speech production. *Ecological Psychology* 1: 333–92.

Schegloff, E. A. 1991. Reflections on talk and social structure. In D. Boden & D.H. Zimmerman, (eds.). *Talk and Social Structure: Studies in Ethnomethodology and Conversation Analysis*. Cambridge: Polity Press: 44–71.

Schegloff, E. A. 1993. Reflections on quantification in the study of conversation. *Research on Language and Social Interaction* 26: 99–128.

Schiller, N. O. 1997. The role of the syllable in speech production. Evidence from lexical statistics, metalinguistics, masked priming, and electromagnetic midsagittal articulography. PhD dissertation, Nijmegen University.

Schouten, J. F. 1970. The residue revisited. In R. Plomp & G. F. Smoorenburg (eds.), *Frequency Analysis and Periodicity Detection in Hearing*. Leiden: Sijthoff, 41–54.

Schutte, H. K. & R. Miller. 1985. Intraindividual parameters of the singer's formant. *Folia Phoniatrica* 37: 31–5.

Scobbie, J. M. 1995. What do we do when phonology is powerful enough to imitate phonetics? Comments on Zsiga. In B. Connell & A. Arvaniti (eds.), *Papers in*

Laboratory IV: Phonology and Phonetic Evidence. Cambridge: Cambridge University Press, 303–14.

Scobbie, J., J. S. Coleman & S. Bird. 1996. Key aspects of declarative phonology. In J. Durand & B. Laks (eds.), *Current Trends in Phonology: Models and Methods.* Vol. 2. Salford: European Studies Research Institute, University of Salford, 685–709.

Scott, S. K. 1993. P-centres in speech: an acoustic analysis. PhD dissertation, University College London.

Selkirk, E. O. 1982. The syllable. In H. van der Hulst & N. Smith (eds), *The Structure of Phonological Representations.* Part II. Dordrecht: Foris, 337–84.

Selkirk, E. O. 1984. *Phonology and Syntax: the Relation between Sound and Structure.* Cambridge, MA: MIT Press.

Shahin, K. N. 1997. Postvelar harmony. An examination of its bases and crosslinguistic variation. PhD dissertation, University of British Columbia.

Shammass, S. 1985. Formant transitions, sspectral shape and vowel context in the perception of voiced stops. Doctoral dissertation, University of Alberta.

Shattuck-Hufnagel, S. & A. Turk. 1996. A prosody tutorial for investigators of auditory sentence processing. *Journal of Psycholinguistic Research* 25: 193–247.

Shepard, R. N. 1987. Toward a universal law of generalization for psychological science. *Science* 237: 1317–23.

Shipman, D. W. & V. W. Zue. 1982. Properties of large lexicons: implications for advanced isolated word recognition systems. In *Conference Record, IEEE International Conference on Speech Acoustics and Signal Processing, Paris, France,* 546–49.

Shriberg, E. 1999. Phonetic conscquences of speech disfluency, In *Proceedings of the XIVth International Congress of Phonetic Sciences,* San Francisco, 1–7 August 1999, Vol.1: 619–22.

Silverman, D. 1997. Laryngeal complexity in Otomanguean vowels. *Phonology* 14: 235–61.

Silverman, D., B. Blankenship, P. Kirk & P. Ladefoged. 1995. Phonetic structures in Jalapa Mazatec. *Anthropological Linguistics* 37: 70–88.

Silverman, K., M. E. Beckman, J. Pitrelli, M. Ostendorf, C. Wightman, P. Price, J. Pierrehumbert & J. Hirschberg. 1992. TOBI: a standard for labeling English prosody. In *Proceedings of the 1992 International Conference on Spoken Language Processing* Vol. 2: 867–70.

Slatcr, A. & J. S. Coleman. 1996. Non-segmental analysis and synthesis based on a speech database. In *Proceedings of ICSLP 96, The Fourth International Conference on Spoken Language Processing* Vol. 4: 2379–82.

Sluijter, A. M. C., V. J. van Heuven & J. J. A. Pacilly. 1997. Spectral balance as a cue in the perception of linguistic stress. *Journal of the Acoustical Society of America* 101: 503–13.

Smalley, W. A. 1976. The problems of consonants and tone: Hmong (Meo, Miao). In W. A. Smalley (ed.), *Phonemes and orthography: Language Planning in Ten Minority Languages in Thailand.* Pacific Linguistics Series C, No. 43.

Smith, C. 1995. Prosodic patterns in the coordination of vowel and consonant gestures. In B. Connell and A. Arvaniti (eds.), *Papers in Laboratory Phonology IV: Phonology and Phonetic Evidence.* Cambridge University Press: Cambridge, 205–23.

References

Soler, A. & J. Romero. 1999. The role of duration in stop lenition in Spanish. In *Proceedings of the XIVth International Congress of Phonetic Sciences*, San Francisco. 1–7 August 1999, Vol. 1: 483–6.

Spencer, A. 1996. *Phonology: Theory and Description*. Oxford: Blackwell.

Sprigg, R. K. 1955. The tonal system of Tibetan (Lhasa dialect) and the nominal phrase. *Bulletin of the School of Oriental and African Studies* 17: 134–53. Reprinted in F. R. Palmer (ed., 1970), *Prosodic Analysis*. London: Oxford University Press, 112–32.

Sproat, R. & O. Fujimura. 1993. Allophonic variation in English /l/ and its implications for phonetic implementation. *Journal of Phonetics* 21: 291–311.

Stahlke, H. 1974. The development of the three-way tonal contrast in Yorùbá. In E. Voeltz (ed.), *Third Annual Conference on African Linguistics*. (Indiana University Publications, African Series, Vol. 7). Bloomington: Indiana University, 138–45.

Steriade, D. 1993. Closure, release, and nasal contours. In M. Huffman & R. Krakow (eds.), *Phonetics and Phonology*. Vol. 5. New York: Academic Press, 401–70.

Steriade, D. 1995. Underspecification and markedness. In J. A. Goldsmith (ed.), *The Handbook of Phonological Theory*. Oxford: Blackwell, 114–74.

Stetson, R. H. 1951. *Motor Phonetics: a Study of Speech Movements in Action*. 2nd edition. Amsterdam: North-Holland.

Stevens, K. N. 1989. On the quantal nature of speech. *Journal of Phonetics* 17: 3–45.

Stevens, K. N. & S. Blumstein. 1981. The search for invariant acoustic correlates of phonetic features. In P. D. Eimas & J. L. Miller (eds.), *Perspectives on the Study of Speech*. Hillsdale, NJ: Lawrence Erlbaum, 1–38.

Stevens, K. N. & S. J. Keyser. 1989. Primary features and their enhancements in consonants. *Language* 65: 81–106.

Stevens, K. N., S. J. Keyser & H. Kawasaki. 1986. Toward a phonetic and phonological theory of redundant features. In J. S. Perkell & D. H. Klatt (eds.), *Invariance and Variability in Speech Processes*. Hillsdale, NJ: Lawrence Erlbaum, 426–49.

Stone, M. 1981. Evidence for a rhythm pattern in speech production: observations of jaw movement. *Journal of Phonetics* 9: 109–20.

Strand, E. 1999. Uncovering the role of gender stereotypes in speech perception. *Journal of Language and Social Psychology* 18: 86–99.

Strange, W. 1972. The effects of training on the perception of synthetic speech sounds: voice onset time. PhD dissertation, University of Minnesota.

Streeter, L. A. & G. N. Nigro. 1979. The role of medial consonant transitions in word perception. *Journal of the Acoustical Society of America* 65: 1533–41.

Summers, W. V. 1988. F1 structure provides information for final-consonant voicing. *Journal of the Acoustical Society of America* 84: 485–92.

Sundberg, J. & P.-E Nordström. 1976. Raised and lowered larynx – the effect on vowel formant frequencies. *Quarterly Progress & Status Report, Speech Transmission Laboratory, Royal Insititute of Technology, Stockholm* 2–3: 35–39.

Sundberg, J. 1987. *The Science of the Singing Voice*. Dekalb, Illinois: Northern Illinois University Press.

Suomi, K. 1993. An outline of a developmental model of adult phonological organization and behaviour. *Journal of Phonetics* 21: 29–60.

Suomi, K., J. M. McQueen & A. Cutler. 1997. Vowel harmony and speech segmentation in Finnish. *Journal of Memory and Language* 36: 422–44.

Sussman, H. M., H. A. McCaffrey & S. A. Matthews. 1991. An investigation of locus equations as a source of relational invariance for stop place categorization. *Journal of the Acoustical Society of America* 90: 1256–68.

Sweet, H. 1877. *A Handbook of Phonetics.* Oxford: Clarendon Press.

Sweet, H. 1908. *The Sounds of English.* Oxford: Clarendon Press.

Tajima, K. 1998. Speech rhythm in English and Japanese: experiments in speech cycling. PhD dissertation, Indiana University, Bloomington.

Taylor, G. P. 1985. *The Student's Grammar of Gujarati.* New Delhi: Asian Educational Services.

Temple, R. A. M. 1999. Phonetic and sociophonetic conditioning of voicing patterns in the stop consonants of French. *Proceedings of the XIVth International Congress of Phonetic Sciences.* San Francisco. 1–7 August 1999, Vol. 2: 1409–12.

Terhardt, E. 1974. Pitch, consonance and harmony. *Journal of the Acoustical Society of America* 55: 1061–9.

Torretta, G. M. 1995. The 'easy-hard' word multi-talker speech database: an initial report. *Research on Spoken Language Processing Progress Report, Speech Research Laboratory, Indiana University* 20: 321–33.

Treiman, R. & C. Danis. 1988. Syllabification of intervocalic consonants. *Journal of Memory and Language* 27: 87–104.

Treiman, R., B. Kessler, S. Knewasser & R. Tincoff. 2000. Adults' sensitivity to phonotactic probabilities. In M. Broe & J. Pierrehumbert (eds.), *Papers in Laboratory Phonology V: Acquisition and the Lexicon.* Cambridge: Cambridge University Press, 269–82.

Trigo, L. 1991. On pharynx-larynx interactions. *Phonology* 8: 113–36.

Tuller, B. & J. A. S. Kelso. 1991. The production and perception of syllable structure. *Journal of Speech and Hearing Research* 34: 501–8.

Tunley, A. 1999. Coarticulatory influences of liquids on vowels in English. PhD dissertation, University of Cambridge.

Turk, A. 1994. Articulatory phonetic clues to syllable affiliation: gestural characteristics of bilabial stops. In P. Keating (ed.), *Papers in Laboratory Phonology III: Phonological Structure and Phonetic Form.* Cambridge: Cambridge University Press, 107–35.

Uchanski, R. M., Choi, S., Braida, L. D., Reed, C. M. & Durlach, N. I. 1996. Speaking clearly for the hard of hearing IV: further studies of the role of speaking rate. *Journal of Speech and Hearing Research* 39: 494–509.

Ueyama, M. 1999. An experimental study of vowel duration in phrase-final contexts in Japanese. *UCLA Working Papers in Phonetics.* 97: 174–82.

Umeda, N. 1977. Consonant duration in American English. *Journal of the Acoustical Society of America* 61: 846–58.

Urua, E-A. E. 1990. Aspects of Ibibio phonology and morphology. PhD dissertation, University of Ibadan.

van Lieshout, P. H., C. W. Starkweather, W. Hulstijn & H. F. M. Peters. 1995. Effects of linguistic correlates of stuttering on EMG activity in nonstuttering speakers. *Journal of Speech and Hearing Research* 38: 360–72.

van Santen, J. P. H., J. S. Coleman & M. A. Randolph. 1992. Effects of postvocalic voicing on the time course of vowels and diphthongs. *Journal of the Acoustical Society of America* 92: 2444.

van Santen, J. P. H. & M. D'Imperio. 1999. Positional effects on stressed vowel duration in Standard Italian. In *Proceedings of the 14th International Congress of Phonetic Sciences*, San Francisco. 1–7 August 1999, 241–4.

Vatikiotis-Bateson, E. & J. A. S. Kelso. 1993. Rhythm type and articulatory dynamics in English, French and Japanese. *Journal of Phonetics* 21: 231–65.

Vaux, B. 1993. Is ATR a laryngeal feature? ATR-voice interactions and the geometry of the lower vocal tract. MS, Harvard University.

Vayra, M. 1992. Phonetic explanations in phonology: laryngealization as the case for glottal stops in Italian word-final stressed syllables. In *Proceedings of Seventh International Phonology Meeting,* Krems, Austria, July 4–7, 1992, 275–94.

Vijver, R. van de. 1998. The iambic issue: iambs as a result of constraint interaction. HIL Dissertations 37. Leiden: Holland Institute of Generative Linguistics.

Vitevitch, M. S., P. A. Luce, J. Charles-Luce & D. Kemmerer. 1997. Phonotactics and syllable stress: implications for the processing of spoken nonsense words. *Language and Speech* 40: 47–62.

Vogel, I. 1978. Raddoppiamento as a resyllabification rule. *Journal of Italian Linguistics* 3: 15–28.

Vogel, I. 1992. Comments on chapters 3 and 4. In G. J. Docherty & D. R. Ladd (eds.), *Papers in Laboratory Phonology II: Gesture, Segment, Prosody.* Cambridge: Cambridge University Press, 124–7.

Vogel, I. 1994. Phonological interfaces in Italian. In M. Mazzola (ed.), *Issues and Theory in Romance Linguistics: Selected Papers from the Linguistic Symposium on Romance Languages XXIII.* Georgetown University Press: Baltimore. 109–26.

Vogel, I. 1997. Prosodic Phonology. In M. Maiden & M. M. Parry (eds.), *The Dialects of Italy.* London: Routledge, 58–67.

Vogel, I., H. T. Bunnell & S. Hoskins. 1995. The phonology and phonetics of the Rhythm Rule. In B. Connell & A. Arvaniti (eds.), *Papers in Laboratory Phonology IV: Phonology and Phonetic Evidence.* Cambridge: Cambridge University Press, 111–27.

Vogel, I. & I. Kenesei. 1990. Syntax and semantics in phonology. In S. Inkelas & D. Zec (eds.), *The Phonology-Syntax Connection.* Chicago: Chicago University Press, 339–64.

Wagner, M. L. 1941. *Fonetica storica del sardo.* Cagliari: Trois.

Wagner, M. L. 1951. *La lingua sarda: storia, spirito, e forma.* Bern: Francke.

Wagner, M. L. 1960–64. *Dizionario Etimologica Sardo.* 3 vols. Heidelberg: Winter.

Wang, Q. E. 1995. Are syllables units of speech motor organization? Unpublished PhD dissertation, University of Connecticut.

Ward, I. C. 1952. *An Introduction to the Yorùbá Language.* Cambridge: W. Heffer and Sons.

Warner, N. 1998. Dynamic cues in speech perception and spoken word recognition. PhD dissertation, University of California at Berkeley.

Warren, P., & W. Marslen-Wilson. 1987. Continuous uptake of acoustic cues in spoken word recognition. *Perception and Psychophysics* 41: 262–75.

Waterson, N. 1971. Child phonology: a prosodic view. *Journal of Linguistics* 7: 179–211.

Watkins, J. 1997. Can phonation types be reliably measured from sound spectra? Some data from Wa and Burmese. *School of Oriental and African Studies Working Papers in Linguistics and Phonetics* 7: 321–39.

Watt, D. J. L. 1998. Variation and change in the vowel system of Tyneside English. PhD dissertation, University of Newcastle upon Tyne.

Wells, J. C. 1982. *Accents of English.* 3 vols. Cambridge: Cambridge University Press.

Wells, J. C. 1990. Syllabification and allophony. In S. Ramsaran (ed.), *Studies in the Pronunciation of English: a Commemorative Volume in Honour of A.C. Gimson.* London: Routledge, 76–86.

West, P. 1999. The extent of coarticulation of English liquids: an acoustic and articulatory study. In *Proceedings of the XIVth International Congress of Phonetic Sciences.* San Francisco. Vol. 3: 1901–4.

Westbury, J. R., M. Hashi & M. J. Lindstrom. 1995. Differences among speakers in articulation of American English /r/: an X-ray microbeam study. In *Proceedings of the XIIIth International Congress of Phonetic Sciences.* Stockholm, Sweden. Vol. 4: 50–7.

Whalen, D. 1989. Vowel and consonant judgments are not independent when cued by the same information. *Perception and Psychophysics.* 46: 284–92.

Whalen, D. H. 1991. Subcategorical phonetic mismatches and lexical access. *Perception and Psychophysics* 50. 351–60.

Whalen, D. H., C. T. Best & J. R. Irwin. 1997. Lexical effects in the perception and production of American English /p/ allophones. *Journal of Phonetics* 25: 501–28.

Whalen, D. H. & Yi Xu. 1992. Information for Mandarin tones in the amplitude contour and in brief segments. *Phonetica* 49: 25–47.

Whorf, B. L. 1943. Phonemic analysis of the English of Eastern Massachusetts. *Studies in Linguistics* 2: 21–40.

Wightman, C. W., S. Shattuck-Hufnagel, M. Ostendorf & P. J. Price. 1992. Segmental durations in the vicinity of prosodic phrase boundaries. *Journal of the Acoustical Society of America* 92: 1707–17.

Wolf, C. G. 1978. Voicing cues in English final stops. *Journal of Phonetics* 6: 299–309.

Wright, R. 1996. Consonant clusters and cue preservation in Tsou. PhD dissertation, UCLA. (Published as: UCLA Dissertations in Linguistics No. 20.)

Wright, S. & P. Kerswill. 1989. Electropalatography in the study of connected speech processes. *Clinical Linguistics and Phonetics* 3: 49–57.

Yip, M. 1993. Tonal register in East Asian languages. In H. van der Hulst & K. Snider (eds.), *The Phonology of Tone. The Representation of Tonal Register.* Berlin and New York: Mouton de Gruyter, 245–68.

Yip, M. 1995. Tone in East Asian languages. In J. A. Goldsmith (ed.), *The Handbook of Phonological Theory.* Oxford: Blackwell, 476–94.

Zawaydeh, B. A. 1997. An acoustic analysis of uvularization spread in Ammani-Jordanian Arabic. *Studies in the Linguistic Sciences* 21 (7): 185–200.

Zawaydeh, B. A. 1998. Gradient uvularization spread in Ammani-Jordanian Arabic. In E. Benmamoun, M. Eid & N. Haeri (eds.), *Perspectives on Arabic Linguistics XI.*

Current Issues in Linguistic Theory, Vol. 167. Amsterdam: John Benjamins, 117–41.

Zawaydeh, B. A. 1999. The phonetics and phonology of gutturals in Arabic. PhD dissertation, Indiana University.

Zipf, G. K. 1935. *The Psycho-biology of Language*. Boston: Houghton Mifflin.

Zsiga, E. C. 1994. Gestural overlap in consonant sequences. *Journal of Phonetics* 22: 121–40.

Zsiga, E. C. 1995. An acoustic and electropalatographic study of lexical and postlexical palatalization in American English. In B. Connell & A. Arvaniti (eds.), *Papers in Laboratory Phonology IV: Phonology and Phonetic Evidence:* Cambridge: Cambridge University Press, 282–302.

Zsiga, E. C. 1997. Features, gestures and Igbo vowels: an approach to the phonetics-phonology interface. *Language* 73: 227–74.

Zwicker, E. & E. Terhardt. 1980. Analytical expressions for critical-band rate and critical bandwidth as a function of frequency. *Journal of the Acoustical Society of America* 68: 1523–24.

Index of names

Index of subjects